# Practical Recording Techniques, Third Edition

# Practical Recording Techniques

## Third Edition

*Bruce Bartlett*
*Jenny Bartlett*

Focal Press

Boston  Oxford  Auckland  Johannesburg  Melbourne  New Delhi

Focal Press is an imprint of Butterworth–Heinemann.

Copyright © 2002 by Butterworth–Heinemann

 A member of the Reed Elsevier group

 Recognizing the importance of preserving what has been written, Butterworth–Heinemann prints its books on acid-free paper whenever possible.

**Library of Congress Cataloging-in-Publication Data**
Bartlett, Bruce.
   Practical recording techniques / Bruce Bartlett, Jenny Bartlett.—3rd ed.
     p.  cm.
   Includes index.
   ISBN 0-240-80473-2 (pbk. : alk. paper)
   1. Magnetic recorders and recording—Handbooks, manuals, etc.  2. Sound—Recorders and reproducing—Handbooks, manuals, etc.  I. Bartlett, Jenny.  II. Title.

   TK7881.6 .B367 2001
   621.389'3—dc21

                           2001040787

**British Library Cataloguing-in-Publication Data**
A catalogue record for this book is available from the British Library.

The publisher offers special discounts on bulk orders of this book.
For information, please contact:
Manager of Special Sales
Butterworth–Heinemann
225 Wildwood Avenue
Woburn, MA 01801-2041
Tel: 781-904-2500
Fax: 781-904-2620

For information on all Focal Press publications available, contact our World Wide Web home page at: http://www.focalpress.com

10 9 8 7 6 5 4 3 2 1

Printed in the United States of America

To family, friends, and music.

# TABLE OF CONTENTS

# 3 Sound, Signals, and Studio Acoustics   43

# 4 Monitoring *63*

# 5 Hum Prevention *75*

# 6 Microphones   95

# 9  Analog Tape Recording   *165*

# 10 Digital Recording and Editing   *189*

# 11  Signal Processors and Effects  *229*

# 12 Recorder–Mixers and Mixing Consoles *259*

# 13 Operating the Multitrack Recorder and Mixer *277*

# 15 Recording the Spoken Word   *317*

# 16 The MIDI Studio: Equipment and Procedures   *325*

# 17 On-Location Recording of Popular Music   *355*

# 20   Surround Sound: Techniques and Media   *419*

# PREFACE

Recording is a highly skilled craft combining art and science. It requires technical knowledge as well as musical understanding and critical listening ability. By learning these skills, you can capture a musical performance and reproduce it with quality sound for the enjoyment and inspiration of others.

Your recordings will become carefully tailored creations of which you can be proud. They will be a legacy that can bring pleasure to many people for years to come.

This book is intended as a hands-on, practical guide for beginning and intermediate recording engineers, producers, musicians—anyone who wants to make better recordings by understanding recording equipment and techniques. I hope to prepare the reader for work in a home studio, a small professional studio, or an on-location recording session.

*Practical Recording Techniques* offers up-to-date information on the latest recording technology, such as digital recording, hard-disk recording, keyboard and digital workstations, SMPTE and MIDI, surround sound, and audio for the Internet. But it also guides the beginner through the basics, showing how to make quality recordings with the new breed of inexpensive home-studio equipment.

The book first overviews the recording-and-reproduction chain to instill a system concept. Next, advice is given on equipping a home studio, from low budget to advanced.

The basics of sound and signals are explained so that you'll know what you're controlling when you adjust the controls on a piece of recording equipment. Studio setup is covered next, including suggestions for improving your studio acoustics, choosing monitor speakers, and preventing hum.

Each piece of recording equipment is explained in detail, as well as the control-room techniques you'll use during actual sessions. Two chapters are devoted to the technology of digital recording and MIDI sequencing. Two sections on remote recording cover techniques for both popular and classical music.

A special chapter explains how to judge recordings and improve them. The engineer must know not only how to use the equipment, but also how to tell good sound from bad.

The latest developments in recording are surround sound and audio for the Internet. Both these topics are covered in detail in their own chapters.

The last chapter answers the question, "Why do we record?"

Finally, four appendices explain the decibel, introduce SMPTE time code, suggest further education, and explain impedance.

Based on my work as a professional recording engineer, the book is full of tips and shortcuts for making great-sounding tapes, whether in a professional studio, on location, or at home. You'll find many topics not covered in similar texts:

How to choose and operate cassette recorder–mixers

Hum prevention

The latest monitoring methods

Chart of microphone types

Microphone selection guide

Miniature microphones

Tonal effects of microphone placement

Glossary of sound-quality descriptions

Documenting the recording session

Audio-for-video techniques

Recording the spoken word

On-location recording

Troubleshooting bad sound; guidelines for good sound

Audio on the Web

Surround sound

# ACKNOWLEDGMENTS

Thank you to Nick Batzdorf of *Recording* magazine for giving me permission to draw from my "Take One" series. Thanks to Pat Brown of Syn-Aud-Con for checking the chapter on hum prevention. For my education, thank you to the College of Wooster, Crown International, Shure Brothers Inc., Astatic Corporation, and all the studios I've worked for.

Thank you to Terri Jadick, Marie Lee, and Maura Kelly at Focal Press and Kristin Landon for working with me on this new edition.

My deepest thanks to Jenny Bartlett for her many helpful suggestions as a layperson consultant and editor. She made sure the book could be understood by beginners.

A note of appreciation goes to the Pat Metheny Group and Samuel "Adagio for Strings" Barber, among many others, whose music inspired the chapter "Music: Why You Record."

Finally, to the musicians I've recorded and played with, a special thanks for teaching me indirectly about recording.

# 1

# THE RECORDING CHAIN

Welcome to the brave new world of 21st-century recording! The digital technologies of the past few years have given us possibilities undreamed of just 10 years ago. This book will show you an overview of current recording technology, help you choose the equipment that best suits your needs, and guide you in using it to create great recordings. And it will explain the technical jargon in plain English.

Thanks to the shift from analog to digital technology, the excitement and satisfaction of recording are accessible to more people than ever before. It used to take a whole roomful—or truckful—of expensive equipment to produce a good recording. But the new generation of smaller, cheaper gear means you may be able to tuck your studio into a corner of your bedroom or the back seat of your Toyota. As a result, many more people are involved in the process of recording—as musicians recording their own albums, or as engineers offering services to others.

As a recording engineer, you are a key player. Your skills help artists realize their visions in sound. Your miking techniques capture the vibrancy of the performance, whether it's the shimmering overtones of a string quartet or the sonic assault of an electric blues band. Your "post" work in the studio—adding effects, tweaking levels, etc.—will take the raw material of the performance and shape and blend it into a polished musical statement.

Mastering the technology, becoming fluent with the audio tools at hand, you will produce exciting recordings that will delight your clients and give you a real sense of pride and achievement.

Be sure to practice what you learn in this book. There's no substitute for hands-on experience. You might offer to record a band's rehearsal for free while you experiment and master the gear. Be patient, let yourself make mistakes, and above all, *listen* to how the sound changes when you move a mic or tweak a knob.

# Types of Recording

Let's get started. Currently there are five main ways to record music:

1. **Live stereo recording:** Record with a stereo microphone or two microphones into a recorder.
2. **Live mixed recording:** Pick up the musicians with several mics plugged into a mixer. Adjust the mic levels and record the mix into a recorder.
3. **Multitrack tape recording:** Record with several mics into a mixer, which is connected to a multitrack tape recorder. Each track or path on tape contains the sound of a different instrument. After the recording is done, you mix or combine the tracks to stereo.
4. **Random-access recording:** Record the music onto a computer hard disk or MiniDisc. You can access any part of the recording instantly, and edit the audio program on-screen.
5. **MIDI sequencing:** A musician performs on a MIDI controller, such as a keyboard or drum pads. The controller puts out a MIDI signal, a series of numbers which indicates which keys were pressed and when they were pressed. The MIDI signal is recorded into computer memory by a sequencer. When you play back the sequence, it plays the tone generators in a synthesizer, or plays *samples*: digital recordings of musical notes.

A sequencer can be synced to a multitrack recorder (tape, hard disk, or MiniDisc). You record MIDI instruments with the sequencer, and record vocals and acoustic instruments with the multitrack recorder. A sequencer can also be part of digital audio recording software.

Let's look at each type of recording in more detail.

# Live Stereo Recording

This method is most commonly used to record an orchestra, symphonic band, pipe organ, small ensemble, quartet, or soloist. The microphones pick up the overall sound of the instruments and the concert-hall acoustics. You might use this minimalist technique to record a folk group, acoustic jazz group, or classical-music ensemble in a good-sounding room.

Figure 1.1 shows the stages of this method—the links in the recording chain. Let's look at each stage from left to right (beginning to end).

1. The musical instruments or voices make sound waves.

2. The sound waves travel through the air and bounce or **reflect** off the walls, ceiling, and floor of the concert hall. These reflections add a pleasing sense of spaciousness.

3. The sound waves from the instruments and the room reach the microphones, which convert the sound into electrical signals.

4. The sound quality is greatly affected by mic technique. Microphone choice and placement are critical in this method because you have no way to adjust the sound later.

5. The signals from the microphones go to a recorder. It may be a cassette deck, open-reel deck, DAT (digital audio tape) recorder, or computer hard drive. The signal changes to a magnetic pattern stored on a magnetic medium. During playback, the magnetic patterns on the tape or disk are converted back into a signal.

   As the tape moves during recording, magnetic signals are stored on tape along a **track**—a path on tape containing a recorded signal. One or more tracks can be recorded side-by-side on a single tape. For example, a 2-track tape recorder can record two tracks on tape, such as the two different audio signals required for stereo recording.

6. To hear the signal you're recording, you need a monitor system: headphones or a stereo power amplifier and loudspeakers. You use the monitors to judge how well your mic technique is working.

The speakers or headphones convert the signal back into sound. This sound resembles that of the original instruments. Also, the acoustics of the listening room affect the sound reaching the listener.

**Figure 1.1**
The recording chain for live stereo recording.

# Recording with Several Mics and a Mixer

Now let's look at a more complex way to record (Figure 1.2).

1. You use several microphones. Each one is placed close to each instrument or singer. As a result, each mic picks up very little room acoustics. This gives a close, clear sound that's desirable in recorded pop music or narration. For more clarity, you might add some sound-absorbent material on the floor, walls, and ceiling.

2. All the mics plug into a mixer, which blends all the microphone signals into one signal, stereo or mono. The mixer also has a volume control for each microphone. While listening to the mixer's signal, you adjust the volume of each instrument to make a pleasing loudness balance.

For example, if the guitar is too quiet relative to the voice, simply turn up the volume control for the guitar microphone until it blends well with the voice. That's a lot easier than grouping the musicians around a single microphone and moving the musicians until you hear a good balance.

Many mixers let you control other aspects of sound besides volume. You can control tone quality (bass and treble), stereo position (left, right, or center), and special effects (such as artificial reverberation, which sounds like room acoustics). You monitor the mixer's signal with headphones or speakers.

3. When the mix sounds okay, you record the mixer's output signal with a tape recorder.

# Multitrack Tape Recording

One problem with the previous setup is that you have to mix while the musicians are playing. If you make a mistake while mixing—say, one

**Figure 1.2**
The recording chain for
several mics and a mixer.

instrument is too quiet—the musicians have to play the song again until you get the balance right. And if you're recording a live gig, there's only one chance to perfect the mix.

The solution is to use a multitrack recorder, which records 4 to 48 tracks side-by-side on a single tape. It's as if several 2-track recorders were locked together. You record the signal of each microphone on its own track, then mix these recorded signals after the performance is done. You can either record a different instrument on each track or record different groups of instruments on each track.

Figure 1.3 shows the stages in this method.

1. Place microphones near the instruments.
2. Plug the mics into a **mixing console**: a big, sophisticated mixer. During multitrack recording, the mixing console amplifies the weak microphone signals up to the level needed by the tape recorder. The console is also used to send each microphone signal to the desired tape track.
3. Record the amplified mic signals on the multitrack tape recorder.

A **recorder–mixer** or **portable studio** combines the mixer and multitrack recorder in a single chassis. It's a convenient system for home studios.

You can record more instruments later on unused tracks—a process called **overdubbing**. Wearing headphones, the performer listens to the recorded tracks to keep his or her place in the song, and plays along with them. You record the performance on an unused track.

4. After the recording is done, play all the tape tracks through the mixing console to mix them with a pleasing balance (Figure 1.4).
5. Play back the multitrack tape of the song several times, adjusting the track volumes and tone controls until the mix is just the way you want

**Figure 1.3**
The recording chain for
multitrack tape recording.

**Figure 1.4**
The recording chain for a multitrack mixdown.

**Figure 1.5**
A small home studio.

it. You can add special effects to enhance the sound quality. Some examples are echo, reverberation, and compression (explained in Chapter 11). Effects are made by **signal processors** which connect to your mixer.

6. Record your final mix on a 2-track stereo recorder (cassette, open-reel, DAT, or computer hard drive).

To illustrate all the equipment mentioned, Figure 1.5 shows a small home studio setup using a recorder–mixer. Figure 1.6 shows a typical layout of a larger recording studio. Often, the tape recorders are operated by remote controls near the mixing console.

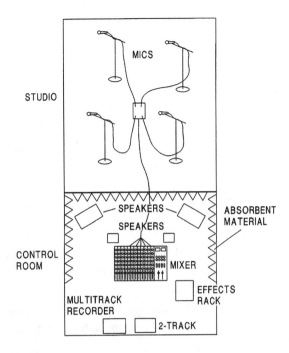

**Figure 1.6**
Typical layout of a larger recording studio.

# Random Access Multitrack Recording

Multitrack tape recording can be slow: you must fast-forward or rewind to the part you want to hear. That's not a problem when you track on a hard drive or MiniDisc. These media have random access: you can instantly go to any part of the recorded program.

Currently, multitrack random access recording comes in four styles:

1. Multitrack recording software.
2. Hard-disk (HD) recorder and a separate mixer.
3. HD recorder–mixer.
4. MiniDisc recorder–mixer.

The first random access setup listed above uses a computer with a sound card and multitrack recording software (Figure 1.7). The sound card converts audio into a signal that is recorded on the computer's hard disk as a magnetic pattern. Instead of a sound card, the recording system might use a **breakout box**: a chassis with input/output connectors, wired to your computer.

Here are the steps in computer multitrack recording:

1. Plug a mic or electric instrument into a mixer or mic preamp to amplify the signal. Plug the mixer output into the sound card. Or,

**Figure 1.7**
Computer with a sound
card and recording/
editing sofware.

plug the mixer output into a breakout box with line inputs. If the breakout box has mic preamps built in, plug the mic directly into the breakout box.

You'll need several sound cards or a card with multiple inputs to record more than two instruments at once.

2. If the sound card has a digital input, but your mixer is analog, first plug the mixer output into an A/D converter (explained in Chapter 10). This device changes the analog signal into a digital one. You might use the A/D converter in a DAT machine for this function.

3. Use the recording software to record the audio onto your hard drive.

4. Overdub more instruments.

5. Mix the tracks with a mouse by adjusting controls that appear on your computer screen. Or mix the tracks with an external **control surface**, which looks like a mixer. The control surface adjusts the virtual controls on-screen.

Here are the steps in recording with an HD (hard-disk) recorder and a separate mixer:

1. Plug a mic or electric instrument into the mixer.

2. Connect the mixer's insert jacks to the HD recorder.

3. Record tracks on the HD recorder.

4. Mix the tracks with the mixer into an external 2-track recorder.

Another option is to record with an HD recorder–mixer. It combines a mixer and a multitrack HD recorder in a single portable chassis (Figure 1.8). A similar option is a MiniDisc recorder–mixer. Here are the steps:

1. Plug a mic or electric instrument into the mixer.
2. Record tracks on the HD recorder or MiniDisc recorder.
3. Mix the tracks with the mixer onto an external 2-track recorder.

# MIDI Sequencing

MIDI sequencing records your performance as moves or gestures rather than as sound. Figure 1.9 shows the process.

1. Play music on a MIDI controller: a keyboard, drum pads, breath controller, or whatever.
2. As you play the controller, it sends a MIDI signal from its MIDI OUT connector. This signal is a string of numbers—computer code—that tells which keys you pressed, when you pressed them, how fast you pressed them, and so on. In other words, the MIDI signal represents your performance gestures. It's not an audio signal.
3. The MIDI signal goes to a synthesizer or sound module. In these devices are tone generators that create musical sounds, such as a bass,

**Figure 1.8**
HD recorder–mixer.

**Figure 1.9**
MIDI sequencing system.

piano, or drums. The MIDI signal plays the tone generators. You hear them with speakers or headphones.

The MIDI signal could also drive a drum machine or sampler. They contain samples, which are recordings in computer memory of single notes played by real musical instruments. The MIDI signal plays the samples.

4. The MIDI signal also goes to a sequencer, a device that records the MIDI signal. Sequencers come in three forms: a circuit in a synth, a stand-alone box, or a computer sequencer program that records MIDI sequences on a hard drive.

5. When you play the sequencer recording, it activates the sound generators or samples to play the same notes you played. You can edit the sequencer recording—for example, fix incorrect notes; change the instrument sounds without having to redo the performance; or change the tempo without changing the pitch.

Want to record MIDI tracks on a MIDI sequencer, and also record audio tracks on a multitrack recorder? A tape synchronizer makes the sequencer and recorder stay together in time. For example, record synth and drum-machine parts with the sequencer. Then while listening to the sequence play, record vocals and acoustic instruments with the multitrack recorder. The synchronizer locks them together in time.

MIDI/digital-audio software lets you record sequences and digital audio on hard disk. First record MIDI sequences onto hard disk, then add several audio tracks: lead vocal, sax solo, or whatever. All these elements stay synchronized.

# Pros and Cons of Each Method

Live stereo recording is simple, cheap, and fast. But it usually sounds too muddy with rock music, and you must adjust balances by moving musicians. It can work well with classical music.

Live-mixed recording is fairly simple and quick. However, loud instruments might sound distant in the recording because of leakage between mics. And if the mix or performance has mistakes, the band has to re-record the entire song.

Multitrack tape recording has many advantages. You can **punch-in**: fix a musical mistake by recording a new, correct part over the mistake. You can **overdub**: record one instrument at a time. This reduces leakage and gives a tighter sound. Also, you can postpone mixing decisions until after the performance. This method is more complex and expensive than live-mixed recording.

Random access multitrack recording has all the advantages of multi-track tape recording. In addition, you can instantly rewind and instantly locate points in a song. You can edit individual tracks. However, hard-disk recordings need to be backed up so that the disk can be erased for new material.

MIDI sequencing lets you edit notes to correct mistakes. Sound quality is excellent, and you can change the instrument sounds after recording the performance. As for drawbacks, you are limited to the sounds of samplers and sound modules. MIDI/digital-audio software lets you add miked instruments to the mix.

# Editing/Mastering

No matter which recording method you use, eventually you'll mix all your songs to a 2-track recorder: cassette, open-reel tape, DAT, or your computer's hard drive.

Then you may want to edit those recorded mixes. Editing is the process where you remove noises and count-offs between songs, put the songs in the desired order, and put a few seconds of silence between songs. You edit an analog open-reel tape recording with a razor blade and splicing tape. You edit a digital recording with your personal computer and editing software (Figure 1.10). This system is called a Digital Audio Workstation or DAW.

The last step is to copy the edited program to tape, DAT, or CD-R. There's your final product, ready to duplicate on CD or cassette.

**Figure 1.10**
A Digital Audio
Workstation (DAW).

# Quality Levels of Recording Formats

Here is a list of various recording formats from lowest sound quality to highest:

1. Cassette (has some hiss, distortion, and wow and flutter that can make wobbly pitch).

2. Analog tape recorded at 7½ips or with narrow width tape (¼-inch, ½-inch) can sound very good but has some tape hiss.

3. MiniDisc (uses data compression that degrades the sound quality slightly—see Chapter 10).

4. Digital (16bit, 44.1kHz). Media that offer 16-bit recording are DAT, CD, MDM, or hard disk.

5. Digital (24bit, 96kHz) or high-speed analog tape, perhaps with noise reduction. Media that offer 24-bit recording are DVD, MDM, or hard disk. Super Audio CD (SACD) is a 1-bit system, but its sound is state-of-the-art.

6. MIDI. Since the sequencer recording is played by sound modules or samplers, it sounds exactly like the original performance. MIDI sequencer recordings reach the public on CD, DVD, or SACD media.

No matter what type of recording you do, each stage contributes to the sound quality of the finished tape. A bad-sounding master tape can be caused by any weak link: low-quality microphones, bad mic placement, improperly set mixer controls, and so on. A great-sounding tape results when you get every stage right. This book will help you reach that goal.

# 2

# EQUIPPING YOUR STUDIO

You want to set up a recording system that's affordable, easy to use, and sonically excellent. With today's wide array of user-friendly sound tools, you can do just that. This chapter is a guide to equipment for a recording studio: what it does, and what it costs.

In this chapter we'll examine:

1. Equipment and costs for budget studios
2. Equipment for higher-end studios
3. Details of each piece of equipment
4. Cable and connections
5. Simple acoustic treatments

What is the bare-bones equipment you need to crank out a decent demo CD? How much does it cost? Thanks to the new breed of affordable equipment, you can put together a complete home recording studio for under $1500.

First you should know the general recording process for popular music:

1. Plug a mic or an instrument into a multitrack recorder.
2. Record the instrument or vocal on one track.
3. Repeat this process with another instrument on another track, and so on—up to 4 or 8 tracks. Or record several instruments at once on several tracks.
4. Mix all these tracks with a mixer, combining them to 2 tracks of stereo music.

5. Record the stereo mix on a 2-track recorder. Repeat these steps for several songs.

6. Edit the mixes to put a few seconds of silence between the songs, and to put the songs in the desired order.

7. Copy the edited mixes onto a CD-R.

This process can be done in several ways; there are many equipment options. For example, you could record with a cassette multitracker, MiniDisc, hard-disk recorder, computer recording software, or a MIDI sequencer. I'll briefly explain what this equipment does.

# Low-Cost Recording Equipment

## *Cassette Multitracker*

Also called a portable studio, a cassette multitracker combines a 4-track cassette recorder with a mixer—all in one portable chassis (Figure 2.1). It lets you record several instruments and vocals, then mix them to stereo. The sound quality of this system is good enough to make demos, or to use as a musical scratchpad for ideas, but is not quite good enough to release commercial albums. Cassettes are old technology. Although they don't sound as clean as digital recordings or open-reel tape, cassette multi-trackers are easy to use and cost little. They are a good choice for beginning recordists.

**Figure 2.1** A cassette recorder–mixer.

## Digital Multitracker

A superior alternative to the cassette multitracker, the digital multitracker combines a digital multitrack recorder (hard disk or MiniDisc) with a mixer in a single chassis (Figure 2.2). It's convenient and portable. Plus it has random access: you can instantly go to any part of the recorded program. With cassettes, you must fast-forward or rewind to the part you want to hear.

## Multitrack Recording Software

Another random-access setup uses a personal computer with a sound card and multitrack recording software (Figure 2.3). The sound card converts audio into a signal that is recorded on the computer's hard disk as a magnetic pattern.

**Figure 2.2**
Digital multitracker.

**Figure 2.3**
Computer with a sound card and multitrack recording software.

You mix the tracks with a mouse by adjusting virtual controls that appear on your computer screen. Or mix the tracks with an external controller, which looks like a mixer. Record the mix on a external 2-track recorder or on your computer's hard drive.

Because software requires computer skills, it is a little harder to learn and use than a cassette or HD multitracker. Software recordings sound as good as HD multitracker recordings and better than cassette.

## MIDI/Digital-Audio Software

This software records both MIDI sequences (keyboard or drum-pad performances) and audio (vocals, sax, etc.) on hard disk.

## Effects Unit

This important device adds special sonic effects such as reverberation, echo, chorus, and flanging (Figure 2.4). Some recorder–mixers and recording software have effects built in.

## Compressor

A compressor is an electronic device that acts like an automatic volume control. It turns down the vocal when it is too loud, and turns up the vocal when it is too soft—making the vocal much easier to listen to.

## Two-Track Recorder

This device records the final stereo mix that you created with your recorder–mixer or computer. A 2-track recorder can be cassette, open-reel (Figure 2.5), MiniDisc, DAT, or a computer sound card and hard disk. Cassette is lowest quality and lowest cost; MiniDisc is better. DAT is CD quality. Computer recording is CD quality or better.

**Figure 2.4**  An effects unit, or signal processor.

**Figure 2.5**  A 2-track open-reel recorder.

## *Editing Software*

After all your songs are mixed to 2-track, you may want to edit the record-ing: remove noises and count-offs between songs, and put the songs in order with a few seconds of silence between them. You edit a digital recording with your personal computer and editing software. This system is called a Digital Audio Workstation (DAW) (Figure 2.3).

After editing the songs, you use a CD-R burner to copy the program to a CD-R. There's your final product—ready to duplicate.

## *Monitor System*

This is a pair of quality headphones or loudspeakers. You can use powered speakers, or use nonpowered speakers with a separate power amplifier.

An essential tool, the monitor system tells you what you're doing to the recorded sound. The sound you hear over the monitors is approxi-mately what the final listener will hear.

## *Microphone*

This device converts the sound of your voice (or any instrument) into an electrical signal that can be recorded. Microphone sound quality varies widely, so be sure to get a good mic costing at least $130 for a dynamic

mic or $250 for a condenser mic. For the latter, you also need phantom power, which is provided either by a phantom power supply or by some recorder–mixers.

# Equipment Costs

Now let's list the equipment for several different types of studios, and see how much it might cost. The following lists omit the acoustic materials, musical instruments, computer, cables, and recording media.

## *Cassette Multitracker Studio*

With this system (Figure 2.6), you might prefer to monitor with head-phones instead of speakers to save money. Don't skimp on headphone quality, because accurate monitoring is essential. You also could use your home stereo or some inexpensive studio monitors.

| | |
|---|---|
| 4-track cassette recorder/mixer | $225–600 |
| Microphone | $130–250 |
| Mic stand and boom | $35 |
| Direct box for bass and synth | $100 |
| Headphones | $170 |
| Effects unit | $135–250 |
| Compressor | $120–300 |
| Sound card | $50–400 |
| Editing software | $70–500 |
| CD-R recorder and software | $250 |
| Total | $1460–2855 |

The sound card, editing software, and CD-R recorder are optional. You might want to take your finished mixes to someone else for editing

**Figure 2.6**
Cassette multitracker studio.

and CD burning. If you want powered speakers, add $650–1000. If you also want a separate 2-track recorder (instead of your computer's hard drive), add $400–975 for a MiniDisc or DAT recorder.

## Digital Recorder–Mixer Studio

This studio is the next step up in quality. Since it records on MiniDisc or a hard drive, there is no tape hiss or distortion. The result is a cleaner sound.

The only difference in equipment is the 8-track digital recorder–mixer, which costs $900 to $1400 (and replaces the 4-track cassette recorder–mixer). All the other equipment is the same as above.

Although the 8-track digital recorder–mixer costs $500–800 more than the 4-track cassette version, the effects are built into the digital unit, so you can probably omit the external effects and compressor for a savings of $255–500. The net price increase over a cassette-based studio is $245–300. As I see it, getting digital sound quality and 8 tracks for $300 more is well worth it.

## Computer Studio

In this studio, the recorder, mixer and effects are in your computer. You need a sound card and multitrack recording software with built-in effects, at a cost of $500–650. All the other equipment is the same as above.

As you can see, the computer studio costs about the same as the cassette studio, but offers digital sound quality. It's a bargain. However, you'll be working with a mouse and a computer screen instead of a physical mixer with knobs and faders. Using a mouse can be fatiguing and can lead to repetitive stress syndrome.

As an alternative to the mouse, you might buy a control surface ($550–3000). It looks like a mixer with faders, but it adjusts the virtual controls you see on the computer screen. That way you can use your computer for recording, and control the software with knobs and faders instead of a mouse.

## MIDI Studio

MIDI stands for Musical Instrument Digital Interface. In this different kind of recording setup, you play synthesized musical instruments—bass, drums, piano, etc.—with a keyboard or drum pads (Figure 2.7).

The recording part of this studio is a sound card and some MIDI/digital-audio software. They let you record both MIDI tracks and

**Figure 2.7**   A simple MIDI studio.

audio tracks. Part of the software, a MIDI sequencer, records the notes you press on the keyboard. Another part of the software records audio signals, such as your vocals or acoustic instruments. Effects are built into the software.

Here's the minimum equipment you need:

| | |
|---|---|
| Keyboard controller | $50 |
| Sound module | $450–1500 |
| Drum machine (optional) | $450–1500 |
| MIDI/digital-audio software or a sequencer | $200–500 |

The keyboard controller is a piano-style keyboard that puts out MIDI signals and triggers the sound module, which simulates musical instruments.

You'll also need headphones, a good mic and mic stand, a CD-R burner, and maybe some powered speakers. Total cost is $1335–3635.

As an alternative, use a keyboard workstation. This is a keyboard synth with a built-in sequencer and effects. Cost is about $2000. The workstation lets you create the entire musical backup on a stereo pair of channels, all in the keyboard.

You need to mix your vocal with the two channels of music from the keyboard workstation. To do that, use the MIDI/digital-audio software.

## Recording System for Classical Music

Suppose you want to record a classical music ensemble. With this recording system (Figure 2.8), you can tape an orchestra, symphonic band, choir, pipe organ, string quartet, duet, or soloist. You also can record small folk or jazz groups if you record in a good-sounding room and balance the musicians by their placement around the mics.

**Figure 2.8**
Low-cost recording system for classical music.

| | |
|---|---:|
| 1 DAT recorder | $700 |
| 2 high-quality condenser mics | $500 |
| 1 stereo phantom-power supply | $125 |
| 1 or 2 mic stands and booms | $80 |
| 2 50-foot mic cables | $50 |
| 1 set high-quality headphones | $80 |
| Total | $1535 |

**Options:** Use two battery-powered boundary mics on the stage floor ($120 to $360/pair) and omit the mic stands. These mics will work for a small musical ensemble such as a quartet or small choir. A pair of mic preamps can give a cleaner sound than the mic preamps built into the DAT recorder.

We've looked at several types of bare-bones recording setups. All can help you create quality demos. You can go much higher in price to get more features and better sound. For example, if you want to record an entire rock band playing all at once, with each instrument having its own mic, you'll need to add more microphones, more tracks, and more headphones.

As we've seen, putting together a home studio or project studio needn't cost much. As technology develops, better equipment is available at lower prices. That dream of owning your own studio is within reach.

# Higher-Cost Recording Equipment

So far we've talked about 2-track recorders, and 4-track/8-track recorder–mixers. The next step up in price, quality, and flexibility are these: a separate mixer and multitrack recorder (Figure 2.9), or a 16-track or 24-track recorder–mixer.

This equipment is good enough to record albums for commercial release. Let's look at the mixer first.

## *Mixer*

A mixer (Figure 2.10) is an electronic device with an elaborate control panel. The mixer is connected to your multitrack recorder. You plug mics

**Figure 2.9**
Mixer/multitrack recorder
studio.

**Figure 2.10** A mixer.

and electric instruments into the mixer, which amplifies their signals. While recording, you use the mixer controls to send those signals to the desired tape tracks, and set recording levels. During mixdown, the mixer combines (mixes) the tracks to stereo. It lets you adjust the sound quality of each track.

A large, complex mixer is called a **mixing console** or **board**. Mixing consoles are explained in more detail in Chapter 12.

## Multitrack Recorders

You have a choice of analog or digital multitrack recorders.

## Analog Multitrack Tape Recorder

An 8-track analog multitrack tape recorder is shown in Figure 2.11. Analog has more tape hiss, distortion, and wow and flutter (unsteady pitch) than digital. But these flaws are pretty much inaudible with high-end analog recorders. Compared to 16-bit 48K digital multitracks, analog multitracks make cymbals sound a little more sweet or gentle, and analog tape distortion adds a fat, warm sound. Analog multitrack uses ¼-inch or wider tape on reels; digital multitrack uses open-reel tape, S-VHS, Hi-8 video cassettes, or a hard drive.

## Digital Multitrack Recorder

There are four types of digital multitrack recorders: open-reel, Modular Digital Multitrack, standalone hard disk, and computer hard disk with multitrack software. Let's consider each one.

- An open-reel digital multitrack recorder records digital audio on open-reel tape and is quite expensive.
- A Modular Digital Multitrack (MDM) is an 8-track digital recorder that records on a video cassette (Figure 2.12). It offers very clean sound and long recording time (40 minutes for ADAT, 1 hour 48

**Figure 2.11**  An 8-track open-reel recorder.

**Figure 2.12**
A Modular Digital
Multitrack (MDM).

minutes for TASCAM DTRs) but costs about $2000 to $3500. You can connect several MDMs together to add more tracks, 8 at a time.

- A standalone Multitrack Hard-Disk Recorder records on a hard disk. It sounds the same as the MDM, but offers random access and is more reliable. However, its data must be backed up to free up space for new projects.
- Multitrack recording software and sound cards can record up to 24 tracks or more, depending on your computer speed and hard-drive speed.

## *Hard-Disk Recorder–Mixer: 16 to 24 Tracks*

As we said before, a multitrack HD recorder can be combined with a mixer in a single chassis, forming an HD recorder–mixer. High-end units can record up to 16 or 24 tracks.

# Equipment Details

Now let's look more closely at each component of the recording studio.

## *Cassette Multitracker*

One of the least expensive ways to record involves the use of a cassette multitracker—also called a cassette recorder–mixer or portable studio. It's a small, portable unit combining a mixer with a multitrack cassette recorder, all in one chassis (Figure 2.1). Also available are MiniDisc and hard-disk recorder–mixers, which we'll cover in Chapter 10.

As we said, a cassette multitracker has two main parts: a mixer and a recorder. You plug microphones and electric musical instruments into the mixer, which amplifies their signals and routes them to tape tracks.

The cassette recorder can record up to 4 tracks. You record one instrument per track or several instruments per track. For example, record piano on track 1, bass on 2, drum machine on 3, and your vocal on 4.

Then after all the tracks are recorded, you play them back through the mixer, which blends or combines them to 2-channel stereo. You balance the tracks—adjust their relative loudness—and record the mix on a separate 2-track recorder. The recording made on that machine is the final product.

Cassette multitracker prices range from about $250 to $800. As price increases, you get cleaner, crisper sound, more inputs, and more features.

Let's take a look at recorder–mixer features.

## Overdubbing

All recorder–mixers have the overdubbing feature. While listening to tracks already recorded, the musician plays along with them and records a new part on an unused track. For example, suppose you've already recorded bass and drums and you want to add a guitar track. The performer listens to a headphone mix of the bass track, drum track, and his or her guitar signal. While the bass and drum tracks play, the musician plays the guitar along with them, and you record the guitar on an unused track.

## Simultaneous Recording on All Tracks

Simultaneous recording is useful especially for recording a live performance. When you record in a studio, you often can record one or two tracks at a time. But when you record a live performance, you need to record all the tracks at once. Not all recorder–mixers let you do this.

## Punch-In/Out

Use the punch-in and punch-out functions to fix mistakes. As the tape is playing, punch into record mode just before the mistake, play a new correct part that is recorded, and punch out of record mode when you're finished. Most recorder–mixers accept a footswitch so you can punch-in with your foot while playing your instrument.

## Bouncing Tracks

When you bounce (or ping-pong) tracks, you mix two or three tracks together and record the result on an unused track. Then you can erase the original tracks, freeing them for recording more instruments. This way you can record up to nine tracks with a 4-track machine. All recorder–mixers permit bouncing.

## Tape Speed

Tape speed is the rate at which tape moves past the record/playback head. In cassette recorders, two speeds are available: $1\frac{7}{8}$ inches-per-second (ips) and/or $3\frac{3}{4}$ ips. On machines running at $1\frac{7}{8}$ ips, you can play standard commercial cassettes which also run at that speed. If your machine can record at $3\frac{3}{4}$ ips, its recordings will sound clearer and crisper than those made at $1\frac{7}{8}$ ips.

## Pitch Control

Pitch control lets you adjust the tape speed up or down so you can match the pitch of recorded tracks to the pitch of new instruments to be recorded. All recorder–mixers have this feature.

## Equalization

Equalization (EQ) means tone control. The simplest units have no EQ; you're stuck with the sound you get from your microphones. Most inexpensive units include a bass and treble control, one set per input. Fancier recorder–mixers have sweepable or semi-parametric EQ, which lets you continuously vary the frequency you want to adjust. This type of EQ offers the most control over the tone quality of each instrument you're recording.

## Effects Loop (Aux Loop)

The effects loop is a set of connectors (labeled "send" and "return") for hooking up an external effects unit, such as a reverb or delay device. Effects add a professional polish to your productions.

If your recorder–mixer has no effects loops, you can still record music, but without any effects. It sounds rather dead and plain. A unit with one effects send lets you add one type of effect; a unit with two effects loops lets you add two for even more sonic interest. A stereo effects loop lets you hear effects in stereo, if your effects device is a stereo unit.

Some recorder–mixers have digital reverb built in so that you don't need to buy an external reverb unit.

## Noise Reduction

A noise reduction circuit reduces the tape hiss that is inherent in cassette tape recording. Dolby C and dbx work best; Dolby B is less effective. But all help you make clean, noise-free recordings.

## Autolocate

With this feature, you can store a certain location on tape in a memory. When you press "locate," the tape rewinds or fast-forwards to that location. You could use this feature to move tape repeatedly between two preset points, such as the beginning and end of a punch-in.

A similar feature is **return-to-zero**, also called "zero stop" or "memory rewind." When you enable return-to-zero, the tape rewinds to a preset point that you mark "000" on the tape counter. This feature makes it easy to practice a punch-in or a mix repeatedly.

## Solenoid Switches

When you push one of your tape-motion controls, the action can be either mechanical or solenoid operated. Solenoid switching ("electronic transport") is gentler to the tape, and often includes logic that protects the tape from rapid changes in tape motion.

## XLR-Type Balanced Inputs

An XLR-type microphone input connector looks like three small holes arranged in a triangle. If your mixer has such inputs, you can run long mic cables without picking up hum. This type of connector is found only in high-end units. Lower-cost recorder–mixers use ¼-inch phone jacks (receptacles) for mic inputs, which are adequate for small studios. But to use them, you also need some female XLR-to-¼-inch impedance-matching adapters, available at Radio Shack.

## Insert Jacks

Insert jack connectors let you plug in a compressor (or other signal processor) in line with an input signal. They make it easy to modify the sound of a single instrument or vocal. Only the more expensive units have this feature.

## Sync Track

A sync track (usually the highest numbered track) records a synchronization tone from a MIDI sequencer. The tone synchronizes tape tracks with sequencer tracks. In this way, you can have your sequencer play synthesized bass, drums, and keyboards while your multitrack recorder plays vocals and acoustic instruments—all in sync.

This is a great way to get extra tracks for little cost. Plus, when you do your mixdown, all the synth tracks play "live" (from the synth outputs) rather than from tape. The result is a cleaner mix.

Any track on any multitrack recorder can record the sync tone. But a dedicated sync track has its own input connector for the sync tone and allows noise reduction to be switched off for more reliable recording.

The sync track also is used for SMPTE (Society of Motion Picture and Television Engineers) time code, another type of synchronizing signal.

### "Notebook" versus "Full-Featured"

A notebook multitracker is very basic. It is used as a scratchpad for musical ideas. Omitting EQ, effects loops, and XLR connectors makes the notebook unit fast and easy to use. In contrast, a full-featured unit is harder to learn, but offers much more control over the sound quality.

## *Microphones*

Another essential item for the studio is one or more microphones. Good mics are essential for quality sound—and you get what you pay for. If you experiment with various types of microphones, you find big differences in fidelity among them. One or more microphones costing at least $125 to $250 each are recommended. Although $250 may seem like a lot of money for a microphone, you can't skimp here and expect to get quality sound. Any distortion or weird tone quality in the microphone may be difficult or impossible to remove later. It's false economy to use a cheap mic.

You may be able to borrow some good microphones, or use the ones you normally use for P.A. Your ears should tell you if the fidelity is adequate for your purpose. Some people are happy to get any sound on tape; others settle for nothing less than professional sound quality.

How many mics and mic inputs do you need? It depends on the instruments you want to record. If you want to mic a drum set, you might need 8 mics and 8 mic inputs, mixing those to 1 or 2 tracks. On the other hand, if you use MIDI instruments, you might need only one good mic for vocals and acoustic instruments. You can use one mic on several different instruments and vocals if you overdub them one at a time.

Probably the most useful mic types for home recording are the cardioid condenser mic and cardioid dynamic mic. The cardioid pickup pattern helps reject room acoustics for a tighter sound. The condenser type is commonly used on cymbals, acoustic instruments, and studio vocals; dynamics are used typically on drums and guitar amps. (For more information on microphones, see Chapter 6.)

If you plan to record solo instruments or musical ensembles in stereo with two mics out front, you need two condenser mics of the same model number, or a stereo microphone. See Chapter 19 for details.

### Phantom-Power Supply

A phantom-power supply powers the circuits in condenser mics. It uses the same cable as the mic's audio signal. You can omit the supply if your condenser mic has a battery, or if your mixer supplies phantom power.

### Mic Preamp

This device amplifies a mic signal up to a higher voltage, called **line level**, which is needed by mixers and tape recorders. A standalone mic preamp provides a little cleaner sound than the mic preamps built into a mixer, but costs much more. Studios on a budget can do without it.

## Direct Box

A direct box is a useful accessory for recorder–mixers with balanced XLR-type mic inputs. A direct box is a small device that connects an electric instrument (guitar, bass, synth) to a mixer XLR-type mic input. It lets you record electric instruments directly into your mixer without a microphone. You can buy a direct box for as little as $50.

A useful feature in a direct box is a filter, which simulates the tone quality of a guitar amplifier/speaker. (See Chapter 8 for more information.)

A direct box or guitar cord picks up a very clean sound, which may be undesirable for electric guitar. If you want to pick up the distortion of the guitar amp, use a microphone instead. Or try a direct box that plugs into the external speaker jack on your guitar amp. It picks up the amp distortion and filters it (reduces the treble) to make it sound more like a guitar speaker.

Some recorder–mixers have "high-impedance" inputs meant for electric guitars. In this case, simply use a short guitar cord between your instrument and the mixer input.

## Monitor System

The monitor system lets you hear what you're recording and mixing. You can use a pair of high-quality headphones, or a pair of loudspeakers and a power amplifier. The power amplifier strengthens the mixer's signal so it can drive loudspeakers. The speakers should be accurate, high-fidelity types costing at least $200 each. Your home stereo might be good enough to serve, but skimping on a monitor system is not a smart move.

Near-field studio monitor speakers (described in Chapter 4) are small, bookshelf-type speakers that are placed about 3 feet apart and 3 feet from you as you sit at your mixer. Also available are powered monitors with built-in amplifiers.

If your monitor speakers are in the same room as your microphones, the mics pick up the sound of the speakers. This causes feedback or a muddy sound. In this case, it's better to monitor with headphones while recording.

If you're recording only yourself, one set of headphones is enough. But if you're recording another musician, you both need headphones. Many recorder–mixers have two headphone jacks for this purpose.

If you want to record or overdub several people at once, you need headphones for all of them. For example, if you're overdubbing three harmony vocalists, each one needs headphones to hear previously recorded tracks to sing with.

To connect all these headphones, you could build a headphone junction box: an aluminum or plastic box that contains several headphone jacks. These are wired to a cable coming from your mixer's headphone jack. Or you could use a splitter cable, which makes two jacks out of one.

## *Effects*

Effects such as reverberation, echo, and chorus can add sonic excitement to a recording. They are produced by devices called **signal processors** (see Figure 2.4).

The most essential effect is **reverberation**, a slow decay of sound such as you hear just after you shout in an empty gymnasium ("HELLO-O-O-o-o-o . . ."). Reverberation adds a sense of space; it can put your music in a concert hall, a small club, or a cathedral. This effect is usually produced by a digital reverb unit, available for $200 and up.

Another popular effect is **echo**, a repetition of a sound ("HELLO hello hello"). It's made by a **delay unit**, which also provides other effects such as chorus, doubling, and flanging.

A **multieffects processor** combines several effects in a single box. These effects can be heard one at a time or several at once. You can even customize the sounds by pushing buttons to change the presets. (See Chapter 11 for more information on effects.)

# Rack and Patch Bay

A rack is an enclosure to mount signal processors and other equipment in. A patch bay or patch panel in a rack is a group of connectors that are wired to equipment inputs and outputs. Neither one is essential, but they are convenient.

# Miscellaneous Equipment

Other equipment for your home studio includes power outlet strips, lighting, tables or studio furniture, mic pop filters, masking tape and a pen to label inputs and cables, head-cleaning fluid and cotton swabs to clean analog recorder tape heads, analog tape head demagnetizer, DAT and MDM cleaning tapes, MIDI equipment stands, session forms, splicing block and splicing tape for analog tape editing, connector adapters, pen and paper, a flashlight, and so on.

# Blank Recording Media

For your recorder you need some blank media to record on. Use the brand suggested by the recorder manufacturer.

Cassette: Brand-name metal or chrome cassette tape

Open-reel multitrack: High-output, low-noise tape of width $\frac{1}{4}$ inch, $\frac{1}{2}$ inch, 1 inch, or 2 inch

MDM: S-VHS video cassettes for Alesis ADAT or Hi-8 video cassettes for TASCAM DTRS

MiniDisc multitrack: MD data disc

Computer: CD-R or CD-RW

HD recorder or HD recorder–mixer: The hard drive recording medium is built in; some units include removable hard drives

# MIDI Studio Equipment

MIDI is covered in detail in Chapter 16. Here are some components in a typical MIDI studio (Figure 2.13).

# MIDI Controller

A MIDI controller is a musical-performance device, such as a keyboard or drum pads, that puts out a MIDI signal when you play it. A MIDI signal

**Figure 2.13**
MIDI/digital-audio
recording system (mixer
not shown).

is a string of numbers that tells which notes you played, when you played them, and so on.

## Synthesizer

A synthesizer (synth) is a piano-style keyboard instrument that simulates the sound of real musical instruments, or generates original sounds. When you play a synth, it puts out a MIDI signal and an audio signal.

## Sequencer

A sequencer is a device, or a computer program, that records the MIDI signal of your performance into computer memory for later editing and playback. A sequence is a computer file of the notes you played and their timing.

## Sampler

A sampler is a device that makes digital recordings of single notes, or short musical phrases, of real musical instruments. The sampler stores the samples in computer memory or on floppy disks. Using a MIDI controller or a sequencer, you trigger the sampler to play notes.

## Sound Module

A sound module is a device that plays prerecorded samples or synthesized sounds when triggered by a MIDI controller or sequencer. It does not record samples.

## Drum Machine

A drum machine is a device that simulates a drummer. It's a sequencer that records a drum performance done on its built-in pads. Each pad plays a different drum sound. When you play back your recorded performance, the samples play. This simulates a drum set and percussion.

## Line Mixer

A line mixer is a small mixer that combines the signals of synths, sound modules, samplers, and drum machines. A line mixer has no mic preamps. If you want to use a mic with your MIDI studio, you also need a mic preamp, or a mixer with mic preamps, or a DAT recorder with a mic preamp.

## MIDI Interface

A MIDI Interface is a circuit card that plugs into a slot in your computer. It converts a MIDI signal into computer data, and vice versa. You use the computer to record and edit sequences of musical notes.

## MIDI Tape-Sync Box

A MIDI tape-sync box is a device that synchronizes a multitrack tape recorder with a sequencer. You record MIDI-instrument parts with the sequencer, record vocals and acoustic instruments with the tape recorder, and sync them together with the tape-sync box. Some recorder–mixers have MIDI tape sync already built in.

## MIDI Software

Listed below are some types of MIDI software.

- **Sequencer software:** Described earlier.
- **Notation software** ($80–600): Displays your performance as a score on screen. You can edit the notes, type in lyrics and chords, and print out the score.
- **Editor/librarian software** ($200): Edits synth patches and stores them on disk.
- **MIDI/digital-audio software** ($50–1000): Also called **digital-audio sequencer** software. This software is part of a system that includes your computer, sound card, and MIDI interface. (Some sound cards

include MIDI interfaces). The system lets you record MIDI sequences (from a MIDI controller) and digital audio tracks (from a mic) on a hard disk. The sequences and digital audio play at the same time in sync. Both can be edited.

Several things happen when you play back what you recorded:

1. The sequencer's MIDI signal comes from the MIDI OUT connector in the MIDI interface.
2. The sequencer's MIDI signal plays notes through a synth, sound module, and/or drum machine.
3. The digital audio—a multitrack mix—plays from the sound-card output.
4. A mixer combines the MIDI-equipment audio with the sound-card audio, and you record the mix on DAT.

# Setting Up Your Studio

Once you have your equipment, you need to connect it together with cables, and possibly install equipment racks and acoustic treatment. Let's consider each step.

## *Cables and Equipment Connectors*

Cables carry electric signals from one audio component to another. They are usually made of one or two insulated conductors (wires) surrounded by a fine-wire mesh shield that reduces hum. Outside the shield is a plastic or rubber insulating jacket.

Cables are either balanced or unbalanced. A **balanced** line is a cable that uses two conductors to carry the signal, surrounded by a shield (see Figure 2.14). An **unbalanced** line has a single conductor surrounded by a shield (see Figure 2.15).

Recording equipment also has balanced or unbalanced connectors. *Be sure your cable connectors match your equipment connectors.* Balanced equipment has a 3-pin (XLR-type) connector (Figure 2.16); unbalanced equipment has a ¼-inch phone jack (Figure 2.17) or phono jack (RCA) connector (Figure 2.18). A jack is a receptacle; a plug inserts into a jack.

The balanced line rejects hum better than an unbalanced line, but an unbalanced line less than 10 feet long usually provides adequate hum rejection and costs less.

**Figure 2.14**
A 2-conductor shielded,
balanced line.

**Figure 2.15**
A 1-conductor shielded,
unbalanced line.

**Figure 2.16**
A 3-pin XLR-type connector
used in balanced
equipment.

**Figure 2.17**
A ¼-inch phone jack
used in unbalanced
equipment.

**Figure 2.18**
A phono (RCA) jack used
in unbalanced equipment.

A cable carries one of these four signal levels or voltages:

- Mic level (about 2 millivolts, or 0.002 volt)
- Electric guitar or keyboard level (about 0.1 volt)
- Line level (0.316 volt for unbalanced equipment, 1.23 volts for balanced equipment)
- Speaker level (about 20 volts)

The term "0.316 volt" also is known as "−10 dBV"; the term "1.23 volts" also is known as +4 dBu (see Appendix A).

## Cable Connectors

There are several types of connectors used in audio. Figure 2.19 shows a ¼-inch phone plug, used with cables for unbalanced microphones, synthesizers, and electric instruments. The tip terminal is soldered to the cable's center conductor; the sleeve terminal is soldered to the cable shield.

Figure 2.20 shows an RCA or phono plug, used to connect unbalanced line-level signals. The center pin is soldered to the cable's center conductor; the cup terminal is soldered to the cable shield.

Figure 2.21 shows a 3-pin pro audio connector (XLR-type). It is used with cables for balanced mics and balanced recording equipment. The

**Figure 2.19**
A ¼-inch phone plug.

**Figure 2.20**
An RCA (phono) plug.

(A) Female

(B) Male

**Figure 2.21**  XLR-type connectors: (A) female; (B) male.

female connector (with holes; Figure 2.21A) plugs into equipment outputs. The male connector (with pins; Figure 2.21B) plugs into equipment inputs. Pin 1 is soldered to the cable shield; pin 2 is soldered to the "hot" red or white lead; and pin 3 is soldered to the remaining lead. This wiring applies to both female and male connectors.

Figure 2.22 shows a stereo phone plug, used with stereo headphones and with some balanced line-level cables. For headphones, the tip terminal is soldered to the left-channel lead; the ring terminal is soldered to the right-channel lead; and the sleeve terminal is soldered to the common lead. For balanced line-level cables, the sleeve terminal is soldered to the shield; the tip terminal is soldered to the hot red or white lead; and the ring terminal is soldered to the remaining lead.

Some mixers have **insert** jacks that are stereo phone jacks; each jack accepts a stereo phone plug. Tip is the send signal to an audio device input; ring is the return signal from the device output; and sleeve is ground.

If you have unbalanced microphone inputs (¼-inch diameter holes) on your recorder or mixer, use a balanced cable (with XLRs on both ends) from mic to input. This reduces hum. At the mixer input, plug an **impedance-matching adapter** into the mic cable, and into the mixer input. Sold at Radio Shack, the adapter has a female XLR connector on one end and a ¼-inch phone plug on the other (see Figure 2.23).

When you connect balanced equipment to unbalanced equipment, use the circuit shown in Figure 2.24 to match their levels. Balanced equipment operates at a relatively high level or voltage (called +4 dBu or +4); unbalanced equipment operates at a lower level (called −10 dBV or −10).

**Figure 2.22**
A stereo phone plug.

**Figure 2.23**
An impedance-matching
adapter.

LOW-TO-HIGH IMPEDANCE MATCHING ADAPTER

**Figure 2.24** A circuit for matching a balanced +4 dBm output to an unbalanced –10 dBV input. It reduces the level 12 dB.

## Cable Types

Cables are also classified according to their function. In a studio, you'll use five types of cables: mic cables, guitar cords, patch cords, MIDI cables, and speaker cables.

A mic cable is usually 2-conductor shielded. It has two wires to carry the signal, surrounded by a fine-wire cylinder or shield that reduces hum pickup. On one end of the cable is a connector that plugs into the microphone, usually a female XLR-type. On the other end is either a ¼-inch phone plug or a male XLR-type connector that plugs into your mixer.

Rather than running several mic cables to your recorder–mixer, you might consider using a **snake**: a box with multiple mic connectors, all wired to a thick multiconductor cable (Figure 2.25). A snake is especially convenient if you're running long cables to recording equipment in a separate room. It's essential for most on-location recording.

A guitar cord is made of 1-conductor shielded cable with a ¼-inch phone plug on each end. Use it to record instruments directly—the electric guitar, electric bass, synthesizer, and drum machine.

Patch cords connect your recorder–mixer to external devices: an effects unit, a 2-track recorder, and a power amplifier. An unbalanced patch cord is made of 1-conductor shielded cable with either a ¼-inch phone plug or a phono (RCA) connector on each end. A stereo patch cord is two patch cords joined together. Professional balanced equipment is interconnected with 2-conductor shielded cable having a female XLR on one end and a male XLR on the other. Professional patch bays use balanced cables with tip-ring-sleeve phone plugs.

STAGE BOX

CONNECTORS TO
MIC CABLES

SNAKE

CONNECTORS
TO MIXER

**Figure 2.25**   A stage box/snake.

A MIDI cable uses a 5-pin DIN connector on each end of a 2-conductor shielded cable. The cable connects MIDI OUT to MIDI IN, or MIDI THRU to MIDI IN.

A speaker cable connects the power amp to each loudspeaker. Speaker cables are normally made of lamp cord (zip cord). To avoid wasting power, speaker cables should be as short as possible and should be heavy gauge (between 12 and 16 gauge). Number 12 gauge is thicker than 14; 14 is thicker than 16.

## Rack/Patch Panel

You might want to mount your signal processors in a **rack**, a wooden or metal enclosure with mounting holes for equipment (Figure 2.26). You also might want to install a **patch panel** or **patch bay**: a group of connectors that are wired to equipment inputs and outputs. Using a patch panel and patch cords, you can change equipment connections easily. You also can bypass or patch around defective equipment. Note that patch bays increase the chance of hum pickup slightly because of the additional cables and connectors.

Figure 2.27 shows some typical patch-panel assignments.

## Equipment Connections

The instruction manuals of your equipment tell how to connect each component to the others. In general, use cables that are as short as possible to reduce hum, but that are long enough to let you make changes.

**Figure 2.26**
A rack and patch panel.

Be sure to label all your cables on both ends according to what they plug into—for example, TRACK 6 OUT or REVERB IN. If you change connections temporarily, or the cable becomes unplugged, you'll know where to plug it back in. A piece of masking tape folded over the end of the cable makes a stay-put label.

Typically, you follow this procedure to connect equipment (see Figure 2.28):

1. Plug audio equipment and electric musical instruments into outlet strips fed from the same circuit breaker.

2. Connect mics and direct boxes to mic cables.

3. Connect mic cables either to the snake junction box, or directly into mixer mic inputs. Connect the snake connectors into mixer mic inputs. If your mixer has phone-jack mic inputs, you probably need to use an impedance-matching adapter (female XLR to phone) between the mic cable and the mic input jack (Figure 2.23).

4. Set the output volume of synthesizers and drum machines about three-quarters up. Connect synthesizers and drum machines to mixer

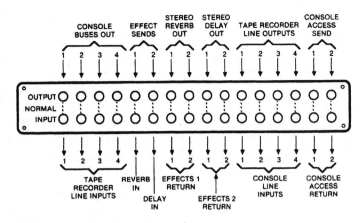

**Figure 2.27** Some typical patch-panel assignments.

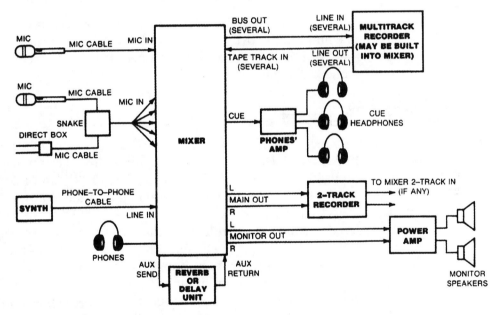

**Figure 2.28** Equipment connections.

line inputs. If this causes hum, use a direct box. If you lack a direct box, and the instrument and mixer both have 3-prong power cords, try cutting or unsoldering the cable shield at the instrument end of the cable.

5. Connect the mixer main outputs to a 2-track recorder.

6. Connect the 2-track recorder outputs to the mixer 2-track inputs (if any).

7. Connect the mixer monitor outputs to the power-amp inputs.
8. Connect the power-amp outputs to loudspeakers.
9. Connect the mixer aux-send connectors to effects inputs.
10. Connect the effects outputs to the mixer aux-return or bus-in connectors.
11. If you're using a separate mixer and multitrack recorder, connect mixer bus 1 to recorder track 1 IN; connect bus 2 to track 2, and so on. Also connect the recorder's track 1 OUT to the mixer's tape-track 1 IN; connect the track 2 OUT to the mixer's tape-track 2 in, and so on.

As an alternative, connect insert jacks to multitrack inputs and outputs. At each insert plug, connect the tip (send) terminal to a track input; connect the ring (return) terminal to the same track's output.

12. If you have several headphones for musicians, connect the cue output to a small amplifier to drive their headphones. Or if the mixer's headphone signal is powerful enough, connect it to a box with several headphone jacks wired in parallel.

## Acoustic Treatment

Along with the recording equipment, you need a quiet room to record in—the larger the better. A basement, living room, or bedroom can work. Many garages have been turned into studios. If the room has a lot of hard surfaces, you might need to place some material in the studio to absorb sound reflections. This treatment reduces the reverberation in the room and gives a clearer recorded sound. For budget or improvised studios, the acoustic treatment has to be limited. Try surrounding the instrument and its mic with thick blankets or sleeping bags hung a few feet away. Maybe hang them on ropes tied between room fixtures. Carpet the floor and nail some egg-crate type mattress foam to wood-paneled walls. You can also try some sound-absorbing cylinders, made commercially.

Add absorbers spaced evenly around the walls until your recordings sound reasonably dry (free of audible room reverberation). There's more on acoustic treatments in Chapter 3.

**Note:** By using close miking, direct boxes and overdubs, you might be able to make good recordings in a room without any acoustic treatment.

This chapter briefly covered the equipment and connectors for a recording studio. The rest of this book explains each piece of equipment in detail and tells how to use it for best results.

# SOUND, SIGNALS, AND STUDIO ACOUSTICS

When you make a recording, you deal with at least two kinds of invisible energy: sound waves and electrical signals. For example, a microphone converts sound into a signal. A signal is a varying voltage that carries information. In our case, it's musical information.

This chapter covers some characteristics of sound and audio signals. These facts will help you know what's going on inside your mixer as you adjust the controls. Better sound is the result.

## Sound Wave Creation

To produce sound, most musical instruments vibrate against air molecules, which pick up the vibration and pass it along as sound waves. When these vibrations strike your ears, you hear sound.

To illustrate how sound waves are created, imagine a vibrating speaker cone in a guitar amp. When the cone moves out, it pushes the adjacent air molecules closer together. This forms a **compression**. When the cone moves in, it pulls the molecules farther apart, forming a **rarefaction**. As shown in Figure 3.1, the compressions have a higher pressure than normal atmospheric pressure; the rarefactions have a lower pressure than normal.

These disturbances pass from one molecule to the next in a springlike motion—each molecule vibrates back and forth to pass the wave

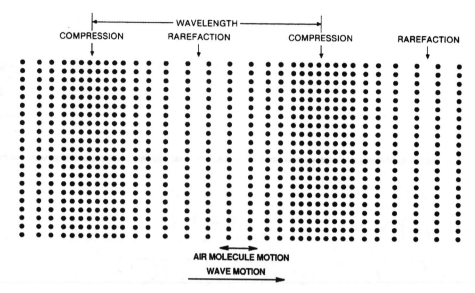

Figure 3.1 A sound wave.

**Figure 3.2**
Sound pressure vs time of
one cycle of a sound
wave.

along. The sound waves travel outward from the sound source at 1130 feet
per second, the speed of sound.

At some receiving point, such as an ear or a microphone, the air pressure varies up and down as the disturbances pass by. Figure 3.2 is a graph
showing how sound pressure varies with time—the "wave" motion. The
high point of the graph is called a **peak**; the low point is called a **trough**.
The horizontal center line of the graph is normal atmospheric pressure.

# Characteristics of Sound Waves

Figure 3.3 shows three waves in succession. One complete vibration from
normal to high to low pressure and back to the starting point is called one
**cycle**. The time it takes to complete one cycle—from the peak of one wave
to the next—is called the **period** of the wave. One cycle is one period long.

**Figure 3.3**
Three cycles of a wave.

# Amplitude

The height of the wave is its amplitude. Loud sounds have high amplitudes (big pressure changes); quiet sounds have low amplitudes (small pressure changes).

# Wavelength

When a sound wave travels through the air, the physical distance from one peak (compression) to the next is called a **wavelength** (refer to Figure 3.1). Low-pitched sounds have long wavelengths (several feet); high-pitched sounds have short wavelengths (a few inches or less).

# Frequency

The sound source (in this case, the guitar-amp loudspeaker) vibrates back and forth many times a second. The number of cycles completed in one second is called **frequency**. The faster the speaker vibrates, the higher the frequency of the sound. Frequency is measured in **hertz (Hz)**, which stands for cycles per second. One-thousand hertz is called "one kilohertz," abbreviated kHz.

The higher the frequency, the higher the perceived pitch of the sound. Low-frequency tones have a low pitch (like low E on a bass, which is 41 Hz). High-frequency tones have a high pitch (like four octaves above middle-C, or 4186 Hz). Doubling the frequency raises the pitch one **octave**.

Children can hear frequencies from 20 Hz to 20 kHz, and most adults with good hearing can hear up to 15 kHz or higher. Each musical instrument produces a range of frequencies, say, 41 Hz to 9 kHz for a string bass, or 196 Hz to 15 kHz for a violin.

# Phase and Phase Shift

The **phase** of any point on the wave is its degree of progression in the cycle—the beginning, the peak, the trough, or anywhere between. Phase

45

**Figure 3.4**
The phases of various points on a wave.

**Figure 3.5**
Two waves that are 90 degrees out-of-phase.

is measured in degrees, with 360 degrees being one complete cycle. The beginning of a wave is 0 degrees; the peak is 90 degrees (one-quarter cycle), and the end is 360 degrees. Figure 3.4 shows the phases of various points on the wave.

If there are two identical waves traveling together, but one is delayed with respect to the other, there is a **phase shift** between the two waves. The more delay, the more phase shift. Phase shift is measured in degrees. Figure 3.5 shows two waves separated by 90 degrees (one-quarter of a cycle) of phase shift. The dashed wave lags the solid wave by 90 degrees.

When there is a 180-degree phase shift between two identical waves, the peak of one wave coincides with the trough of another. If these two waves are combined, they cancel out. This phenomenon is called **phase cancellation**.

Suppose you have a signal with a wide range of frequencies, such as the singing voice. If you delay this signal and combine it with the original undelayed signal, some frequencies will be 180 degrees out-of-phase and will cancel. This makes a hollow, filtered tone quality.

Here's an example of how this can happen. Suppose you're recording a singer/guitarist with one mic near the singer and another mic near the guitar. Both mics pick up the singer. The singer's mic is close to the mouth, and you hear it with no delay in the signal. The guitar mic is farther from the mouth, so its voice signal is delayed. When you mix the two mics, you often hear a funny tone quality caused by phase cancellations between the two mics.

Suppose you're recording a stage play with a mic on a short stand on the floor. The mic picks up the direct sound from the actors, but it also picks up delayed reflections off the floor. Direct and delayed sounds combine at the mic, causing phase cancellations. You hear it as a hollow, filtered sound that changes when the actor walks while talking.

## *Harmonics*

The type of wave shown in Figure 3.2 is called a **sine wave**. It is a pure tone of a single frequency, like a signal from a tone generator. In contrast, most musical tones have a complex waveform, which has more than one frequency component. All sounds are combinations of sine waves of different frequencies and amplitudes. Figure 3.6 shows sine waves of three frequencies combined to form a complex wave.

The lowest frequency in a complex wave is called the **fundamental frequency**. It determines the pitch of the sound. Higher frequencies in the complex wave are called **overtones** or **upper partials**. If the overtones are multiples of the fundamental frequency, they are called **harmonics**. For example, if the fundamental frequency is 200 Hz, the second harmonic is 400 Hz, and the third harmonic is 600 Hz.

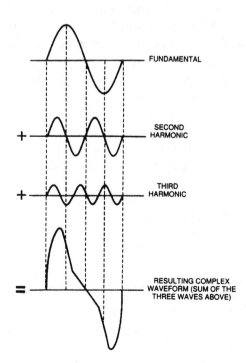

FUNDAMENTAL

SECOND HARMONIC

THIRD HARMONIC

RESULTING COMPLEX WAVEFORM (SUM OF THE THREE WAVES ABOVE)

**Figure 3.6**
Adding fundamental and harmonic waveforms to form a complex waveform.

**Figure 3.7**
The four sections of the envelope of a note.

The harmonics and their amplitudes help determine the tone quality or **timbre** of a sound, and help to identify the sound as a trumpet, piano, organ, voice, etc.

**Noise** (such as tape hiss) contains a wide band of frequencies and has an irregular, nonrepeating waveform.

## *Envelope*

Another characteristic that identifies a sound is its envelope. When a note sounds, it doesn't last forever. It rises in volume, lasts a short time, then falls back to silence. This rise and fall in volume of one note is called the note's **envelope**. The envelope connects the peaks of successive waves that make up a note. Each musical instrument has a different envelope.

Most envelopes have four sections: **attack, decay, sustain**, and **release** (see Figure 3.7). During the attack, a note rises from silence to its maximum volume. Then it decays from maximum to some midrange level. This middle level is the sustain portion. During release, the note falls from its sustain level back to silence.

Percussive sounds, such as drum hits, are so short that they have only a rapid attack and decay. Other sounds, such as organ or violin notes, last longer. They have slower attacks and longer sustains. Guitar plucks and cymbal crashes have quick attacks and slow releases. They hit hard then fade out slowly.

You can shorten a guitar string's decay or ringing by damping the string with the side of your hand. You can press a blanket against a kick drum head to damp the decay and get a tighter sound.

# **Signal Characteristics of Audio Devices**

When a mic converts sound to electricity, this electricity is called the **signal**. It has the same frequency and the same amplitude changes as the incoming sound wave.

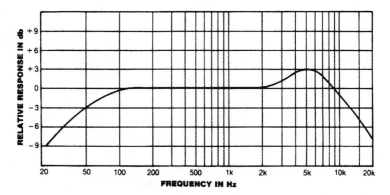

**Figure 3.8** An example of a frequency response.

When this signal passes through an audio device, the device may alter the signal. It might change the level of some frequencies, or add unwanted sounds that are not in the original signal. Let's look at some of these effects.

## *Frequency Response*

Suppose you have an audio device—a mic, mixer, effects unit, recorder, or speaker. You send a musical signal through the device. Usually the music contains some high frequencies and some low frequencies.

The device might respond differently to different frequencies. It might amplify the low notes and weaken the high notes. You can graph how the device responds to different frequencies by plotting its output level vs frequency. This graph is called a **frequency response** (Figure 3.8). The level in the graph is measured in dB (decibels), while frequency is measured in Hz (hertz). Generally, one dB is the smallest change in loudness that we can hear.

Suppose the level is the same at all frequencies. Then the graph forms a horizontal straight line, and so is called a "flat frequency response" (Figure 3.9). All the frequencies are reproduced at an equal level. In other words, the device passes all the frequencies without changing their relative levels. You get out the same amount of bass and treble that went in. A flat response does not affect the tonal balance of the incoming sound.

Many audio devices do not have a flat response across the audio band from 20 Hz to 20,000 Hz. They have a limited range of frequencies that they can reproduce at an equal level (within a tolerance, such as ±3 dB). In Figure 3.8, the frequency response shown by the solid line is 50 Hz to 12,000 Hz ± 3 dB. That means the audio device passes all frequencies from

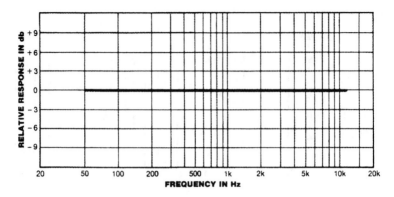

**Figure 3.9** A flat frequency response.

50 Hz to 12,000 Hz at a nearly equal level—within 3 dB. It reproduces low sounds and high sounds equally well. The response is down 3 dB at 50 Hz and 12,000 Hz, and is up 3 dB at 5000 Hz.

Usually, the more extended or "wide" the frequency range is, the more natural and real the recording sounds. A wide, flat response gives accurate reproduction. A frequency response of 200 Hz to 8000 Hz (±3 dB) is narrow (poor fidelity); 80 Hz to 12,000 Hz is wider (better fidelity), and 20 Hz to 20,000 Hz is widest (best fidelity).

Also, the flatter the frequency response, the greater the fidelity or accuracy. A response deviation of ±3 dB is good; ±2 dB is better; and ±1 dB is excellent. There are exceptions to this statement, which we'll look at in Chapter 11 in the section on equalization.

When you turn a bass or treble knob on your guitar amp, mixer EQ, or stereo, you're changing the frequency response. If you turn up the bass, the low frequencies rise in level. If you turn up the treble, the high frequencies are emphasized. The ear interprets these effects as changes in tone quality—warmer, brighter, thinner, duller, and so on.

Figure 3.8 shows a non-flat frequency response. Toward the right side of this line, the response at high frequencies "rolls off" or declines. This shows that the upper harmonics are weak. The result is a dull sound. Toward the left side, the response at low frequencies rolls off. That means the fundamentals are weakened and the result is a thin sound.

The frequency response of an audio device might be made non-flat on purpose. For example, you might cut low frequencies with an equalizer to reduce breath pops from a microphone. Also, a microphone may sound best with a non-flat response—such as boosted high frequencies that add presence and sizzle.

# *Noise*

Noise is another characteristic of audio signals. Every audio component produces a little noise—a rushing sound like wind in trees. Noise in a recording is undesirable unless it's part of the music.

You can make noise less audible by keeping the signal level in a device relatively high. If the level is low, you have to turn up the listening volume in order to hear the signal well. Turning up the volume of the signal also turns up the volume of the noise, so you hear noise along with the signal. But if the signal level is high, you don't have to turn up the listening level so much. Then the noise remains in the background.

# *Distortion*

If you turn up the signal level too high, the signal distorts and you hear a gritty, grainy sound. This type of distortion is sometimes called "clipping" because the peaks of the signal are clipped off so they are flattened. To hear distortion, simply record a signal at a very high recording level (with the meters going well into the red area) and play it back.

# *Optimum Signal Level*

You want the signal level high enough to cover up the noise, but low enough to avoid distortion. Every audio component works best at a certain optimum signal level, and this is usually indicated by a "0" on a meter or lights that show the signal level.

Figure 3.10 shows the range of signal levels in an audio device. At the bottom is the noise floor of the device—the level of noise it produces with no signal. At the top is the distortion level—the point at which the signal distorts and sounds grungy. In between is a range in which the signal sounds clean. The idea is to maintain the signal around the 0 point on the average.

# *Signal-to-Noise Ratio*

The level difference in dB between the signal level and the noise floor is called the "signal-to-noise ratio" or S/N (see Figure 3.10). The higher the signal-to-noise ratio, the cleaner the sound. A signal-to-noise ratio of 50 dB is fair, 60 dB is good, and 70 dB or greater is excellent.

To illustrate signal-to-noise ratio, imagine a person yelling a message over the sound of a train. The message being yelled is the signal; the noise

**Figure 3.10**
The range of signal levels
in an audio device.

is the train. The louder the message, or the quieter the train, the greater the S/N. And the greater the S/N, the clearer the message.

## *Headroom*

The level difference in dB between the normal signal level and the distortion level is called "headroom" (see Figure 3.10). The greater the headroom, the greater the signal level the device can pass without running into distortion. If an audio device has a lot of headroom, it can pass high-level peaks without clipping them.

You want to set your mixer controls so that the signal has some headroom, is well above the noise floor, and is below distortion. Here's how. During recording:

1. Set master faders and group faders to 0 (the shaded portion of fader travel).
2. Set the bass player's fader to 0.
3. Have the bassist play the loudest part of the song.
4. Adjust the input trim to set the recording level.
5. Repeat for the other faders and instruments.

During mixdown:

1. Set master faders and group faders to 0.
2. Set up a mix with the channel faders.
3. Keeping the master and group faders near 0, adjust the channel faders' overall level so that the mixer's stereo meters peak around 0. (The more faders in use, the lower the fader levels should be.)

With these settings, the signal levels in the mixer should be just about right, with no audible noise or distortion. And the mixer should have enough headroom so that loud peaks won't distort.

# Behavior of Sound in Rooms

Because most music is recorded in rooms, you need to understand how room surfaces affect sound.

## *Echoes*

Musical instruments make sound waves that travel outward in all directions. Some of the sound travels directly to your ears (or to a microphone) and is called **direct sound**. The rest strikes the walls, ceiling, floor, and furnishings of the recording room. At those surfaces, some of the sound is absorbed, some is transmitted through the surface, and the rest is reflected back into the room.

Because sound waves take time to travel (moving at about 1 foot per millisecond), the reflected sound reaches you after the direct sound. The reflection repeats the original sound after a short delay. If the sound is delayed about 50 milliseconds or more, we call it an **echo** (Figure 3.11). In some concert halls we hear single echoes; in small rooms we often hear a short, rapid succession of echoes called flutter echoes. You can detect them

*(A) Echo formation.*

*(B) Intensity vs. time of direct sound and its echoes.*

**Figure 3.11**  Echoes.

by clapping your hand next to a wall. **Flutter echoes** happen when sound bounces back and forth between two parallel walls.

## *Reverberation*

Sound reflects many times from all the surfaces in the room. These reflections sustain the sound of each note the musician plays. This persistence of sound in a room after the original sound has stopped is called **reverberation (reverb)**. For example, reverberation is the sound you hear just after you shout in an empty gymnasium. The sound of your shout stays in the room and gradually dies away (decays).

Reverb is hundreds of echoes that gradually get quieter. The echoes follow each other so rapidly that they merge into a single continuous sound. Eventually, the room surfaces completely absorb the echoes. The timing of the echoes is random, and the echoes increase in number as they decay. Figure 3.12 shows how reverberation develops in a recording room.

Reverberation is a continuous fade-out of sound ("HELLO-O-O-o-o"), while an echo is a discrete repetition of a sound ("HELLO hello hello hello").

Reverberation time (RT60) is the time it takes for reverb to decay 60 dB. Too long a reverb time makes a recording sound distant, muddy,

(A) Multiple sound reflections create reverberation.

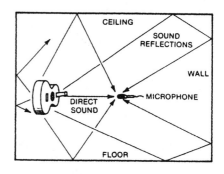

(B) Intensity vs. time of direct sound, early reflections, and reverberation.

**Figure 3.12** Reverberation.

and washed-out. That's why pop-music recordings are made in a fairly "dead" or nonreverberant studio, which has an RT60 of about 0.4 seconds or less. In contrast, classical music is recorded in "live," reverberant concert halls (RT60 about 1 to 3 seconds) because we want to hear reverb with classical music—it's part of the sound.

Reverberation comes to you from every direction because it is a pattern of many sound reflections off the walls, ceiling, and floor. Since we can tell where sounds come from, we can distinguish between the direct sound of an instrument coming to us from a single location and the reverberation coming to us from everywhere else. So we can ignore the reverb and concentrate on the sound source. In fact, we normally are not aware of reverberation.

But record an instrument in that room and play back the recording. You'll hear a lot more reverb than what you heard live. What's going on? The reverb you recorded on tape is not all around you. Instead, it's all up front between the speakers. So it's more audible; you can't discriminate against the reverb spatially. To reduce the amount of reverb in your recordings, you need to place mics close to instruments, and maybe add some sound-absorbing materials to the room.

## Leakage

Sound from an instrument travels to the nearest mic, and also "leaks" into the mics intended for other instruments (Figure 3.13). This overlap of an instrument's sound into the mic of another instrument is called **leakage** (or **bleed** or **spill**).

It's very important to minimize leakage—to ensure that each mic picks up only its intended instrument. Suppose that you're miking a drum set and an acoustic piano. As the musicians play, you monitor what the mics pick up. When you turn up just the drum mics, the drums sound close-up or "tight." But when you also turn up the piano mic, the drum

**Figure 3.13**
Example of leakage. The piano mic picks up leakage from the drums—changing the close drum sound to distant.

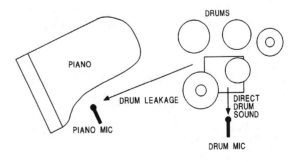

sound becomes distant or muddy. That's because the piano mic picks up drum leakage at a distance.

# How to Tame Echoes, Reverb, and Leakage

Echoes, reverb, and leakage can make your recordings sound mushy and distant. There are two ways to prevent these problems: with recording techniques and with acoustic treatment.

## Controlling Room Problems with Recording Techniques

Sometimes you can make clean recordings in an ordinary room, such as a club, living room, or basement, if you follow these suggestions:

- Mike close. Place each mic 1 to 6 inches from each instrument or voice. Then the mics will hear more of the instruments and less of the room reflections. You might want to use mini mics, which attach directly to instruments.
- Use directional mics—cardioid, supercardioid, or hypercardioid— which reject room acoustics.
- Record bass guitar and synth directly with a guitar cord or a direct box. Since you omit the microphone, you pick up no room acoustics. To get a good sound when recording electric guitar direct, record off the effects boxes or use a guitar-amp simulator.
- Overdub instruments one at a time rather than recording them all at once. You'll pick up a much cleaner sound. However, this loses the emotional interaction that occurs when all the musicians play together. You might record all the loud instruments at once: drums, bass, and electric guitar. Then overdub the quiet instruments: acoustic guitars, sax, piano, vocals.
- Record in a large room. This lets you spread the musicians farther apart, and weakens the sound reflections from the walls into the mics.

## Controlling Room Problems with Acoustic Treatments

When should you apply acoustic treatment to a room, or build a studio?

- You clap your hands next to a wall and you hear flutter echoes (a fluttering sound). These are caused by sounds bouncing back and forth between hard parallel walls.
- Your studio is a very live environment, such as a garage or concrete-block basement, so you hear too much room reverberation.
- Your studio is very small.
- You hear outside noises in your recordings.
- Bass-guitar amps and monitor speakers sound boomy.
- You want the freedom to mike several feet away without picking up noise or excess room reverb.
- You hear a lot of leakage in the mic signals.

If these conditions apply, check out the following suggestions on upgrading the acoustics of your studio.

Reverb and echoes are caused by sound reflections off room surfaces. So any surface that is highly sound-absorbent helps to reduce those problems.

To absorb high frequencies, use porous materials such as convoluted (bumpy) foam mattresses. Nail or glue them to the walls, or mount them on frames. Thick foam works better than thin. Four-inch foam on the wall absorbs frequencies from about 800 Hz up. Leave some space between the foam panels; this helps to diffuse or spread out the sound in the room (Figure 3.14).

Don't overdo the foam padding. A stuffed, dead room is uncomfortable to play in. Keep some reflections because they add "air" and liveliness to the sound.

Other high-frequency absorbers are sleeping bags, carpeting, curtains, and fiberglass insulation covered with muslin or burlap. If possible, space these materials several inches from the wall. The spacing helps them absorb mid-bass frequencies.

Start with just a little absorption behind or above the musician you're recording. Add more absorbers, a few at a time, until your recordings sound as dead as you wish.

To absorb low frequencies, you can make bass traps. Here are three types:

1. **Resonant tube trap:** Take a 35- to 55-gallon rubber trashcan, stuff it with fiberglass insulation (wear a dust mask and gloves), and cover the open end with muslin or canvas. This tube trap absorbs frequencies near $1130/2H$, where $H$ is the height of the trashcan in feet. For

**Figure 3.14** Acoustic treatments.

example, a 3-foot-high trashcan absorbs 188 Hz. Placement is not critical.

2. **Frictional tube trap:** Make a 2-foot-diameter canvas bag, 8 feet tall, and fill it with fiberglass insulation. Hang one bag a few feet out from each room corner (Figure 3.14). The distance should be 1130/4F, where F is the frequency in Hz that you want to absorb. For example, to absorb 80 Hz, hang the bag 3.5 feet out from a room corner. (Thanks to David Moulton for those ideas).

3. **Lattice:** Build a 3-foot-wide lattice frame of wood slats, the same height as the ceiling (Figure 3.14). Cover the frame with muslin or burlap. Put the frame diagonally across a room corner and fill it with R-30 insulation. Leave the foil on, foil side out toward the room. Put one assembly in each corner. (Thanks to Chips Davis for this idea).

There are other ways to absorb bass. Wood paneling works well. It also helps to open closet doors and place couches and books a few inches from the walls. In a basement studio, nail acoustic tile to the ceiling joists, with fiberglass insulation in the air space between tiles and ceiling.

You may not need any bass traps if you don't put any bass into the room. For example, don't turn up the bass guitar amp—just record the bass direct and have the musicians wear headphones to hear the bass.

# Controlling Standing Waves

Let's look at another acoustic problem: standing waves. If you play an amplified bass guitar through a speaker in a room, and do a bass run up the scale, you may hear some notes that boom out in the room. The room is resonating at those frequencies. These resonance frequencies, which are strongest below 300 Hz, occur in patterns called "standing waves." They can give a tubby or boomy coloration to musical instruments and monitor speakers.

Room resonances are worst in a cubical room. They are less of a problem if the room's length, width, and height are not multiples of each other. The table below shows several room dimensions in feet that reduce boomy-sounding standing waves.

| Height | Width | Length |
|--------|-------|--------|
| 8  | 9.1  | 11.1 |
| 8  | 9.4  | 11.8 |
| 8  | 10.1 | 11.3 |
| 8  | 10.2 | 12.3 |
| 8  | 11.6 | 16.8 |
| 8  | 11.8 | 13.6 |
| 8  | 12.8 | 18.6 |
| 8  | 13.0 | 21.0 |
| 10 | 11.4 | 13.9 |
| 10 | 11.7 | 14.7 |
| 10 | 12.6 | 14.1 |
| 10 | 12.8 | 15.4 |
| 10 | 14.5 | 21.0 |
| 10 | 14.7 | 17.0 |
| 10 | 16.0 | 23.3 |
| 10 | 16.2 | 26.2 |

For example, if the room width is 9.1 feet, and the ceiling is 8 feet high, the length should be 11.1 feet for best reduction of boominess.

Try to record in a large room because the room resonance frequencies are likely to be below the musical range. Use bass traps to absorb room resonances. Contrary to popular opinion, nonparallel walls don't prevent standing waves.

# Making a Quieter Studio

The following tips will keep noises out of your recordings:

- Turn off appliances and telephones while recording.
- Pause for ambulances and airplanes to pass.
- Close windows. Consider covering them with thick plywood.
- Close doors and seal with towels.
- Remove small objects that can rattle or buzz.
- Weather-strip doors all around, including underneath. (Leave the doors open for ventilation when not recording.)
- Replace hollow doors with solid doors.
- Block openings in the room with thick plywood and caulking.
- Put several layers of plywood and carpet on the floor above the studio, and put insulation in the air space between the studio ceiling and the floor above.
- Place microphones close to instruments and use directional microphones. This won't reduce noise in the studio, but it will reduce noise picked up by the microphones.

When building a new studio, you might want to make the walls of plastered concrete block because massive walls reduce sound transmission. Or make the walls of gypsum board and staggered studs. Nail gypsum board to 2 × 4 staggered studs on 2 × 6 footers as shown in Figure 3.15. Staggering the studs prevents sound transmission through the studs. Fill the airspace between walls with insulation.

The ideal home-recording room for pop music is a large, well-sealed room with optimum dimensions. This room is in a quiet neighborhood. It should have some soft surfaces (carpet, acoustic-tile ceiling, drapes,

**Figure 3.15**
Staggered-stud construction
to reduce noise
transmission.

couches), and some hard vibrating surfaces (wood paneling or gypsum-board walls on studs).

Your home studio may not need acoustic treatment. Do some trial recordings to find out. But if your room could stand some improvement, the suggestions here should point you in the right direction.

For better results and a more professional appearance, consider buying some acoustic treatments from these companies:

http://tubetrap.com

http://www.acousticalsolutions.com

http://www.illbruck-sonex.com

http://www.rpginc.com

http://www.fstechnologies.com

# 4

# MONITORING

One of the most exciting moments in recording comes when the finished mix is played over the studio monitor speakers. The sound is so clear you can hear every detail, and so powerful you can feel the deep bass throbbing in your chest.

You use the monitor system to listen to the output signals of the console or the tape recorders. It consists of the console monitor mixer, the power amplifiers, loudspeakers, and the listening room. Each power amplifier boosts the electrical power of a console signal to a sufficient level to drive a loudspeaker. The speaker converts the electrical signal into sound, and the listening-room acoustics affect the sound from the speaker.

A quality monitor system is a must if you want your mixes to sound good. The power amp and speakers tell what you're doing to the recorded sound. According to what you hear, you adjust the mix and judge your mic techniques. Clearly, the monitor system affects the settings of many controls on your mixer, as well as your mic selection and placement. And all those settings affect the sound you're putting on tape. So, using inadequate monitors can result in a poor-sounding product coming out of your studio.

It's important to use accurate speakers that have a flat frequency response. If your monitors are weak in the bass, you will tend to boost the bass in the mix until it sounds right over those monitors. But when that mix is played over speakers with a flatter response, it will sound too bassy because you boosted the bass on your mixer. So, using monitors with weak bass results in bassy recordings; using monitors with exaggerated treble results in dull recordings, and so on. In general, colorations in the monitors will be inverted in your mixdown tape.

That's why it's so important to use an accurate monitor system—one with a wide, smooth frequency response. Such a system lets you hear exactly what's on the tape.

# Speaker Requirements

The requirements for an accurate studio monitor are these:

- **Wide, smooth frequency response.** To ensure accurate tonal reproduction, the on-axis response of the direct sound should be ±4 dB or less from 40 Hz to 15 kHz. The low-frequency response of a small monitor speaker should extend to at least 70 Hz.

- **Uniform off-axis response.** The high-frequency output of a speaker tends to diminish off-axis. Ideally the response at 30 degrees off-axis should be only a few dB down from the response on-axis. That way, a producer and engineer sitting side-by-side will hear the same tonal balance. Also, the tonal balance will not change as the engineer moves around at the console.

- **Good transient response.** This is the ability of the speaker to accurately follow the attack and decay of musical sounds. If a speaker has good transient response, bass guitar sounds tight, not boomy. Drum hits have sharp impact. Some speakers are designed so that the woofer and tweeter signals are aligned in time. This aids transient response.

- **Clarity and detail.** You should be able to hear small differences in the sonic character of instruments, and to sort them out in a complex musical passage.

- **Low distortion.** Low distortion is necessary because it lets you listen to the speaker for a long time without your ears hurting. A good spec might be: Total harmonic distortion under 3% from 40 Hz to 20 kHz at 90 dB SPL.

- **Sensitivity.** Sensitivity is the sound pressure level a speaker produces at 1 meter when driven with 1 watt of pink noise. **Pink noise** is random noise with equal energy per octave. This noise is either band-limited to the range of the speaker or is a one-third-octave band centered at 1 kHz. Sensitivity is measured in dB/W/m (dB sound pressure level per 1 watt at 1 meter). A spec of 93 dB/W/m is considered high; 85 dB/W/m is low. The higher the sensitivity, the less amplifier power you need to get adequate loudness.

- **High output capability.** This is the ability of a speaker to play loudly without burning out. You often need to monitor at high levels to hear quiet details in the music. Plus, when you record musicians who play loudly in the studio, it can be a letdown for them to hear a quiet playback. So you may need a maximum output of 110 dB SPL.

This formula calculates the maximum output of a speaker (how loud it can play):

$$dBSPL = 10\log(P) + S$$

where dB SPL is the sound pressure level at 1 meter, $P$ is the continuous power rating of the speaker in watts, and $S$ is the sensitivity rating in dB/watt/meter.

For example, if a speaker is rated at 100 watts maximum continuous power, and its sensitivity is 94 dB SPL/watt/meter, its maximum output SPL is $10\log(100) + 94 = 114$ dB SPL (at 1 meter from the speaker). The level at 2 meters will be about 4 to 6 dB less.

# Nearfield™ Monitors

Many professional recording studios use large monitor speakers that have deep bass. However, they are expensive, heavy, and difficult to install, and they are affected by the acoustics of the control room.

If you want to avoid this hassle and expense, consider using a pair of **Nearfield monitor speakers** (Figure 4.1). A Nearfield monitor is a small, wide-range speaker typically using a cone woofer and dome-shaped tweeter. You place a pair of them about 3 or 4 feet apart, on stands just behind the console, about 3 or 4 feet from you. Nearfields are far more popular than large wall-mounted speakers.

This technique, developed by audio consultant Ed Long, is called **Nearfield monitoring**. Because the speakers are close to your ears, you hear mainly the direct sound of the speakers and tend to ignore the room acoustics. This way, the speakers tend to sound about the same in any environment, so you may not need to acoustically treat your control room. Plus, Nearfield monitors sound very clear and provide sharp stereo imaging. They are normally used without equalization. Some units have bass or treble tone controls built in.

Nearfield monitors are designed for close listening—they have enough bass to sound full when placed far from walls. Although most Nearfields lack deep bass, they can be supplemented with a subwoofer to reproduce the complete audio spectrum. Or you can check the mix occasionally with headphones that have deep bass.

**Figure 4.1**
A Nearfield monitor
speaker.

Some Nearfields are in a **satellite–subwoofer** format. The two satellite speakers are small units, typically including a 4-inch woofer and ³/₄-inch dome tweeter. The satellites are too small to produce deep bass, but that is handled by the subwoofer. It is a single cabinet with one or two large woofer cones. Typically, the subwoofer (sub) produces frequencies from 100 Hz down to 40 Hz or below. Since we do not localize sounds below about 100 Hz, all the sound seems to come from the satellite speakers.

The sub–satellite system is more complicated to set up than two larger speakers, but offers deeper bass.

# Powered Monitors

Some monitors have a power amplifier built in. You feed them a line-level signal (labeled MONITOR OUT) from your mixing console. Some powered monitors are bi-amplified: they have one amplifier for the woofer and one for the tweeter. The advantages of bi-amplification are:

- Distortion components caused by clipping the woofer power amplifier will not reach the tweeter, so there is less likelihood of tweeter burnout if the amplifier clips. In addition, clipping distortion in the woofer amplifier is made less audible.

- Intermodulation distortion is reduced.
- Peak power output is greater than that of a single amplifier of equivalent power.
- Direct coupling of amplifiers to speakers improves transient response—especially at low frequencies.
- Bi-amping reduces the inductive and capacitive loading of the power amplifier.
- The full power of the tweeter amp is available regardless of the power required by the woofer amp.

# The Power Amplifier

If your monitor speakers are not powered, you need a power amplifier (Figure 4.2). It boosts your mixer's line-level signal to a higher power in order to drive the speakers.

How many watts of power do you need? The monitor speaker's data sheet gives this information. Look for the specification called "Recommended amplifier power." A power amp of 50 watts per channel continuous is about the minimum for Nearfield monitors; 150 watts is better. Too much power is better than too little, because an underpowered system is likely to clip or distort. This creates high frequencies that can damage tweeters.

A good monitor power amp has distortion under 0.05% at full power. It should have a high damping factor—at least 100—to keep the bass tight. The amp should be reliable. Look for separate level controls for left and right channels. The amplifier should have a clip or peak light that flashes when the amp is distorting.

**Figure 4.2** A power amplifier.

# Speaker Cables and Polarity

When you connect the power amp to the speakers, use good wiring practice. Long or thin cables waste amplifier power by heating. So put the power amp(s) close to the speakers and use short cables with thick conductors—at least 16 gauge. The low resistance of these cables helps the power amplifier to damp the speaker motion and tighten the bass.

If the two speakers are wired in opposite polarity, one speaker's cone moves out while the other speaker's cone moves in. This causes vague stereo imaging, weak bass, and a strange sense of pressure on your ears. Be sure to wire the speakers in the same polarity as follows: In both channels, connect the amplifier positive (+ or red) terminal to the speaker positive (+ or red) terminal. Setting the correct polarity is also called "speaker phasing."

# Control-Room Acoustics

The acoustics of the control room affect the sound of the speakers. Sound waves leaving the speaker strike the room surfaces. At those surfaces, some frequencies are absorbed, while other frequencies are reflected. At your ears, the sound waves reflected from the room surfaces combine with the direct sound. Reflections that arrive within 20 to 65 milliseconds (msec) after the direct sound blend with the direct sound and affect the tonal balance you hear.

Suppose the walls are covered with carpet so that they absorb only the high frequencies. Then the walls will reflect mainly the low frequencies. When you listen to a speaker playing in such a room, you hear the direct sound from the speaker plus the bassy wall reflections. The combined sound will be bass-heavy. Now suppose the walls are made of wood paneling mounted on studs. Such a vibrating surface absorbs lows and reflects highs. The sound you hear probably will be thin and overly bright.

Clearly, the room surfaces should reflect (or absorb) all frequencies about equally to avoid coloring the sound of the speakers. Equal absorption (±25%) from about 250 Hz to 4000 Hz is usually adequate. As described in Chapter 3, you can use flexible panels to absorb lows, in combination with fibrous materials or foam to absorb highs. Or use thick fibrous material spaced from the wall and ceiling.

**Room resonances** or **standing waves** can cause some notes to blare out and cause other notes to disappear. Be sure to control these resonances as suggested in Chapter 3.

Room acoustics also affect the decay-in-time of the sound coming from the speakers. Whenever the speakers play a note that ends suddenly, the sound of that note continues to bounce around the room. This causes echoes and reverberation that prolong the sound. This long decay of sound is not part of the recording. So the control room should be relatively **dead**—that is, it should have a short reverberation time. A typical living room has a reverb time of about 0.4 second; the control room should, too, so the engineer will hear about the same amount of room reverb that a home listener will hear. A totally dead room is uncomfortable to listen in.

Using Nearfield monitors makes the room acoustics less important, but it still helps to treat the room acoustics. To prevent sound reflections from the wall behind the speakers, apply muslin-covered fiberglass insulation or acoustic foam. This treatment improves the monitors' sound. Stereo imaging and depth are greatly improved, the sound is clearer, and the frequency response is flatter. The treatment will reduce boominess and ringing, and make transients sharper. Also, your recordings will translate better to other speakers.

If your control room is separate from the studio, the control room should be built to keep out sound from the studio. You want to hear only the sound from the monitors, not the live sound from the musicians. In a home studio, you can achieve isolation simply by putting the control-room equipment in a room far removed from the studio, with the doors closed.

A control room built next to the studio needs good isolation. Use double-wall construction with staggered studs (see Figure 4.3). Put fiberglass insulation between the two walls. The door between the two rooms should be solid wood and should be weatherstripped all around—including underneath. Use a double-pane window (mounted in rubber) between the control room and studio.

In some home or project studios, the control room is the same room as the studio. Since no isolation is used, the cost of building the studio is much less. The engineer records while listening with headphones, and does the critical monitoring mostly during the playback and the mixdown.

**Figure 4.3**
Staggered-stud construction to reduce noise transmission.

# Speaker Placement

Once you have acquired the speakers and worked on the room acoustics, you can install the speakers.

Mount them at ear height so the mixer doesn't block their sound. To prevent sound reflections off the mixer, place the speakers on stands behind the meter bridge, rather than putting them on top. For best stereo imaging, align the speaker drivers vertically and mount the speakers symmetrically with respect to the side walls. Place the two speakers as far apart as you're sitting from them; aim them toward you, and sit exactly between them (Figure 4.4).

Try to position the monitors several feet from the nearest wall. Wall reflections can degrade the frequency response and stereo imaging. The closer to the wall the speakers are, the more bass you hear.

# Using the Monitors

You've treated the room acoustics, and you've connected and placed the speakers as described earlier. Now it's time to adjust the stereo balance.

1. Play a mono musical signal and assign it to channels 1 and 2 in your mixer.

2. Adjust the channel 1 and 2 master faders so that the signal reads the same on the channel 1 and 2 meters.

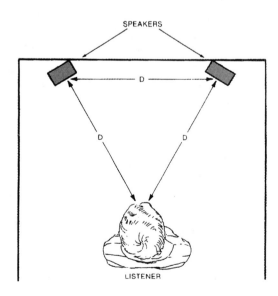

**Figure 4.4**
The recommended speaker/listener relationship for best stereo imaging.

3. Place the two speakers the same distance from you.

4. Sit at the mixer exactly midway between the speakers, and listen to the image of the sound between the speaker pair. You should localize it midway between the monitors—that is, straight ahead.

5. If necessary, center the image by adjusting the left or right volume control on your power amp. (Note: An off-center listener will hear the image shifted toward one side.)

When you do a mixdown, try to keep the listening level around 85 dB SPL—a typical home listening level. As discovered by Fletcher and Munson, we hear less bass in a program that is played quietly than in the same program played loudly. If you mix a program while monitoring at, say, 100 dB SPL, the same program will sound weak in the bass when heard at a lower listening level—which is likely in the home. So, programs meant to be heard at 85 dB SPL should be mixed and monitored at that level.

Loud monitoring also exaggerates the frequencies around 4 kHz. A recording mixed loud may sound punchy, but the same recording heard at a low volume will sound dull and lifeless.

Here's another reason to avoid extreme monitor levels: Loud sustained sound can damage your hearing or cause temporary hearing loss at certain frequencies. If you must do a loud playback for the musicians (who are used to high SPLs in the studio), protect your ears by wearing earplugs or leaving the room.

You can get a low-cost sound level meter from Radio Shack. Play a musical program at 0 VU on the mixer meters and adjust the monitor level to obtain an average reading of 85 dB SPL on the sound level meter. Mark the monitor-level setting.

Before doing a mix, you may want to play some familiar records over your monitors to remind yourself what a good tonal balance sounds like. Listen to the amount of bass, midrange, and treble, and try to match those in your mixes. But listen to several records, since they vary.

While mixing, monitor the program alternately in stereo and mono to make sure there are no out-of-phase signals that cancel certain frequencies in mono. Also beware of center-channel buildup: Instruments or vocals that are panned to center in the stereo mix sound 3 dB louder when monitored in mono than they do in stereo. That is, the balance changes in mono—the center instruments are a little too loud. To prevent this, don't pan tracks hard left and hard right. Bring in the side images a little so they will be louder in mono.

You'll mix the tracks to sound good on your accurate monitors. But also check the mix on small inexpensive speakers to see whether anything is missing or whether the mix changes drastically. Make sure that bass instruments are recorded with enough edge or harmonics to be audible on the smaller speakers. It's a good idea to make a cassette copy of the mix for listening in a car, boom box, or compact stereo.

# Headphones

Quality headphones are a low-cost alternative to loudspeakers for a home studio. You may find that headphones provide adequate isolation if the music you're recording is quiet.

Many home studios have the mixer and monitors in the same room as the musicians. In this case, you monitor with headphones while recording and overdubbing, then monitor with speakers when you mix. If you're monitoring as the musicians are playing, block out their sound by using closed-cup headphones or in-the-ear earphones.

Compared to speakers, headphones have several advantages:

- They cost much less.
- There is no coloration from room acoustics.
- The tone quality is the same in different environments.
- They are convenient for on-location monitoring.
- It's easy to hear small changes in the mix.
- Transients are sharper due to the absence of room reflections.

The disadvantages of headphones are:

- They become uncomfortable after long listening sessions.
- Cheap headphones have inaccurate tone quality.
- Headphones don't project bass notes through your body.
- The bass response varies due to changing headphone pressure.
- The sound is in your head rather than out front.
- You hear no room reverberation, so you may add in too much or too little artificial reverb.
- It's difficult to judge the stereo spread. Over headphones, panned signals tend to sound not as far off center as the same signals do heard over speakers. The same is true of stereo recordings made with a coincident pair of mics.

Even though headphones may not sound like speakers, you can do your mixes over headphones to match commercial records heard over those same headphones. Then your mixes should sound commercial over speakers, too.

# The Cue System

The cue system is a monitor system for musicians to use as they're recording. It includes the cue or monitor knobs in your mixer, a small amplifier, a headphone connector box, and headphones. Musicians often can't hear each other well in the studio, but they can listen over headphones to hear each other in a good balance. Also, they can listen to previously recorded tracks while overdubbing.

Headphones for a cue system should be durable and comfortable. They should be closed-cup to avoid leakage into microphones. This is an ideal situation; open-air phones may work well enough. Also, the cue "phones" should have a smooth response to reduce listening fatigue, and should play loud without burning out. Make sure they are all the same model so each musician hears the same thing. A built-in volume control is convenient.

A suggested cue system is shown in Figure 4.5. Connect a power amp to the cue or monitor output of your mixer. The amp drives several resistor-isolated headphones, which are in parallel.

Sometimes you can get by with four headphone jacks in a small metal box, wired in parallel and connected to your mixer's headphone jack.

Although some consoles can provide several independent cue mixes, the ideal situation is to set up individual cue mixers near each musician. Then they can set their own cue mix and listening level. The inputs of these mixers are fed from the console output buses.

Suppose a vocalist sings into a microphone and hears that mic's signal over the cue headphones. If the singer's voice and the headphone's sound are opposite in polarity, the voice partially cancels or sounds funny in the "phones." Make sure that the voice and headphones are the same polarity.

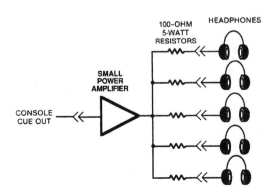

**Figure 4.5**
A cue system.

Here's how. While talking into a mic and listening to it on headphones, reverse the ground and signal leads to the headphones connector. The position that gives the fullest, most solid sound in the headphones is correct.

All the headphones in your studio should be the same model, so that everyone will hear with correct polarity.

# Conclusion

Ultimately, what you hear from the monitors influences your recording techniques and affects the quality of your recordings. So take the time to plan and adjust the control-room acoustics. Choose and place the speakers carefully. Monitor at proper levels and listen on several systems. You'll be rewarded with a monitor system you can trust.

# **5**

# HUM PREVENTION

You patch in a piece of audio equipment, and there it is—HUM! It's a low-pitched tone or buzz. This annoying sound is a tone at 60 Hz (50 Hz in Europe) and multiples of that frequency.

What's causing it? How can you get rid of it? This chapter answers those questions.

## Grounding Definitions

To understand the information in this chapter, you need a few definitions related to grounding.

**Grounding:** Connecting pieces of electronic equipment to ground.

**Ground:** A point designated as a zero-voltage reference. Voltages and signals in the system are measured relative to this ground point.

**Earth ground** or **physical ground:** A connection to moist dirt usually made through a copper ground rod.

**Power ground (safety ground):** An earth ground connection to equipment chassis made through the power cord. If you look at a modern AC outlet, you'll see three holes. The U-shaped hole is the safety ground. This terminal connects by a long wire to the power company's earth ground: a copper rod driven into the earth or a building's underground steel structure.

Many electronic devices have 3-wire power cords; the round ground pin on the cord is connected to the equipment chassis. A **chassis** is a metal housing that surrounds the circuitry in a piece of audio equipment. When you plug a device's 3-prong power cord into an outlet, the chassis of the device is connected to the safety ground. If a short circuit accidentally occurs between the chassis and a hot power line, the chassis current will flow to the safety ground rather than through someone touching the chassis, preventing shocks.

**AC mains:** The 60 Hz, 120/240 V AC power wiring supplied by the power company (sometimes a type called 3-phase).

**Phase:** One part or one leg of a 3-phase power wiring.

# Preventing Hum Pickup in Audio Cables

One source of hum is your studio's power wiring, which radiates hum fields that vibrate at 60 Hz or higher. Your audio cables can pick up these hum fields. Let's explain how.

## *Electrostatic Interference*

Power lines act as one plate of a capacitor, while the conductors in audio cables act as the other plate. An oscillating electrostatic field is set up between these two plates, causing hum to be transmitted (coupled) from the power lines to the cable conductors. An electrostatic field couples best at high frequencies, and so is heard as a buzz primarily made of the upper harmonics of 60 Hz.

To block hum fields, each audio cable has a shield—a cylinder of foil or fine wires that surrounds the signal wires in the center of the cable. A **shield** is a conductive enclosure around signal-carrying conductors, used to keep out electrostatic hum fields and radio frequency interference (RFI). Metal racks, equipment chassis, and microphone handles also are shields.

A shield works only when connected to a ground, such as the ground terminal of a chassis-mounted connector. That way, hum currents induced in the shield go to ground instead of getting into your audio. The ground provides a drain path for shield charges caused by the electrostatic fields.

If a cable shield is broken (usually at a connector), you might hear hum because there is no path to ground for the induced hum currents. So if you hear hum, check for broken shield connections in your cables. Also, use good-quality cables that have a high percentage of shielding (90% or better). The greater the shield coverage, the better it rejects hum.

# Magnetic Interference

Power lines and transformers also act as electromagnets, radiating magnetic lines of force that oscillate at 60 Hz and its harmonics. These lines of force "cut" through the conductors in audio cables, causing the conductors to generate electricity at 60 Hz and its harmonics. Magnetic fields couple best at low frequencies, and so are usually heard as a low tone at 60 Hz. A magnetic hum field is directional, so you can detect it by rotating the device that is picking up hum. If the hum level varies, the hum is induced magnetically.

A shield must be made of a magnetic material (such as steel) to block magnetic hum fields. This shield need not be grounded unless you also want to use it for electrostatic shielding.

There are a number of steps you can take to avoid magnetic interference:

- Avoid using fluorescent lights in the studio.
- Install your equipment at least several inches (or feet) from the large power transformers in power amplifiers. Keep cables away from computer monitors.
- Extension cords, power cords, and lighting cables radiate hum fields that audio cables can pick up. So separate your audio cables from those other types by at least one foot. If you must cross those cables, do so at right angles and space them vertically; this reduces the coupling between cables.

Coiled AC cords radiate more hum than straight cords. You might want to shorten unused AC cable to avoid coiling it.

---

CAUTION: This may void your warranty or UL approval.

---

# Balanced and Unbalanced Lines

The kinds of cables you use—balanced or unbalanced—affect the amount of hum pickup. A balanced line is a cable made of two conductors that carry the signal, surrounded by a shield (Figure 5.1). The shield does not carry the signal; it is connected to ground and keeps hum fields out of the conductors. Balanced equipment uses 3-pin pro audio connectors (XLR type). Professional audio equipment uses balanced connectors. Pin 1 is ground or shield, pin 2 is audio in-polarity (hot), and pin 3 is audio return (cold).

**Figure 5.1**
Balanced line.

**Figure 5.2**
Unbalanced line.

In a balanced line, the two conductors pick up equal amounts of hum interference. The cable plugs into a balanced input, which is sensitive to the voltage difference between the two conductors. Because there is little or no difference in hum voltage between the two conductors, hum picked up by the cable is not amplified, or is cancelled in the process.

Twisted-pair cable picks up less magnetically induced hum than non–twisted pair cable. This is because twisted conductor pairs occupy the same point in space on the average, so they are the same distance from the hum source and receive equal hum interference. This equal interference is then cancelled by the balanced input circuitry of the equipment.

An **unbalanced line** is a cable that uses a single conductor surrounded by a shield (see Figure 5.2). An unbalanced cable has either an RCA (phono) plug or a ¼-inch 2-conductor phone plug. Unbalanced equipment has RCA (phono) jacks, or has ¼-inch phone jacks. Home stereos and semipro recording equipment use unbalanced connectors.

Both the conductor and the shield carry the audio signal, so the shield isn't as effective in blocking electrostatic hum as it is in a balanced line. Also, the inner conductor and outer shield are at different impedances to ground, so they pick up different amounts of hum interference. This difference in induced hum voltage is amplified by the equipment the cable is plugged into.

Unbalanced lines pick up more hum than balanced lines. However, if you use unbalanced lines less than 10 feet long, hum is usually inaudible. You can get by with unbalanced lines in a small home studio where everything is close together. But if you need to run long mic cables (over 25 feet), consider getting a mixer with balanced (XLR-type) mic inputs to reject hum.

When connecting balanced equipment to unbalanced equipment, you may want to add a 1:1 audio isolation transformer at the unbalanced input or output (see Figure 5.3). This allows most of the interconnecting cable to be balanced.

**Figure 5.3** Transformer connections between balanced and unbalanced equipment.

# Preventing "Dirty" AC Power

The AC power from wall outlets is seldom a clean sine wave. Distortion, spikes, RFI, and "hash" appear on the waveform and can cause buzzes in your audio. To ensure clean power:

- Avoid silicon control rectifier (SCR) light dimmers. Instead, use multiway incandescent bulbs to vary the studio lighting levels.
- Install a power conditioner, AC isolation transformer, or line filter between the AC power outlets and the audio-equipment power cords.
- Use a balanced AC power supply. It cancels hum by using balanced AC power from a center-tapped power transformer. Instead of one 120 V line and one 0 V line, it has two 60 V lines. They are in phase with each other, and sum to 120 V. But they are connected to the center-tap ground out of phase (one is +60 V; the other is −60 V). Any hum and noise on the grounding system cancel out.

# Preventing Ground Loops

A major cause of hum is the **ground loop**. It is the circuit loop that is formed when equipment is connected to ground through more than one path. It occurs when two pieces of audio gear are connected to each other through a shield and also through the AC safety ground. Ground loops sound like a 60 Hz tone.

Figure 5.4 shows a ground loop. Two equipment chassis are connected to two separate safety grounds by their AC cords. Also, the equip-

**Figure 5.4** A ground loop.

ment chassis are connected together by the shield of the audio cable. The shield and safety-ground wires form a ground loop. A ground loop also can be created between two cable shields connected to the same piece of equipment.

Here is a real-world example of a ground loop situation. Suppose you're recording a synthesizer. The synth and your mixer have 3-prong power cords that connect to the safety ground. The synth is plugged into an AC outlet across the room, and your mixer is plugged into a nearby outlet. When you connect the synth to your mixer with a guitar cord, and monitor the signal, you hear hum.

Figure 5.4 shows what's happening. Chances are that the outlets are fed from different circuit breakers, so the outlets are at different ground voltages. When you plug your synth and mixer into these separated outlets, and connect the equipment together with a guitar cord, the difference in ground voltages makes a 60 Hz hum current flow between the synth and mixer. That's a ground loop.

There are several ways to prevent ground loops, and we'll look at each one.

## *Isolate the Grounds*

One solution is to use a transformer-isolated direct box between the synth and your mixer's balanced mic input. Unlike a guitar cord, the transformer passes the signal without connecting the two chassis together. On the direct box, flip the ground-lift switch to the position where you hear the least hum.

**Figure 5.5** Wiring an isolation transformer between two unbalanced devices.

A similar solution works for two pieces of unbalanced gear. If you hear hum after connecting them with a cable, try wiring a 1:1 isolation transformer between them (see Figure 5.5).

## Connect Everything to the Same Ground

Another cure for ground loops is to plug all your equipment into one or more outlet strips fed from the same circuit breaker. That way, the ground voltage for all the equipment is about the same, so no hum current can flow between their chassis. Plug the electric musical instruments and recording gear into the same strips. Use thick extension cords for distant equipment.

There still may be a slight voltage difference between components because their power supplies reflect different voltages onto their chassis. A balanced AC power supply can eliminate this problem.

Before you plug in all those power cords, make sure that the sum of the equipment fuse ratings does not exceed the amperage rating for that circuit. In most cases, a single 20-amp breaker will handle a small home studio.

## Break the Loop

Suppose that the synth and mixer are plugged into the same outlet strip. If you hear hum when you connect them together, unsolder or cut the shield at one end of the cable between them. This breaks the ground loop. The safety-ground leads, instead of the shield, serve as the signal return path. If you still hear hum, use a direct box.

Some people try to prevent ground loops by putting a 3-to-2 adapter on each power cord. This breaks the loop by removing the safety ground. It's a quick fix, but it creates a serious shock hazard and is not recommended.

What if you connect two unbalanced devices that have 2-prong power cords? Leave the shield connected at both ends because it carries the signal. Ground loops aren't normally a problem with this type of equipment. The orientation of 2-prong AC cords in nonpolarized outlets makes a difference. For each piece of audio gear, rotate the 2-prong power cord in its outlet to find the minimum-hum position.

In balanced line-level cables, you can break the loop by cutting or unsoldering the cable shield in one connector. Then no hum current can flow between equipment. The shield still drains electrostatic interference to ground through its single ground connection. Connect the shield only in the female XLR connector. Leave the shield unsoldered in the male connector—cut it short and shrink-tube it so that it doesn't short to other contacts.

> CAUTION: Don't lift (remove) the shield unless you are sure that the connected end is to a chassis ground, not a signal ground.

To disconnect the shield temporarily—as in on-location work—insert a ground-lift adapter (Figure 5.6) in the male cable connector.

If you hear radio stations or other type of RFI with a lifted-ground cable, solder a 0.01 µF capacitor between the unconnected shield and pin 1 of the XLR-type connector.

Don't use ground-lift adapters with mic cables. In mic cables, the shield must be connected to pin 1 on both ends, or else the mic housing won't be grounded. If the mic housing is not grounded, it won't shield the mic circuitry, so you'll hear hum.

In some situations, the shield *should* be connected to pin 1 on both ends of the cable:

- When the cable is a mic cable between a microphone and another device.
- When you use balanced AC power.
- When pin 1 of the equipment connector is grounded to the equipment chassis (check this with an ohmmeter).

## Connect Shields to Grounded Chassis

The following method is the recommended way to prevent ground loops in an audio system with balanced equipment. Connect the cable shield

**Figure 5.6**  A ground-lift adapter for balanced line-level cables.

**Figure 5.7**
Wiring an XLR-type
connector to tie the shield
to chassis.

only to the equipment chassis on both ends of the cable. Ground all equipment chassis by the power-cord safety ground.

If pin 1 is tied (connected) only to the chassis (not to signal ground), solder the cable shield to pin 1 in the connectors that plug into that component. If pin 1 is tied to the signal ground on an internal PC board, wire the XLR-type connector as shown in Figure 5.7.

## Keep the Loop Area Small

A ground loop can be created between two cables connected to the same piece of equipment. If these two cables are widely separated, they form a big loop or circle that can pick up radiated hum fields like an antenna.

To reduce this kind of hum pickup, make the loop area small. Keep your equipment close together and use short audio cables. When running send-and-return cables to a signal processor, tape these cables together. When you run left-channel and right-channel cables for a stereo hookup, use a single stereo cable.

## Prevent Ground Loops in Racks

A rack is a grounded metal cabinet used to hold audio equipment and patch panels. The equipment bolts onto rack channels, which are vertical metal strips with holes in them. Inside the rack is an AC outlet strip to power the rack equipment. Also inside the rack, near the bottom, is a **rack ground** securely bonded to the rack.

Try to put all unbalanced equipment in a single rack to shorten the cables between them. There are two opposite approaches to mounting unbalanced equipment in a rack. One is to isolate the chassis from the rack; the other is to ground the chassis to the rack.

According to the "isolate" approach, a ground loop can occur when two chassis of unbalanced equipment contact each other through a rack. To prevent this, put unbalanced equipment in a wooden rack with wooden rack channels, and keep the chassis separated (insulated) from each other with electrical tape. If you must use a rack with metal rails, isolate all the unbalanced pieces of rack equipment from the rack (and each other) by using electrical tape, nylon mounting bolts, and nylon washers. You can buy isolation tabs made for this purpose.

In contrast, some engineers prefer to ground all chassis to the rack channels, which are tied to safety ground. That way, equipment with "wall wart" power supplies will be grounded.

There are two opposite approaches to grounding at a patch panel:

1. Connect corresponding pairs of input and output jack sleeves together, but isolate the shields from the rack (see Figure 5.8). An example of a corresponding pair is "Tape Track 7 Out" and "Mixer Tape Input 7."

2. Don't connect anything to sleeves of patch bay jacks wired to equipment inputs. In addition, connect input cable shields to the rack ground bus (see Figure 5.9).

**Figure 5.8**
A method of wiring a patch bay to prevent ground loops.

**Figure 5.9**
Another method of wiring
a patch bay to prevent
ground loops.

## *Prevent Accidental Ground Loops*

Ground loops can happen when a connector shell or a snake box touches a metal surface. Inside an XLR-type cable connector is a ground lug that contacts the metallic connector shell. If the ground lug is soldered to pin 1 (the shield's pin), the shell is connected to the shield through the ground lug and pin 1. Ground loops may occur if the shell touches a grounded metallic surface. So don't wire the ground lug to pin 1.

If you locally ground a microphone snake box, this will create a ground loop. So don't ground the snake box except through its cable shield. Make sure the snake box doesn't touch any metal surfaces.

Each audio cable should have an insulating rubber or plastic jacket to prevent ground loops. If the shield is exposed, it can contact grounded metallic surfaces at more than one point, creating a ground loop.

# Reducing Hum with Mics and Electric Guitars

Microphones and electric guitars are sensitive to hum pickup because they produce low-level signals. These signals need a lot of amplification, which also amplifies any hum picked up by these devices and their cables.

## *Microphone Hum*

Use these tips to minimize microphone hum pickup:

- Use low-impedance microphones (150–600 ohms), which pick up less hum than high-impedance microphones.

- Use microphones with balanced outputs (3-pin connectors), which pick up less hum than unbalanced mics (hot conductor plus shield).
- Use a balanced cable from the mic to the input. If you have unbalanced mic inputs on your recorder or mixer, solder the shield and pin-3 lead to the phone plug sleeve or ground terminal; solder the pin-2 lead to the plug's hot or tip terminal.
- If the mic cable still picks up hum, unbalance the cable through a 1:1 transformer that is plugged directly into the input (refer to Figure 5.3).
- If hum pickup is severe with a dynamic microphone, use a dynamic mic with a humbucking coil built in. Or change to a condenser mic.
- Use twisted-pair mic cable to reduce pickup of magnetically induced hum. The more shield coverage, the less pickup of electrostatically induced hum. **Braided shield** generally offers the best coverage; **double-spiral wrapped** is next best, and **spiral-wrapped** is worst.
- Use star-quad cables such as those made by Canare, Mogami, or Belden.
- Routinely check mic cables to make sure the shield is connected at both ends.
- Check that the mic-connector set screw is securely screwed clockwise into the mic handle. This set screw is in the handle near the connector.
- For outdoor work, tape over cracks between connectors to keep out dust and rain.

## Electric-Guitar Hum

Electric guitars are high-impedance, unbalanced devices, which makes them very susceptible to hum. Try the following suggestions to reduce hum associated with electric guitars:

- Replace or repair guitar cords that have broken shields. Use only high-quality cords with metal-jacket plugs.
- Flip the polarity switch (if present) on the guitar amp to the lowest-hum position.
- Flip the ground-lift switch on each direct box to the lowest-hum position.
- Have the guitarist turn up the volume of the guitar all the way, and then turn down the gain on the guitar amp.

- Have the guitarist move around or turn around (rotate) to find a spot with minimum hum pickup.
- Replace any defective tubes in the guitar amp. If the power-supply filter capacitors in the guitar amp are corroded, replace them. This replacement should be done by an authorized technician.
- Use guitars with humbucking pickups, or install modern humbuckers in older guitars.
- Use a quieter amplifier.

# Reducing Radio Frequency Interference (RFI)

RFI is heard as buzzing, clicks, radio programs, or "hash" in the audio signal. It's caused by CB transmitters, computers, lightning, radar, radio and TV transmitters, industrial machines, auto ignitions, stage lighting, and other sources. Many of the following techniques are the same used to reduce hum from other sources. To reduce RFI:

- Use wide copper straps or braids, rather than wires, for ground connections, to reduce the high ground resistance caused by **skin effect**—the tendency of RF signals to travel on the outside of a conductor.
- Install high-quality RFI filters in the AC power outlets. The cheap types available from local electronics shops are generally ineffective.
- Physically separate the lighting power wiring from the audio cables.
- Avoid SCR dimmers—instead, use multiwatt incandescent bulbs to vary the studio lighting levels.
- Use enclosed equipment racks. The metal enclosure acts as a shield.
- Avoid long ground leads and unbalanced lines that are over 10 feet long.

Also, for each unbalanced mic input, consider connecting a $0.01\,\mu F$ capacitor between the hot terminal and ground (if the mixer lacks such a capacitor). Then, if the shell of the mic-input connector isn't grounded to the mixer chassis, connect a $0.001\,\mu F$ Mylar capacitor between the shell terminal and the mixer chassis (if the mixer lacks such a capacitor).

Long speaker cables can act as an RF antenna. If you suspect the cables to be the source of the RFI, bypass the RF to ground at the power-amp speaker terminals. Connect a $0.01\,\mu F$ to $0.03\,\mu F$ disk capacitor between one speaker lead and the amplifier chassis ground. Use one capacitor per channel. Do the same for the "ground" side of the amp's speaker terminals, if they are above chassis ground.

In connectors that have the shield floating (*not* tied to pin 1), connect the shield to pin 1 through a 0.01 µF capacitor. This bypasses the RFI to ground without connecting the audio signal to ground. Also, for balanced lines in mic junction boxes, solder a 0.01 µF capacitor between pins 1 and 2, and between pins 1 and 3. You also could do this at the mixer at each balanced mic input.

# Special Considerations for On-Location Work

In a remote recording job, you're outside the controlled environment of a studio. You need to take special precautions with power distribution, electric-guitar grounding, and interconnecting multiple sound systems.

## *Power-Distribution System*

A touring sound company should carry its own single-phase power distribution system because the building ground wiring on location is unreliable. See Figure 5.10 for a suggested AC power distribution system.

## *Electric-Guitar Grounding*

At times, electric-guitar players can receive a shock when they touch their guitar and a mic simultaneously. This occurs when the guitar amp is plugged into an electrical outlet on stage, and the mixing console (to which the mics are grounded) is plugged into a separate outlet across the room. As stated before, these two power points may be at widely different

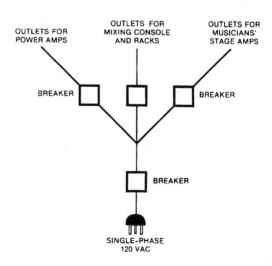

**Figure 5.10**
An AC power distribution system for a touring sound system.

ground voltages, so a current can flow between the grounded mic housing and the grounded guitar strings.

> CAUTION: Electric guitar shock is especially dangerous when the guitar amp and the console are on different phases of the AC mains.

It helps to power all instrument amps and audio gear from the same AC distribution outlets. That is, run a heavy extension cord from a stage outlet back to the mixing console (or vice versa). Plug all the power-cord ground pins into grounded outlets. That way, you prevent shocks and hum at the same time.

If you're picking up the electric guitar direct, use a transformer-isolated direct box and set the ground-lift switch to the minimum-hum position.

Using a neon tester or voltmeter, measure the voltage between the electric-guitar strings and the metal grille of the microphones. If there is a voltage, flip the polarity switch on the amp. Use foam windscreens for additional protection against shocks.

## Interconnecting Multiple Sound Systems

When you record a concert, three mixers are commonly in use: house, monitor, and recording. On stage, a mic splitter takes the signal from each mic and sends it three ways to the three mixers (see Figure 5.11).

To avoid ground loops between the three systems, ground the mic-cable shields to only one mixer. At the splitter, use the ground-lift switches to disconnect the shields going to the other two mixers. Ground to the mixer that provides the least hum. You might need to power two of the

**Figure 5.11** Using a mic splitter to feed three sound systems.

mixers from outlets near the other mixer. That way, the three mixers share a common ground.

If you encounter an unknown system where balanced audio cables might be grounded at both ends, use some cable ground-lift adapters (Figure 5.5) to float (remove) the extra ground connection at equipment inputs.

Often, a radio station or video crew will take an audio feed from a studio's mixing console. In this case, you can prevent a hum problem by using a console with transformer-isolated inputs and outputs. Or you can use a 1:1 audio isolation transformer between the console and the feeds.

# Special Considerations for Small Studios

If you have a small studio with fewer than 20 power cords in use, you can use the wall-outlet power ground to ground your audio equipment. Plug your equipment into 3-wire grounded outlet strips powered by the same wall-outlet circuit breaker. If your equipment has 2-prong power cords, you probably won't have any ground-related problems if you connect the equipment as described earlier. In particular, review the section on preventing ground loops.

# Special Considerations for Large Studios

The following suggestions are for large professional installations using balanced audio lines. If you have a small studio, you may want to skip this section or just read it for the advice it contains.

## *AC Power Wiring*

Hum prevention starts with properly designed power wiring. Sound-system equipment should be powered on its own circuit separate from others, such as those used for lighting or air-conditioning, which can put noise spikes on the AC line.

Listed below are four ways to power the audio system. The first is most effective but most expensive; the last is least effective but least expensive:

- Power the audio system from its own power transformer on a telephone pole outside the studio.
- Get power from an independent breaker box.

- Have an electrician put the audio system on a different phase of the incoming AC mains than the phase(s) other equipment is connected to.
- Power the audio from its own circuit breaker.

In any case, all the audio equipment (including guitar amps in the studio or on stage) should be on the same phase of the power line to prevent hum.

## Ground Wiring

Even if your wall outlets have a safety ground, you can't always trust these grounds to have a low-resistance connection to earth ground. If you suspect that the earth ground at the electrical service entrance is insufficient, have an electrician replace it.

Large studios often require special wiring of the safety ground to prevent ground loops. Although studio power wiring must meet electrical code requirements, the ground wiring may be nonstandard; confer with the electrician to make sure the work is done as described in this section and also meets code.

If you're installing a system in a building or home that is already wired for AC power, use a balanced AC power supply to power the studio. Plug all the 3-prong power cords into outlet strips that are fed from the balanced supply. This eliminates ground-loop problems.

If you're installing new power wiring, use AC outlets with isolated-ground terminals. That is, use special wall outlets that float (isolate) the ground terminal from the wall box; the wall box is grounded through the conduit. Such outlets are available from electrical supply houses.

Typical AC outlets with modern wiring contain three wires: hot (black), neutral (white), and ground (bare or green). The ground wire goes to the U-shaped hole in the outlet. Substitute your own ground wire for the bare or green one by following this procedure:

1. Have an electrician run a low-resistance (No. 10 gauge) insulated wire from each outlet's ground receptacle back to the ground bus bar: a copper plate in the bottom of the circuit-breaker box. Try to keep the lengths of all the ground leads about equal for equal resistance to earth ground. These ground wires should not short to the conduit, or you get ground loops.
2. Plug the rack equipment into the rack's AC outlet strip.
3. Plug the 3-prong AC power cord of each piece of equipment (and rack outlet strip) into an isolated-ground AC outlet.

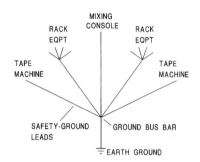

**Figure 5.12**
Recommended layout of safety-ground wires.

You may want to enclose the power wiring in a grounded metal conduit to prevent hum radiation from the power lines into audio circuits.

A proper grounding scheme resembles a tree (see Figure 5.12). The earth ground is the roots, the safety-ground wires are the big branches, and the rack safety-ground wires are the small branches. This is also called a **star** or **single-point** grounding system.

# Summary

For unbalanced equipment in a small studio, and using short connecting cables, these are the most important points to remember about hum prevention:

- Plug all equipment into outlet strips powered by the same breaker.
- Put unbalanced equipment in a single rack, isolated from the rack and each other (say, by using a wooden rack). Some engineers prefer instead to ground all chassis to the rack rails.
- Use balanced mic cables if possible.

  For balanced equipment in a large installation:

- Put audio equipment on a separate power feed.
- Use AC isolation transformers or AC line filtering if necessary.
- Consider installing a balanced AC power supply, such as made by Equi = Tech or Furman.
- In each balanced line-level cable, connect the shield to pin 1 in the female XLR; disconnect the shield from pin 1 in the male XLR. Leave the shield connected on both ends if the equipment chassis are tied to pin 1, or if you use balanced AC power.
- As an alternative, ground cable shields only to equipment chassis as shown in Figure 5.7.

92

- If you're installing new power wiring, use isolated-ground outlets. Connect an insulated low-resistance wire from each outlet's ground receptacle to a single ground point. Plug all the rack equipment into the same AC outlet strip in the rack. Plug all the power cords into 3-prong outlets.

# Hum-Fixing Checklist

Even if your system is wired properly, a hum or buzz may appear when you make a connection. Follow these tips to stop the hum:

- Check cables and connectors for broken leads.
- Remove audio cables from your devices and monitor each device by itself. It may be defective.
- Use a direct box instead of a guitar cord between instrument and mixer.
- Try a 1:1 isolation transformer between the two devices.
- Add ground-lift adapters to line-level balanced cables at the male XLR end. **Caution:** Lifted shields can act as an RF antenna.
- Try the connection shown in Figure 5.7.
- Make sure that the snake box is not touching metal.
- Tighten the mic-connector screws.
- Try another mic.
- Flip AC polarity switches or ground-lift switches.
- Have the guitarist move or aim in a different direction.
- Route mic cables away from power cords; separate them vertically where they cross.

By following all these tips, you should be able to connect audio equipment without introducing any hum. Good luck!

# 6

# MICROPHONES

What microphone is best for recording an orchestra? What's a good snare mic? Should the microphone be a condenser or dynamic, omni or cardioid?

You can answer these questions more easily once you know the types of microphones and understand their specs. First, it always pays to get a high-quality microphone—which costs at least $125. The mic is a source of your recorded signal. If that signal is noisy, distorted, or tonally colored, you'll be stuck with those flaws through the whole recording process. Better get it right up front.

Even if you have a MIDI studio and get all your sounds from samples or synthesizers, you still might need a good microphone for sampling, or to record vocals, sax, acoustic guitar, and so on.

A microphone is a **transducer**—a device that changes one form of energy into another. Specifically, a mic changes sound into an electrical signal. Your mixer amplifies and modifies this signal.

## Transducer Types

Mics for recording can be grouped into three types depending on how they convert sound to electricity: dynamic, ribbon, or condenser.

A **dynamic** mic capsule, or transducer, is shown in Figure 6.1. A coil of wire attached to a diaphragm is suspended in a magnetic field. When sound waves vibrate the diaphragm, the coil vibrates in the magnetic field and generates an electrical signal similar to the incoming sound wave. Another name for a dynamic mic is moving-coil mic, but this term is seldom used.

**Figure 6.1**
A dynamic transducer.

**Figure 6.2** A ribbon transducer.

In a **ribbon** mic capsule, a thin metal foil or ribbon is suspended in a magnetic field (Figure 6.2). Sound waves vibrate the ribbon in the field and generate an electrical signal.

A **condenser** or **capacitor** mic capsule has a conductive diaphragm and a metal backplate placed very close together (Figure 6.3). They are charged with static electricity to form two plates of a capacitor. When sound waves strike the diaphragm, it vibrates. This varies the spacing between the plates. In turn, this varies the capacitance and generates a signal similar to the incoming sound wave.

Two types of condenser mics are true condenser and electret condenser. In a **true condenser** mic (externally biased mic), the diaphragm and backplate are charged with a voltage from a circuit built into the mic. In an **electret condenser** mic, the diaphragm and backplate are charged by an **electret** material, which is in the diaphragm or on the backplate.

**Figure 6.3**
A condenser transducer.

Electrets and true condensers can sound equally good, although some engineers prefer true condensers, which tend to cost more.

A condenser mic needs a power supply to operate, such as a battery or phantom power supply. **Phantom power** is 12 to 48 V DC applied to pins 2 and 3 of the mic connector through two equal resistors. The microphone receives phantom power and sends audio signals on the same two conductors. Many mixing consoles supply phantom power at their mic input connectors. You simply plug the mic into the mixer to power it.

Dynamics and ribbons need no power supply. You can plug these types of mics into a phantom supply without damage, unless either signal conductor is accidentally shorted to the mic housing. Because of its lower diaphragm mass and higher damping, a condenser mic responds faster than a dynamic mic to rapidly changing sound waves (transients).

Figure 6.4 shows a cutaway view of a typical dynamic mic and condenser mic.

## *General Traits of Each Transducer Type*

### Condenser

- Wide, smooth frequency response
- Detailed sound, extended highs
- Omni type has excellent low-frequency response
- Transient attacks sound sharp and clear
- Preferred for acoustic instruments, cymbals, studio vocals
- Can be miniaturized

**Figure 6.4** Inside a typical dynamic mic and condenser mic.

## Dynamic

- Tends to have rougher response, but still quite usable
- Rugged and reliable
- Handles heat, cold, and high humidity
- Handles high volume without distortion
- Preferred for guitar amps and drums
- If flat response, can take the "edge" off woodwinds and brass

## Ribbon

- Prized for its warm, smooth tone quality
- Delicate
- Complements digital recording

There are exceptions to the tendencies listed above. Some dynamics have a smooth, wide-range frequency response. Some condensers are rugged and handle high SPLs. It depends on the specs of the particular mic.

# Polar Pattern

Microphones also differ in the way they respond to sounds coming from different directions. An **omnidirectional** microphone is equally sensitive to sounds arriving from all directions. A **unidirectional** mic is most sensitive to sound arriving from one direction—in front of the mic—but softens sounds entering the sides or rear of the mic. A **bidirectional** mic is most sensitive to sounds arriving from two directions—in front of and behind the mic—but rejects sounds entering the sides.

There are three types of unidirectional patterns: cardioid, super-cardioid, and hypercardioid. A mic with a **cardioid** pattern is sensitive to sounds arriving from a broad angle in front of the mic. It is about 6 dB less sensitive at the sides, and about 15 to 25 dB less sensitive in the rear. The **supercardioid** pattern is 8.7 dB less sensitive at the sides and has two areas of least pickup at 125 degrees away from the front. The **hypercardioid** pattern is 12 dB less sensitive at the sides and has two areas of least pickup at 110 degrees away from the front.

To hear how a cardioid pickup pattern works, talk into a cardioid mic from all sides while listening to its output. Your reproduced voice is loudest when you talk into the front of the mic, and softest when you talk into the rear.

The supercardioid and hypercardioid reject sound from the sides more than the cardioid—they are more directional. But they pick up more sound from the rear than the cardioid does.

A microphone's polar pattern is a graph of its sensitivity vs the angle at which sound comes into it. The polar pattern is plotted on polar graph paper. Sensitivity is plotted as distance from the origin. Figure 6.5 shows various polar patterns.

## *Traits of Different Polar Patterns*

### Omnidirectional

- All-around pickup
- Most pickup of room reverberation
- Not much isolation unless you mike close
- Low sensitivity to pops (explosive breath sounds)
- Low handling noise
- No up-close bass boost (proximity effect)
- Extended low-frequency response in condenser mics—great for pipe organ or bass drum in an orchestra or symphonic band
- Lower cost in general

### Unidirectional (Cardioid, Supercardioid, Hypercardioid)

- Selective pickup
- Rejection of room acoustics, background noise, and leakage

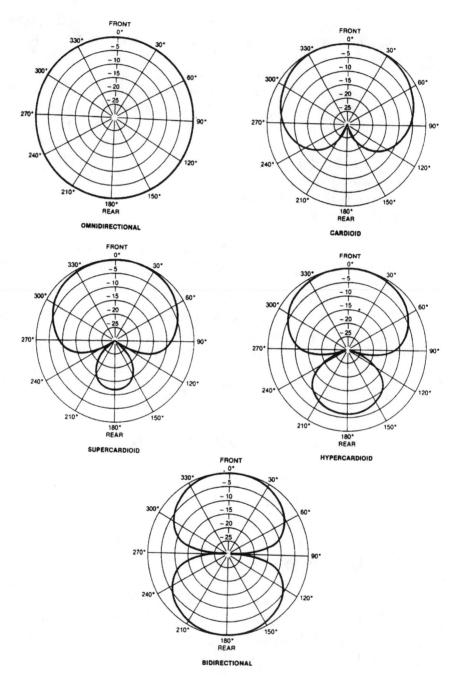

**Figure 6.5** Various polar patterns. Sensitivity is plotted vs angle of sound incidence.

- Good isolation—good separation between tracks
- Up-close bass boost (except in mics that have holes in the handle)
- Better gain-before-feedback in a sound-reinforcement system
- Coincident or near-coincident stereo miking (explained in Chapter 7)

## Cardioid

- Broad-angle pickup of sources in front of the mic
- Maximum rejection of sound approaching the rear of the mic

## Supercardioid

- Maximum difference between front hemisphere and rear hemisphere pickup (good for stage-floor miking)
- More isolation than a cardioid
- Less reverb pickup than a cardioid

## Hypercardioid

- Maximum side rejection in a unidirectional mic
- Maximum isolation—maximum rejection of reverberation, leakage, feedback, and background noise

## Bidirectional

- Front and rear pickup, with side sounds rejected (for across-table interviews or two-part vocal groups, for example)
- Maximum isolation of an orchestral section when miked overhead
- Blumlein stereo miking (two bidirectional mics crossed at 90 degrees)

In a good mic, the polar pattern should be about the same from 200 Hz to 10 kHz. If not, you'll hear **off-axis coloration**: the mic will have a different tone quality on and off axis. Small-diaphragm mics tend to have less off-axis coloration than large-diaphragm mics.

You can get either the condenser or dynamic type with any kind of polar pattern (except bidirectional dynamic). Ribbon mics are either bidirectional or hypercardioid. Some condenser mics come with switchable patterns. Note that the shape of a mic does not indicate its polar pattern.

If a mic is **end addressed**, you aim the end of the mic at the sound source. If a mic is **side addressed**, you aim the side of the mic at the sound source. Figure 6.6 shows a typical side-addressed condenser mic with switchable polar patterns.

**Figure 6.6**
A typical multi-pattern mic
that is side-addressed.

Boundary mics that mount on a surface have a pattern that is half-omni (hemispherical), half-supercardioid, or half-cardioid (like an apple sliced in half through its stem). The boundary mounting increases the directionality of the mic, thus reducing pickup of room acoustics.

# Frequency Response

As with other audio components, a microphone's frequency response is the range of frequencies that it will reproduce at an equal level (within a tolerance, such as ±3 dB).

The following is a list of sound sources and the microphone frequency response that is adequate to record the source with high fidelity. A wider-range response works, too.

- Most instruments: 80 Hz to 15 kHz
- Bass instruments: 40 Hz to 9 kHz
- Brass and voice: 80 Hz to 12 kHz
- Piano: 40 Hz to 12 kHz
- Cymbals and some percussion: 300 Hz to 15 or 20 kHz
- Orchestra or symphonic band: 40 Hz to 15 kHz

If possible, use a mic with a response that rolls off below the lowest fundamental frequency of the instrument you're recording. For example, the frequency of the low-E string on an acoustic guitar is about 82 Hz. A mic used on the acoustic guitar should roll off below that frequency to avoid picking up low-frequency noise such as rumble from trucks and air conditioning. Some mics have a built-in low-cut switch for this purpose. Or you can filter out the unneeded lows at your mixer.

A **frequency-response curve** is a graph of the mic's output level in dB at various frequencies. The output level at 1 kHz is placed at the 0 dB line on the graph, and the levels at other frequencies are so many dB above or below that reference level.

The shape of the response curve suggests how the mic sounds at a certain distance from the sound source. (If the distance is not specified, it's probably 2 to 3 feet). For example, a mic with a wide, flat response reproduces the fundamental frequencies and harmonics in the same proportion as the sound source. So a flat-response mic tends to provide accurate, natural reproduction at that distance.

A rising high end or a "presence peak" around 5 to 10 kHz sounds more crisp and articulate because it emphasizes the higher harmonics (Figure 6.7). Sometimes this type of response is called **tailored** or **contoured**. It's popular for guitar amps and drums because it adds punch and emphasizes attack. Some microphones have switches that alter the frequency response.

Most unidirectional and bidirectional mics boost the bass when used within a few inches of a sound source. You've heard how the sound gets bassy when a vocalist sings right into the mic. This low-frequency boost related to close mic placement is called the **proximity effect**, and it's often

**Figure 6.7** An example of the frequency response of a microphone with proximity effect and a presence peak around 5 kHz.

plotted on the frequency-response graph. Omni mics have no proximity effect; they sound tonally the same at any distance.

The warmth created by proximity effect adds a pleasing fullness to drums. In most recording situations, though, the proximity effect lends an unnatural boomy or bassy sound to the instrument or voice picked up by the mic. Some mics—multiple-D or variable-D types—are designed to reduce it. These types have holes or slots in the mic handle. Some mics have a bass-rolloff switch to compensate for the bass boost. Or you can roll off the excess bass with your mixer's equalizer until the sound is natural. By doing so, you also reduce low-frequency leakage picked up by the microphone.

Note that mic placement can greatly affect the recorded tone quality. A flat-response mic does not always guarantee a natural sound because mic placement has such a strong influence. Tonal effects of mic placement are covered in Chapter 7.

# Impedance (Z)

This spec is the mic's effective output resistance at 1 kHz. A mic impedance between 150 and 600 ohms is low; 1000 to 4000 ohms is medium; and above 25 kilohms is high.

Always use low-impedance mics. If you do, you can run long mic cables without picking up hum or losing high frequencies. The input impedance of a mixer mic input is about 1500 ohms. If it were the same impedance as the mic, about 250 ohms, the mic would "load down" when you plug it in. Loading down a mic makes it lose level, distort, or sound thin. To prevent this, a mic input has an impedance much higher than that of the microphone. But it's still called a low-Z input.

More information on impedance is in Appendix D.

# Maximum SPL

To understand this spec, first we need to understand SPL. Sound pressure level is a measure of the intensity of a sound. The quietest sound we can hear, the threshold of hearing, is 0 dB SPL. Normal conversation at 1 foot measures about 70 dB SPL; painfully loud sound is above 120 dB SPL.

If the maximum SPL spec is 125 dB SPL, the mic starts to distort when the instrument being miked is putting out 125 dB SPL at the mic. A maximum SPL spec of 120 dB is good, 135 dB is very good, and 150 dB is excellent.

Dynamic mics tend not to distort, even with very loud sounds. Some condensers are just as good. Some have a pad you can switch in to prevent distortion in the mic circuitry. Since a mic pad reduces signal-to-noise ratio, use it only if the mic distorts.

# Sensitivity

This spec tells how much output voltage a mic produces when driven by a certain SPL. A high-sensitivity mic puts out a stronger signal (higher voltage) than a low-sensitivity mic when both are exposed to an equally loud sound.

A low-sensitivity mic needs more mixer gain than a high-sensitivity mic. More gain usually results in more noise. When you record quiet music at a distance (classical guitar, string quartet), use a mic of high sensitivity to override mixer noise. When you record loud music or mike close, sensitivity matters little because the mic signal level is well above the mixer noise floor. That is, the signal-to-noise ratio is high. Listed below are typical sensitivity specs for three transducer types:

- Condenser: 5.6 mV/Pa (high sensitivity)
- Dynamic: 1.8 mV/Pa (medium sensitivity)
- Ribbon or small dynamic: 1.1 mV/Pa (low sensitivity)

The louder the sound source, the higher the signal voltage the mic puts out. A very loud instrument, such as a kick drum or guitar amp, can cause a microphone to generate a signal strong enough to overload the mic preamp in your mixer. That's why most mixers have pads or input-gain controls—to prevent preamp overload from hot mic signals.

# Self-Noise

**Self-noise** or **equivalent noise level** is the electrical noise or hiss a mic produces. It's the dB SPL of a sound source that would produce the same output voltage that the noise does.

Usually the self-noise spec is A-weighted. That means the noise was measured through a filter that makes the measurement correlate more closely with the annoyance value. The filter rolls off low and high frequencies to simulate the frequency response of the ear.

An A-weighted self-noise spec of 18 dB SPL or less is excellent (quiet); a spec around 28 dB SPL is good; and a spec around 35 dB SPL is fair—not good enough for quality recording.

Because a dynamic mic has no active electronics to generate noise, it has very low self-noise (hiss) compared to a condenser mic. So most spec sheets for dynamic mics do not specify self-noise.

# Signal-to-Noise Ratio

This is the difference in dB between the mic's sensitivity and its self-noise. The higher the SPL of the sound source at the mic, the higher the S/N ratio. Given an SPL of 94 dB, an S/N spec of 74 dB is excellent; 64 dB is good. The higher the S/N ratio, the cleaner (more noise-free) is the signal, and the greater is the reach of the microphone.

"Reach" is the clear pickup of quiet, distant sounds due to high S/N. Reach is not specified in data sheets because any mic can pick up a source at any distance if the source is loud enough. For example, even a cheap mic can reach several miles if the sound source is a thunderclap.

# Polarity

The polarity spec relates the polarity of the electrical output signal to the acoustic input signal. The standard is "pin 2 hot." That is, the mic produces a positive voltage at pin 2 with respect to pin 3 when the sound pressure pushes the diaphragm in (positive pressure).

Be sure that your mic cables do not reverse polarity. On *both* ends of each cable, the wiring should be pin 1 shield, pin 2 red, pin 3 white or black. Or the wiring on both ends should be pin 1 shield, pin 2 white, pin 3 black.

If some mic cables are correct polarity and some are reversed, and you mix their mics to mono, the bass may cancel.

# Special Microphone Types

The following sections describe three types of recording mics used for special purposes: the **boundary microphone**, **miniature microphone**, and **stereo microphone**.

## *Boundary Microphone*

Boundary mics are designed to be used on surfaces. Tape them to the underside of a piano lid, or tape them to the wall for pickup of room ambience. They can be used on hard baffles between instruments, or on panels to make the mics directional. A boundary mic uses a mini condenser mic capsule mounted very near a sound-reflecting plate or boundary. Because of this construction, the mic picks up direct sound and reflected sound at the same time—in-phase at all frequencies. So you get a smooth response free of phase cancellations. A conventional mic near a surface sounds colored; a boundary mic on a surface sounds natural.

One example of a boundary mic is the Crown Pressure Zone Microphone (PZM) series (Figure 6.8). The claimed benefits are a wide, smooth frequency response free of phase cancellations, excellent clarity and "reach," and the same tone quality anywhere around the mic. The polar pattern is half-omni or hemispherical. Some boundary mics have a half-cardioid or half-supercardioid polar pattern. They work great on a conference table, or near the front edge of a stage floor to pick up drama or musicals.

## Miniature Microphone

Mini condenser mics can be attached to drum rims, flutes, horns, acoustic guitars, and so on. Their tone quality is about as good as larger studio microphones and the price is relatively low. With these tiny units you can mike a band in concert without cluttering the stage with boom stands (Figure 6.9). Or you can mike a whole drum set with two or three of these. Although you lose individual control of each drum in the mix, the cost is

**Figure 6.8** Typical PZM construction.

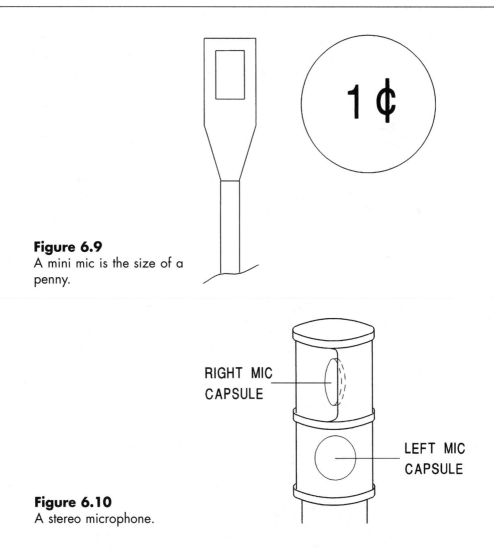

**Figure 6.9**
A mini mic is the size of a penny.

**Figure 6.10**
A stereo microphone.

low and the sound is quite good with some bass and treble boost. Compared to large mics, mini mics tend to have more noise (hiss) in distant-miking applications.

## Stereo Microphone

A stereo microphone combines two directional mic capsules in a single housing for convenient stereo recording (Figure 6.10). Simply place the mic a suitable distance and height from the sound source, and you'll get a stereo recording with little fuss.

Because there is no spacing between the mic capsules, there also is no delay or phase shift between their signals. Coincident stereo microphones are mono-compatible—the frequency response is the same in mono and stereo—because there are no phase cancellations if the two channels are combined.

## Microphone Selection

Table 6.1 is a guide to choosing a mic based on your requirements.

Suppose you want to record a grand piano playing with several other instruments. You need the microphone to reduce leakage. Table 6.1 recommends a unidirectional mic or an omni mic up close. For this particular piano, you also want a natural sound, for which the table suggests a mic with a flat response. You want a detailed sound, so a condenser mic is the choice. A microphone with all these characteristics is a flat-response, unidirectional condenser mic. If you're miking close to a surface (the piano lid), a boundary mic is recommended.

Now suppose you're recording an acoustic guitar on stage, and the guitarist roams around. This is a moving sound source, for which the table recommends a mini mic attached to the guitar. Feedback and leakage are not a problem because you're miking close, so you can use an omni mic. Thus, an omni condenser mic is a good choice for this application.

For a home studio, a suggested first choice is a cardioid condenser mic with a flat frequency response. This type of mic is especially good for studio vocals, cymbals, percussion, and acoustic instruments. Remember that the mic needs a power supply to operate, such as a battery or phantom power supply.

Your second choice of microphone for a home studio is a cardioid dynamic microphone with a presence peak in the frequency response. This type is good for drums and guitar amps. I recommend cardioid over omni for a home studio. The cardioid pattern rejects the leakage, background noise, and room reverb often found in home studios. An omni mic, however, can do that, too, if you mike close enough. Also, omni mics tend to provide a more natural sound at lower cost, and they have no proximity effect.

## Mic Accessories

There are many devices used with microphones to route their signals or to make them more useful, including pop filters,

**Table 6.1** Mic application guide

| Requirements | Characteristic |
| --- | --- |
| Natural, smooth tone quality | Flat frequency response |
| Bright, present tone quality | Rising high-frequency response |
| Extended lows | Omni condenser or dynamic with low-frequency response |
| Extended highs (detailed sound) | Condenser |
| Reduced "edge" or detail | Dynamic |
| Boosted bass up close | Single-D cardioid |
| Flat bass response up close | Omnidirectional, multiple-D cardioid, or single-D cardioid with bass rolloff |
| Reduced pickup of leakage, feedback, and room acoustics | Unidirectional, or omni up close |
| Enhanced pickup of room acoustics | Omnidirectional, or unidirectional farther away |
| Miking close to a surface, even coverage of moving sources or large sources, inconspicuous mic | Boundary mic or miniature mic |
| Coincident or near-coincident stereo (see Chapter 18) | Unidirectional mics or stereo mic |
| Extra ruggedness | Moving coil (dynamic) |
| Reduced handling noise | Omni, or unidirectional with shock mount |
| Reduced breath popping | Omni, or unidirectional with pop filter |
| Distortion-free pickup of very loud sounds | Condenser with high maximum SPL spec, or dynamic |
| Noise-free pickup of quiet sounds | Low self-noise, high sensitivity |

stands and booms, shock mounts, cables and connectors, stage boxes and snakes, and splitters.

## Pop Filters

A much needed accessory for a vocalist's microphone is a pop filter or windscreen. It usually is a foam "sock" which you put over the mic.

Why is it needed? When a vocalist sings a word starting with "p," "b," or "t" sounds, a turbulent puff of air is forced from the mouth. A microphone placed close to the mouth is hit by this air puff, resulting in a thump or little explosion called a **pop**. The windscreen reduces this problem.

Some microphones have pop filters or ball-shaped grilles built in. The best type of pop filter is a nylon screen in a hoop placed a few inches from the mic.

You can also reduce pop by placing the mic above or to the side of the mouth, or by using an omni mic.

## Stands and Booms

Stands and booms hold the microphones and let you position them as desired. A mic stand has a heavy metal base that supports a vertical pipe. At the top of the pipe is a rotating clutch that lets you adjust the height of a smaller telescoping pipe inside the large one. The top of the small pipe has a standard $^5/_8$-inch 27 thread, which screws into a mic stand adapter.

A boom is a long horizontal pipe that attaches to the vertical pipe. The angle and length of the boom are adjustable. The end of the boom is threaded to accept a mic stand adapter, and the opposite end is weighted to balance the weight of the microphone.

## Shock Mounts

A shock mount holds a mic in a resilient suspension to isolate the mic from mechanical vibrations, such as bumps to the mic stand and floor thumps.

Many mics have an internal shock mount that isolates the mic capsule from its housing; this reduces handling noise as well as stand thumps.

## Cables and Connectors

Mic cables carry the electrical signal from the mic to the mixing console or tape recorder. With low-impedance mics, you can use hundreds of feet of cable without hum pickup or high-frequency loss. Some mics have a permanently attached cable for convenience and low cost; others have a connector in the handle to accept a separate mic cable. The second method is preferred for serious recording because if the cable breaks, you have to repair or replace only the cable, not the whole microphone.

Mic cables are made of one or two insulated conductors surrounded by a fine-wire mesh shield to keep out electrostatic hum. If you hear a loud buzz when you plug in a microphone, check that the shield is securely soldered in place.

After acquiring a microphone, you may need to wire its 2-conductor shielded cable to a 3-pin audio connector. Here are the solder connections:

- Pin 1: Shield
- Pin 2: "Hot" lead (usually red or white)
- Pin 3: "Cold" lead (usually black)

If the mic output is 3-pin balanced, but your recorder or mixer mic input is an unbalanced phone jack, a different wiring is needed:

Phone-plug tip: Hot lead

Phone-plug long ground lug: Shield and cold lead

Wind your mic cables onto a large spool, which can be found in the electrical section of hardware stores. Plug the cables together as you wind them.

## Snakes

It is messy and time-consuming to run mic cables from several mics all the way to a mixer. Instead, you can plug all your mics into a stage box with several connectors (Figure 2.25). The snake—a thick multi-conductor cable—carries the signals to the mixer. At the mixer end, the cable divides into several mic connectors that plug into the mixer.

## Splitters

When you record a band in concert, you need to feed each mic's signal to your recording mixer and to the band's PA and monitor mixers. A mic splitter does the job. It has one input for each microphone and two or three isolated outputs per microphone to feed each mixer.

# Summary

We talked about some mic types, specs, and accessories. You should have a better idea about what kind of microphone to choose for your own applications.

Mic manufacturers are happy to send you free catalogs and application notes. Your dealers may have this literature. You can get the company addresses from them or from the World Wide Web.

Remember, you can use any microphone on any instrument if it sounds good to you. Just try it and see if you like it. To make high-quality recordings, though, you need good mics with a smooth, wide-range frequency response, low noise, and low distortion.

# 7

# MICROPHONE TECHNIQUE BASICS

Suppose you're going to mike a singer, or a sax, or a guitar. Which mic should you choose? Where should you place it?

Your mic technique has a powerful effect on the sound of your recordings. In this chapter we'll look at some general principles of miking that apply to all situations. Chapter 8 covers common mic techniques for specific instruments.

## Which Mic Should I Use?

Is there a "right" mic to use on a piano, a kick drum, or a guitar amp? No. Every microphone sounds different, and you choose one that gives you the sound you want. Still, it helps to know about two main characteristics of mics that affect the sound: frequency response and polar pattern.

Most condenser mics have an extended high-frequency response—they reproduce sounds up to 15 or 20 kHz. This makes them great for cymbals, or other instruments that need a detailed sound, such as acoustic guitar, strings, piano, and voice. Dynamic moving-coil microphones have a response good enough for drums, guitar amps, horns, and woodwinds. Loud drums and guitar amps sound dull if recorded with a flat-response mic; a mic with a presence peak (a boost around 5 kHz) gives more edge or punch.

The polar pattern of a mic affects how much leakage and ambience it picks up. Leakage is unwanted sound from instruments other than the one the mic is aimed at. Ambience is the acoustics of the recording room, its early reflections and reverb. The more leakage and ambience you pick up, the more distant the instrument sounds.

An omni mic picks up more ambience and leakage than a directional mic when both are the same distance from an instrument. So an omni tends to sound more distant. To compensate, you have to mike closer with an omni.

# How Many Mics?

The number of mics you need varies with what you're recording. If you want to record an overall acoustic blend of the instruments and room ambience, use just two microphones or a stereo mic (Figure 7.1). This method works great on an orchestra, symphonic band, choir, string quartet, pipe organ, small folk group, or a piano/voice recital. Stereo miking is covered in detail later in this chapter.

To record a pop-music group, you mike each instrument or instrumental section. Then you adjust the mixer volume control for each mic to control the balance between instruments (Figure 7.2).

To get the clearest sound, don't use two mics when one will do the job. Sometimes you can pick up two or more sound sources with one mic (Figure 7.3). You could mike a brass section of four players with one mic on four players, or with two mics on every two players.

**Figure 7.1** Overall miking of a musical ensemble with two distant microphones.

**Figure 7.2** Individual miking with multiple close mics and a mixer.

**Figure 7.3** Multiple miking with several sound sources on each microphone.

Picking up more than one instrument with one mic has a problem: during mixdown, you can't adjust the balance among instruments recorded on the same track. You have to balance the instruments before recording them. Monitor the mic, and listen to see if any instrument is too quiet. If so, move it closer to the mic.

# How Close Should I Place the Mic?

Once you've chosen a mic for an instrument, how close should the mic be? Mike a few inches away to get a tight, present sound; mike farther away for a distant, spacious sound. (Try it to hear the effect.) The farther a mic is from the instrument, the more ambience, leakage, and background noise it picks up. So mike close to reject these unwanted sounds. Mike farther away to add a live, loose, airy feel to overdubs of drums, lead-guitar solos, horns, etc.

Close miking sounds close; distant miking sounds distant. Here's why. If you put a mic close to an instrument, the sound at the mic is loud. So you need to turn up the mic gain on your mixer only a little to get a 0 VU recording level. And since the gain is low, you pick up very little reverb, leakage, and background noise (Figure 7.4A).

If you put a mic far from an instrument, the sound at the mic is quiet. You'll need to turn up the mic gain a lot to get a 0 VU recording level. And since the gain is high, you pick up a lot of reverb, leakage, and background noise (Figure 7.4B).

If the mic is very far away—maybe 10 feet—it's called an ambience mic. It picks up mostly room echoes and reverb. A popular mic for ambience is a boundary microphone taped to the wall. You mix it with the usual close mics to add a sense of space. Use two for stereo. When you record a live concert, you might want to place ambience mics over the audience, aiming at them from the front of the hall, to pick up the crowd reaction and the hall acoustics.

Classical music is always recorded at a distance (about 4 to 20 feet away) so that the mics will pick up reverb from the concert hall. It's a desirable part of the sound.

(A) A close microphone picks up mainly direct sound, resulting in a close sound quality.

(B) A distant microphone picks up mainly reflected sound, resulting in a distant sound quality.

**Figure 7.4**

## Reducing Leakage

Suppose you're close-miking a drum set and a piano at the same time (Figure 7.5). When you listen to the drum mics alone, you hear a close, clear sound. But when you mix in the piano mic, that nice, tight drum sound degrades into a distant, muddy sound. That's because the drum sound leaked into the piano mic. The piano mic picked up a distant drum sound from across the room.

There are many ways to reduce leakage:

- Mike each instrument closely. That way the sound level at each mic is high. Then you can turn down the mixer gain of each mic, which reduces leakage at the same time.
- Overdub each instrument one at a time.
- Record direct.
- Filter out frequencies above and below the range of each instrument.
- Use directional mics (cardioid, etc.) instead of omnis.
- Record in a large, fairly dead studio. In such a room, leakage reflected from the walls is weak.
- Put portable walls (goboes) between instruments.

## Don't Mike Too Close

Miking too close can color the recorded tone quality of an instrument. If you mike very close, you might hear a bassy or honky tone instead of a natural sound.

Why? Musical instruments are designed to sound best at a distance, at least $1\frac{1}{2}$ feet away. The sound of an instrument needs some space to develop. A mic placed a foot or two away tends to pick up a well-balanced, natural sound. That is, it picks up a blend of all the parts of the instrument that contribute to its character or timbre.

**Figure 7.5**
Example of leakage. The piano mic picks up leakage from the drums— changing the close drum sound to distant.

Think of a musical instrument as a loudspeaker with a woofer, midrange, and tweeter. If you place a mic a few feet away, it will pick up the sound of the loudspeaker accurately. But if you place the mic close to the woofer, the sound will be bassy. Similarly, if you mike close to an instrument, you emphasize the part of the instrument that the microphone is near. The tone quality picked up very close may not reflect the tone quality of the entire instrument.

Suppose you place a mic next to the sound hole of an acoustic guitar, which resonates around 80 to 100 Hz. A microphone placed there hears this bassy resonance, giving a boomy recorded timbre that does not exist at a greater miking distance. To make the guitar sound more natural when miked close to the sound hole, you need to roll off the excess bass on your mixer, or use a mic with a bass rolloff in its frequency response.

The sax projects highs from the bell, but projects mids and lows from the tone holes. So if you mike close to the bell, you miss the warmth and body from the tone holes. All that's left at the bell is a harsh tone quality. You might like that sound, but if not, move the mic out and up to pick up the entire instrument. If leakage forces you to mike close, change the mic or use EQ.

Usually, you get a natural sound if you put the mic as far from the source as the source is big. That way, the mic picks up all the sound-radiating parts of the instrument about equally. For example, if the body of an acoustic guitar is 18 inches long, place the mic 18 inches away to get a natural tonal balance. If this sounds too distant or hollow, move in a little closer.

# Where Should I Place the Mic?

Suppose you have a mic placed a certain distance from an instrument. If you move the mic left, right, up or down, you change the recorded tone quality. In one spot, the instrument might sound bassy; in another spot, it might sound natural, and so on. So, to find a good position, simply place the mic in different locations—and monitor the results—until you find one that sounds good to you.

Here's another way to do the same thing. Close one ear with your finger, listen to the instrument with the other ear, and move around until you find a spot that sounds good. Put the mic there. Then make a recording and see if it sounds the same as what you heard live. Don't try this with kick drums or screaming guitar amps!

Why does moving the mic change the tone quality? A musical instrument radiates a different tone quality in each direction. Also, each part of

**Figure 7.6**
Microphone placement affects the recorded tonal balance.

the instrument produces a different tone quality. For example, Figure 7.6 shows the tonal balances picked up at various spots near a guitar.

Other instruments work the same way. A trumpet radiates strong highs directly out of the bell, but does not project them to the sides. So a trumpet sounds bright when miked on-axis to the bell and sounds more natural or mellow when miked off to one side. A grand piano miked one foot over the middle strings sounds fairly natural; under the soundboard sounds bassy and dull, and in a sound hole sounds constricted.

It pays to experiment with all sorts of mic positions until you find a sound you like. There is no one right way to place the mics because you place them to get the tonal balance you want.

# On-Surface Techniques

Sometimes you're forced to place a mic near a hard reflecting surface. Examples:

- Recording drama or opera with the mics near the stage floor.
- Recording an instrument that has hard surfaces around it.
- Recording a piano with the mic close to the lid.

In these cases, you'll often pick up an unnatural, filtered tone quality. Here's why. Sound travels to the microphone via two paths: directly from the sound source, and reflected off the nearby surface (Figure 7.7). Because of its longer travel path, the reflected sound is delayed compared to the direct sound. The direct and delayed sound waves combine at the mic, which causes phase cancellations of various frequencies. The series of peaks and dips in the response is called a **comb-filter** effect, and it sounds like mild flanging.

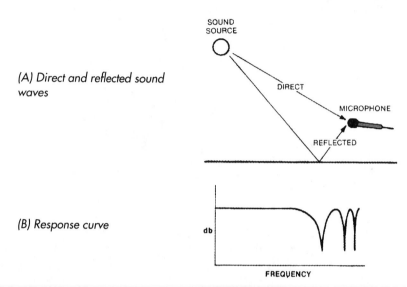

(A) Direct and reflected sound waves

(B) Response curve

**Figure 7.7** A mic placed near a surface picks up direct sound and delayed reflections, giving a comb-filter frequency response.

(A) Direct and reflected sound waves

(B) Response curve

**Figure 7.8** A boundary mic on a surface picks up direct and reflected sounds in phase.

Boundary mics solve the problem. In a boundary mic, the diaphragm is very close to the reflecting surface so that there is no delay in the reflected sound. Direct and reflected sounds add in-phase over the audible range of frequencies, resulting in a flat response (Figure 7.8).

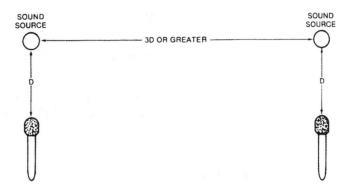

**Figure 7.9**   The 3:1 rule of microphone placement avoids phase interference between microphone signals.

You might tape an omni boundary mic to the underside of a piano lid, to a hard-surfaced panel, or to a wall for ambience pickup. A unidirectional boundary mic works great on a stage floor to pick up drama. A group of these mics will clearly pick up people at a conference table.

# The Three-to-One Rule

Let's say you're miking several instruments, each with its own mic. If you place the musicians too close together, the sound will be blurred. But if you spread out the musicians and mike them close, the sound will be clearer.

Specifically, try to space the mics at least three times the mic-to-source distance (as in Figure 7.9.) This is called the 3:1 rule. For example, if two mics are each placed 1 foot from their sound sources, the mics should be at least 3 feet apart. This will prevent the blurred, colored sound caused by phase cancellations between mics.

The mics can be closer than 3:1 if you use two cardioid mics aiming in opposite directions.

Suppose you're recording a singer/guitarist. There's a mic on the singer and a mic on the acoustic guitar. The vocal picked up by the guitar mic is delayed because the vocal sound travels a longer path to that mic. The two vocal signals in the mix—direct and delayed—interfere with each other and make a hollow sound.

Try these solutions:

1. Mike the voice and guitar very close. Roll off the excess bass with your mixer's EQ. Maybe use a pickup on the guitar instead of a mic.

2. Place two bidirectional mics so the tops of their grilles touch. This gets rid of any delay between their signals. Aim the "dead" side of the

vocal mic at the guitar; aim the dead side of the guitar mic at the mouth.

3. Use just one mic midway between the mouth and guitar. Adjust the balance by changing the mic's height.

4. Delay the vocal mic signal by about 1 msec. Then the two mics' signals will be in phase, preventing phase cancellations when they are mixed to the same channel.

# Off-Axis Coloration

Some mics have **off-axis coloration**: a dull or colored effect on sound sources that are not right in front of the mic. Try to aim the mic at sound sources that put out high frequencies, such as cymbals. When you pick up a large source such as an orchestra, use a mic that has the same response over a wide angle. Such a mic has similar polar patterns at middle and high frequencies. Most large-diaphragm mics have more off-axis coloration than smaller mics ($^3/_4$-inch or under).

# Stereo Mic Techniques

Stereo mic techniques capture the sound of a musical group as a whole, using only two or three microphones. When you play back a stereo recording, you hear **phantom images** of the instruments in various spots between the speakers. These image locations—left to right, front to back—correspond to the instrument locations during the recording session.

Stereo miking is the preferred way to record classical-music ensembles and soloists. In the studio, you can stereo-mike a piano, drum set cymbals, vibraphone, harmony singers, or other large sound sources.

# Goals of Stereo Miking

One goal is accurate localization. That is, instruments in the center of the group are reproduced midway between the two speakers. Instruments at the sides of the group are heard from the left or right speaker. Instruments halfway to one side are heard halfway to one side, and so on.

Figure 7.10 shows three stereo localization effects. Figure 7.10A shows some instrument positions in an orchestra: left, left-center, center, right-center, right. In Figure 7.10B, the reproduced images of these instruments are accurately localized between the speakers. The stereo spread, or stage width, extends from speaker to speaker. (You might want to record a string quartet with a narrower spread).

(A) Orchestra instrument locations (top view).

(B) Images localized accurately between speakers (the listener's perception).

(C) Narrow stage width effect.

(D) Exaggerated separation effect.

**Figure 7.10** Stereo localization effects.

If you space or angle the mics too close together, you get a narrow stage width (Figure 7.10C). If you space or angle the mics too far apart, you hear exaggerated separation (Figure 7.10D). That is, instruments halfway to one side are heard near the left or right speaker.

To judge stereo effects, you have to sit exactly between your monitor speakers (the same distance from each). Sit as far from the speakers as the spacing between them. Then the speakers appear to be 60 degrees apart. This is about the same angle an orchestra fills when viewed from a typical ideal seat in the audience (say, tenth row center). If you sit off-center, the images shift toward the side on which you're sitting and are less sharp.

# Types of Stereo Mic Techniques

To make a stereo recording, you use one of these basic techniques:

- Coincident pair (XY or MS)
- Spaced pair (AB)
- Near-coincident pair (ORTF, etc.)
- Baffled pair (sphere, OSS, SASS, PZM wedge, etc.)

Let's look at each technique.

## *Coincident Pair*

With this method, you mount two directional mics with grilles touching, diaphragms one above the other, and angled apart (Figure 7.11). For example, mount two cardioid mics with one grille above the other, and angle them 120 degrees apart. You can use other patterns too: supercardioid, hypercardioid, or bidirectional. The wider the angle between mics, the wider the stereo spread.

How does this technique make images you can localize? A directional mic is most sensitive to sounds in front of the mic (on-axis) and progressively less sensitive to sounds arriving off-axis. That is, a directional mic puts out a high-level signal from the sound source it's aimed at, and produces lower-level signals from other sound sources.

The coincident pair uses two directional mics that are angled symmetrically from the center line (Figure 7.11). Instruments in the center of the group make the same signal from each mic. During playback, you hear a phantom image of the center instruments midway between your speakers. That's because identical signals in each channel produce an image in the center.

If an instrument is off-center to the right, it is more on-axis to the right-aiming mic than to the left-aiming mic. So the right mic will produce a higher-level signal than the left mic. During playback of this recording, the right speaker will play at a higher level than the left speaker. This reproduces the image off-center to the right—where the instrument was during recording.

The coincident pair codes instrument positions into level differences between channels. During playback, the brain decodes these level differ-

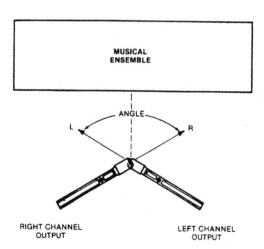

**Figure 7.11**
Coincident-pair technique.

ences back into corresponding image locations. A pan pot in a mixing console works on the same principle. If one channel is 15 to 20 dB louder than the other, the image shifts all the way to the louder speaker.

Suppose we want the right side of the orchestra to be reproduced at the right speaker. That means the far-right musicians must produce a signal level 20 dB higher from the right mic than from the left mic. This happens when the mics are angled far enough apart. The correct angle depends on the polar pattern.

Instruments partway off center produce interchannel level differences less than 20 dB, so you hear them partway off center.

Listening tests have shown that coincident cardioid mics tend to reproduce the musical group with a narrow stereo spread. That is, the group does not spread all the way between speakers.

A coincident-pair method with excellent localization is the Blumlein array. It uses two bidirectional mics angled 90 degrees apart and facing the left and right sides of the group.

A special form of the coincident-pair technique is Mid-Side or MS (Figure 7.12). In this method, a cardioid or omni mic faces the middle of the orchestra. A matrix circuit sums and differences the cardioid mic with a bidirectional mic aiming to the sides. This produces left- and right-channel signals. You can remote-control the stereo spread by changing the ratio of the mid signal to the side signal. This remote control is useful at live concerts, where you can't physically adjust the mics during the concert. MS localization can be accurate.

To make coincident recordings sound more spacious, boost the bass 4 dB (+2 dB at 600 Hz) in the L-R or side signal.

A recording made with coincident mics is mono-compatible. That is, the frequency response is the same in mono or stereo. Since the mics occupy almost the same point in space, there is no time or phase difference between their signals. And when you combine them to mono, there

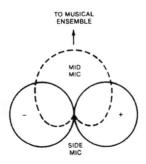

**Figure 7.12**
Mid-Side (MS) technique.

RIGHT CHANNEL = MID + SIDE
LEFT CHANNEL = MID − SIDE

are no phase cancellations to degrade the frequency response. If you expect that your recordings will be heard in mono (say, on TV), then you'll probably want to use coincident methods.

## *Spaced Pair*

Here, you mount two identical mics several feet apart and aim them straight ahead (Figure 7.13). The mics can have any polar pattern, but omni is most popular for this method. The greater the spacing between mics, the greater the stereo spread.

How does this method work? Instruments in the center of the group make the same signal from each mic. When you play back this recording, you hear a phantom image of the center instruments midway between your speakers.

If an instrument is off-center, it is closer to one mic than the other, so its sound reaches the closer microphone before it reaches the other one. Both mics make about the same signal, except that one mic signal is delayed compared with the other.

If you send a signal to two speakers with one channel delayed, the sound image shifts off center. With a spaced-pair recording, off-center instruments produce a delay in one mic channel, so they are reproduced off center.

The spaced pair codes instrument positions into time differences between channels. During playback, the brain decodes these time differences back into corresponding image locations.

A delay of 1.2 msec is enough to shift an image all the way to one speaker. You can use this fact when you set up the mics. Suppose you want to hear the right side of the orchestra from the right speaker. The sound from the right-side musicians must reach the right mic about 1.2 msec before it reaches the left mic. To make this happen, space the mics about

**Figure 7.13**
Spaced-pair technique.

2 to 3 feet apart. This spacing makes the correct delay to place right-side instruments at the right speaker.

Instruments partway off center make interchannel delays less than 1.2 msec, so they are reproduced partway off center.

If the spacing between mics is, say, 12 feet, then instruments that are slightly off center produce delays between channels that are greater than 1 msec. This places their images at the left or right speaker. I call this "exaggerated separation" or a "ping-pong" effect (Figure 7.10D).

On the other hand, if the mics are too close together, the delays produced will be too small to provide much stereo spread. Also, the mics will tend to emphasize instruments in the center because the mics are closest to them.

To record a good musical balance of an orchestra, you need to space the mics about 10 or 12 feet apart. But then you get too much separation. You could place a third mic midway between the outer pair and mix its output to both channels. That way, you pick up a good balance, and you hear an accurate stereo spread.

The spaced-pair method tends to make off-center images unfocused or hard to localize. Why? Spaced-pair recordings have time differences between channels. Stereo images produced solely by time differences are unfocused. You still hear the center instruments clearly in the center, but off-center instruments are hard to pinpoint. Spaced-pair miking is a good choice if you want the sonic images to be diffuse or blended, instead of sharply focused.

Another flaw of spaced mics: If you mix both mics to mono, you may get phase cancellations of various frequencies. This may or may not be audible.

Spaced mics, however, give a "warm" sense of ambience, in which the concert-hall reverb seems to surround the instruments and, sometimes, the listener. Here's why: The two channels of recorded reverb are incoherent; that is, they have random phase relationships. Incoherent signals from stereo speakers sound diffuse and spacious. Since spaced mics pick up reverb incoherently, it sounds diffuse and spacious. The simulated spaciousness caused by the phasiness is not necessarily realistic, but it is pleasant to many listeners.

Another advantage of the spaced pair is that you can use omni mics. An omni condenser mic has deeper bass than a uni condenser mic.

## Near-Coincident Pair

In this method, you angle apart two directional mics, and space their grilles a few inches apart horizontally (Figure 7.14). Even a few inches of spacing

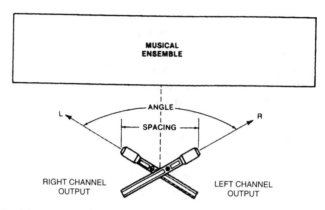

**Figure 7.14** Near-coincident pair technique.

increases the stereo spread and adds a sense of ambient warmth or air to the recording. The greater the angle or spacing between mics, the greater the stereo spread.

How does this method work? Angling directional mics produces level differences between channels. Spacing mics produces time differences. The level differences and time differences combine to create the stereo effect.

If the angling or spacing is too great, you get exaggerated separation. If the angling or spacing is too small, you'll hear a narrow stereo spread.

A common near-coincident method is the ORTF system, which uses two cardioids angled 110 degrees apart and spaced 7 inches (17 cm) horizontally. Usually this method gives accurate localization. That is, instruments at the sides of the orchestra are reproduced at or very near the speakers, and instruments halfway to one side are reproduced about halfway to one side.

## Baffled Omni Pair

This method uses two omni mics, usually ear-spaced, and separated by either a hard or soft baffle (Figure 7.15). To create stereo, it uses time differences at low frequencies and level differences at high frequencies. The spacing between mics creates time differences. The baffle creates a sound shadow (reduced high frequencies) at the mic farthest from the source. Between the two channels, there are spectral differences—differences in frequency response.

Some examples of baffled-omni pairs are the Schoeps or Neumann sphere microphones, the Jecklin Disk, and the Crown SASS-P MKII.

**Figure 7.15**
Baffled-omni technique.

## Comparing the Four Techniques

Coincident pair:

- Uses two directional mics angled apart with grilles touching.
- Level differences between channels produce the stereo effect.
- Images are sharp.
- Stereo spread ranges from narrow to accurate.
- Signals are mono compatible.

Spaced pair:

- Uses two mics spaced several feet apart, aiming straight ahead.
- Time differences between channels produce the stereo effect.
- Off-center images are diffuse.
- Stereo spread tends to be exaggerated unless a third center mic is used, or unless spacing is under 2 to 3 feet.
- Provides a warm sense of ambience.
- Tends not to be mono compatible, but there are exceptions.
- Good low-frequency response if you use omni condensers.

Near-coincident pair:

- Uses two directional mics angled apart and spaced a few inches apart horizontally.
- Level and time differences between channels produce the stereo effect.

- Images are sharp.
- Stereo spread tends to be accurate. Provides a greater sense of air than coincident methods.
- Tends not to be mono compatible.

  Baffled omni pair:

- Uses two omni mics, usually ear-spaced, with a baffle between them.
- Level and time differences (spectral differences) produce the stereo effect.
- Images are sharp.
- Stereo spread tends to be accurate.
- Good low-frequency response.
- Good imaging with headphones.
- Provides more air than coincident methods.
- Tends not to be mono compatible, but there are exceptions.

# Hardware

A handy device is a stereo mic adapter or stereo bar. It mounts two mics on a single stand, and lets you adjust the angle and spacing. You might prefer to use a stereo mic instead of two mics. It has two mic capsules in a single housing for convenience.

# How to Test Imaging

Here's a way to check the stereo imaging of a mic technique.

1. Set up the stereo mic array in front of a stage.
2. Record yourself speaking from various locations on stage where the instruments will be—center, half-right, far right, half-left, far left. Announce your position.
3. Play back the tape over speakers.

You'll hear how accurately the technique translated your positions, and you'll hear how sharp the images are.

We looked at several mic arrays to record in stereo. Each has its pros and cons. Which method you choose depends on the sonic compromises you're willing to make.

# 8

# MICROPHONE TECHNIQUES

This chapter describes some ways to select and place mics for musical instruments and vocals. These techniques are popular, but they're just suggested starting points. Feel free to experiment.

Before you mike an instrument, listen to it live in the studio, so you know what sound you're starting with. You might want to duplicate that sound through your monitor speakers.

## Electric Guitar

Let's start by looking at the chain of guitar, effects, amplifier, and speaker. At each point in the chain where you record, you'll get a different sound (Figure 8.1).

1. The electric guitar puts out an electrical signal that sounds clean and clear.
2. This signal might go through some effects boxes, such as distortion, wah wah, compression, chorus, or stereo effects.
3. Then the signal goes through a guitar amp, which boosts the signal and adds distortion. At the amplifier output (preamp out or external speaker jack), the sound is very bright and edgy.
4. The distorted amp signal is played by the speaker in the amp. Since the speaker rolls off above 4 kHz, it takes the edge off the distortion and makes it more pleasant.

You can record the electric guitar in many ways (Figure 8.1):

**Figure 8.1** Recording an electric guitar.

- With a mic in front of the guitar amp
- With a direct box
- Both miked and direct
- Through a signal processor

The song you're recording will tell you what method it wants.

Just mike the amp when you want a rough, raw sound with tube distortion and speaker coloration. Rock 'n' roll or heavy metal usually sounds best with a miked amp. If you record through a direct box, the sound is clean and clear, with crisp highs and deep lows. That might work for quiet jazz or R&B. Use whatever sounds right for the particular song you're recording.

First, try to kill any hum you hear from the guitar amp. Turn up the guitar's volume and treble controls so that the guitar signal overrides hum and noise picked up by the guitar cable. Ask the guitarist to move around, or rotate, to find a spot in the room where hum disappears. Flip the polarity switch on the amp to the lowest-hum position. To remove buzzes between guitar notes, try a noise gate, or ask the player to keep his or her hands on the strings.

## Miking the Amp

Small practice amplifiers tend to be better for recording than large, noisy stage amps. If you use a small one, place it on a chair to avoid picking up sound reflections from the floor (unless you like that effect).

A common mic for the guitar amp is a cardioid dynamic type with a "presence peak" in its frequency response (a boost around 5 kHz). The cardioid pattern reduces leakage (off-mic sounds from other instruments). The dynamic type handles loud sounds without distorting, and the presence peak adds "bite." Of course, you can use any mic that sounds good to you.

As a starting point, try miking the amp about an inch from the grille over a speaker cone, slightly off-center—where the cone meets the dome.

The closer you mike the amp, the bassier the tone. The farther off-center the mic is, the duller the tone.

Often, distant miking sounds great when you overdub a lead guitar solo played through a stack of speakers in a live room. Try a boundary mic on the floor or on the wall, several feet away.

## *Recording Direct*

Now let's look at recording direct (also known as direct injection or DI). The electric guitar produces an electrical signal which you can plug into your mixer. You bypass the mic and guitar amp, so the sound is clean and clear. Just remember that amp distortion is desirable in some songs.

Mixer mic inputs tend to have an impedance (Z) around 1500 ohms. But a guitar pickup is several thousand ohms. So if you plug a high-Z electric guitar directly into a mic input, the input will load down the pickup and give a thin or dull sound.

To get around this loading problem, use a direct box between the guitar and your mixer (Figure 8.2). The DI box has a high-Z input and low-Z output, thanks to a built-in transformer or circuit. Some mixers have a high-Z input jack built in, so you can plug the electric guitar or bass directly into this jack.

Some direct boxes let you record off the amp's external-speaker jack to pick up distortion. The sound at that jack is really annoying—edgy and

**Figure 8.2**
Typical direct box.

sizzly. To compensate, some DI boxes include a circuit that filters the highs out of that signal to simulate the effect of the speaker.

The direct box should have a ground-lift switch to prevent ground loops and hum. Set it to the position where you monitor the least hum. You might try a mix of direct sound and miked sound.

## Electric Guitar Effects

If you want to record the guitarist's special effects, connect the output of the effects boxes into the direct-box input. Many players have a rack of signal processors that creates their unique sound, and they just give you their direct feed. Be open to their suggestions, and diplomatic about changing the sound. If they are studio players, they often have a better handle on effects than you might as the engineer.

You might want a "fat" or spacious lead-guitar sound. Here are some ways to get it:

- Send the guitar signal through a digital delay set to 10 to 20 msec. Pan guitar left, delay right. Adjust levels for nearly equal loudness from each speaker. (Watch out for phase cancellations in mono.)
- Send the guitar signal through a pitch-shifter, set for just a few cents of pitch bending. Pan guitar left, pitch-shifted guitar right.
- Record two guitarists playing identical parts, and pan them left and right. This works great for rhythm-guitar parts in heavy metal.
- Double the guitar. Have the player re-record the same part on an unused track while listening to the original part. Pan the original part left and pan the new part right.
- Add stereo reverb or stereo chorus.

Some guitar processors add many effects to an electric guitar, such as distortion, EQ, chorus, and compression. You simply plug the electric guitar into the processor, adjust it for the desired sound, and record the signal direct. You wind up with a fully produced sound with a minimum of effort.

# Electric Bass

BWAM, dik diddy bum. Do your bass tracks sound that clear? Or are they more muddy, like, "Bwuh, dip dubba duh"? Here's how to record the electric bass so it's clean and easy to hear in a mix.

As always, first you work on the sound of the instrument itself. Put on new strings if the old ones sound dull. Adjust the pickup screws (if any) for equal output from each string. Also adjust the intonation and tuning.

Usually, you record the electric bass direct for the cleanest possible sound. A direct pickup gives deeper lows than a miked amp, but the amp gives more midrange punch. You might want to mix the direct and miked sound. Use a condenser or dynamic mic with a good low-frequency response, placed 1 to 6 inches from the speaker.

When mixing a direct signal and a mic signal, make sure they are in-phase with each other. To do this, set them to equal levels and reverse the polarity of the direct signal or the mic signal. The polarity that gives the most bass is correct.

Have the musician play some scales to see if any notes are louder than the rest. You might set a parametric equalizer to soften these notes, or use a compressor.

The bass guitar should be fairly constant in level (a dynamic range of about 6 dB) to be audible throughout the song, and to avoid saturating the tape on loud peaks. To do this, run the bass guitar through a compressor. Set the compression ratio to about 4:1; set the attack time fairly slow (8–20 msec) to preserve the attack transient; and set the release time fairly fast ($\frac{1}{4}$ to $\frac{1}{2}$ second). If the release time is too fast, you get harmonic distortion.

EQ can make the bass guitar clearer. Try cutting around 200 to 400 Hz. Don't boost the extreme lows. A boost at 1500 to 5000 Hz adds edge or slap, and a boost at 700 to 800 Hz adds "growl" and harmonic clarity.

Here are some ways to make the bass sound clean and well defined:

- Record the bass direct.
- Use no reverb or echo on the bass.
- Have the bass player turn down the bass amp in the studio, just loud enough to play adequately. This reduces muddy-sounding bass leakage into other mics.
- Better yet, don't use the amp. Instead, have the musicians monitor the bass (and each other) with headphones.
- Have the bass player try new strings or a different guitar. Some guitars are better for recording than others.
- Ask the bass player to use the treble pickup near the bridge.
- Be sure to record the bass with enough edge or harmonics so the bass will be audible on small, cheap speakers.
- Try a bass-guitar signal processor such as the Bass Rockman.

If the bass part is full and sustained, it's probably best to go for a mellow sound without much pluck. Let the kick drum define the rhythmic pattern. But if both the bass and kick are rhythmic and work independently, then you should hear the plucks. Listen to the song first, then get a bass sound appropriate for the music. A sharp, twangy timbre is not always right for a ballad; a full, round tone will get lost in a fusion piece.

Often, a musician plays bass lines on a synth or sound module. The module is triggered from a keyboard, a sequencer, or a bass guitar plugged into a pitch-to-MIDI converter. Connect the module output to your mixer line in.

Two effects boxes for the electric bass are the octave box and the bass chorus. The octave box takes the bass signal and drops it an octave in pitch. That is, it divides the bass signal's fundamental frequency in two. You put 82 Hz in; you get 41 Hz out. This gives an extra deep, growly sound.

A bass chorus gives a wavy, shimmering effect. Like a conventional chorus box, it detunes the signal and combines the detuned signal with the direct signal. Also, it removes the lowest frequencies from the detuned signal, so that the chorus effect doesn't thin out the sound.

# Synthesizer, Drum Machine, Electric Piano

For the most clarity, you usually DI a synth, MIDI sound module, drum machine, or electric piano. Set the volume on the instrument about ¾ up to get a strong signal. Try to get the sound you want from patch settings rather than EQ.

Plug the instrument into a phone jack input on your mixer, or use a direct box. If you connect to a phone jack and hear hum, you probably have a ground loop. Here are some fixes:

- Power your mixer and the instrument from the same outlet strip. If necessary, use a thick extension cord between the outlet strip and the instrument.
- Use a direct box instead of a guitar cord, and set the ground-lift switch to the position where you monitor the least hum.
- To reduce hum from a low-cost synth, use battery power instead of an AC adapter.

A synth can sound dry and sterile. To get a livelier, funkier sound, you might run the synth signal into a power amp and speakers, and mic the speakers a few feet away.

If the keyboard player has several keyboards plugged into a keyboard mixer, you may want to record a premixed signal from that mixer's output. Record both outputs of stereo keyboards.

You don't need to record MIDI instruments to multitrack. Just use your sequencer and sync it to tape (see Chapter 16).

# Leslie Organ Speaker

This glorious device has a rotating dual-horn on top for highs and a woofer on the bottom for lows. Only one horn of the two makes sound; the other is for weight balance. The swirling, grungy sound comes from the phasiness and Doppler effect of the rotating horn, and from the distorted tube electronics that drive the speaker. Here are a few ways to record it (Figure 8.3):

- In mono: Mic the top and bottom separately, 3 inches to 2 feet away. Aim the mics into the louvers. In the top mic's signal, roll off the lows below 150 Hz.
- In stereo: Record the rotating horn in stereo with a mic on either side. Problem: The horn will sound like it's rotating twice as fast, because the mics will pick up the horn twice per rotation.
- In stereo: Record the top horn with a stereo mic or a pair of mics out front. Put a mic with a good low end on the bottom speaker, and pan it to center.

When you record the Leslie, watch out for wind noise from the rotating horn and buzz from the motor. Mic farther away if you monitor these noises.

# Drum Set

The first step is to make the drums sound good live in the studio. If the set sounds poor, you'll have a hard time making it sound great in the

**Figure 8.3**
Miking a Leslie organ speaker.

control room! You might put the drum set on a riser 1½ feet high to reduce bass leakage and to provide better eye contact between the drummer and the rest of the band. To reduce drum leakage into other mics, you could surround the set with goboes: padded thick-wood panels about 4 feet tall. For more isolation, place the set in a drum booth, a small padded room with windows. It's also common to overdub the set in a live room.

# Tuning

One secret of creating a good drum sound lies in careful tuning. It's easier to record a killer sound if you tune the set to sound right in the studio before miking it.

First let's consider drum heads. Plain heads have the most ring or sustain, while heads with sound dots or hydraulic heads dampen the ring. Thin heads are best for recording because they have crisp attack and long sustain. Old heads become dull, so use new heads.

When you tune the toms, first take off the heads and remove the damping mechanism, which can rattle. Put just the top head on and hand-tighten the lugs. Then, using a drum key, tighten opposite pairs of lugs one at a time, one full turn. After you tighten all the lugs, repeat the process, tightening one-half turn. Then press on the head to stretch it. Continue tightening a half-turn at a time until you reach the pitch you want. You'll get the most pleasing tone when the heads are tuned within the range of the shell resonance.

To reduce ugly overtones, try to keep the tension the same around the head. While touching the center of the head, tap with a drumstick on the head near each lug. Adjust tension for equal pitch around the drum. If you want a downward pitch bend when the head is struck, loosen one lug.

Keep the bottom head off the drum for the most projection and the broadest range of tuning. In this case, pack the bottom lugs with felt to prevent rattles. But you may want to add the bottom head for extra control of the sound. Projection is best if the bottom head is tighter than the top head—say, tuned a fourth above the top head. There will be a muted attack, an "open" tone, and some note bending. If you tune the bottom head looser than the top, the tone will be more "closed," with good attack.

With the kick drum (bass drum), a loose head gives lots of slap and attack, and almost no tone. The opposite is true for a tight head. Tune the head to complement the style of music. For more attack or click, use a hard beater.

Tune the snare drum with the snares off. A loose batter head or top head gives a deep, fat sound. A tight batter head sounds bright and crisp. With the snare head or bottom head loose, the tone is deep with little snare buzz, while a tight snare head yields a crisp snare response. Set the snare tension just to the point where the snare wires begin to "choke" the sound, then back off a little.

## Damping and Noise Control

Usually the heads should ring without any damping. But if the toms or snare drum rings too much, put some plastic damping rings on them. Or tape some gauze pads, tissues, or folded handkerchiefs to the edge of the heads. Put masking tape on three sides of the pad so that the untaped edge is free to vibrate and dampen the head motion. Don't overdo the damping, or the drum set will sound like cardboard boxes.

Oil the kick drum pedal to prevent squeaks. Tape rattling hardware in place.

Sometimes a snare drum buzzes in sympathetic vibration with a bass-guitar passage or a tom-tom fill. Try to control the buzz by wedging a thick cotton wad between the snares and the drum stand. Or tune the snare to a different pitch than the toms.

## Drum Miking

Now you're ready to mike the set. For a tight sound, place a mic near each drum head. For a more open, airy sound, use fewer mics or mix in some room mics placed several feet away. Typical room mics are omni condensers or boundary mics. Figure 8.4 shows typical mic placements for a rock drum set. Let's look at each part of the kit.

### Snare

The most popular type of mic for the snare is a cardioid dynamic with a presence peak. The cardioid pattern reduces leakage; its proximity effect boosts the bass for a fatter sound. The presence peak adds attack. You might prefer a cardioid condenser for its sharp transient response.

Bring the mic in from the front of the set on a boom. Place the mic about 1 inch in from the rim, 1 or 2 inches above the head (Figure 8.5). Angle the mic down to aim where the drummer hits. Or attach a mini condenser mic to the side of the snare drum so it "looks at" the top head over the rim.

Some engineers mike both the top and bottom heads of the snare drum, with the microphones in opposite polarity. A mic under the snare drum gives a zippy sound; a mic over the snare drum gives a fuller sound.

141

**Figure 8.4** Typical mic placements for a drum set.

**Figure 8.5**
Snare-drum miking.

Whenever the hi-hat closes, it makes a puff of air that can "pop" the snare-drum mic. Place the snare mic so the air puff doesn't hit it. To prevent hi-hat leakage into the snare mic:

- Mike the snare closely.
- Bring the snare boom in under the hi-hat, and aim the snare mic away from the hi-hat.
- Use a piece of foam to block sound from the hi-hat.
- Use a de-esser on the snare.
- Overdub the hi-hat.

## Hi-Hat

Try a cardioid condenser mic about 6 inches over the cymbal edge that's farthest from the drummer (Figure 8.6). To avoid their puff just mentioned, don't mike the hi-hat off its side; mike it from above aiming down. This also reduces snare leakage. You may not need a hi-hat microphone, especially if you use room mics.

## Tom-Toms

You can mike the toms individually, or put a mic between each pair of toms. Place a cardioid dynamic about 1 inch over the drumhead and 1 inch in from the rim, angled down about 45 degrees toward the head (Figure 8.7). Again, the cardioid's proximity effect gives a full sound. Another way:

**Figure 8.6**
Hi-hat miking.

**Figure 8.7**
Tom-tom miking.

clip mini condenser mics to the toms, peeking over the top rim of each drum. Or you might try a bi-directional mic between two tom-toms.

If the tom mics pick up too much cymbals, aim the "dead" rear of the tom mics at the cymbals. If you use a supercardioid or hypercardioid mic, aim the null of best rejection at the cymbals.

Another way to reduce cymbal leakage: Remove the bottom heads from the toms and mike them inside a few inches from the head, off-center. This also keeps the mics out of the drummer's way. The sound picked up inside the tom-tom has less attack and more tone than the sound picked up outside.

## Kick Drum

Place a blanket or carpet pad inside the drum, pressing against the beater head to dampen the vibration and tighten the beat. The blanket shortens the decay portion of the kick-drum envelope. Tune the drum low.

A popular mic for kick drum is a large-diameter, cardioid dynamic type with an extended low-frequency response. Some mics are designed specifically for the kick drum. For starters, place the kick mic inside on a boom, a few inches from where the beater hits (Figure 8.8). Mic placement close to the beater picks up a hard beater sound; off-center placement picks up more skin tone, and farther away picks up a boomier shell sound.

**Figure 8.8**
Kick-drum miking.

**Figure 8.9**
Overhead cymbal miking.

Other miking tips: Hang a mini omni condenser mic inside near the beater, or place an omni condenser a few inches from the beater. These mics respond to very deep frequencies and have sharp transient response, which helps the attack.

How should the recorded kick drum sound? Well, they don't call it kick drum for nothing. THUNK! You should hear a powerful low-end thump plus an attack transient.

Kick drum often needs a fair amount of EQ to sound good. Typically you cut several dB around 400 to 600 Hz to remove the "papery" sound, and boost around 2.5 kHz to 10 kHz to add click or snap. Don't overdo the high-frequency boost; usually you don't want too much "point" on the kick sound.

## Cymbals

To capture all the crisp "ping" of the cymbals, a good mic choice is a cardioid condenser with a flat, extended high-frequency response. Place the overhead mics about 2 to 3 feet above the cymbal edges; closer miking picks up a low-frequency ring (Figure 8.9.) The cymbal edges radiate the most highs. Place the cymbal mics to pick up all the cymbals equally. If your recording will be heard in mono, you might want to mount the mic grilles together and angle the mics apart (Figure 8.4, position "A"). Or use a stereo mic.

Recorded cymbals should sound crisp and smooth, not muffled or harsh.

## Room Mics

Besides the close-up drum mics, you might want to use a distant pair of room mics when you record drum overdubs. Place the mics about 10 or 20 feet from the set to pick up room reverb. When mixed with the close-up mics, the room mics give an open, airy sound to the drums. Popular room mics are omni condensers or boundary mics taped to the control-room window. You might compress the room mics for special effect. If you don't have enough tracks for room microphones, try raising the overhead mics.

## Boundary Mic Techniques

Boundary mics let you pick up the set in unusual ways. You can strap one on the drummer's chest to pick up the set as the drummer hears it. Tape them to hard-surfaced goboes surrounding the drummer. Put them on the floor under the toms and near the kick drum, or hang a pair over the cymbals.

## Recording with Two to Four Mics

Sometimes you can mike the set simply. Place a stereo mic (or two mics) overhead and put another mic in the kick. If necessary, add a snare-drum mic. This method works well for acoustic jazz. If you want the toms to sound fuller, boost the lows in the overhead mics.

Another setup is shown in Figure 8.10. It uses only one mini omni condenser mic and one kick-drum mic. This method sometimes works well on small drum sets.

Clip a mini omni condenser mic to the snare-drum rim about 4 inches above the rim, in the center of the set, aiming at the hi-hat. Also mike the kick drum.

The mini mic will pick up the snare, hi-hat, and toms all around it, and will pick up the cymbals from underneath. Move the mic closer or farther from the toms, and raise or lower the cymbals, until you hear a pleasing balance. Add a little bass and treble. You'll be surprised at the good sound and even coverage you can get with this simple setup.

Want a stereo effect? Tape another mini mic just over the floor-tom rim, on the side farthest from the drummer (Figure 8.11). Pan the mini mics left and right.

146

**Figure 8.10** Miking a small drum set with two mics (one in the kick drum).

**Figure 8.11** Miking a small drum set with three mics (one clipped onto the snare-drum rim, the other in the kick drum).

## Drum Recording Tips

After you set up all the mics, ask the drummer to play. Listen for rattles and leakage by soloing each microphone. Try not to spend much time getting a sound; otherwise you waste the other musicians' time and wear out the drummer.

147

To keep the drum sound tight, turn off mics not in use in particular tune, use a noise gate on each drum mic, or overdub the drums.

One effect for the snare drum is gated reverb. It's a short splash of bright-sounding reverberation, which is rapidly cut off by a noise gate or expander. Many effects units have a gated-reverb program.

Another trick is recording "hot." Using an analog multitrack, record the drums at a high level so they distort just a little. It's also common to compress the kick.

A drummer might use drum pads, or drum triggers, fed into a sound module. Record direct off the module. You might want to mike the cymbals anyway for best sound.

If you're recording a drum machine and it sounds too mechanical, add some real drums. The machine can play a steady background while the drummer does other things.

When miking drums on stage for P.A., you don't need a forest of unsightly mic stands and booms. Instead, you can use short mic holders that clip onto drum rims and cymbal stands, or use mini condenser mics.

In a typical rock mix, the drums either are the loudest element, or are slightly quieter than the lead vocal. The kick drum is almost as loud as the snare. If you don't want a wimpy mix, keep those drums up front!

Try these EQ settings to enhance the recorded sound of the drums:

- Snare and rack toms: Fat at 200 Hz, crack at 5 kHz. If the sound is too tubby, cut around 200 Hz.
- Floor toms: Fullness at 80 to 100 Hz.
- Cymbals: Sizzle at 10 kHz or higher. Roll off the lows below 500 Hz to reduce low-frequency leakage.
- Kick drum: Boost at 2.5 kHz to 10 kHz for click. Filter out highs above 9 kHz to reduce leakage from cymbals. To remove the "cardboard" sound, cut at 300 to 600 Hz.

A typical track assignment for drums might be:

1. Kick
2. Snare
3 & 4. Toms in stereo
5 & 6. Overheads in stereo

# Percussion

Let's move on to percussion, such as the cowbell, triangle, tambourine, or bell tree. A good mic for metal percussion is a condenser type because it has sharp transient response. Mike at least 1 foot away so the mic doesn't distort.

You can pick up congas, bongoes, and timbales with a single mic between the pair, a few inches over the top. A cardioid dynamic with a presence peak gives a full sound with a clear attack.

For xylophones and vibraphones, place two cardioid mics 1½ feet above the instrument, aiming down. Cross the mics 135 degrees apart or place them about 2 feet apart. You'll get a balanced pickup of the whole instrument.

# Acoustic Guitar

The acoustic guitar has a delicate timbre that you can capture through careful mic selection and placement. First prepare the acoustic guitar for recording. To reduce finger squeaks, try commercial string lubricant, a household cleaner/waxer, talcum powder on fingers, or smooth-wound strings. Ask the guitarist to play louder; this increases the "music-to-squeak" ratio!

Replace old strings with new ones. Experiment with different kinds of guitars, picks, and finger picking to get a sound that's right for the song.

For acoustic guitar, a popular mic is a condenser with a smooth, extended frequency response from 80 Hz up. This kind of mic has a clear, detailed sound. You can hear each string being plucked in a strummed chord. Usually the sound picked up is as crisp as the real thing.

Now let's look at some mic positions. To record a classical guitar solo in a recital hall, mike about 3 to 6 feet away to pick up room reverb. Try a stereo pair (Figure 8.12A), such as XY, ORTF, MS, or spaced pair (described in Chapter 7).

When you record pop, folk, or rock music, try a spot about 6 to 12 inches from where the fingerboard joins the guitar body—at about the 12th fret (Figure 8.12B). That's a good starting point for capturing the acoustic guitar accurately. Still, you need to experiment and use your ears. Close to the bridge, the sound is woody and mellow.

In general, close miking gives more isolation, but tends to sound harsh and aggressive. Distant miking lets the instrument "breathe"; you hear a gentler, more open sound.

Another spot to try: Tape a mini omni mic onto the body, halfway between the sound hole and bridge, about ½ inch from the low E string (Figure 8.12C).

The guitar will sound more real if you record in stereo. Try one mic near the 12th fret, and another near the bridge (Figures 8.12D, 8.12E). Pan

**Figure 8.12**
Some mic techniques for
acoustic guitar.

left and right. Another way to record stereo is with an XY pair of cardioid mics about 6 inches from the end of the fingerboard, mixed with a 3-foot-spaced pair of omni mics about 3 feet away.

Is feedback or leakage a problem? Mike close to the sound hole (Figure 8.12F). The tone there is very bassy, so turn down the low-frequency EQ on your mixer until the sound is natural. Also cut a few dB around 3 kHz to reduce harshness.

You get the most isolation with a contact pickup. It attaches to the guitar, usually under the bridge. The sound of a pickup is something like an electric guitar. You can mix a mic with a pickup to add air and string noise to the sound of the pickup. That way, you get good isolation and good tone quality.

# Singer/Guitarist

Normally you overdub the guitar and vocal separately. But if you have to record both at once, the vocal might sound filtered or hollow because of phase cancellations between the vocal mic and guitar mic. This can happen whenever two mics pick up the same source at approximately equal levels, at different distances, and both mixed to the same channel. Try one of these methods to solve the problem:

- Angle the vocal mic up and angle the guitar mic down to isolate the two sources. Follow the 3:1 rule.
- Use a pickup or mini mic on the guitar.

- Delay the vocal mic about 1 msec. This keeps the two mic signals in phase, preventing phase cancellations. Some multitrack recorders have a track-delay feature for this purpose.
- Use a coincident pair of figure eights crossed at 90 degrees. Aim the front of one mic at the voice; aim the front of the other mic at the guitar.
- Use a stereo mic or stereo pair about 1 foot out front; raise or lower the mics to adjust the voice/guitar balance.

# Grand Piano

This magnificent instrument is a challenge to record well. First have the piano tuned, and oil the pedals to reduce squeaks. You can prevent thumps by stuffing some foam or cloth under the pedal mechanism.

For a classical-music solo, record in a reverberant room such as a recital hall or concert hall. Reverb is part of the sound. Set the piano lid on the long stick. Use condenser mics with a flat response. Place a stereo mic, or a stereo pair of mics, about 7 feet away and 7 feet high, up to 9 feet away and 9 feet high (Figure 8.13). Move the mics closer to reduce reverb, farther to increase it. You might need to mix in a pair of hall mics: Try cardioids aiming away from the piano about 25 feet away.

When recording a piano concerto, give the piano a spot mic about 3 feet away. Put the mic in a shock mount.

Pop music demands close miking. Close mics pick up less room acoustics and leakage, and give a clear sound that cuts through the mix. Try not to mike the strings closer than 8 inches, or else you'll emphasize the strings closest to the mics. You want equal coverage of all the notes the pianist plays.

One popular method uses two spaced mics inside the piano. Use omni or cardioid condensers, ideally in shock mounts. Put the lid on the long stick. If you can, remove the lid to reduce boominess. Center one mic over the treble strings and one over the bass strings. Typically, both mics are 8 to 12 inches over the strings and 8 inches horizontally from the hammers (Figure 8.14, top, bass and treble mics). Aim the mics straight down or angle them to aim at the hammers. Pan the mics partly left and right for stereo. As an alternative, try two ear-spaced omni condensers about 12 to 18 inches above the strings.

The spaced mics might have phase cancellations when mixed to mono, so you might want to try coincident miking (Figure 8.14, top, stereo pair). Boom-mount a stereo mic, or an XY pair of cardioids crossed at 120

151

**Figure 8.13**
Suggested grand-piano miking for classical music.

degrees. Miking close to the hammers sounds percussive; toward the tail has more tone.

For more clarity and attack, boost EQ around 10 kHz or use a mic with a rising high-frequency response.

Boundary mics work well, too. If you want to pick up the piano in mono, tape a boundary mic to the underside of the raised lid, in the center of the strings, near the hammers. Use two for stereo over the bass and treble strings. Put the bass mic near the tail of the piano to equalize the mic distances to the hammers (Figure 8.14, bottom). If leakage is a problem, close the lid and cut EQ around 250 Hz to reduce boominess.

# Upright Piano

Here are some ways to mike an upright piano:

(A) Remove the panel in front of the piano to expose the strings over the keyboard. Place one mic near the bass strings and one near the treble strings about 8 inches away. Record in stereo and pan the signals left and

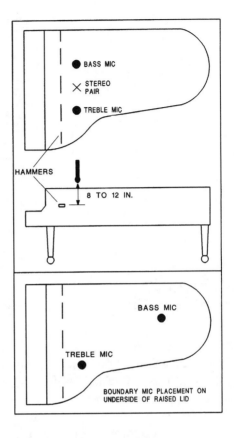

**Figure 8.14**
Suggested grand-piano
miking for popular music.

right for the desired piano width. If you can spare only one mic for the piano, just cover the treble strings.

(B) Remove the top lid and upper panel. Put a stereo pair of mics about 1 foot in front and 1 foot over the top. If the piano is against a wall, angle the piano about 17 degrees from the wall to reduce tubby resonances.

(C) Aim the soundboard into the room. Mike the bass and treble sides of the soundboard a few inches away. In this spot, the mics pick up less pedal thumps and other noises. Try cardioid dynamic mics with a presence peak.

# Acoustic Bass

The acoustic bass (string bass, bass viola) can be recorded many ways. This instrument puts out frequencies as low as 41 Hz, so use a mic with an extended low-frequency response.

It's common to mix a pickup with a mic. For a well-defined sound, place the mic a few inches in front of the bridge, on the side toward the G

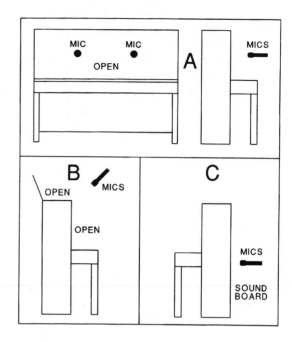

**Figure 8.15**
Some mic techniques for upright piano.

string (top string). For more fullness, move the mic toward the f-hole. Another spot is a few inches from the top of the treble f-hole. Watch out for proximity effect (up-close bass boost) if you use a directional mic up close.

If you need more isolation, place a cardioid dynamic mic near the treble f-hole and roll off the excess bass on your mixer.

Here are some methods that isolate the bass and let the player move around. They work well for P.A.:

- Wrap a mini omni condenser mic in foam rubber (or in a foam windscreen) and mount it in an f-hole.
- Tape the cable of a mini omni mic to the bridge.
- Wrap a regular mic in foam padding (except the front grille) and squeeze it behind the bridge or between the tailpiece and the body.
- Try a direct feed from a pickup. This method adds clarity and edge, but might sound electric.
- Wrap a mini omni condenser in foam and stuff it in an f-hole. Mix this mic with the pickup to round out the tone. You may need to roll off the bass of the f-hole mic. Flip the polarity of the mic and use whatever setting sounds best.

# Banjo

Try a flat-response mic about 1 foot away. If you need more isolation, mike closer and roll off some bass. The banjo sounds pleasantly mellow when miked toward the edge of the head, near the resonator holes (if the banjo has them). Cloth stuffed inside will reduce feedback in P.A. situations.

For the most isolation, tape a mini omni condenser mic to the head about 1 inch in from the bottom edge, or on the tailpiece, or on the bridge. You can wedge a pickup between the strings below the bridge and the banjo head. Put the pickup flat against the head surface.

# Mandolin, Dobro, Bouzouki, Lap Dulcimer

Mike these about 8 to 12 inches away with a condenser mic. If you need more lows and more isolation, mike close to an f-hole. You can tape a mini omni condenser mic near an f-hole and tweak EQ for the best sound.

# Hammered Dulcimer

Place a flat-response condenser mic about 2 feet over the center of the soundboard (Figure 8.16A). On stage, place a cardioid dynamic or condenser 6 to 12 inches over the middle of the top end (Figure 8.16B). For the best gain-before-feedback in a P.A. system, mix in a mini omni condenser mic (or a cardioid with bass rolloff) very near the sound hole (Figure 8.16C).

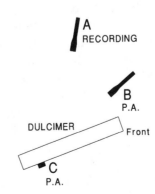

**Figure 8.16**
Some mic techniques for hammered dulcimer.

155

# Fiddle (Violin)

Listen to the fiddle itself to make sure it sounds good. Correct any instrument problems before miking.

First try a flat-response condenser mic (omni or cardioid) about 2 feet over the bridge. This distant miking gives an airy, silky sound. Close miking sounds more nasal and scratchy, which might be desirable in some music styles. If the ceiling is low, reflections might color the sound. In that case, cover the ceiling over the fiddle with a sleeping bag or foam. Or have the fiddle player sit down.

If you have to mike close—say, for a singing fiddler—aim the mic horizontally at the mouth about 6 inches away. The mic will pick up both the singer and the fiddle.

Other methods: Get a mini omni mic, and clip its holder to the violin's tailpiece. Mount the mic a few inches from an f-hole over the bridge. Or clip the mini omni to the strings between the bridge and tailpiece; aim the mic at the fiddle body. If necessary, cut a little at 3 kHz to reduce harshness and boost around 200 Hz for warmth.

A good spot for a pickup is on the left side of the top (player's view), on the player's side of the bridge.

To record a classical violin solo, try a stereo mic (or a stereo pair) 12 to 20 feet away in a reverberant room.

# String Section

Place the strings in a large, live room and mike them at distance to pick up a natural acoustic sound. A common mic choice is a condenser with a flat response. First try a stereo mic or stereo pair of mics about 4 to 20 feet behind the conductor, raised about 15 feet.

If the room is noisy or too dead, or the balance is poor, you'll need to mike close and add digital reverb. Try one mic on every two to four violins, 6 feet off the floor, aiming down. Same for the violas. Mike the cello about 1–2 feet from the bridge, to the right side between the bridge and f-hole. When you mix the strings to stereo, pan them evenly between the monitor speakers. Spread them left, center, and right to make a "curtain of sound." If you can spare only one track for the strings, use a stereo-izer effect during mixdown.

# String Quartet

Record a quartet in stereo using a stereo mic or a pair of mics. Place them about 6 to 10 feet away to capture the room ambience. The monitored instruments should not spread all the way between speakers. If you want to narrow the stereo stage, angle or space the mics closer together.

# Bluegrass Band, Old-Time String Band

Suppose you're recording a group that has a good acoustic balance. Try a stereo mic or stereo pair of mics about 3 feet away and 6 feet high (lower if the group is seated). Move the players toward or away from the mics to adjust their balance.

You'll have more control if you mike all the instruments up close and mix them. This also gives a more "commercial" sound. The production style aims for a natural timbre on all the instruments, either with no effects or with slight reverb.

# Harp

Use a condenser mic with a flat response. If the harp is playing with an orchestra, mike the harp about 18 inches from the front of the soundboard, or 18 inches from the player's left hand. You can mike a harp solo about 4 feet over the top.

Tape a mini omni condenser mic to the soundboard if you need more isolation. A mic on the inside of the soundboard has more isolation; a mic on the outside sounds more natural. Also try a cardioid condenser wrapped in foam, stuck into the center hole from the rear.

# Horns

"Horns" in studio parlance refers to the brass instruments: trumpets, cornets, trombones, baritones, french horns, and tubas.

All the brass radiate strong highs straight out from the bell, but do not project them to the sides. A mic close to and in front of the bell picks up a bright, edgy tone. To mellow out the tone, mike the bell off-axis with a flat-response mic (Figure 8.17). The sound on-axis to the bell has a lot of

**Figure 8.17**
Miking for trumpet tone control.

spiky high harmonics that can overload a condenser mic, mixer input, or analog tape. That's another reason to mike off-axis.

Mike the trumpet with a dynamic—a moving coil or ribbon—to take the edge off the sound. Use a condenser mic if you want a lot of sizzle. Mike about 1 foot away for a tight sound; mike several feet away for a fuller, more dramatic sound.

You can pick up two or more horns with one microphone. Several players can be grouped around a single omni mic, or around a stereo pair of mics. The musicians can play to a pair of boundary mics taped on the control-room window or on a large panel.

Record a classical brass quartet in a reverberant room. Use a stereo mic, or a stereo pair of mics, about 6 to 12 feet away.

# Saxophone

A sax miked very near the bell sounds bright, breathy, and rather hard (Figure 8.18). Mike it there for best isolation. To get a warm, natural sound, mike the sax about 1½ feet away, halfway down the wind column (Figure 8.18). Don't mike too close, or else the level varies when the player moves. A compromise position for a close-up mic is just above the bell, aiming at the holes. You can group a sax section around one mic.

# Woodwinds

With woodwinds, most of the sound radiates not from the bell, but from the holes. So aim a flat-response mic at the holes about 1 foot away.

When miking a woodwind section within an orchestra, you need to reject nearby leakage from other instruments. To do that, try aiming a

**Figure 8.18**
Two ways to mike a
saxophone.

**Figure 8.19**
One effective placement
for flute miking.

bi-directional mic down over the woodwind section. The side nulls of the mic cut down on leakage.

To pick up a flute in a pop-music group, try miking a few inches from the area between the mouthpiece and the first set of finger holes (Figure 8.19). You may need a pop filter. If you want to reduce breath noise, roll off high frequencies or mike farther away. You also can attach a mini omni mic to the flute a few inches above the body, between the mouthpiece and finger holes.

For classical music solos, try a stereo pair 4 to 12 feet away.

# Harmonica, Accordion, Bagpipe

One way to mike a harmonica (harp) is to use a cardioid dynamic mic with a ball grille. Place the mic very close to the harmonica or have the player hold it. A condenser mic about 1 foot away gives a natural sound. To get a bluesy, dirty sound, use a "bullet"-type harmonica mic or play the harmonica through a miked guitar amp.

For accordion, try a mic about 6 to 12 inches from the sound holes near the keyboard. Some accordions have sound holes on both sides, so you'll need two mics. Follow the 3:1 rule. The distance between mics should be at least 3 times the mic-to-source distance.

A bagpipe has two main sound sources: the chanter, which the musician plays with the fingers, and the drone pipes, which make a steady tone. Mike the chanter about a foot away from the side, and mike the drone pipes a foot from the end. Again, follow the 3:1 rule. You could also mike the bagpipe a few feet away with one mic.

# Lead Vocal

The lead vocal is the most important part of a pop song, so it's critical to record it right. First set up a comfortable environment for the singer. Put down a rug, add some flowers or candles, dim the lights. Set up a good cue mix with effects to help the singer get into the mood of the song.

With any vocal recording, there are some problems to overcome, but we can deal with them. Among these are proximity effect, breath pops, wide dynamic range, sibilance, and sound reflections from the music stand. Let's look at these in detail.

## Miking Distance

When you sing or talk close to most directional mics, the microphone boosts the bass in your voice. This is called the proximity effect. We've come to accept this bassy sound as normal in a P.A. system, but the effect just sounds boomy in a recording.

To prevent boomy bass, mike the singer at a distance, about 8 inches away (Figure 8.20). A popular mic choice is a flat-response condenser mic with a large diaphragm (1¼-inch diameter). As always, you can use any mic that sounds good to you. If the mic has a bass rolloff switch, set it to "flat."

Singers should maintain their distance to the mic. I ask the singer to spread the fingers, touch lips with the thumb, and touch the mic with the pinky. The hand forms a spacer for keeping constant distance.

Some singers can't help but "eat" the mic. You can mike them at distance, and also give them a dummy mic to hold while singing.

If you must record the singer and the band at the same time—as in a concert—you'll have to mike close to avoid picking up the instruments with the vocal mic. Try a cardioid mic with a bass rolloff and a foam pop filter. The sound will be bassy because of proximity effect, so roll off the excess lows at your mixer. For starters, try −6 dB at 100 Hz. Some mics have

**Figure 8.20**
Typical miking technique
for a lead vocal.

a bass filter switch for this purpose. Aim the mic partly toward the singer's nose to prevent a nasal or closed-nose effect. This closeup method works well if you want an intimate, breathy sound.

When recording a classical-music singer who is accompanied by an orchestra, place the mic about 1 to 2 feet away. If the singer is a soloist (maybe accompanied by piano), use a stereo pair about 8 to 15 feet away to pick up room reverb.

## Breath Pops

When you sing a word with "p" or "t" sounds, a turbulent puff of air shoots out of the mouth. The puff hits the mic and makes a thump or small explosion called a **pop**. To reduce it, put a foam-plastic pop filter on the mic. Some mics have a ball grille screen to cut pops, but foam works better. The pop filter should be made of special open-cell foam to pass high frequencies. For best pop rejection, allow a little air space between the foam and the front of the mic grille.

Foam pop filters reduce the highs a little. So they should be left off instrument mics, except for outdoor recording or dust protection. Pop filters do not reduce breathing sounds or lip noises. To get rid of these problems, mike farther away or roll off some highs.

The most effective pop filter is a hoop with a nylon stocking stretched over it. You can buy this type, or make one with a coat hanger and a crochet hoop. A similar pop filter is a disk of perforated metal. Place the filter a few inches from the mic.

Another way to get rid of pop is to put the mic at forehead height, aiming at the mouth (Figure 8.20). This way the puffs of air shoot under the mic and miss it. Make sure the vocalist sings straight ahead, not up at the mic, or the mic will pop.

## Wide Dynamic Range

During a song, vocalists often sing too loud or too soft. They blast the listener or get buried in the mix. That is, many singers have a wider dynamic range than their instrumental backup. To even out these extreme level variations, ask the singer to use proper mic technique. Back away from the mic on loud notes; come in closer for soft ones. Or you can **ride gain** on singers: gently turn them down as they get louder, and vice versa.

The best solution is to pass the vocal signal through a compressor, which acts like an automatic volume control. Plug the compressor into the vocal channel's insert jacks. A typical compressor setting is 2:1 ratio, −10 dB threshold.

If the singer moves toward and away from the mic while singing, the average level will go up and down. Try to mike the singer at least 8 inches away, so that small movements of the singer won't affect the level.

If you must mike close to prevent leakage or feedback, ask the vocalist to sing with lips touching the pop filter to keep the same distance to the mic. Turn down the excess bass using your mixer's low-frequency EQ (typically −6 dB at 100 Hz).

## Sibilance

Sibilance is the emphasis of "s" or "sh" sounds, which are strongest around 5 kHz to 10 kHz. They help intelligibility. In fact, many producers like sizzly "s" sounds, which add a bright splash to the vocal reverb. But the sibilance should not be piercing or strident.

If you want to reduce sibilance, use a mic with a flat response—rather than one with a presence peak—or cut the highs little around 8 kHz on your mixer. Better yet, use a **de-esser** signal processor, which cuts the highs only when the singer makes sibilant sounds.

## Reflections from the Music Stand and Ceiling

Suppose that a lyric sheet or music stand is near the singer's mic. Some sound waves from the singer go directly into the mic. Other sound waves reflect off the lyric sheet or music stand into the mic (Figure 8.21, top). The delayed reflections will interfere with the direct sound, making a colored tone quality like mild flanging.

To prevent this, lower the music stand and tilt it almost vertically (Figure 8.21, bottom). This way, the sound reflections miss the mic. Or tape the lyric sheet behind the singer's cardioid mic (Figure 8.20). The cardioid mic will reject reflections that enter the mic from the rear.

If your studio has a low ceiling, the recorded vocal might have a colored tone quality due to phase cancellations from ceiling reflections. Try putting the mic lower and use a hoop-type pop filter. Also put a 3-foot square of acoustic foam on the ceiling over the singer and mic.

## Vocal Effects

Some popular vocal effects are stereo reverb, echo, and doubling.

You can record real room reverb by miking the singer at a distance in a hard-surfaced room. Slap echo provides a 1950's rock 'n' roll effect. Often

**Figure 8.21**
Preventing reflections from
a music stand.

a vocal is mixed dry, with no reverb. A little distortion might even be effective on some songs.

Doubling a vocal gives a fuller sound than a single vocal track. Overdub a second take of the vocal on an empty track, in sync with the original take. During mixdown, mix the second vocal take with the original, at a slightly lower level than the original. Or double the vocal by running it through a digital delay set to 15–35 msec.

# Background Vocals

When you overdub background vocals (harmony vocals), you can group two or three singers in front of a mic. The farther they are from the mic, the more distant they will sound in the recording. Pan the singers left and right for a stereo effect. Since massed harmonies can sound bassy, roll off some lows in the background vocals.

If you want independent control of each background singer, give each one a close-up mic and record them with separate mixer channels or separate tracks.

Barbershop or gospel quartets with a good natural blend can be recorded with a stereo mic or stereo pair of mics about 2 to 4 feet away. If their balance is poor, close-mike each singer about 8 inches away, and balance them with your mixer. This also gives a more "commercial" sound. If you close-mike, spread the singers at least 2 feet apart to prevent phase cancellations.

# Summary

We can sum up mic placement like this: If leakage or feedback are problems, place the mic near the loudest part of the instrument, and add EQ to get a natural sound. Otherwise, place the mic in various spots until you find a position that sounds good over your monitors. There is no single "correct" mic technique for any instrument. Just place the mic where you hear the desired tonal balance and amount of room reverb.

Try the techniques described here as a starting point, then explore your own ideas. Trust your ears! If you capture the power and excitement of electric guitars and drums, if you capture the beautiful timbre of acoustic instruments and vocals, you've made a successful recording.

# ANALOG TAPE RECORDING

Thanks to the tape recorder, a musical performance can be captured permanently and relived again and again. In this chapter we'll look at these aspects of tape recording:

1. The analog tape recorder—parts, functions, alignment, cleaning
2. Noise reduction systems (Dolby and dbx)
3. Tape handling, storage, and editing

Although the analog tape recorder might seem outdated in these days of digital recording, it is still a viable format. Many top engineers prefer the sound of analog, claiming smoother and more extended highs, and a gentler, warmer sound than digital. However, digital recorders that operate at 24-bit/96 kHz can sound as smooth as analog. See Chapter 10 for more detail.

How does the analog tape recorder work? As it records, it changes the incoming audio signal into a magnetic signal on tape. The tape itself is a strip of plastic, usually Mylar, with a thin coating of magnetic particles: ferric oxide, ferric-cobalt, or chromium dioxide. Each particle is a tiny magnet. These particles aim in random directions. During recording, an external magnetic field aligns them into magnetic patterns. During playback, the magnetic patterns on tape generate the original audio signal.

## Tape Recorder Parts and Functions

A tape recorder has three main parts: the heads, the electronics, and the transport.

- The heads are electromagnets that change electric signals to magnetic fields, and vice versa.
- The electronics amplify and equalize the signals going to and from the heads.
- The transport pulls the tape past the heads, which contact the tape.

Let's look more closely at each of the three main parts.

## *The Heads*

Professional open-reel recorders have three heads placed left-to-right: erase, record, and playback (Figure 9.1). Semi-pro recorders and cassette multitrackers use a single head to record and play back.

The **erase head** makes a magnetic field that vibrates at an ultrasonic frequency. As the tape rolls past the erase head, the tape is exposed to this vibrating magnetic field, which weakens as the tape moves away from the head. This action orients the magnetic particles randomly and erases any signal on tape.

The **record head** changes the incoming electric signal into a magnetic field that varies as the signal does. As the tape passes the record head, the head magnetizes or aligns the tape particles in a pattern that corresponds to the audio signal. This pattern stays on the tape forever unless it's erased.

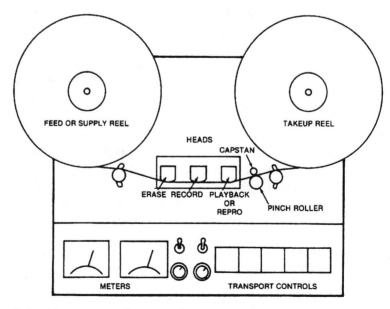

**Figure 9.1** Major parts of a typical tape recorder.

The pattern stored on tape is a varying magnetic field. As the tape passes the playback head, the head picks up this magnetic field and changes it back into a similar electric signal. This signal is amplified and is sent to the recorder's output connectors.

In the center of the head's front face, where it contacts the tape, is the **gap**: a vertical line that is the break in the electromagnet. The record-head gap puts the signal on the tape as it passes the head; the playback-head gap reads the signal off the tape as it passes the head. Most heads have more than one gap: one gap per track (Figure 9.2).

There are limits to the signal level you can put on tape. When the signal is strong enough to align all the magnetic particles, higher levels can't increase the magnetic signal on tape. This is called **tape saturation**. It causes the fuzzy, grungy sound of distortion.

If the recording level is too low, though, you start to hear tape noise (hiss). **Hiss** is the random noise signals generated by nonaligned particles. You hear hiss when the recorded signal is weak compared to the tape noise. So, you should record most signals at as high a level as possible without distortion. That way, you get a clean recording with no grunge and almost no hiss. But sometimes a little tape saturation sounds good on drums.

## *The Electronics*

Recorder electronics have these functions:

- Amplify and equalize the incoming audio signal
- Send the audio signal to the record head
- Amplify and equalize the signal from the playback head

The equalization done by the electronics is called **record equalization** and **playback equalization**. Record equalization is a slight boost at low and high frequencies to improve the signal-to-noise ratio at those fre-

**Figure 9.2** Gaps in a tape head.

quencies. Part the of playback equalization is a bass cut to compensate for the bass boost during recording.

During playback, the output from the playback head rises 6 dB per octave because the head's output depends on the rate of change of magnetic flux, which doubles with each higher octave. (Magnetic flux is the lines of magnetic force.) To compensate for this rise, playback equalization falls 6 dB per octave.

The magnetism on tape tends to slightly erase the high frequencies on tape. But playback equalization has a high-frequency boost to compensate for this, and for high-frequency losses within the head.

The frequency response of the playback EQ has been standardized in the United States to a curve called the NAB (National Association of Broadcasters) curve. Other countries may use different playback EQ.

An ultrasonic oscillator in the electronics drives the erase head. The ultrasonic signal, called **bias**, is also mixed with the audio fed to the record head. Adding bias is needed to reduce distortion. The amount of bias is adjustable. It affects the recording's level, frequency response, distortion, and **drop-outs** (short signal losses).

The bias setting is critical. Too high a setting reduces the level recorded on tape and rolls off high frequencies. Too low a setting also reduces the level on tape, results in distortion and drop-outs, and raises the highs. The bias is set at the factory for a particular type of tape. That's why it's important to use the type of tape your user manual recommends. If your cassette deck has a bias adjustment, set it according to the user manual. We'll describe how to set the bias in pro machines later in this chapter.

## The Tape Transport

The job of the transport is to move the tape past the heads. During recording and playback, the transport should move the tape at a constant speed and with constant tape tension. During rewind or fast forward, the tape shuttles rapidly from one reel to the other.

Most pro open-reel decks have three motors in the transport: two for shuttling and tape tension, and a third to drive the capstan. The **capstan** is a post that rotates against a rubber **pinch roller**. The tape is pressed between the capstan and pinch roller. As the capstan rotates, it pulls the tape past the heads. Also in the transport are rollers that reduce **wow** (a slow periodic variation in tape speed) and **flutter** (rapid variation in tape speed).

The **tape counter** usually shows the elapsed time on tape. You can mark a particular point on tape—say, the beginning of a song—by resetting the tape counter to zero. On some machines, a return-to-zero button shuttles the tape to the zero point and then stops automatically. This function is useful when you want to repeatedly practice an overdub or a mix.

A pro open-reel tape deck moves tape at $7\frac{1}{2}$, 15, or 30 ips (inches per second). Cassette decks run at $1\frac{7}{8}$ ips or $3\frac{3}{4}$ ips. Faster speeds sound better. As tape speed increases, cymbals sound cleaner, there's less tape hiss, and the pitch is more stable. But a slower tape speed consumes less tape and allows more running time.

## Tracks

A track is a path on tape containing a single channel of audio. The wider the track (that is, the more tape it covers), the greater the signal-to-noise ratio (S/N). Doubling the track width improves the S/N by 3 dB.

Some tape-recorder heads have one gap that records and plays one track over the full width of the tape. Other heads have several gaps that record and play two or more tracks. Each track covers part of the tape width. Figure 9.3 shows some track-width standards for $\frac{1}{4}$-inch tape.

- A full-track mono head records over nearly the full width of the tape in one direction (Figure 9.3A).

- A half-track mono head records one track in one direction and one track in the opposite direction when the tape is flipped over (Figure 9.3B). Each track covers about one-third of the tape. The unused third between the tracks is a guard band to prevent crosstalk between tracks.

- A 2-track stereo or half-track stereo head records 2 tracks in one direction (Figure 9.3B). This format is used for stereo master tapes. Track widths are the same as half-track mono.

- A quarter-track stereo head records 2 tracks in one direction and 2 tracks in the opposite direction when the tape has been flipped over (Figure 9.3C). Stereo cassette decks use this format on $\frac{1}{8}$-inch wide tape.

- A multitrack head records 4 more tracks in one direction (Figure 9.3C). Depending on the width of the tape, the number of tracks can be 4, 6, 8, 16, 24, 32, or 48. Cassette recorder–mixers use this format (4 or 8 tracks only).

## Tape Width

Magnetic recording tape comes in various widths to accommodate the track formats:

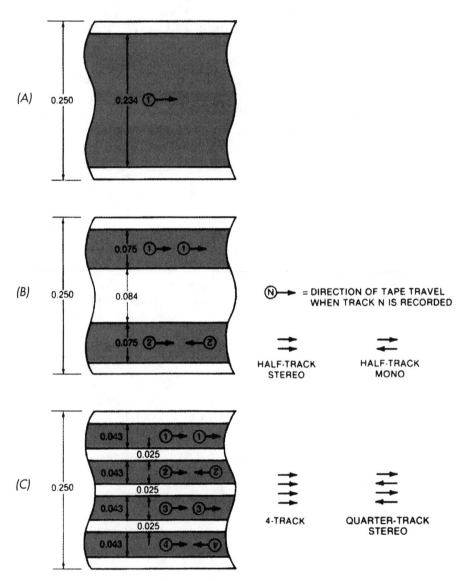

**Figure 9.3** Some track-width standards for ¼-inch tape.

- ⅛-inch for ¼-track stereo, and cassette (4-or-8-track)
- ¼-inch for full-track mono, half-track mono, quarter-track stereo, 2-track stereo, 4-track, and 8-track
- ½-inch for 4, 8, or 16 tracks
- 1-inch for 8, 16, or 24 tracks
- 2-inch for 16, 24, 32, or 48 tracks

## *Cassette Deck*

The cassette deck from a home stereo is a low-cost, convenient way to make proof tapes and demos. The sound is not good enough, though, for masters that will be duplicated commercially. You can get an excellent deck for $200 and up. Some useful features are Dolby B, C, and S, which reduce tape hiss, and Dolby HX, which reduces high-frequency distortion. Look for a wow and flutter spec below 0.05%, or you may hear wobbly pitch. Also look for a front-mounted adjustable bias control, so you can fine-tune the bias to the type of tape you're using.

## *Multitrack and Synchronous Recording*

The multitrack recorder can be either a standalone unit or can be built into a recorder–mixer. Chapter 2 describes the features of the multitrack recorders used in recorder–mixers.

Multitrack machines are available that record 4, 6, 8, 16, 24, 32, or 48 tracks side-by-side on a single tape. It's like having several stereo tape decks in sync. Each track contains the signal of a different instrument, or a different mix of instruments. You can record the tracks all at once, one at a time, or in any combination. After you record the tracks, you combine and balance them through a mixing console. Unlike 2-track recording, multitrack recording lets you fine-tune the mix after the recording session. You can practice the changes in the mix until you get them right.

Multitrack recordings can sound clearer than live-to-2-track recordings because you can overdub instruments without mic leakage rather than recording them all at once. If you record several instruments and vocals at the same time, leakage or off-mic sound can add a muddy, loose sound to the mix. But when you overdub there is no leakage, so the final mix can be cleaner.

Multitrack recording, though, needs an extra generation, since you must record the multitrack mix onto a 2-track tape. Each generation or tape copy adds 3 dB of tape hiss. In addition, every time the number of tracks used in the mix doubles, the noise increases 3 dB. It's not a lot, but it is audible.

Another trade-off of multitrack recording is that the recording process takes much longer. With live-to-2-track recording, the recording is done when the performance is done. But with multitrack recording, you must record first and then do a mixdown. Overdubbing is optional, but is the norm, and adds more time. Plus, multitrack equipment is more complicated and expensive, and is more time-consuming to set up. Still, the ability to fine-tune the mix after the session makes multitrack the preferred choice for pop-music recording.

# Overdubbing

One advantage of multitrack recorders is that tape tracks can be recorded at different times. For instance, a musician can listen to recorded tracks off the playback head and overdub a new part. During playback, the new part is delayed relative to the original tracks because the playback head is located a small distance from the record head.

To remove the delay caused by overdubbing, and to sync the original tracks with the overdub, you play the original tracks through the record head temporarily. At the same time, the record head records the overdub on an open track. This process is called **simul-sync**, **selsync**, or **synchronous recording**. To enable it, set each track's tape-monitor switch to the SYNC position. When you play a tape through the record head, the signal loses highs but is adequate for synching.

Semi-pro tape decks and cassette multitrackers combine the record and playback functions in one head. So there's no sync problem; recorded tracks and overdubs are always in sync. The same is true of digital multitracks.

# Meters and Level Setting

Meters on the tape recorder (one per track) show the record and playback levels. These meters may be VU meters, VU meters with built-in peak LEDs, or LED bargraph indicators showing peak levels.

## The VU Meter

A VU meter is a voltmeter that shows approximately the relative volume or loudness of the audio signal. The meter is calibrated in VU or Volume Units. The Volume Unit is the same as a decibel, only when you're measuring a steady sine-wave tone. That is, 1 VU = 1 dB only when you apply a steady tone.

A **0 VU recording level** (0 on the record level meter) is the normal operating level of a recorder. It indicates that the magnetic signal is being recorded on tape at the optimum level.

Recording levels that are too high (greater than +3 VU) saturate or overload the tape, which causes distortion. Too-low levels (say, consistently below –10 VU) result in audible tape hiss.

When you apply a rapidly changing signal to a VU meter, the meter reads less than the peak voltage of the waveform. This is because the response of a VU meter is not fast enough to accurately track rapid transients, such as drum beats.

This inaccuracy can cause problems with level setting. For example, if you record drums at 0 VU on the meter, peaks may be 8 to 14 dB higher, resulting in tape distortion. So, whenever you record instruments having sharp attacks or a high peak-to-average ratio (such as drums, piano, percussion, or horns), record at −6 to −8 VU to prevent tape distortion. Note that mild distortion on drum peaks (recording "hot") may give a desirable effect. Instruments with a low peak-to-average ratio, such as organ or flute, can be recorded around +3 VU without audible distortion.

## Peak Indicators

Unlike the VU meter, the peak indicator shows peak recording levels more accurately because it responds very rapidly. If your recorder has an LED peak light in each VU meter, set the levels so the LEDs flash only occasionally. For setting recording levels, an LED flash takes precedence over the VU meter reading. If the recorder has LED bargraph peak indicators, set all tracks to peak at 0 to +6 dB, according to the user manual.

## Matching Mixer and Recorder Meters

If you're using a separate mixer and recorder, it's common practice to set the mixer meters and recorder meters to match each other. That way you have to watch only the mixer meters while recording. Also, when the mixer and recorder are both peaking around 0 VU, this minimizes the noise and distortion in both units.

If your mixer meters and recorder meters have the same ballistics (the same speed), match the meters with a steady 1 kHz tone from a signal generator or a synthesizer note (C or B two octaves above middle C). Otherwise, hum a steady tone into a mic plugged into your mixer, and set the levels on the mixer and tape deck to 0.

If your tape-deck meters move faster or slower than your mixer meters, follow this procedure:

Play a program with a lot of loud drum hits through your mixer, peak the mixer at 0, and set your recorder level to peak at 0 on its meters. Then play a 0 VU tone through your mixer, and note the level on the recorder meters for future reference.

At this point you could watch just the mixer meters. But you get the most accurate reading by watching your recorder meters. Once the mixer and recorder meters match each other, leave the recorder controls alone. Set levels only with the mixer faders or mixer gain trim controls.

# Judging Machine Specifications

The following specs indicate excellent performance:

- Wow and flutter 0.04% or less.
- S/N 70 dB with Dolby C, 85 dB with Dolby S or SR.
- Record/play response 40 Hz–18 kHz (±3 dB).

# Operating Precautions

Here are some operating tips for tape recorders that may prevent some accidents:

- Don't put the machine in record mode until levels are set. If you record an extremely high-level high-frequency signal, the crosstalk within the head might erase other tracks.
- Keep the tape away from recorder heads when turning the machine on or off, or you may put a click on the tape.
- Keep degaussers and bulk tape erasers several feet from tapes you don't want to erase.
- Before you start recording on a track, make sure you won't be erasing something you wanted to keep. Listen to the track first or refer to your track sheet.
- Edge tracks of multitrack tapes are prone to drop-outs due to edge damage. Since drop-outs occur mostly at high frequencies, use the edge tracks only to record instruments with little high-frequency output (such as bass or kick drum).
- Repeated passes of a recording past the heads may gradually erase high frequencies. You may want to make a copy of the multitrack tape (or a quick 2-track mix) for musicians to practice overdubs with. Then go back to the original tape when the musicians are ready to record.
- Bouncing or ping-ponging tracks tends to lose high-frequency response and increase tape hiss, so try to limit bounced tracks to bass or midrange instruments.

# Noise Reduction

An analog tape recorder adds undesirable tape hiss and print-through to the recorded signal, degrading its clarity. **Print-through** is the transfer of a magnetic signal from one layer of tape to the next, causing an echo. Tape hiss is especially easy to hear when you do a multitrack mixdown, because every track mixed in adds to the overall noise level. Noise increases 3 dB whenever the number of tracks in use doubles, assuming they are mixed at equal levels.

Fortunately, noise-reduction devices such as Dolby and dbx can reduce tape hiss and print-through. However, these units do not remove noise in the original signal from the mixing console. If your signal is noisy before you record it, Dolby or dbx will not remove this noise. They work only on tape noise.

Dolby is used with consumer cassette decks, Fostex cassette multi-trackers, and open-reel recorders. dbx is used with TASCAM cassette multitrackers. You need one channel of noise reduction per tape track. Noise-reduction units connect between the mixer output busses and the corresponding tape-track inputs, and also between the tape-track outputs and the mixer tape inputs (Figure 9.4). Some open-reel recorders and most cassette recorders have built-in noise reduction; it is permanently connected.

These noise-reduction devices compress the signal during recording and expand it in a complementary way during playback. The compressor part of the circuit boosts the recorded level of quiet musical passages. During playback, the expander part works in a complementary way, turning down the volume during quiet passages, reducing noise added by the tape. During loud passages (when noise is masked by the program), the gain returns to normal.

A compressed tape is called **encoded**; the expanded tape is called **decoded**. If an encoded tape is played without decoding, it sounds compressed and trebley.

The encode and decode sections must track each other. For example, a 10 dB level change at the input of the encode section should yield a 10 dB level change at the output of the decode section. Otherwise, the dynamics sound unnatural. To prevent this problem, avoid excessive recording levels and adjust the noise-reduction unit for correct tracking if it can be adjusted (see the operating manual for instructions).

## *dbx*

With dbx noise reduction, the compression ratio is 2:1. That is, a program with a 90 dB dynamic range is compressed to 45 dB, which is easily handled by a tape recorder with a 60 dB S/N. During playback, dbx expands the dynamic range back to the original 90 dB. Use of dbx improves S/N by 30 dB and increases headroom by 10 dB. The dbx circuit also includes pre-emphasis (treble boost) of 12 dB during recording and complementary

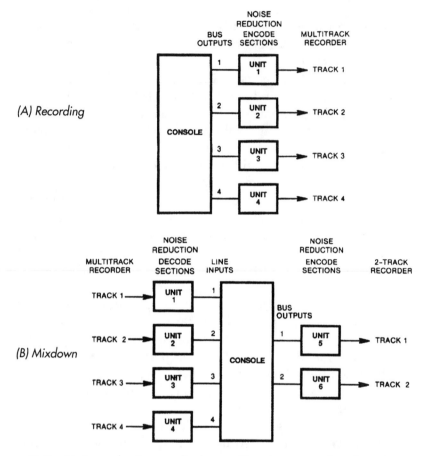

**Figure 9.4** Noise reduction applied to multitrack tape and to 2-track master tape.

de-emphasis (treble cut) during playback to reduce modulation noise. dbx operates at all signal levels and across the entire audible spectrum.

## Dolby

Dolby operates only on quiet passages—those below −10 VU. High-level passages do not need noise reduction because the program masks the noise. There are five different types of Dolby noise reduction (listed in increasing order of effectiveness):

- Dolby B
- Dolby C
- Dolby A

- Dolby S
- Dolby SR

Dolby B is a lower-cost system for cassette decks and operates only at high frequencies to reduce tape hiss by up to 10 dB.

Dolby C, for cassette and open-reel, works over a slightly wider range and reduces noise by up to 20 dB.

Dolby A, an early system for open-reel, divides the audible spectrum into four separate frequency bands that are compressed and expanded independently. This system reduces noise by 10 dB below 5 kHz and up to 15 dB at 15 kHz.

Dolby S for cassettes reduces tape hiss by 24 dB and low-frequency noise by 10 dB.

Dolby SR (Spectral Recording), for open-reel, is the most effective Dolby system, reducing noise by more than 25 dB over most of the audible spectrum. As a result, a recorder operated at 15 ips with Dolby SR can have a maximum S/N exceeding 105 dB. During recording, Dolby SR boosts the gain of parts of the spectrum that are low-to-medium in level. During playback, it reduces the gain of the same regions in a complementary way.

When using Dolby A, you must record a calibration signal called a **Dolby tone** on tape before the regular program. An oscillator in the Dolby unit generates this tone. During playback, the level of the recorded Dolby tone is indicated on a Dolby meter. You set the Dolby input level so that the meter indication lines up with the Dolby-level mark on the meter. Then the expander circuitry tracks the recording properly.

If the level is set improperly, the frequency response and dynamic range are slightly changed. Fortunately, there is room for some error since these changes occur in low-level signals and so are hard to hear.

## Dolby versus dbx

Both Dolby and dbx have pros and cons. Compared to Dolby, dbx gives more noise reduction. On the other hand, dbx exaggerates dropouts more than Dolby does. Dolbyized recordings are relatively free of noise "breathing"—hiss or fuzziness that varies with the signal level, especially on bass or percussion tracks. dbx can change the dynamics at low frequencies.

Many professional engineers record at 30 ips, without noise reduction, or use Dolby SR. Dolby-encoded and dbx-encoded tapes are not compatible with each other and cannot be played properly without decoding through the appropriate unit. So, if you plan to send your tapes to another studio, check that the studio has the same type of noise reduction that you want to use. On mass-produced cassettes, use either no noise reduction or

Dolby B because most consumer stereo cassette decks have Dolby B. You can use whatever you want on your multitrack tape.

When using noise reduction, avoid saturating the tape while recording. Otherwise, the attack transients may be altered during playback through the noise-reduction unit. If you are using noise reduction, you can record at 3 VU lower than normal for 3 dB more headroom. When you copy a tape, switch in the noise reduction on the playback deck (if it has been recorded with noise reduction), and also on the recording deck. Be sure to copy the Dolby tone if the master tape has one.

# Preventive Maintenance

The analog tape recorder needs periodic maintenance—cleaning, demagnetizing, alignment, and calibration—for best performance.

## Cleaning the Tape Path

Over time, dust and oxide shed from the tape build up on your deck's heads. This layer of deposits separates the tape from the heads, causing high-frequency loss and drop-outs. In addition, buildup of oxide on the tape guides, capstan, and pinch roller can cause flutter. So it's very important to clean the entire tape path before every recording session. Use the cleaning fluid recommended in your recorder manual. Denatured alcohol (from hardware stores or drugstores) and a dense-packed cotton swab are often used. Don't use rubbing alcohol or isopropyl alcohol because they can leave a film on the head, and they contain water. Use rubber cleaner on rubber parts—rather than alcohol—to prevent swelling or cracking. Allow the cleaning fluid to dry before putting in a cassette or threading on a tape.

## Demagnetizing the Tape Path

Tape heads and tape guides can build up a magnetic field that can partly erase high frequencies, add tape hiss, and cause clicks at splices. You can get rid of this magnetism with a tape-head **demagnetizer** or **degausser** (such as the R.B. Annis Han-D-Mag). It's an electromagnet with a probe tip. Generally, only the gapped types are strong enough to be effective; the pencil-shaped types may cost less but don't work as well. The demagnetizer produces a magnetic field that vibrates at 60 Hz. You touch the probe tip to the head in order to magnetize it, then slowly pull the tip away so that the magnetism tapers off until none is left.

The technique of using a demagnetizer is critical:

1. If necessary, cover the probe tip with electrical tape or a handkerchief to avoid scratching the heads.

2. Turn off your recorder. Be sure that no tapes are near the demagnetizer.

3. With the demagnetizer at least 1 foot from your recorder, plug it in.

4. Bring the demagnetizer slowly to the part to be demagnetized.

5. After touching the part with the probe tip, remove the demagnetizer *slowly* to at least 1 foot away. In this way, the induced magnetic field diminishes to zero gradually. Move slowly. If you touch the demagnetizer to a head and quickly remove it, you'll magnetize the head worse than when you started!

Demagnetize each tape head and tape guide in this manner—one at a time. Finally, withdraw the degausser at least 1 foot away and unplug it. Demagnetize your machines after every 8 hours of use and before playing an alignment tape. The same precautions about slow operation apply to a bulk tape eraser.

## Alignment and Calibration for a Cassette Deck

For the best high-frequency response (brilliance and clarity), the gap in each head must be exactly at a right angle to the tape edge. This is called **azimuth alignment** (Figure 9.5). The azimuth is the left–right head angle relative to the tape edge. Cassette decks are aligned at the recorder factory, and they usually stay aligned if you treat the recorder gently and avoid bumping it. In pro studios, however, engineers align the heads periodically with the aid of a **standard alignment tape** (described later).

In a home studio, if you clean and demagnetize the heads, and still think that the high-frequency response of your recorder is diminished, con-

**Figure 9.5**
Azimuth alignment.

sider aligning the heads yourself or letting a professional technician do it. You need either a standard alignment tape or a commercially recorded cassette. You may need to remove the cassette door cover first.

Look for a small spring-loaded screw next to the record/playback head. This screw affects the azimuth. If you have an alignment tape, put it in your cassette deck and play the 15 kHz tone. Adjust the azimuth screw for maximum signal level as shown on your meters.

If you lack an alignment tape, put on a good commercially recorded cassette that has lots of cymbals or hi-hat. Adjust the azimuth screw to the point where these instruments sound the most crisp and clear. You'll find a peak in the clarity at a certain screw rotation, and a duller sound on either side of that.

Before a cassette deck or recorder–mixer is shipped to your dealer, its electronics are factory calibrated—adjusted for best performance from a certain brand of tape. If your machine is calibrated correctly, the playback signal should sound just like the input signal (except for some added tape hiss, and perhaps a little loss of clarity or high end). The calibration is usually left alone, and you use the brand of tape for which the machine was adjusted.

Occasionally, these circuit adjustments drift, so the circuit may need to be recalibrated. It's a complicated procedure best left to a service technician. In fact, some home and semi-pro recorders are not designed for easy calibration. The internal parts to be adjusted may not be easily accessible.

## *Alignment and Calibration for Professional Tape Machines*

Professional recording engineers align and calibrate their machines periodically. This ensures flat frequency response, the best S/N, and the least distortion. They also align and calibrate to correctly reproduce tapes made at other studios, using the alignment tones on those tapes.

To perform a complete alignment, you need:

- A small screwdriver
- An audio-frequency generator
- A standard playback alignment tape

Information about standard playback alignment tapes is available from various tape-recorder manufacturers, and from Standard Tape Laboratory (415-851-6600) or Magnetic Reference Laboratory (415-969-8187).

Follow your owner's manual about calibration. Clean and demagnetize the tape heads before starting. Basically, you follow these steps:

1. Using the alignment tape, play the 15 kHz tone and adjust playback-head azimuth for maximum output or for best phase match between channels (using an oscilloscope).

2. Adjust the high-frequency playback equalization (if any) to achieve the same output level at 700 Hz and 10 kHz. Or try for the flattest overall response if several tones are on the tape. Don't adjust the low-frequency equalization yet.

3. The magnetic field strength on tape (the fluxivity) is measured in nanowebers per meter (nWb/m). If you're using an alignment tape made at a standard operating level of 185 nWb/m (old Ampex standard level), set the playback level to read −3 VU or −6 VU as recommended by the tape manufacturer. If you're using an elevated-level alignment tape that uses a standard operating level of 250 nWb/m or 320 nWb/m, set the playback level to read 0 VU (or as recommended by the tape or recorder manufacturer). Do not touch the playback level for the rest of the calibration.

4. Thread on some blank tape of the desired brand.

5. Record a 15 kHz tone and adjust record-head azimuth for maximum playback output, or for best phase match between channels. (Skip this step if your recorder combines the record and playback functions in a single head.)

6. While recording a 1 kHz tone, set the bias to achieve maximum playback level. Then go back to 10 kHz, and turn up the bias past that point (**overbias**) until the output drops 0.5 to 1 dB. Overbiasing reduces drop-outs and modulation noise. For other overbias settings, read the suggestions on the tape box.

7. While recording tones of 10 kHz, 100 Hz, and 700 Hz, adjust the high-frequency record equalization and low-frequency playback equalization (if any) to achieve the same playback output level at all frequencies. Or use many tones to achieve the flattest overall response. Record the tones at 0 VU for 15 ips, −10 VU for 7½ ips, and −20 VU for cassettes. The slower tape speeds need lower recording levels to prevent tape saturation at high frequencies.

8. Feed a 1 kHz tone at 0 VU from the mixing console to the recorder. Record the tone. Set the record level so the recorder reads 0 VU on playback.

9. Set the "record cal" or "meter cal" so that the meter reads 0 VU on "input" or "source."

After calibration, your tape machine will operate as well as possible with the particular type of tape you're using. The playback signal should sound identical to the input signal (except for some added tape hiss).

# Using Magnetic Tape

Now that you have been introduced to tape recording hardware, it's time to consider the tape itself—its editing, handling, and storage.

## *Editing and Leadering*

When you edit a tape, you cut and rejoin the tape to delete unwanted material, to insert leader tape, or to rearrange material into the desired sequence. If you're doing all your work on cassettes, or if you're editing with a digital audio workstation, you can skip this section.

### Equipment and Preparation

To edit, you need these materials: demagnetized single-edge razor blades, a light-colored grease pencil, splicing tape, **leader tape**, and an **editing block**. Leader tape is plastic or paper tape without an oxide coating, which is used for a spacer between takes (i.e., silence between recorded songs). Paper leader is preferred over plastic because plastic can generate static electricity pops. An editing block holds the tape during the splicing operation. It's easier to use than a tape splicer with hold-down tabs and allows more precise cutting.

Before editing, wash your hands to avoid getting oily spots on the tape. Cut several 1-inch pieces of splicing tape and stick them on the edge of the tape deck or table. Also cut several sections of leader at the 45-degree slot in the editing block. A typical leader length between songs is 4 seconds, which is 60 inches long for 15 ips or 30 inches long for 7$\frac{1}{2}$ ips. While editing, try to hold the magnetic tape lightly by the edges.

### Leadering

Suppose you've recorded a reel full of takes and you want to remove the out-takes, count-offs, and noises between the good takes. You also want to insert leader between each song. This process, called **leadering**, can be done like this:

1. Wind several turns of leader onto an empty take-up reel and cut the leader at the 45-degree slot.

2. Remove this take-up reel, put on an empty one, and play the tape to be edited.

3. Locate the beginning of the first song's best take. Stop the tape there.

4. Put the machine in cue or edit mode so the tape presses against the heads.

5. While monitoring the tape-recorder output, rock the tape back and forth over the heads by rotating both reels by hand—first rapidly, then more and more slowly. You'll hear the music slowed down and low in pitch.

6. Find the exact point on tape where the song starts—that is, where it passes over the playback-head gap. Align the beginning sound with the gap.

7. Using the grease pencil, mark the tape about $\frac{1}{2}$ inch to the right of the gap (that is, at a point on tape just before the song starts).

8. Loosen or "dump" the tape by rotating the supply reel counterclockwise and the take-up reel clockwise simultaneously.

9. Remove the tape from the tape path and press it into the splicing block, oxide side down.

10. Align the mark with the 45-degree-angled slot (Figure 9.6).

11. Slice through the tape with a razor blade, drawing the blade toward you. Don't use the 90-degree slot because such an abrupt cut can cause a pop noise at the splice.

12. Remove the unwanted tape to the right of the cut and put the take-up reel aside.

13. Slide the cut end of the tape to the right of the editing-block slot (Figure 9.7).

14. Put on the take-up reel containing the turns of leader tape, and insert the end of the leader into the right half of the block.

15. Slide together the ends of the leader tape and magnetic tape so that they butt or touch together with no overlap.

16. Take a piece of splicing tape and stick a corner of it onto a hand-held razor blade.

17. Align the splicing-tape piece parallel to the recording tape.

18. Apply the piece over the cut onto the non-oxide side, and stick it down by rubbing with your fingernail.

19. Slide the splice out of the block. Gently pop the tape out of the block by pulling up on the ends of the tape extending from both sides of the block. Twist the tape toward you while pulling.

(A) Mark for beginning of song.

MARK FOR BEGINNING OF SONG

(B) Mark for end of song.

MARK FOR END OF SONG

**Figure 9.6** Aligning edit marks with cutting slot.

MAGNETIC
TAPE

LEADER
TAPE

**Figure 9.7**
Applying splicing tape.

20. Check that there is no gap or overlap at the splice.

21. Wind the tape onto the take-up reel and locate the ending of the first song.

22. As it ends, turn up the monitors and listen for the point where the reverberant "tail" of the music fades into tape hiss. Stop the tape there and mark it lightly at the playback-head gap (at the center line of the head).

23. After pressing the tape into the block, cut the tape at the mark. Remove the tape to the left of the cut.

24. Splice the end of the first song to a 4-second length of leader and again check the splice.

25. Wind the first song and the leader onto the take-up reel and remove it.

26. Put on the take-up reel containing unwanted material you set aside previously. Splice it to the rest of the master tape.

27. Locate the beginning of the next good take you want in the program. Mark it and cut the tape.

28. Put the reel containing the first song on the take-up spindle.
29. Splice the tail end of the leader onto the beginning of the second song, then wind the second song onto the take-up reel. You now have two songs joined by leader tape.

Repeat these steps until all the good takes are joined by leader. You then have a reel of tape with several songs separated by white leader, which makes it easy to find the desired selection.

## Joining Different Takes

What if you want to join the verse of Take 1 to the chorus of Take 2? You have to cut into both takes at the same point in the song, then join them. It takes practice to make an inaudible splice in this manner, but it's done every day in professional studios. The two takes must match in tempo, balance, and level for the edit to be undetectable. To mask any clicks occurring at the splice, cut the tape just before a beat—at the beginning of a drum attack, for instance. An alternative is to cut into a silent pause. If you cut into a continuous sound such as a steady chord, a cymbal ring, or reverberation, the splice is noticeable.

Follow these steps to join different takes:

1. Play Take 1 and locate the point where you want Take 1 to stop and Take 2 to start—at the beginning of the chorus, for instance. Stop the tape there.
2. Put the recorder in cue or edit mode, rock the tape, and try to identify a beat or attack transient.
3. At the point on tape where this beat just starts to cross the playback-head gap, mark the tape.
4. Cut the tape at the mark and remove the take-up reel containing the verse of Take 1.
5. Put on an empty take-up reel, thread the master tape, and fast-wind to Take 2.
6. Find the same spot in Take 2 that you marked in Take 1. Mark and cut it.
7. Using splicing tape, join Take 2 (in the supply reel) to Take 1 (in the take-up reel you just set aside). Again, check that there is no gap and no overlap at the splice.

Play the spliced area to see if the edit is detectable. If not, congratulations! It should sound like a single take. If Take 2 comes in a little late, carefully remove the splice and cut out just a little tape surrounding the cut. Resplice and listen again.

Suppose you've recorded most of a good take, but the musicians make a mistake and stop playing. Rather than repeating the entire song, the musicians can start playing a little before the point where they stopped and then finish the song. You splice the two segments into a complete and perfect take. Editing is also useful for inserting sound effects in the middle of a song, or for making tape loops. You can even record a difficult mix-down in segments and then edit the segments together.

## Reducing Print-Through

Print-through is the transfer of a magnetic signal from one layer of tape to the next, causing an echo. If the echo follows the program, it is called **post-echo**. If the echo precedes the program, it is called **pre-echo**. Print-through is easy to hear in recordings that have many silent areas, such as narration. To minimize print-through:

- Demagnetize the tape path (because stray magnetic fields increase print-through).
- Use $1\frac{1}{2}$ mil tape (thinner tapes increase print-through). C-60 cassette tape is thicker than C-90, so C-60 is preferred.
- Use noise-reduction devices (discussed earlier in this chapter).
- Store tapes at temperatures under 80 degrees Fahrenheit, and don't leave tapes on a hot machine (heat increases print-through).
- Rewind tapes in storage at least once a year. This action allows print-through to decay by separating and realigning adjacent layers of tape.
- Store tapes tail out. That is, after playing or recording a tape, leave it on the take-up reel. Rewinding a tape about 15 minutes before playing helps to reduce print-through that may have occurred during storage. Also, tail-out storage results mainly in post-echo, which is less audible than the pre-echo you get in tapes stored rewound.

## Tape Handling and Storage

Tape reels must be handled and stored carefully to avoid damaging the tape and the signals recorded on it. If you examine a reel of used recording tape, you may see some edges or layers of tape sticking out of the tape pack. These edges can be crushed by pressure from the reel flanges, causing dropouts and high-frequency loss. Figure 9.8 shows how to hold reels to prevent tape damage.

**Figure 9.8**
Handling tape reels.

To prevent edge damage during storage, leave tapes tail-out after playing or recording to ensure a smooth tape pack. Repair or discard reels with a bent flange. Reels left out in the open can collect dust, so keep them in boxes. Store tape boxes vertically, not stacked. The preferred storage conditions are 60 to 75 degrees Fahrenheit and 35 to 50% relative humidity. Keep tapes away from magnetic fields such as those caused by speakers, headphones, or telephones.

# 10

# DIGITAL RECORDING

The types of recorders described so far are analog recorders. That is, the magnetic particles on tape are oriented in patterns analogous to the audio waveform. Digital recorders convert the audio signal to a numerical code of ones and zeros.

Let's venture into the world of digital audio. We'll overview digital recording, DAT recorders, digital editing with DAWs, CD-R recorders, Modular Digital Multitracks, hard-disk recorders, MO recorders, MiniDisc recorders, and IC recorders.

## Analog versus Digital

Analog and digital recorders don't sound the same. Analog decks sound reasonably accurate, but they add a little warmth to the sound. It's due to slight third harmonic distortion, head bumps (bass boost), and tape compression. Analog decks also add some tape hiss, frequency response errors, wow and flutter, modulation noise, and print-through.

Digital recorders don't have these problems, so they sound very clean. Although some digital recorders sound harsh compared to analog, they are improving with each generation. In particular, digital recorders that can record at 24 bits and 96 kHz can sound just as smooth as analog. Both analog and digital have their colorations. Just use whatever works artistically for the particular music you're recording.

Compared to analog recorders and open-reel tape, digital recorders and their tape tend to cost less, are smaller, allow easier location of timing information, and allow easier tape loading.

# Digital Recording

Like an analog tape deck, a digital tape recorder puts audio on magnetic tape, but in a different way. Here's what happens.

1. The signal from your mixer (Figure 10.1A) is run through a lowpass filter (**anti-aliasing filter**) which removes all frequencies above 20 kHz.

2. Next, the filtered signal passes through an **analog-to-digital (A/D) converter**. This converter measures (samples) the voltage of the audio waveform several thousand times a second (Figure 10.1B).

(A) The audio waveform enters the A/D converter.

(B) The voltage is measured at regular intervals.

(C) The voltage measurements are quantized.

(D) The binary numbers are stored in memory or on tape.

**Figure 10.1** Digital recording (pulse code modulation or PCM).

3. Each time the waveform is measured, a binary number (made of 1's and 0's) is generated that represents the voltage of the waveform at the instant it is measured (Figure 10.1C). This process is called **quantization**. Each 1 and 0 is called a **bit**, which stands for binary digit.

4. These binary numbers are stored magnetically on tape or disk as a modulated square wave recorded at maximum level (Figure 10.1D).

The playback process is the reverse:

1. The binary numbers are read from tape.

2. The **digital-to-analog (D/A) converter** translates the numbers back into an analog signal made of voltage steps.

3. An **anti-imaging filter** (lowpass filter) smooths the steps in the analog signal, resulting in the original analog signal.

Since the digital playback head reads only 1's and 0's, it is insensitive to tape hiss and tape distortion. Numbers are read into a buffer memory and read out at a constant rate, eliminating speed variations. **Reed–Solomon error correction** corrects most errors. A process called **interpolation** restores lost data. If a bit is missing, an error-correction circuit "guesses" at its correct value based on the bytes that came before and after.

All digital recording devices employ the same A/D, D/A conversion process, but use different storage media. A DAT machine records on tape; a hard-disk drive records on magnetic hard disk; an MO drive records on a magneto-optical disc; a compact disc and DVD recorder record on an optical disc; and a sampler records into computer memory. The sound quality of any of these devices depends mainly on its A/D and D/A converters.

As we said, the audio signal is measured many thousand times a second to generate a string of binary numbers (called "words"). The longer each word is (the more bits it has), the greater is the accuracy of each measurement. Short words give poor resolution of the signal voltage (high distortion); long words give good resolution (low distortion). A **word length** of 16 bits is adequate (but not optimum) for hi-fi reproduction. It is the current standard for compact disc. Some digital recorders offer 18-, 20-, or 24-bit word lengths. **Bit depth** or **resolution** are other terms for word length.

**Sampling rate** is the rate at which the A-to-D converter samples or measures the analog signal while recording. For example, a rate of 48 kHz is 48,000 samples per second. That is, 48,000 measurements are generated for each second of sound. The higher the sampling rate, the wider the frequency response of the recording. The upper frequency limit is slightly less than half the sampling rate. If the sampling rate is 44.1 kHz, this gives a flat response up to 20 kHz. A 96 kHz sampling rate can be used on the DVD (Digital Versatile Disc).

Sampling rates of 44.1K and 48K sound almost identical, and tend to sound "brittle" with high-level, high-frequency sounds. Rates of 88.2K or 96K sound almost the same, and both sound more transparent than 44.1K or 48K. A bit depth of 24 bits sounds more transparent than 16 bits. Even 16-bit CDs sound better when made from 24-bit masters.

In summary, a digital audio system samples the analog signal and quantizes (assigns a value to) each sample. Sampling rate affects the high-frequency response; bit depth affects the dynamic range, noise, and distortion. According to the Nyquist theorem, the upper frequency limit is one-half the sampling rate. Compact discs use a 44.1 kHz sampling rate and so their frequency response extends to 22.05 kHz.

In a digital transmission, the two channels of a stereo program are **multiplexed**. That is, one word from channel 1 is followed by one word from channel 2, which is followed by one word from channel 1, and so on.

# The Clock

Each digital audio device has a **clock** that sets the timing of its signals. The clock is a series of pulses running at the sampling rate. When you transfer digital audio from one device to another, their clocks must be synchronized. One device **must** provide the master clock and the other must be the slave. If you send digital audio from one device, the receiver syncs to the sender's clock, which is embedded in its digital signal. If you send data from many sources at once, use a separate cable to connect one device's **word clock** output to all other devices.

# Digital Audio Signal Formats

Digital audio signals come in four basic formats: AES/EBU, S/PDIF, ADAT lightpipe, and TDIF. Let's look at each one.

- AES/EBU (also called AES3-1985): 2-channel professional format. Uses a balanced 110-ohm shielded twisted-pair cable with XLR-type connectors. (Regular mic cable adds jitter, explained later.) The signal contains digital audio plus a word clock, or a separate word clock on another cable. The AES/EBU cable can be up to 200 feet long, but the word clock cable should be 20 feet maximum.
- S/PDIF Sony/Philips Digital Interface (also called EIAJ CP-340 Type II or IEC 958): 2-channel consumer or semi-pro format. The signal

contains digital audio plus a word clock. Uses a 75-ohm coaxial cable with RCA or BNC connectors, or a fiber optic cable with a Toslink connector. Optical interfaces prevent ground loops and cable losses. AES/EBU signals are higher voltage than S/PDIF, and S/PDIF sometimes has SCMS copy protection.

- ADAT lightpipe: The Alesis ADAT modular digital multitracks use a **lightpipe**, which sends 8 channels of digital audio in and out on a single optical cable with TOSLINK connectors.
- TASCAM TDIF (TASCAM Digital Interface): The TASCAM DA-88 and similar modular digital multitracks use a multiconductor cable with standard DB-25 connectors. TDIF sends 8 channels of digital audio in and out on a single cable, which can be up to 5 meters long.

## *Converting Signal Formats*

AES and S/PDIF signals are similar but not necessarily compatible. You can convert one to the other using a **format converter**. Some sound cards and digital mixers do this conversion. Lightpipe and TDIF signals can be converted as well.

Some digital audio devices do not implement AES or S/PDIF correctly, so they do not interface with some other devices.

# Dither

Digital audio processing—such as level changes, EQ, or reverb—is done in a processor chip that performs mathematical calculations on each sample. These calculations create longer word lengths than existed in the original program. But the processor must output the same word length as the original signal. For example, a 16-bit audio file might result in words 32 bits long after processing. These 32-bit words must be converted back to 16 bits at the processor output. The extra bits could be truncated or cut off, but this causes distortion.

One DAW solves the problem by scaling back the output level of the digital mix until it is 16 bits maximum. The "scaling back" or level reduction is done with 64-bit precision. Another solution is to add **dither** (low-level noise) to the digital signal before converting it back to analog.

Let's explain dither. Each digital word is made of a certain number of bits. During quantization, the A/D converter assigns the closest possible digital number to represent the measured voltage of each sample. The last or rightmost bit toggles on or off depending on whether the processor rounds the word value up or down. This toggling results in **quantization error** or **quantization noise**.

Dithering is the process of adding low-level noise—a random signal of 1's and 0's—to a digital audio signal. This randomizes the on/off state of the last bit in the words. The result is less quantization noise.

The idea is to dither down to 16 bits the long internal length words. This dithering is best done once, just before the output of the processor. It is done automatically in the A/D, D/A converters, but can be set manually in some digital editing programs and outboard D/A converters.

**Noise shaping** is applied to a digital signal as its word length is reduced before being converted into an analog signal. First the digital signal is dithered by adding low-level noise to each sample. After the extra bits are removed, the noise is raised in pitch to the high end of the audio spectrum, and beyond to ultrasonic frequencies. This makes the noise less audible.

Dithering is also done when converting 24-bit recordings down to 16 bits for CD release, because CD is a 16-bit medium. With good dithering algorithms, it's possible to preserve most of the 24-bit quality (ultralow distortion and noise) when converting to 16 bits. Currently the best system is considered to be the POW-r™ Psychoacoustically Optimized Word-length Reduction algorithm from the Pow-r Consortium L.L.C. It reduces the high-resolution, higher word lengths (20 to 32 bit) to CD-standard 16-bit format while retaining the transparency of the high-resolution recording. In other words, the 16-bit CD sounds like the original 24-bit recording. (Thanks to Matt Lesko for this information.)

In addition, you could send audio through a multitrack 24-bit A/D converter, process it with POW-r, and record the result onto a 16-bit multitrack. The playback would sound like a 24-bit recording.

# Jitter

**Jitter** is an instability in the timing of digital bits. It causes small changes in the audio waveform's shape, resulting in a slight veiling of the sound (low-level distortion). A jitter spec under 250 picoseconds is considered inaudible. Jitter is caused by timing errors in digital I/O driver circuits, CD-R transport speed, word clocks, transformers, and cables.

To reduce jitter, use high-quality, well-shielded digital cables of the correct impedance, and keep their length as short as possible. Avoid ground loops. Keep analog and digital cabling separate. Try to sync all devices in your studio to the same master clock, because this distributed clock has less jitter than local clocks. If you use a separate word-clock cable, make it the same length as the digital audio cable.

# Digital Transfers or Copies

When you send a digital signal from one device to another, they must be set to the same sampling rate. For example, if the digital signal from a multitrack recorder is 48 kHz, the digital mixer it feeds must also be set to 48 kHz. In a digital transfer, the sending device usually is the master, and the receiving device is the slave. Normally you can set the slave to automatically lock onto the sampling rate of the master. Set the master device to Internal Clock, and set the slave device to External Clock. Or set the slave's clock source to whatever device the master is.

The word length (number of bits) of digital transfers is less critical. As long as the two machines handle the same digital format—S/PDIF, AES/EBU, ADAT lightpipe, TDIF—transfers of any word length can be done.

It's okay to send a lower-bit signal to a higher-bit device. For instance, feed a 16-bit signal from a DAT into a 24-bit digital mixer. The mixer will add more zeroes to fill out the digital word, with no effect on sound quality. It's also no problem to feed a device more bits than it can hold. The receiving device ignores the extra bits. For example, send a 24-bit signal to a 16-bit recorder. The last 8 bits will be truncated or cut off.

Truncation adds slight distortion, but this can be reduced by adding dither—low-level noise—to the signal before truncating. So it's best to keep the word length as long as possible as you're working on a project. Always apply dither before you reduce the word length.

Note that many devices do their internal processing at a higher resolution than their A/D converters have.

The following digital copies result in perfect clones of the original audio file:

- Inside a computer from one hard drive location to another
- From one computer's hard drive to another computer's hard drive
- Backing up data to a tape drive, Jaz, or Zip drive

The following digital copies might or might not be perfect clones, because of inadequate error correction or interpolation errors:

- To or from DAT or MDM tape
- To or from CD-Rs

Copying digitally from one digital device to another does not introduce any jitter. Jitter may occur during an A-to-D conversion.

The following data compression algorithms do not lose any data, so they do not degrade audio quality:

- Emagic's Zap
- Waves' TrackPac
- PKWare's PKZIP
- WinZip Computing's WinZip
- Aladdin Systems' StuffIt
- Meridian Lossless Packing (MLP)

When you make a digital copy, always use high-quality cables intended for digital audio.

# DAT

Like analog recorders, digital recorders come in 2-track and multitrack formats. Currently, 2-track open-reel digital recorders are quite expensive. There's a low-cost alternative: a DAT or R-DAT recorder. R-DAT stands for Rotating-head Digital Audio Tape. Costing $700 and up, a DAT machine records 2 tracks of audio digitally on a small cassette. This convenient format has become a standard for mastering and audio backup. However, DAT is likely to be replaced by rewritable CD-R. For example, the Alesis MasterLink can burn CDs at 24-bit word length.

DAT sound quality is at least as good as a compact disc. What you put in, you get out, virtually without any added hiss, distortion, or wow and flutter. Sonic drawbacks might include a little phase shift at high frequencies, quantization error (imprecise measurement of the analog signal), and jitter (unstable timing of the samples). All these can make the sound slightly harsh or veiled. It's a subtle effect, though.

Some DATs' A/D converters sound better than others. Some engineers prefer to use a high-quality external A/D converter and plug it into the DAT's digital input. Another option is an external mic preamp/A/D converter.

The DAT machine records on a small cassette about half the size of a standard analog cassette. The shell has a hinged door that flips open to expose the tape. Thanks to the DAT's fast transport, a 2-hour tape winds in about 45 seconds.

When you load the cassette, two spindles enter the two hubs from below the cassette and lock it into place. Then the tape is drawn into the machine and wraps around a rotating drum, which holds the record and playback heads (Figure 10.2).

As the tape moves past the rotating heads, they scan diagonally across the tape as they write the digital signal by pulse code modulation. The

**Figure 10.2**
Inside a DAT recorder.

tracks laid down by the rotating heads are about one-tenth the thickness of a human hair! Although the linear tape speed is slow, the tape speed as seen by the record head is very high, so the ultrasonic digital signal can be recorded. Tape drop-outs can cause data losses, but most of these are restored by a circuit that corrects the errors.

As the DAT machine records, it writes **absolute time** (ABS) on tape. ABS time is the running time in hours, minutes, and seconds, where 00:00:00 is at the head of the tape. You use ABS time to locate selections and time them.

## DAT Tape

A DAT cassette measures 73 × 54 × 10.5 mm. Its tape is 3.81 mm (⅛ inch) wide. On one end of the shell is a hinged door that flips open to expose the tape so it can be drawn around the rotating head drum. The cassette has a sliding safety tab on one end to prevent accidental erasure. If the little door is closed, you can record on the tape. If it's open, you can't.

DAT machines can record up to 2 hours on a 60-meter tape. Using a metal-powder oxide, DAT tapes come in various lengths. Avoid tapes over 60 meters because some DAT transports can't handle long tapes. Computer-grade DAT tapes (DDS) are more error-free than audio-grade DAT tapes.

Before recording on a DAT tape, it's a good idea to exercise the tape: Fast forward to the end and rewind to the top. This distributes the tape lubricants more evenly, aligns the tape with your machine's tape guides, and loosens the tape pack so it travels more freely. If audible errors occur, clean the heads with a dry cleaning cassette.

# DAT Subcodes

A **subcode** is information on tape that is independent of the audio data. Subcodes tell the number of each song, where it starts, and whether to play it. You can record or erase subcodes without affecting the audio program. The three main types of subcodes are **Start IDs**, **Program Numbers**, and **Skip IDs**.

- A Start ID marks the beginning of each song. You can write it manually or automatically. Manual Start IDs can be placed anywhere, say, to mark cues. You can set the DAT machine to record a Start ID automatically whenever a signal appears after a silence of three or more seconds. You should record manual Start IDs after recording all your mixes onto a DAT tape. Like other subcodes, Start IDs can be recorded or erased without altering the audio program. You can enter them during recording or playback. If the cassette's safety tab is set to prevent accidental erasure, you can't record or erase subcodes.

- A Program Number is the number of each song. A DAT machine can automatically assign Program Numbers to the Start IDs in consecutive order. Then you can locate a particular song quickly by having the DAT recorder search for the song's program number.

- A Skip ID makes the machine skip the song. This ID can only be written manually. Whenever the machine senses a Skip ID during playback, it stops and fast winds to the next Start ID, and begins playing. You can turn this function on or off.

# DAT Features

A DAT recorder has the usual transport controls, and some unique features, indicators, and controls. Some DAT machines include these features:

- Search: When you enable the search function, the machine fast winds to the selected program number.

- Memory Rewind or Return to Zero: When enabled, this function rewinds the tape to a preset "0" position on the tape counter.

- Renumber: This function automatically numbers the Start IDs consecutively from 1 upwards.

- SMPTE time code: This is available on a few models, digitally encoded as part of the subcode. It's used to synchronize the DAT audio program with a video tape or a MIDI sequencer.

- Mic inputs: These let you plug two mics directly into the DAT recorder. Generally the sound quality of the DAT mic preamps is not as good as that of an external mixer or mic preamp. You have a choice of pro-type balanced XLR connectors or consumer-type unbalanced phone jacks.

- Digital inputs and outputs: These let you make digital copies with no A/D–D/A conversion required. A copy made from a digital in/out is a clone of the original recording, with no loss in sound quality (unlike an analog copy).
- Confidence head playback: Some units have an extra head so you can hear the tape playback as you're recording.

Other features: a built-in monitor speaker, a clock/calendar, phantom power for condenser mics, an input attenuator to prevent mic preamp overload, a limiter to prevent recording beyond 0 dB, and a stereo mic. Some DAT recorders are portable, and they run off batteries or AC.

## DAT Indicators

The DAT recorder has an LED or LCD display window which shows various aspects of the recording.

- Time: Absolute time, remaining time on the tape, or elapsed time for the current selection.
- Meters: Peak-reading bargraph meters that show recording level. Unlike with an analog tape deck, "0" on the meter is the absolute maximum recording level. It's called 0 dBFS, or 0 dB full scale. When the signal level hits 0, all 16 bits are on.
- Error: If this indicator flashes, there was a loss of data. Usually the electronics can correct for this loss. Some units show the error rate.
- Sampling rate: The frequency at which the machine is sampling audio signals, such as 44.1 kHz. This indicator works both during recording and playback.
- Subcodes: Program number, Start ID, and Skip ID.
- Search mode: This shows whether the search mode is on.

## DAT Controls

- Sampling frequency: This is the rate at which the DAT's A-to-D converter samples or measures the analog signal while recording. On most models you can switch between 48 kHz and 44.1 kHz. Some units can also record at 32 kHz.

  Which rate should you use? For CD release, use 44.1K (same as the CD). Otherwise, use 48K for better sound. For longer playing time or four channels, use 32K. During playback, a DAT recorder senses the sampling rate on tape and automatically switches to that rate.

What if you have a 48K tape that you want to release on CD? The CD mastering engineer can (1) convert the 48K digital signal to 44.1K, which might degrade the sound, or (2) use the analog output of his or her DAT machine, and convert the analog signal to digital at 44.1K. This may or may not sound better.

- Analog/digital input selector: This chooses between analog and digital input signals.

- Emphasis: Used in older consumer DAT recorders, this boosts high frequencies during recording and turns them down during playback. The result is lower noise. When you play a DAT tape recorded with emphasis, the DAT machine detects it and turns on de-emphasis.

  Don't use both emphasized and non-emphasized recordings in the same project. If you copy them to hard disk, they all will play with emphasis, or without it. Then some recordings will sound too bright or too dull.

- Copy protect: This puts a flag in the subcode that prevents the tape from being digitally copied. A DAT deck will identify a copy-inhibit flag in its subcode, and will not digitally copy that recording. Be sure copy inhibit is OFF if you want to duplicate your DAT master digitally.

Consumer DAT machines have a copy inhibit system called **SCMS** (Serial Copy Management System). This feature lets you make a digital-to-digital copy, but prevents regenerations from that copy. That is, you can't make digital copies of the copy. Most compact-disc duplicators can disable or ignore the SCMS copy-code bit.

For more on DAT, check out the DAT-head's mailing list on the Internet. Subscribe to DAT-heads-request@fedney.near.net.

When you edit a DAT recording, splicing the tape doesn't work because the tracks won't align perfectly after the splice, and you may remove some data. Instead, you can copy from one DAT machine to another, changing the order of selections during the copying process.

Tight edits are impossible unless you use a digital audio workstation (DAW), covered next.

# The Digital Audio Workstation

The digital audio workstation (DAW) allows you to record, edit, and mix audio programs entirely in digital form, providing the highest sound quality. The DAW can store up to several hours of digital audio or MIDI data. You can edit this data with great precision on a computer monitor screen. What's more, you can add digital effects and perform automated mixdowns.

DAWs are available in three general forms:

1. A self-contained system (a portable hard-disk recorder–mixer)
2. A computer, sound card, and editing software (Figure 10.3). The editing software is controlled by a mouse.
3. A computer DAW with a controller interface: real faders and switches instead of a mouse.

All three systems record digital audio on a hard drive. The self-contained system has a mixer with real controls—faders and pushbuttons—while the computer DAW uses **virtual controls** simulated on your monitor screen. The computer DAW with a controller surface also has virtual controls on screen, but you adjust them with a **controller surface** that has physical faders, buttons, and transport controls and buttons.

What are the advantages of each format? The standalone DAW is portable, requires no computer, and is less likely to crash than a computer. The computer DAW offers more flexibility, such as more tracks, more hard-drive space, and more choices of plug-in effects. If you already own a computer, you can upgrade it to a DAW by purchasing editing software, which costs less than a self-contained DAW. The controller surface is less fatiguing to use than a mouse, but costs more.

The computer workstation includes editing software and a sound card you plug into the computer. The sound card converts audio into computer data that is recorded on hard disk. The card also converts hard-disk data back into audio. Some cards have an A/D converter built in; others

**Figure 10.3**
A computer digital audio workstation.

accept a digital signal directly from your DAT or digital mixer. Although most cards handle 2 to 4 inputs, some offer 8 inputs—either on cables or in a TDIF connector.

Once the audio data is on hard disk, it can be read by the read head in the hard drive. Since the head can be controlled to jump to any particular location on disk, it allows **random access**—nearly instant access to different parts of the audio program. You can quickly locate or edit any portion of the program. To rearrange or repeat song sections, you simply tell the computer the order in which you want them played.

Multitrack computer DAWs often use a breakout box (I/O box or audio interface) to get several channels of audio into and out of the computer. A typical I/O box has 8 analog input and 8 analog output connectors, as well as digital connectors such as SPDIF, ADAT lightpipe, TASCAM TDIF, or AES/EBU. The I/O box connects to a card in the computer, usually via a USB or FireWire port.

Regarding the hard drive, you need about 11 megabytes per minute of stereo program, plus more for temporary audio files and regular programs. A 1.2-gigabyte hard drive is big enough to record a full-length CD program. The drive should be an A/V (audio/video) type with embedded servo. It postpones thermal recalibration until the drive is idle. The drive should be capable of high throughput (at least 1000 kilobytes/second for 2 tracks, and 2000 to 4000 kilobytes/second for 4 stereo tracks.)

One function of a DAW is for compact disc pre-mastering. You start with your rough DAT mixdown master containing music, studio noises, and long spaces between songs. After copying it to hard disk, edit this program with the workstation. That is, define the start and stop points of each song. Finally you dump the edited program onto DAT, and that is your CD pre-master. You can record your own CDs off the workstation with a compact disc recorder (CD-R writer).

Below is a general editing procedure for DAWs:

1. Play the DAT tape containing your program, and record it onto the hard disk. This recording might be just one song, several sound effects, or an entire album. You might prefer to record your mixer's output directly to your hard drive as you are mixing—bypassing the DAT tape.

2. The waveform of the audio program appears on your monitor screen (Figure 10.4). You can **zoom out** to see the entire program, or **zoom in** to see individual samples.

3. Using a mouse, mark the beginning and end of **regions** in the audio waveform. These are sections of the program that you want to keep. In Figure 10.4, a region is highlighted. Examples of regions are an

entire song, the chorus of a song, a drum riff, or a vocal lick. The computer keeps track of these start/stop points—called **pointers**—which are addresses on your hard disk. Also define some regions of silence— 4 seconds, for example—to insert between songs.

4. Once you have defined the regions, put them into a stereo track, or into a playlist. A **playlist** (**Edit Decision List**, **EDL**, or **Sequence View**) is a list of the regions in the order you want them to play (Figure 10.5).

   While editing, you can delete regions, move them around, copy them, insert silences, and re-sequence the playlist so that the songs progress in any desired order.

   Some edits may be **destructive**: They change the data on disk. Most edits are **nondestructive**: They change only the pointers, so the data on disk is not changed or destroyed. Nondestructive edits are not permanent. If you don't like an edit, you can undo it and do it over.

5. Once the program is edited the way you want it, copy it in real time onto a DAT tape, or to a stereo file on your hard drive that will be

**Figure 10.4** A waveform editing screen.

used to burn a CD-R. During this process, the software plays the program by running down the playlist of pointers. The pointers tell the hard-disk head where on the disk to read the data from (Figure 10.5). That is, the playlist tells the head to jump around from point to point on the disk to play selected portions in the desired order.

More information on computer recording can be found at http://www.pcrecording.com.

## DAW Functions

Here are some of the functions found in most digital audio workstations:

**Multitrack digital recording:** From 2 tracks on up.

**Cut and paste:** Remove a section of a song and put it somewhere else in the song.

**Copy:** Duplicate a section of a song (say, a chorus) and put it somewhere else in the song.

**Crossfade:** Fade out of one song while fading into another.

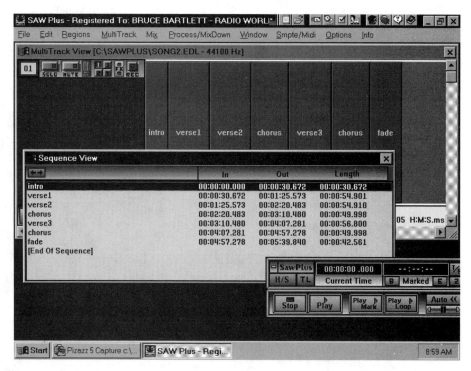

**Figure 10.5** A sequence view (EDL) screen.

**Fade-in, fade-out:** Do an automated fade.

**Virtual tracks:** Extra takes of a single instrument's performance, recorded on the hard drive. During mixdown you can choose the best takes to use. Some DAWs have 256 virtual tracks, but 16 real tracks. In that case you can mix 16 tracks during mixdown, but some of those 16 tracks might have several virtual tracks or alternate takes that can be accessed during mixdown.

**Slip:** Move a song, or a section of a song, in time—either within or across tracks. Or adjust the start times of sound effects by moving them on-screen with a mouse. You can slip one track forward or backward in time, independent of other tracks.

**Scrub:** Play the program slowly forward and backward (like rocking tape reels to move the tape back and forth across the head). This lets you find edit points accurately.

**Trim:** Remove or truncate unwanted portions of the waveform or program.

**Time/pitch compression/expansion:** This makes an audio program shorter or longer without changing its pitch. It's useful for making radio spots fit their allotted time. You can also change the pitch of a track without changing its duration.

**Variable pitch:** Adjust the pitch up or down, while also changing the duration.

**Automated mixing:** The computer remembers your mix moves and sets the mixer controls accordingly during the mixdown. For more information, see the section on Automated Mixing in Chapter 16.

**Spectrum analysis:** A display of level versus frequency of the audio program as it progresses in time.

**MIDI sequencer:** This lets you import or record several tracks of MIDI performance data.

**Sync:** Synchronization to SMPTE time code or MIDI time code.

**Number of simultaneous tracks:** Some units can record up to 8 tracks simultaneously, but play 16 tracks during mixdown. If you want to record an entire band at once, the DAW must be able to record at least 8 tracks simultaneously.

**Locate and marker points:** Enter the times of several points in a song, and return to them instantly.

**Routing or virtual patchbay:** Assign any input to any track.

**PQ editing:** This allows you to add song start-and-stop times and index points to create a pre-master tape for compact discs.

**CD recording capability:** Record edited CDs, either on an external or internal CD burner.

**DSP (Digital Signal Processing):** Digital control and effects such as mixing, volume adjustments, panning, surround panning, equalization, reverberation, echo, chorus, limiting, looping, compression, expansion, noise removal, and noise gating.

**Plug-ins:** A plug-in is a software module that adds DSP effects to DAW editing programs. When you install the plug-in software, it becomes part of the DAW editing program, and you can call it up when you need it. Your DAW becomes the "host," and the plug-in provides extra effects that did not come originally with the host program. Most plug-ins are provided by third-party manufacturers.

With the click of a mouse, you can load in the right plug-in for the job, with no external processors or patch cords needed. Parameters (such as reverb time, chorus depth, or compression ratio) can be adjusted, and most parameters can be saved and automated.

Digidesign's ProTools multitrack editing system uses plug-ins in two forms: TDM and Audio Suite. TDM works in real time, while Audio Suite processes a sound file and creates a new one—as with normalization or time compression/expansion.

Recent plug-ins can simulate or model the sound of hardware processors. For example, Amp Farm by Line 6 is a guitar-amp modeling plug-in, while Antares Microphone Modeler can simulate the sound of popular studio mics. Vintage compressors, tube mic preamps, and analog tape recorders have been modeled as well.

Plug-ins come in several formats, the most popular for Windows being VST and DirectX. DirectX is a group of application-program interfaces that enhance multimedia (video and audio) on Windows systems. The latest version, DirectX 8, lets you automate effects in your mix, and supports software-synth plug-ins.

## *Optimizing Your Computer for Digital Audio*

If your editing projects on a DAW involve just two tracks, computer speed is not too important. But as productions become increasingly elaborate—more bits, more tracks, more effects—speed becomes critical.

The data flow of multitrack digital audio places high demands on computer speed. Recording and playback of digital audio requires long, continuous periods of streaming audio data. The more tracks in use, and the higher the bit depth and sampling rate, the faster the data flow has to be. And the more effects plug-ins that are in use, the greater the load on the CPU.

Clearly, you need a fast computer for high-end audio editing. But you also need to optimize its settings for best results. I will cover some ways to speed up the data flow and to reduce the CPU usage. If you follow these tips, you will have a faster system that handles more plug-ins and more tracks at once. And clicks or audio glitches will be less likely in CD burns or in file playback.

## Speeding Up Your Hard Drive

The hard drive should have a fast average access time (under 9 msec) and a high internal sustained transfer rate. What transfer rate is needed? In general, the data rate of digital audio is the Number of tracks × Sampling rate × Bytes (where 8 bits = 1 byte). If the result is in kilobytes, divide it by 1.024. If the result is in megabytes, divide it by 1.04. So the data rate of 8 tracks of 44.1K/16-bit audio (2 bytes) is 689 kB/second. For 48K/24-bit it is 1.1MB/second. For 96K/24-bit the rate is 2.2MB/second. A full-blown production of 96K/24-bit and 24 tracks reaches 6.6MB/second.

Real-time DSP processing for effects may increase the rate by 3 to 5 times. So the actual transfer rate needed ranges from about 3.5MB/second (8 tracks of 44.1K/16-bit) to 33MB/second (24 tracks of 96K/24-bit). The best current hard drives can transfer about 40MB/second with a PCI bus and an Ultra ATA/66 or Ultra ATA/100 interface (for EIDE drives), or a SCSI interface for SCSI drives. Do not use an ISA bus interface—its rate tops out at 2MB/second.

Hard drives with high rotational speed or spindle rate (7200 rpm or greater) tend to have a faster transfer rate. A rate of 10,000 rpm is recommended for 24-bit multitrack productions. SCSI drives tend to be faster than IDE, but SCSI costs more, and many IDE drives are fast enough.

Use one hard drive for audio files only, and another hard drive for programs. Or use one disk partition for audio files and another partition for programs. If possible, use the lower-letter partition for audio files because it is the faster part of the disk. Two separate drives are generally faster than one partitioned drive.

Defragment the audio file drive often, or reformat it when you are finished with all the files on it. Defragmenting reorganizes files into contiguous areas on the disk so that each audio file can be accessed with minimum head movements.

Format the audio-file disk or partition using the command FORMAT [drive letter]: /z:32 or /z:64 (the largest possible for your disk). That /z switch creates bigger cluster sizes that reduce the number of read/write operations and reduce file fragmentation.

**Important:** Use drivers that allow bus mastering. Install bus-mastering drivers for your hard drives, and enable DMA (Direct Memory Access) for IDE drives. Both these options can greatly speed data transfer and reduce CPU usage.

To check for bus mastering in Windows, go to Control panel > System > Device manager > Hard disk controllers, and look for Bus master controller. To enable DMA, go to Control panel > System > Device manager > Disk drives. Double-click your hard drive, go to Settings, and check the DMA box. You'll need to reboot if you changed the DMA setting.

If you have both a master and a slave IDE drive, record on the master drive—it's faster.

Go to Control panel > System > Performance > File system > Hard disk. Set Read-ahead optimization to minimum. Set Typical Role to Network Server because it gives higher priority to disk use. In Performance > File system > Troubleshooting, disable write-behind caching for all drives.

You can also speed the data transfer of CD-ROM drives and CD burners. Go to Control panel > System > Device manager, and double-click CD-ROM. Select your model of CD-ROM. Under Settings, check Disconnect, Sync data transfer, and DMA. Do *not* check Auto-insert notification.

Go to Control Panel > System > Performance > File system > CD-ROM. Set Supplemental cache size to maximum.

## Increasing Processing Speed

Install lots of memory—64 MB is minimum, 128 MB is better, and 256 MB or more is better yet. The idea is to have your programs running in RAM, rather than swapping data to your hard drive. Get the fastest CPU you can afford (the highest clock speed in MHz).

Consider using a non-accelerated video card, because faster cards place high demands on system timing. Don't multitask (run other programs) while the audio is streaming. Each additional task slows down the system.

The following tips apply only to Windows on a PC:

- Shut down background applications such as screen savers, System Agent, virus checkers, and Windows sounds. These apps can interrupt data flow. In BIOS and in Windows, turn off power management. Otherwise the system might shut down at the wrong time. You can reclaim memory space by removing startup programs: Select

Start/Run and open MSCONFIG. Select the Startup tab, and uncheck all programs except for the System Tray. Reboot.

- On the Web, download the latest drivers for your video card and hard-disk adapter.
- Go to Control panel > Display > Settings. Set Colors to 16-bit because 24-bit wastes CPU cycles.
- Go to Start > Run > and type Sysedit to open System.ini in a text editor. Find [vcache]. Under [vcache], make sure MinFileCache and MaxFileCache are both set to 4096 (if your computer has 32MB of RAM) or 8192 (if your computer has 64MB or more of RAM). Save System.ini and reboot. These settings do not affect audio performance, but they keep your file cache from taking up too much memory.
- Go to Control panel > System > Performance > Graphics > Advanced. Sometimes, setting Hardware Acceleration less than maximum can speed up audio throughput.
- Set up a permanent swap file (virtual memory) on drive C for faster performance. Follow these steps:
  1. Go to Performance > Virtual Memory.
  2. Select "Let me specify my own virtual memory settings."
  3. Select "Disable virtual memory" > OK > Yes > Close.
  4. Reboot your system.
  5. Defragment drive C.
  6. Again, go to Control panel > System > Performance > Virtual Memory.
  7. Uncheck "Disable virtual memory."
  8. Select Hard disk:C.
  9. Set Minimum to 2 times the size of your RAM.
  10. Set Maximum the same as Minimum.
  11. Click "OK" and restart Windows.
- The more effects plug-ins you use, the fewer tracks you can mix, because effects put a big load on the CPU. You might be able to get around this problem by installing a Digital Signal Processing (DSP) card, such as the TC Works Powercore. It handles the processing for the plug-ins. The plug-ins access the card rather than the CPU. You can install multiple cards to expand the system. Pro Tools includes its own DSP cards.

If you have a program that measures disk throughput (read and write times), you might want to measure your system's speed before and after each change mentioned above. That way you will know which changes were effective. After I tweaked the settings on my own computer system, the disk sustained transfer rate became three times faster! I hope your changes will be as effective.

# CD Recordable

So far we've looked at DAT and DAW. Another form of digital recording is the compact disc. On your own desktop, you can cut a compact disc by using a CD-R recorder. It's exciting to hear one of these CDs playing your music with the purity of digital sound. The sound quality meets or exceeds compact disc standards, and the expected lifetime is about 70 years.

CD-R stands for Compact Disc Recordable. This optical medium is a **write-once** (nonerasable) format. CD-RW stands for Compact Disc Re-Writable; you can erase it and record a new program. While a CD-R will play in any CD player or CD-ROM drive, a CD-RW will play only in a CD-ROM drive. CD-RW blank discs cost more than CD-R blank discs.

How can you use the CD-R format? You could make demos that sound much cleaner than cassettes. Or make a one-off copy of your stereo mixes for clients. Use the CD-R as a pre-master to send to a CD replicator. Another function is to compile sound libraries of production music, samples, and sound effects. The CD format is a more dependable storage medium than DAT, so it's a great way to archive your recordings.

## *CD-R Formats*

Want to try CD-R? First you'll be faced with two basic choices of CD-R recorder:

1. A **standalone CD-R recorder**, sometimes called a **consumer CD recorder**.

2. A **computer peripheral CD-R recorder**, also called a computer CD burner. You plug it into your computer system.

Both types produce discs that sound equally good. They are not compatible with each other: a consumer disc will not play in a computer CD burner, and vice versa. But both types of discs will play on any audio CD player.

The standalone CD recorder has everything you need in one chassis. Inside is a CD transport, laser, and microprocessor. On the back are analog and digital ins and outs. On the front are the level meters, record-level knob, display, and keypad. Because the standalone unit needs no external computer, it's user-friendly. Just connect your audio source containing an edited program, either on DAT or analog tape. Set the recording level and start recording.

The standalone unit can write audio but not data. The 63-minute blank discs it uses are "CD for Consumer" format and sell for around $3. (An exception is the Marantz CDR610, which can use cheaper blanks.) Prices for standalone CD-R writers start around $400.

A computer CD recorder costs less: about $150 and up. The unit plugs into an EIDE or SCSI connector in your computer. It can write audio or computer data.

Its blank discs, in the "CD for Professionals" format, cost less than $1 in quantity. Disc length is 74 minutes (650 MB), 63 minutes (550 MB), or 80 minutes (700 MB). Some discs permit recording at up to 4 times real time; others can record up to 16× if your computer and hard drive are fast enough.

The peripheral CD-R recorder also requires a CD recording program, usually packaged with the recorder. You don't have to use that program; other ones are available that you might prefer. Be sure the program is compatible with your recorder. Most software requires at least a 486DX2-66 computer with 16 MB RAM. You'll also need a sound card (44.1 K, 16-bit), and some software to record audio onto hard disk.

Regarding the hard-disk drive, use an A/V (audio/video) type of at least 1 GB capacity and high throughput. If you want to burn more than one CD at once, you can daisy-chain CD-R recorders together, or buy a multi-drive CD burner.

## *CD-R Technology*

While conventional CD players follow the Sony–Philips Red Book standard, CD-R's conform to the Orange Book part II standard. Once recorded, a CD-R disc meets the Red Book standard.

A recordable CD is the same size as a standard compact disc, but is more colorful. On top is a layer of gold; on the bottom is a recording layer made of blue cyanine dye. Actually, the blue layer appears green because of the gold layer behind it. Some CD-R discs use a yellow (gold) dye of phthalocyanine. Yellow dye lasts a little longer in accelerated aging tests, and it may work better with high-speed CD-R drives. Still, most CD-R writers are optimized for green cyanine disks, which can handle a wider range of laser power. Black CD-Rs can record up to 16× real-time speed.

A blank CD-R is made of four layers:

1. Clear plastic (protects the gold layer)
2. Gold (reflects laser light)
3. Dye (for the recording)
4. Clear plastic (protects the dye layer)

The dye fills a spiral groove which is etched in the bottom clear-plastic layer. This groove guides the laser.

To record data on disc, the laser melts holes in the dye layer. The plastic layer flows into the holes to form pits. During playback, the same laser reads the disc at lower power. At each pit, laser light reflects off the gold layer. The reflected light enters the laser reader, which detects the varying reflectance as the pits go by.

In contrast with a standard CD, a CD-R disc has two more data areas:

- The **Program Calibration Area** (PCA). The CD recorder uses this area to make a test recording, which determines the right amount of laser power to burn the disc (4 to 8 milliwatts).

- The **Program Memory Area** (PMA). This area stores a temporary table of contents (TOC) as the CD-R tracks are being assembled. The TOC is a list of the tracks, their start times, and the total program time. The recorder uses the PMA for this information until it writes the final TOC.

## CD-R Sessions, Disc-at-Once, Track-at-Once

Before we look at the differences among CD-R recorders, we need to understand the concept of a **session**. A session on disc is a lead-in, program area, and lead-out. Each session has its own TOC. Each lead-in and lead-out consumes 13 MB of disc space.

With the **multisession** feature, you can write several sessions on a disc at different times. This feature comes in handy when you need to add information to a disc a little at a time. Only the first session on disc will play on an audio CD player, so the discs are just for your own use—not for distribution.

Some CD-R recorders permit **Disc-at-Once** recording, in which the entire disc must be recorded nonstop. You can't add new material once you write to the disc. With the right software, Disc-at-Once lets you set the length of silence between tracks (down to 0 seconds), and lets you control how the tracks are laid out on disc. Disc-at-Once is the pro audio format.

Most CD-R recorders allow **Track-at-Once** recording. They can record one track (or a few tracks) at a time—up to 99 tracks. You can play a partly recorded disc on a CD-R recorder. But the disc will not play on a regular CD player until the final TOC is written. Track-at-Once is not recommended for audio because it puts 2-second spaces and clicks between audio tracks.

If you want no pauses between tracks (as on a live album), get a CD-R writer with Disc-at-Once. Also get some software that can adjust the pause length down to zero, or that can set the Start ID of each song anywhere in the program. Note that a self-contained CD-R writer will copy your edited program as it is, with or without pauses.

A good CD-R writer has a buffer of at least 2 MB. Some writers include SCMS copy code. Be sure that you can return the CD-R writer if it proves to be unreliable.

## *How to Use a Standalone CD-R Writer*

Let's say that you've compiled a DAT of song mixes. You want to copy them onto a CD by using a self-contained CD-R writer. The first step is to edit your mixes into a finished program. To do this you'll need a sound card and a 2-track digital editing program. Here are the steps:

1. Connect your DAT recorder to the sound card. Transfer your mixes from DAT to hard disk.
2. While viewing the soundfile waveform, mark each song as a region (a selected segment of audio). Using a mouse, fine-tune the start and stop points of each region so that there are no noises between songs.
3. Assemble the songs in order into an Edit Decision List (a playlist or cue sheet). The total playing time should be under 60 minutes to fit on the CD-R disc.
4. Between songs, put silent spaces or crossfades. Three to four seconds of space is typical.
5. Have the computer change the level of songs that need it.
6. Start recording on your DAT. Play the cue list off the hard drive and copy it to DAT.
7. Once your edited program is on DAT, write a start ID $\frac{1}{2}$ second before each song. Renumber the program numbers.

Now you're ready to play the edited DAT into the CD-R writer. Connect the DAT's output to the CD-R writer's input. Set your levels and begin recording. Your program will copy to disc in real time.

Depending on the CD-R writer, the DAT start IDs may or may not convert to CD track numbers. If not, you can use a converter box, or add the track numbers manually while you record.

# *How to Use a Computer CD-R Recorder*

The procedure for this type of CD-R is different. First make the right connections. If your mixes are on hard disk, you're all set. If your mixes are on DAT, plug the DAT's digital output into your sound card's digital input. If your sound card has no digital input, plug your DAT's analog output to your sound card's analog input. Other sources can be analog tape, LPs, or cassettes. Just connect the analog source signal to the sound card's analog input.

You'll need two types of software: sound recording/editing software and CD-R recording software. There are two ways to proceed:

**Method 1**. Use this method if your CD-R burning program requires a separate WAV file for each song:

1. Start the computer recording/editing software.
2. Record each song to hard disk as a separate WAV file. Note: The spacing between songs will be set to a fixed length by the CD-R recording software. If you want to have extra seconds of silence at the end of a song, record the silence as part of the song's WAV file.
3. Start the CD-R recording software.
4. Select which WAV files you want to put on the CD-R, and arrange them in order in your playlist.
5. Start recording the CD-R. The WAV files will transfer in order to the CD-R disc.

**Method 2**. Use this method if your CD-R burning program can create CD tracks from a single WAV file by following pointers to song start times. Method 2 gives you more control over the songs' levels, EQ, and spacing. With this method, you can create CD track start IDs that occur during a continuous program, such as a live concert recording.

1. Start the computer recording/editing software.
2. Record several songs as one long WAV file.
3. Edit each song's start/stop times and define each song as a region.
4. Assemble the regions in order in your playlist. Note the start time of each song.
5. Build the mix to a new soundfile. That is, your computer will play the playlist and will create a WAV-type soundfile of your edited program on the hard drive.
6. Write a cue list text file that tells the start time of each song within the WAV file.

214

7. Start the CD-R recording software.

8. Load in the cue list and record the CD-R. The program writes the cue-list start times in the CD-R's table of contents.

The total playing time must be less than the CD-R length. CD-R discs cannot be erased and used over again, so try to make everything right before you burn a disc. You could do a practice burn on a CD-RW.

Track-at-Once inserts a 2-second gap between each song whether you want it or not. To make the gaps longer, record silence onto each song's end.

## CD-R Recording Settings

When you record a CD-R, you can either burn a disc **on-the-fly** or create a **disk image**. When recording **on-the-fly**, the computer grabs the sound files from random locations on hard disk and puts them in order as the CD-R does a burn.

When recording a **disk image**, the computer rewrites the sound files to a single, contiguous space on your hard disk and puts them in order. Then you copy the disk image from hard disk to CD-R.

A disk image takes up disk space and takes longer, but it increases throughput, which reduces the chance of errors. On-the-fly CD burning is faster and takes no extra disk space, but requires a fast Pentium.

You might have a choice of transfer speed—up to 16 times normal speed, depending on the throughput of your hard drive and on the blank CD-R characteristics. A 16× recorder can burn a 74-minute CD in less than 5 minutes. Some CD burners automatically select the optimum speed based on what the blank CD-R can handle. High speeds do not degrade sound quality seriously, but they tend to increase errors—which the CD player may or may not correct accurately. Normal speed is 172 kilobytes per second, double speed is 344 KBps, etc. The recommended speed is 2× when making a final master CD to be sent out for replication, as it has fewer errors than faster speeds.

At high speeds, a disk-image burn is more likely to copy without errors than an on-the-fly burn. Also at high speeds, a yellow blank is more likely to write without errors than a green blank.

As soon as the recording is done, the display will indicate that the TOC is being written. Eventually, the system will beep and eject the disc. To prevent error-causing fingerprints, be sure to handle the disc only by the edges. Pop the disc in an audio CD player, press Play, and check that all the tracks play correctly.

215

If you are intending the CD for commercial release, I recommend using a professional CD checker such as the Clover QA1010 or EC-2. It will catch unacceptably high error rates. Their web site has a lot of useful information on CD-Rs (http://www.cloversystems.com).

You can identify the CD either by writing on the label side with a felt-tip marker, or by sticking on a paper label. Use label design software and a label applicator device. Some software can even print liner notes, including the track numbers, titles, and timing.

# MDM: Modular Digital Multitrack

So far we've covered DAT, DAW, and CD-R. Another digital recording format is the MDM (Figure 10.6). It records 8 digital tracks on a videocassette, using a rotating drum like a DAT recorder. Two popular models are the Alesis ADAT-XL which records on S-VHS tape, and the Tascam DA-88 or DA-78, which records on Hi-8 mm tape. ADAT records up to 40 minutes on a single tape; DA-88 records up to 1 hour 48 minutes. It's great for recording concerts nonstop.

With both types, you can sync several 8-track units by a cable to add more tracks, 8 at a time. Unlike SMPTE time code, MDM sync does not use up any tracks. MDM options include remote controls, remote editors, circuit boards with enhanced converters, and circuit boards that allow sync to SMPTE and MIDI.

To prevent data errors, be sure to format the MDM tape correctly. Fast-forward the tape to the end, rewind to the top, then format the tape. Clean the heads with a dry cleaning tape only when an error signal appears, because cleaning tapes are abrasive and can wear out the heads.

It's common to record music on an MDM, dump the MDM tracks to computer hard disk for editing, then dump the edited tracks back to MDM. Sound cards are available with Alesis Lightpipe or TASCAM TDIF connectors for this purpose.

**Figure 10.6**
A Modular Digital
Multitrack (MDM).

# Random-Access Multitracks

Let's turn to another type of digital recorder. While MDMs record on tape, random-access units record on hard disk (HD), magneto-optical (MO) disk, or MiniDisc. All these units allow editing and can undo edits. Multitrack random-access units come in five formats:

- Computer DAW (Digital Audio Workstation)
- HD recorder (Hard-Disk recorder)
- MO recorder (Magneto-Optical recorder)
- HD recorder–mixer (Figure 10.7)
- MiniDisc recorder–mixer

Later we'll explain all these in detail.

## *Random-Access Units versus MDMs*

How do random-access units compare to MDMs? Random access offers instant locating of song parts, instant computer editing of tracks, and fewer errors than tape. But tape costs much less than a disk of the same recording time. MDMs make it easy to remove a project and start a new one: Just change the tapes. With a DAW or HD recorder, you must back up the project on a removable hard drive, then delete the project on disk to make room for the new one (unless you have lots of hard drive space).

Listed below are the characteristics of each type of random-access recorder.

**Figure 10.7**
A hard-disk
recorder–mixer.

# Computer DAW

- Includes a computer, recording/editing software, and one or more sound cards. You send audio from your mixer to the sound card, which converts the audio to a signal that can be recorded on the computer's hard drive. The sound card has analog or digital inputs and outputs.

- A DAW can also be used to edit multitrack recordings that were made originally on a Modular Digital Multitrack. Sound cards are available with Alesis Lightpipe or Tascam TDIF connectors, so that you can transfer 8 or more tracks at once from the MDM to your hard drive for editing.

- Some DAWs use a **breakout box** instead of a sound card. Also called an **audio interface** or **I/O interface**, a breakout box is a chassis with four or more input/output connectors, wired to the computer. Some breakout boxes accept line-level signals from your mixer; others have mic preamps built in. Some even have Hi-Z inputs for electric guitars and inserts to connect outboard effects.

- Records 2 to 24 tracks at a time. Some can record an unlimited number of tracks by overdubbing. The number of tracks you can record and play back depends on the speed of your computer and hard drive.

- Mixes to stereo in the computer. The mix can be stored externally on DAT or CD-R, or internally on your hard drive.

- Has a large screen for graphical editing of the waveform.

- Uses on-screen faders that you control with a mouse.

- Many can use an external **control surface**, which replaces the mouse. A control surface looks like a mixer with real faders and knobs. It attaches to the computer through a USB port and controls the "virtual" faders and knobs you see on the monitor screen. Control surfaces also include mic inputs, transport controls, and sometimes MIDI connectors.

- The more effects plug-ins you use, the fewer tracks you can mix, because effects put a big load on the CPU. You might be able to get around this problem by installing a Digital Signal Processing (DSP) card. It handles the processing for the plug-ins. The plug-ins access the card rather than the CPU. You can install multiple cards to expand the system. Example: TC Works Powercore.

# Hard-Disk (HD) Recorder

- Records and plays up to 24 tracks at once on a built-in hard drive, just like the drive in your computer. The latest units record with 24-bit resolution and up to 96 kHz sampling rate. Some record 24 tracks of 24-bit programs at sample rates of 44.1 and 48 kHz. They record 12 tracks of 24-bit recording at 88.2 and 96 kHz.
- Requires an external mixer.
- Allows track editing, either on a built-in LCD screen or on a plug-in computer monitor.
- Some have built-in removable hard drives for backing up projects.
- Compared to a DAW, an HD recorder is less likely to crash, is cheaper and more portable, and tends to have better converters.

# MO Recorder

- The Magneto Optical recorder has the same features as the hard-disk recorder. In an MO recorder, a laser heats the disc surface so it can be easily magnetized, and a laser reads the data. Data can be erased and rewritten. The MO cartridge can store 100 MB to several gigabytes.
- An MO disk is convenient, reliable, and low-cost, but slower than a hard disk.
- MO format is 2-track or multitrack.

# HD Recorder–Mixer

This device (also known as a standalone digital workstation, or digital multitracker) records and plays up to 24 tracks at once on a built-in hard drive. The mixer includes faders (volume controls) for mixing, EQ or tone controls, and aux sends for effects (such as reverb). An LCD screen displays recording levels, waveforms for editing, and other functions.

Compared to a DAW, an HD recorder–mixer is self-contained, is less likely to crash, is cheaper and more portable, and tends to have better converters. It also allows hands-on mixing with real controls.

Listed below are some features to look for in HD recorder–mixers.

- Number of tracks: 8 to 24. The more tracks you have, the more instruments and vocals you can record on individual tracks.
- Number of virtual tracks (extra takes): Up to 800. I'll explain virtual tracks later.

- Number of tracks that can be recorded simultaneously: 8 to 24. If you want to record an entire band at once, you need to record many tracks at the same time.

- Number of mixer channels: 8 to 24.

- Bit depth: 16 to 24 bit. The more bits, the higher the sound quality.

- Sampling rate: 44.1 kHz to 96 kHz. The higher the sampling rate, the higher the sound quality. The latest units record with 24-bit resolution and up to 96 kHz sampling rate. Some record 24 tracks of 24-bit programs at sample rates of 44.1 and 48 kHz. They record 12 tracks of 24-bit recording at 88.2 and 96 kHz.

- Number and type of analog inputs and outputs, and digital inputs and outputs. XLR mic connectors are preferred over $\frac{1}{4}$-inch phone jack connectors. XLRs let you run long mic cables without hum pickup, and they can provide phantom power that condenser mics need in order to work.

- Number of built-in digital effects: Up to 8 stereo or 16 mono. Examples of effects are reverberation, echo, flanging, chorus, and compression. They add sonic excitement and a professional touch to your productions.

- Types of EQ: 2-band or 3-band, fixed or parametric. EQ or equalization means tone control. A 2-band EQ adjusts bass and treble; a 3-band adjusts bass, midrange, and treble. A fixed-frequency EQ is less flexible than a parametric or sweepable EQ, which lets you adjust the frequency range you want to work on.

- Backup options: Removable hard drive, DAT, ADAT, CD-R.

- Levels of undo: Up to 1000. The Undo function lets you undo an editing change you just did. If you don't like how an edit sounded, you can press Undo and go back to the way things were before you made the change.

- Number of locate points: Up to 1000. A locate point is a point in time in the recording that you can have the recorder memorize and locate later. For example, you might want to mark the time where the beginning of a song is, so you can tap a button and go there instantly.

- Expansion ports for SMPTE and MTC sync, MDM interface, and extra ins and outs. Beginners probably don't need these features, but they let you connect your multitracker to other devices.

- MIDI implementation: MIDI Machine Code (MMC), Control Change (CC). These features let you control the mixer via MIDI commands.

- Types of synchronization: SMPTE, Word Clock, MTC, MIDI Clock with Song Position Pointer, ADAT, DA-88, RS-422. These are various formats that you might want your multitracker to sync with.

- Jog/shuttle wheel to "scrub" audio—play it slowly forward and backward to locate an edit point.

- Remote control.

- Automated mixing. A memory circuit in the multitracker remembers your song-mix settings and mix changes. The next time you play the song, the memory circuit resets the mixer to those settings automatically. Some multitrackers have motorized faders, so that the faders move up and down just as they did when you adjusted them while mixing.

- Editing (cut and paste, etc.). Editing lets you do all sorts of things with the song arrangement. You might remove parts of songs that you don't want to keep, loop a drum part so that it repeats continuously, or copy a chorus to several points in a song.

- Video output to plug into a computer monitor screen. During editing, it's a lot easier to see details in the sound waveform if you can plug a large monitor into your multitracker.

- Mastering tools and CD-burning ability. In mastering you compile a playlist of mixed songs from which you can create an album. Some multitrackers include programs that let you record your songs on a CD-R recorder, either external or built-in.

## MiniDisc Recorder–Mixer

Introduced by Sony in 1991, the MiniDisc (MD) is a convenient recording medium that is removable, low cost, and near-CD quality. A MiniDisc recorder-mixer is a multitrack MD recorder and mixer in a single, affordable package. It records and plays 4 or 8 audio tracks at once on a removable MD data disc. About the size of a floppy disk, an MD data disc records 8 tracks for 18.5 minutes or 4 tracks for 37 minutes. The built-in mixer has faders and knobs and includes a small LED screen for non-graphical editing.

Both MiniDisc and hard-disk multitrackers let you record virtual tracks. A **virtual track** is a 1-channel recording of a single take or performance on a random-access medium. Most random-access recorders let you record several virtual tracks or takes of a single instrument, then select which take you want to hear during mixdown. For example, suppose you have a 16-track hard-disk recorder. You could record up to 255 virtual tracks of a vocal on hard disk. Then during mixdown, choose which virtual track will play as one of those 16 tracks. Some recorders can be set up to select parts of different virtual tracks during playback. For example, play vocal take 15 for the verse, play vocal take 3 for the chorus, and so on.

In other words, you can associate several virtual tracks, or takes, with a single "real" track. You might play 8 tracks at once, and you can choose which virtual track (take) plays on each track. For example, you can record several takes of a guitar solo—keeping each one—and choose the best take during mixdown. You also can create a **composite track**, which is made of the best parts of several takes.

## MiniDisc Editing

Let's go over MiniDisc editing in detail. **Song Copy** duplicates a song at a new location, while **Track Copy** copies data from one track to another. **Song Divide** lets you divide a song in two at the current counter location. With this function, you can create sections—verse, chorus, etc.—that you can play or repeat in any order. You can also remove noises before and after songs. **Song Combine** joins divided parts from the same song. Some units let you move individual tracks in time. The **Cue List** feature is a list of the song sections in the order you want them played. Sections can be looped or repeated. The recorder will play down the cue list, assembling the song from its sections. A **Program Play List** is a list of the songs in the order you want them played. **Scale Factor Edit** can be used to match the volume of tracks recorded at different levels, or to create fade-ins and fade-outs.

## Advantages of MiniDisc and Hard-Disk Multitrackers over Cassette Multitrackers

Although a cassette multitracker costs little and is relatively easy to use, MiniDisc and hard-disk multitrackers offer several advantages.

MD and HD have cleaner sound: no tape hiss, wow and flutter, or crosstalk and much less distortion.

MD and HD recorders are faster to work with than cassette recorders. That's because they have random access: You can instantly go to and play any part of the recorded program. In contrast, a cassette recorder is slower because its data is sequential. You must fast-forward or rewind to the part you want to hear.

Unlike cassette, MD and HD require no open track for bouncing. You can bounce 4 tracks down to 2 tracks on the same disc.

Other advantages:

- Able to write disc titles and track titles on the disc
- No need to clean heads
- Less generation loss
- More accurate recording timer
- More durable medium
- Tighter punch-ins
- Jog/shuttle wheel
- Markers (pointers or locate points) can be added
- Cue list playback and Program Play List
- Editing: Track and song copy/erase, song divide, song combine, etc.

## MD versus MDM

How does a MiniDisc recorder compare to a Modular Digital Multitrack recorder, such as the Alesis ADAT or TASCAM DA-88? The MiniDisc's random access offers instant locating of song parts, instant nondestructive editing of tracks, and fewer errors than tape. But MDM sounds very slightly better than MD because the MDM does not compress the data. MiniDisc is more reliable and lasts longer than MDM tape.

The MDM allows longer nonstop recording time, as shown in the table below:

| | | |
|---|---|---|
| TASCAM DA-88 | 8 tracks | 108+ minutes |
| 140 MB MD Data disc | 8 tracks | 18.5 minutes |
| 140 MB MD Data disc | 4 tracks | 37.0 minutes |
| 160 MB 74-min. MiniDisc | 2 tracks | 74.0 minutes |
| Iomega Jaz 2 GB drive | 2 tracks | 192.0 minutes |

## MiniDisc versus DAW

In a DAW you can change projects quickly by using a removable hard drive—such as an Iomega Jaz drive—but MiniDiscs cost much less. A Jaz 2 GB disk costs about $99, while a MiniDisc costs about $2. (The Jaz disk holds more data, though; see the table above.) A DAW has higher sound quality than the MiniDisc and allows much more extensive editing at the waveform level.

## MiniDisc versus Hard Disk

HD sounds a little cleaner than MD because MD uses ATRAC data compression, but HD does not. Although MiniDisc is more reliable and lasts longer than hard disk, hard disk wins over MiniDisc in the area of editing. WAV files stored on a hard disk can be edited in your computer; a MiniDisc's ATRAC data file cannot. However, you can do simple edits in the MD recorder itself.

Cassette and MiniDisc have the advantage that, once you are done with a project, you simply remove the cassette or MiniDisc and put in a blank one for the next project. With an HD recorder–mixer, you must back up the project on a removable hard drive, then erase the project on disk to make room for the next one.

Which format is right for you? A cassette multitracker features low cost and ease of use. MiniDisc offers fast access, editing, near-CD sound quality, fairly low cost, and no need to back up data. A hard-disk recorder–mixer provides the best sound and the most powerful features, although it can be challenging to learn and requires a backup device.

For more information on random-access multitrackers, see these Web sites: minidisc.org, yamaha.com, fostex.com, akai.com, tascam.com, rolandus.com, and korgusa.com.

## MiniDisc Technology

Let's look at the MiniDisc format in more detail.

A blank MiniDisc is a rewritable, magneto-optical medium read by a laser. The disc itself is like a miniature compact disc inside a 2.5-inch square housing. A write-protect tab on the housing prevents accidental erasure. Estimated disc life is 30 years, but a strong magnet near the disc can erase data.

Two types of blank discs are available: the regular 74-minute MiniDisc used in 2-track recorders, and the MD Data disc used in multitrack recorders.

Most MiniDisc devices record audio at 44.1 kHz, 16 bits, but 24-bit recording is available in some units.

To fit all this data on a small disc, MD recorders use a data compression scheme called ATRAC: Adaptive Transform Acoustic Coding. It reduces by 5:1 the storage needed for digital audio. ATRAC is a perceptual coding method, which omits data deemed inaudible due to masking.

For example, if an audio signal has two sounds that are about the same frequency, and one sound is louder than the other, the quieter sound will be inaudible due to masking. So ATRAC removes the quieter sound, which would be inaudible anyway.

ATRAC has had several revision levels; the latest version (as of August 2000) is 4.5. The higher the version number, the better the sound. Some reviewers have claimed that version 4.5 sounds essentially the same as compact discs when playing a musical program. Earlier versions are said to be near-CD in quality, and much better than MP3. All versions are compatible.

Sound quality depends not only on the ATRAC version, but also on the quality and bit depth of the A/D converter in the recorder. Although the MiniDisc format uses data compression, its stereo digital output is standard 16-bit S/PDIF.

There is a slight generation loss when tracks are copied or bounced. The signal is ATRAC-processed with each copy. After more than five copies or so, the sound cumulatively begins to take on a mid-to-low rumble and a high-frequency squeak.

MiniDisc recorders can make ATRAC-compressed copies of CDs directly from the CD player's digital output.

### Two-Track MiniDisc Recorders

Two-track recorders come in portable style or component style. The portable MiniDisc Walkman™ format is becoming popular with news reporters who need to carry a small, high-quality recorder in the field. Reporters can edit the recording using buttons on the recorder.

Portable 2-track MD recorders have been used for documenting musical groups at folk festivals. The recordist walks around the festival, recording various groups of musicians (with their permission, let's hope!). MiniDisc also offers an easy way to record school concerts, sound effects, or your band's gigs.

Can you use a 2-track MiniDisc to record a stereo master of your mixdowns? You could, but CD-R and DAT masters are preferred for their higher sound quality. Also, many mastering houses do not accept MiniDisc masters.

# Portable IC Recorder

This is a digital recorder with no moving parts. The first device of this type was the Denon DN-F20R. Intended mainly for field recording and electronic news gathering, it records audio digitally on a CompactFlash Type I IC memory card. Each card has a memory capacity of up to 192 MB. Up to 999 audio programs can be recorded in stereo or mono, and in MPEG2 layer 2, MPEG1 layer 2 or linear PCM (.WAV) formats.

The Marantz PMD680 PC Card Recorder is a mono IC recorder with $1/4$-inch and XLR inputs, SPDIF and analog outputs, and a telephone jack. A slot contains static RAM cards, which can be fed into a card reader attached to a PC. The recorder offers a choice of MP2, Broadcast Wave, or WAV file formats and three bit rates.

The Zoom PS-02 Palmtop Studio includes three audio tracks, drum and bass machines, guitar multi-effects, mixer, a built-in mic, and a tuner in a chassis that fits in your pocket. Effective as a digital sketchpad recorder, the PS-02 stores over 2 hours of program on a 128 MB Smart-Media card.

The Nagra RCX220 is a handheld audio recorder that digitizes audio with Digigram MPEG1 layer 2 compression. It records to Flash RAM and transfers the audio via USB to a computer for editing.

# Backup

So far we've looked at several types of digital recording devices. With any device, it's important to back up or make a copy of your recordings. The hard drive on which you store your projects will eventually crash. DAT tapes and video tapes have a limited lifespan as well. So it's vital to back up your data periodically.

Some backup systems are ADAT, TASCAM DTRS, MO (magneto-optical), CD-R, CD-RW, tape drives, Iomega Zip drive (100 MB), Jaz drive (2 GB), DVD-RAM, and DVD-RW. It's common to back up DAW projects on removable hard drives. CD and DVD are perhaps the most long-lasting formats for archiving. Many engineers prefer to archive audio programs on analog tape as well as digital.

# Digital Recording Options

Having covered several types of digital recording devices, let's briefly describe some options that apply to all of them.

- Sampling frequency for high-quality audio can be 44.1 kHz, 48 kHz, 96 kHz, or 192 kHz. Higher sampling frequencies sound better but need more disk storage space and faster throughput.
- Word length (bit depth or resolution) for high-quality audio can be 16, 20, or 24 bits. More bits sound better but need more storage and throughput.
- CD quality is 44.1 kHz/16 bits. State of the art is Super Audio CD or linear PCM at 192 kHz/24 bits (but you're more likely to see 96 kHz/24 bits).
- Number of tracks or channels (not including virtual tracks):

2 tracks in DAT, CD, DVD, and portable IC recorder.

2 to 8 tracks in MO recorders.

8 or 16 tracks in hard-disk recorder–mixers.

8, 16, or 24 tracks in hard-disk recorders (some combine to make 48 tracks).

2, 8, 16, 24, or 32 tracks in DAWs.

2 to 48 tracks in reel-to-reel recorders.

8 to 128 tracks in modular digital multitracks.

- Storage media: Hi-8 videocassette (TASCAM DTRS), SVHS video-cassette (ADAT), hard drive, MO, DAT, CD, DVD, MiniDisc, open-reel tape, flash memory card.
- Other options:

  Built-in mixer

  Controller surface

  LCD screen versus computer monitor

As we've seen, there is a wide variety of digital recording formats. Learn all you can about digital technology, then choose the formats that meet your needs.

# EFFECTS AND SIGNAL PROCESSORS

With effects, your mix sounds more like a real "production" and less like a bland home recording. You might simulate a concert hall with reverb. Put a guitar in space with stereo chorus. Make a kick drum punchy by adding compression. Used on all pop-music records, effects can enhance the basic sounds on tape by adding spaciousness and excitement. They are essential if you want to produce a commercial sound. But many jazz, folk, and classical groups sound fine without any effects.

To add an effect to a track, you feed its signal from your mixer's aux send to an effects device, or **signal processor** (Figure 11.1). It modifies the signal in a controlled way. Then the modified signal returns to your mixer.

This chapter describes the most popular signal processors and suggests how to use them.

## Equalizer

Recall from Chapter 2 that an equalizer (usually in the mixer) is a sophisticated tone control, something like the bass and treble controls in a stereo system.

Equalization (EQ) lets you improve on reality: add crispness to dull cymbals; add bite to a wimpy electric guitar. Or EQ can make a track sound more natural: For instance, remove tubbiness from a close-miked vocal.

To understand how EQ works, we need to know the meaning of a spectrum. Each instrument or voice produces a wide range of frequencies

**Figure 11.1** A signal processor.

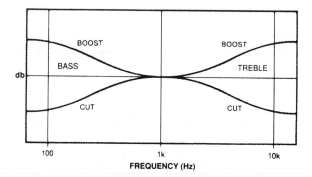

**Figure 11.2**
The effect of the bass and
treble control.

called its **spectrum**—the fundamentals and harmonics. The spectrum gives
each instrument its distinctive tone quality or timbre.

If you boost or cut certain frequencies in the spectrum, you change
the tone quality of the instrument. EQ adjusts the bass, treble, and
midrange of a sound by turning up or down certain frequency ranges. That
is, it alters the frequency response. For example, a boost (a level increase)
in the range centered at 10 kHz makes percussion sound bright and crisp.
A cut at the same frequency dulls the sound.

## *Types of EQ*

Equalizers range from simple to complex. The most basic type is a **bass
and treble control** (labeled LF EQ and HF EQ). Figure 11.2 shows its effect
on frequency response. Typically, this type has up to 15 dB of boost or cut
at 100 Hz (for the low-frequency EQ knob) and at 10 kHz (for the high-
frequency EQ knob).

With a three-band EQ you can boost or cut the lows, mids, and highs
at fixed frequencies (Figure 11.3). Sweepable EQ is more flexible because
you can "tune in" the exact frequency range needing adjustment (Figure
11.4). If your mixer has sweepable EQ, one knob sets the center frequency
while another sets the amount of boost or cut.

Parametric EQ lets you set the frequency, amount of boost/cut,
and bandwidth—the range of frequencies affected. Figure 11.5 shows how
a parametric equalizer varies the bandwidth of the boosted part of the
spectrum.

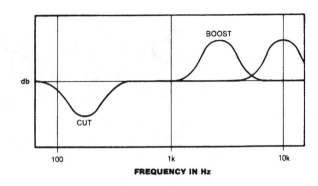

**Figure 11.3**
The effect of multiple-frequency equalization.

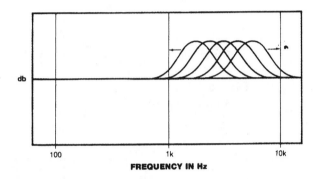

**Figure 11.4**
The effect of sweepable equalization.

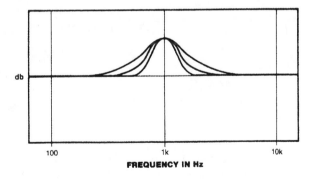

**Figure 11.5**
Curves that illustrate varying the bandwidth of a parametric equalizer.

A graphic equalizer (Figure 11.6) is usually outside the mixing console. This type has a row of slide pots that work on 5 to 31 frequency bands. When the controls are adjusted, their positions graphically show the resulting frequency response. Usually, a graphic equalizer is used for monitor-speaker EQ, or is patched into a channel for sophisticated tonal tweaking.

Equalizers can also be classified by the shape of their frequency response. Peaking EQ shapes the response like a hill or peak when set for

**Figure 11.6** A graphic equalizer.

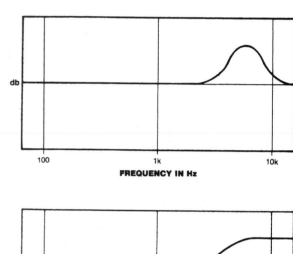

**Figure 11.7**
Peaking equalization at
7 kHz.

**Figure 11.8**
Shelving equalization at
7 kHz.

a boost (Figure 11.7). With shelving EQ, the shape of the frequency response resembles a shelf (Figure 11.8).

A filter causes a rolloff at the frequency extremes. It sharply rejects (attenuates) frequencies above or below a certain frequency. Figure 11.9 shows three types of filters: lowpass, highpass, and bandpass.

For example, a 10 kHz lowpass filter (high-cut filter) removes frequencies above 10 kHz. Its response is down 3 dB at 10 kHz and more above that. This reduces hiss-type noise without affecting tone quality as much as a gradual treble rolloff would. A 100 Hz highpass filter (low-cut filter) attenuates frequencies below 100 Hz. Its response is down 3 dB at 100 Hz and more below that. This removes low-pitched noises such as air-

**Figure 11.9**
Lowpass, highpass, and bandpass filters.

handler rumble or breath pops. A 1 kHz bandpass filter cuts frequencies above and below a frequency band centered at 1 kHz.

The crossover filter in most monitor speakers consists of lowpass, highpass, and bandpass filters. They send the lows to the woofer, mids to the midrange, and highs to the tweeter.

A filter is named for the steepness of its rolloff: 6 dB per octave (first order), 12 dB/octave (second order), 18 dB/octave (third order), and so on.

## *How to Use EQ*

If your mixer has bass and treble controls, their frequencies are preset (usually at 100 Hz and 10 kHz). Set the EQ knob at 0 to have no effect ("flat" setting). Turn it clockwise for a boost; turn it counterclockwise for a cut. If your mixer has multiple-frequency EQ or sweepable EQ, one knob sets the frequency range and another sets the amount of boost or cut.

Table 11.1 shows the fundamentals and harmonics of musical instruments and voices. The harmonics given represent an approximate range. For each instrument, turn up the lower end of the fundamentals to get warmth and fullness. Turn down the fundamentals if the tone is too bassy or tubby. Turn up the harmonics for presence and definition; turn down the harmonics if the tone is too harsh or sizzly.

Percussion, cymbals and muted trumpet actually have some energy up to 80 to 100 kHz.

Here are some suggested frequencies to adjust for specific instruments. If you want the effects described below, apply boost. If you don't, apply cut. Try these suggestions and accept only the sounds you like:

- Bass: Full and deep at 60 Hz, growl at 600 Hz, presence at 2.5 kHz, string noise at 3 kHz and up.
- Electric guitar: Thumpy at 60 Hz, full at 100 Hz, puffy at 500 Hz, presence or bite at 2 to 3 kHz, sizzly and raspy above 6 kHz.
- Drums: Full at 100 Hz, wooly at 250 to 600 Hz, trashy at 1 to 3 kHz, attack at 5 kHz, sizzly and crisp at 10 kHz.

**Table 11.1**   Frequency Ranges of Musical Instruments and Voices

| Instrument | Fundamentals | Harmonics |
|---|---|---|
| Flute | 261–2349 Hz | 3–8 kHz |
| Oboe | 261–1568 Hz | 2–12 kHz |
| Clarinet | 165–1568 Hz | 2–10 kHz |
| Bassoon | 62–587 Hz | 1–7 kHz |
| Trumpet | 165–988 Hz | 1–7.5 kHz |
| French horn | 87–880 Hz | 1–6 kHz |
| Trombone | 73–587 Hz | 1–7.5 kHz |
| Tuba | 49–587 Hz | 1–4 kHz |
| Snare drum | 100–200 Hz | 1–20 kHz |
| Kick drum | 30–147 Hz | 1–6 kHz |
| Cymbals | 300–587 Hz | 1–15 kHz |
| Violin | 196–3136 Hz | 4–15 kHz |
| Viola | 131–1175 Hz | 2–8.5 kHz |
| Cello | 65–698 Hz | 1–6.5 kHz |
| Acoustic bass | 41–294 Hz | 1–5 kHz |
| Electric bass | 41–300 Hz | 1–7 kHz |
| Acoustic guitar | 82–988 Hz | 1–15 kHz |
| Electric guitar | 82–1319 Hz | 1–3.5 kHz (through amp) |
| Electric guitar | 82–1319 Hz | 1–15 kHz (direct) |
| Piano | 28–4196 Hz | 5–8 kHz |
| Bass (voice) | 87–392 Hz | 1–12 kHz |
| Tenor (voice) | 131–494 Hz | 1–12 kHz |
| Alto (voice) | 175–698 Hz | 2–12 kHz |
| Soprano (voice) | 247–1175 Hz | 2–12 kHz |

- Kick drum: Full and powerful below 60 Hz, papery at 300 to 800 Hz (cut at 400 to 600 Hz for better tone), click or attack at 2 to 6 kHz.
- Sax: Warm at 500 Hz, harsh at 3 kHz, key noise above 10 kHz.
- Acoustic guitar: Full or thumpy at 80 Hz, presence at 5 kHz, pick noise above 10 kHz.
- Voice: Full at 100 to 150 Hz (males), full at 200 to 250 Hz (females), honky or nasal at 500 Hz to 1 kHz, presence at 5 kHz, sibilance ("s" sounds) above 6 kHz.

Example: A vocal track sounds too full or bassy. Reach for the LF EQ knob (say, 100 Hz) and turn it down until the voice sounds natural. To reduce muddiness on snare, bass, electric guitar, or vocal, cut around 300 Hz.

Set EQ to the approximate frequency range you need to work on. Then apply full boost or cut so the effect is easily audible. Finally, fine-tune the frequency and amount of boost or cut until the tonal balance is the way you like it.

What if an instrument sounds honky, tubby, or harsh, and you don't know what freq to tweak? Set a sweepable equalizer for extreme boost. Then sweep the frequencies until you find the frequency range matching the coloration. Cut that range by the amount that sounds right. For example, a piano miked with the lid closed might have a tubby coloration—maybe too much output around 300 Hz. Set your low-frequency EQ for boost, and vary the center frequency until the tubbiness is exaggerated. Then cut at that frequency until the piano sounds natural.

In general, avoid excessive boost because it can distort the signal. Try cutting the lows instead of boosting the highs. To reduce muddiness or enhance clarity, cut 1 to 2 dB around 300 Hz—either on individual instruments or on the entire mix. Don't boost everything at the same frequency.

## When to Use EQ

Before using EQ, try to get the desired tone quality by changing the mic or its placement. This gives a more natural effect than EQ. Many purists shun the use of EQ, complaining of excessive phase shift or ringing caused by the equalizer—a "strained" sound. Instead, they use high-quality microphones, carefully placed, to get a natural tonal balance without EQ.

Suppose you still need some EQ. Should you EQ while recording or mixing? If you mix more than one instrument to the same track, you can't EQ them independently during mixdown unless their frequency ranges are far apart. To explain, suppose a recorded track contains lead guitar and vocals. If you add a midrange boost to the guitar, you'll hear it on the vocals, too. The only solution is to EQ the lead guitar by itself when you record it.

If you assign each instrument to its own track, the usual practice is to record flat (without EQ) and then equalize the track during mixdown.

Sometimes the instruments need a lot of EQ to sound good. If so, you might want to record with EQ so that the playback for the musicians will sound good. When you play the multitrack recording through your monitor mixer, the recording may not sound right unless the tracks are already EQ'd. (That's assuming the monitor mixer in your board has no EQ.)

When you do a bass cut or treble boost, you'll get a better S/N by applying this EQ during recording, instead of during mixdown. But if you're doing a treble cut, apply it during mixdown to reduce tape hiss.

## *Uses of EQ*

Here are some applications for EQ:

- **Improve tone quality.** This is the main use of EQ: to make an instrument sound better tonally. For example, you might use a high-frequency rolloff on a singer to reduce sibilance, or on a direct-recorded electric guitar to take the "edge" off the sound. You could boost 100 Hz on a floor tom to get a fuller sound, or cut around 250 Hz on a bass guitar for clarity. Cut around 100 Hz to reduce bass buildup on massed harmony vocals. The frequency response and placement of each mic affect tone quality as well.

  Although you can set the EQ for each track when it is soloed, a better way is to set the equalizers when the entire mix is playing. That's because one instrument can mask or hide certain frequencies in another instrument. For example, the cymbals might mask the "s" sounds in the vocal, making the vocal sound dull—even though it might sound fine when soloed.

- **Create an effect.** Extreme EQ reduces fidelity, but it also can make interesting sound effects. Sharply rolling off the lows and highs on a voice, for instance, gives it a "telephone" sound. A 1 kHz bandpass filter does the same thing. To make a mono keyboard track sound stereo, send it to two mixer channels. Boost lows and cut highs in one channel panned left; cut lows and boost highs in the other channel panned right.

- **Reduce noise and leakage.** You can reduce low-frequency noises—bass leakage, air-conditioner rumble, mic-stand thumps—by turning down the lows below the range of the instrument you're recording.

For example, a fiddle's lowest frequency is about 200 Hz, so you'd set the equalizer's frequency range to 40 or 60 Hz and apply cut. This rolloff won't change the fiddle's tone quality because the rolloff is below the range of frequencies that the fiddle produces. Similarly, a kick drum has little or no output above 9 kHz, so you can filter out highs above 9 kHz on the kick drum to reduce cymbal leakage. If you do this filtering during mixdown, it will also reduce tape hiss. Filtering out frequencies below 100 Hz on most instruments reduces air-conditioning rumble and breath pops. Try rolling off the lows on audience mics to prevent muddy bass.

- **Compensate for the Fletcher–Munson effect.** As discovered by Fletcher and Munson, the ear is less sensitive to bass and treble at low volumes than at high volumes. So, when you record a very loud instrument and play it back at a lower level, it might lack bass and treble. To restore these, you may need to boost the lows (around 100 Hz) and the highs (around 4 kHz) when recording loud rock groups. The louder the group, the more boost you need. It also helps to use cardioid mics with proximity effect (for bass boost) and a presence peak (for treble boost).

- **Make a pleasing blend.** If you mix two instruments that sound alike, such as lead guitar and rhythm guitar, they tend to mush together— it's hard to tell what each is playing. You can make them more distinct by equalizing them differently. For example, make the lead guitar edgy by boosting 3 kHz, and make the rhythm guitar mellow by cutting 3 kHz. Then you'll hear a more pleasing blend and a clearer mix. The same philosophy applies to bass guitar and kick drum. Since they occupy about the same low-frequency range, they tend to mask or cover each other. To make them distinct, either fatten the bass and thin out the kick a little, or vice versa. The idea is to give each instrument its own space in the frequency spectrum. For example: the bass fills in the lows, synth chords emphasize midbass, lead guitar adds edge in the upper mids, and cymbals add sparkle in the highs.

- **Compensate for mic placement.** Sometimes you are forced to mike very close to reject background sounds and leakage. But a close mic emphasizes the part of the instrument that the mic is near. This gives a colored tone quality, but EQ can partly compensate for it. Suppose you had to record an acoustic guitar with a mic near the sound hole. The guitar track will sound bassy because the sound hole radiates strong low frequencies. But you can turn down the lows on your mixer to restore a natural tonal balance. This use of EQ can save the day by fixing poorly recorded tracks in live concert recordings.

During a concert, the stage monitors might be blaring into your recording/P.A. microphones, so you're forced to mike close in order to reject monitor leakage and feedback. This close placement, or the monitor leakage itself, can give the recording an unnatural tone quality. In this case, EQ is the only way to get usable tracks.

- **"Re-mix" a single track.** If you have a track that contains two different instruments, sometimes you can change the mix within that track by using EQ. Imagine a track that has both bass and synth. By using LF EQ, you can bring the bass up or down without affecting the synth very much. Mixing with EQ is more effective when the two instruments are far apart in their frequency ranges.

Whenever you record, the ideal situation is to use the right mic in the right position, and in a good-sounding room. Then you don't need or want equalization. Otherwise, though, your recordings will sound better with EQ than without it.

# Compressor

A compressor acts like an automatic volume control, turning down the volume when the signal gets too loud. Here's why it's necessary:

Suppose you're recording a female vocalist. Sometimes she sings too softly and gets buried in the mix; other times she hits loud notes, blasting the listener and saturating the tape. Or she may move toward and away from the mic while singing, so that her average recording level changes.

To control this problem, you can **ride gain**—turn her down when she gets too loud; turn her up when she gets too quiet. But it's hard to anticipate these changes. You might prefer to use a compressor, which does the same thing automatically. It reduces the gain (amplification) when the input signal exceeds a preset level (called the **threshold**). The greater the input level, the less the gain. As a result, loud notes are made softer, so the dynamic range is reduced (Figure 11.10).

Compression keeps the level of vocals or instruments more constant, so they are easier to hear throughout the mix. And it prevents loud notes that may saturate the tape. Also, it can be used for special effects— say, to make drums sound fatter, or to increase the sustain on a bass guitar. In pro studios, compression is used almost always on vocals; often on bass guitar, kick drum, and acoustic guitar; and sometimes on other instruments.

Doesn't compression rob the music of its expressive dynamics? Yes, if overdone. But a vocal that gets too loud and soft is annoying. You need to tame it with a compressor. Even then, you can tell when the vocalist is

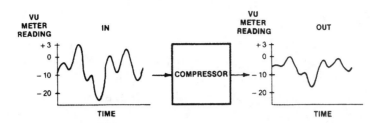

**Figure 11.10** Compression.

singing loudly by the tone of the voice. It also helps to compress the bass and kick drum to ensure a uniform, driving beat.

You can avoid vocal compression if the singer uses proper mic technique. He or she should back away from the mic on loud notes, and come in close on soft notes. To tell whether you need a compressor, listen to your finished mix. If you can understand all the words, and no notes are too loud, omit the compressor.

## *Using a Compressor*

Normally, you compress individual tracks or instruments, not the entire mix. You want to compress only the stuff that needs it. Compressing the overall mix is wise when your mix will be duplicated on cassette, because cassettes have a small dynamic range. To compress a stereo mix, you need a 2-channel compressor with a stereo link, which keeps the left–right balance from changing.

Should you compress while tracking or mixing? If you compress while tracking, that improves the S/N of the tape track, but you must decide on compressor settings during the recording session. If you compress tracks during mixdown, you can change the settings at will.

Let's describe the controls on the compressor. Some compressors have few controls; most of their settings are preset at the factory.

### Compression Ratio or Slope

This is the ratio of the change in input level to the change in output level. For example, a 2:1 ratio means that for every 2 dB change in input level, the output changes 1 dB. A 20 dB change in input level results in a 10 dB change in the output, and so on.

Typical ratio settings are 2:1 to 4:1. A "soft knee" or "over easy" characteristic is a low compression ratio for low-level signals and a high ratio for high-level signals. Some manufacturers say that this characteristic sounds more natural than a fixed compression ratio.

## Threshold

This is the input level above which compression occurs. Set the threshold high (about −5 VU) to compress only the loudest notes; set it low (−10 or −20 VU) to compress a broader range of notes. A setting of −10 is typical. If the compressor has a fixed threshold, adjust the amount of compression with the input level control.

## Gain Reduction

This is the number of dB that the gain is reduced by the compressor. It varies with the input level. You set the ratio and threshold controls so that the gain is reduced on loud notes by an amount that sounds right. The amount of gain reduction shows up on a meter. Three to 6 dB is typical.

## Attack Time

This is how fast the compressor reduces the gain when it's hit by a musical attack. Typical attack times range from 0.25 to 10 msec. Some compressors adjust the attack time automatically to suit the music; others have a factory-set attack time. The longer the attack time, the larger the peaks that are passed before gain reduction occurs. So, a long attack time sounds punchy; a short attack time reduces punch by softening the attack.

## Release Time

This is how fast the gain returns to normal after a loud passage ends. It's the time the compressor takes to reach 63% of its normal gain. You can set the release time from about 50 msec to several seconds. For bass instruments, the release time must be longer than about 0.4 second to prevent harmonic distortion.

Short release times make the compressor follow rapid volume changes in the music, and keep the average level higher. But since the noise rises along with the gain, short release times can give a pumping or breathing sound. Long release times sound more natural. If the release time is too long, though, a loud passage will reduce the gain during a subsequent quiet passage. In some units, the release time varies automatically, or is factory-set to a useful value.

## Output-Level Control

Also called **make-up gain**, this sets the compressor's output signal to the level your mixer wants to see. Some compressors keep the output level constant when other controls are varied. Spend some free time playing with all the settings so you learn how they affect the sound. Play various instruments and vocals through a compressor, vary the settings, and take notes on what you hear.

Some compressors have a **side chain**. This is a pair of in/out jacks for connecting an equalizer. To compress only the sibilant sounds on a vocal track, boost the side-chain EQ around 10 kHz. To compress only the breath pops on a vocal track, boost the side-chain EQ around 20 Hz.

A **multiband** or **split-frequency** compressor divides the audio band into three or four bands (bass, mids, treble) and compresses each band separately. That way, the compressor can squash a loud bass note, or soften "s" sounds, without bringing down the overall level. Multiband compressors are often applied to the final mix of each song during mixdown or mastering.

## Connecting a Compressor

Connect a compressor in series with the signal you want to compress, in one of the following ways:

- To compress one instrument or voice while recording: Locate the input module of the instrument you want to compress. Connect the compressor between the insert send-and-return jacks (Chapter 12 explains these terms). Or, take a signal from the input module's direct out. Feed that into the compressor, and feed the compressor output to the tape track.

- To compress a group of instruments while recording: Locate the bus output of the instruments you want to compress. Go from bus out to compressor in, and go from compressor out to tape-track in. If the bus has insert jacks, you could connect to them instead.

- To compress one tape track during mixdown: Go from track out to compressor in, and go from compressor out to mixer tape in. Or just patch into the insert jacks for that track's mixer module.

# Limiter

A limiter keeps signal peaks from exceeding a preset level. Limiters are used to prevent DAT overload during field recording, or to prevent P.A. power amps from clipping. In a digital audio workstation, you might use limiting to reduce the level of signal peaks. Then raise the overall level—bring it up to maximum level by normalization. Limiting and normalization create a louder program on your finished CD, but without compressing the song's dynamics.

The compression ratio in a limiter is very high—10:1 or greater—and the threshold is set high, say at 0 VU. For input levels up to 0 VU, the output level matches the input. For input levels above 0 VU, the output level stays at 0 VU. This prevents overload in the device following the limiter.

While a compressor reduces the overall dynamic range of the music, a limiter affects only the highest peaks (Figure 11.11). To act on these rapid peaks, limiters have a very fast attack time—1 microsecond to 1 millisecond.

A compressor/limiter carries out both of the functions in its name. It compresses the average signal levels over a wide range, and limits peaks to prevent overload. It has two thresholds: one low for the compressor and one high for the limiter.

# Noise Gate

A noise gate (expander) acts like an on–off switch that removes noises during pauses in an audio signal. It reduces the gain when the input level falls below a preset threshold. That is, when an instrument stops playing for a moment, the noise gate drops the volume—removing any noise and leakage during the pause (Figure 11.12).

**Note:** The gate does *not* remove noise while the instrument is playing.

Where is it used? The noise gate helps to clean up drum tracks by removing leakage between beats. It can shorten the decay time of the drums, giving a very tight sound. During a mixdown, you might gate each track of an analog recorder to reduce tape hiss. If you're recording a noisy guitar amp, try a gate to cut out the buzz and hiss between phrases.

How do you use a noise gate? Patch it between a tape-track output and a mixer tape input. Play the tape. Set the gate's threshold so that hiss and leakage go away during pauses. If the gate chops off each note, grad-

**Figure 11.11** Limiting.

**Figure 11.12** Noise gating.

ually turn down the threshold. Set the release time short for drums and longer for instruments that have a long sustain.

Excellent tapes can be made without gating. But if you want a tighter sound, gates come in handy. Some signal processors have compression, limiting, and noise gating in a single package.

Some gates have a side-chain input or key input. It's an input for an external signal that controls the gating action. The control signal triggers the output of the gate's main audio path. For example, you could feed a bass guitar through the noise gate, and gate the bass with a kick-drum signal fed into the side chain. Then the bass will follow the kick drum's envelope.

# Delay: Echo, Doubling, Chorus, Flanging

A digital delay (or a delay program for a computer) takes an input signal, holds it in a memory chip, then plays it back after a short delay—about 1 msec to 1 second (Figure 11.13). Delay is the time interval between the input signal and its repetition at the output of the delay device.

If you listen to the delayed signal by itself, it sounds the same as the undelayed ("dry") signal. But if you combine the delayed and dry signals, you may hear two distinct sounds: the signal and its repetition. By delaying a signal, a processor can create several effects such as echo, repeating echo, doubling, chorus, and flanging.

## *Echo*

If the delay is about 50 msec to 1 second, the delayed repetition of a sound is called an **echo**. This is shown in Figure 11.14 by the two pulses. Echoes occur naturally when sound waves travel to a distant room surface, bounce off, and return later to the listener—repeating the original sound. A delay unit can mimic this effect.

**Figure 11.13** Delaying the signal.

**Figure 11.14** Echo.

In setting up a mix with echo, you want to hear both the dry sound and its echo. You do this by creating an effects loop: from the mixer, to the effects box, back to the mixer. Here's how:

1. On the delay unit, set the dry/wet mix control all the way to "wet." Then the output of the delay unit will be only the delayed signal.

2. Suppose you want to use aux1 as the echo control. Connect aux1 send to delay unit IN. Connect delay unit OUT to bus 1 and 2 IN (or to the effects-return jacks).

3. Find the mixer module for the instrument you want to add echo to.

4. Assign the instrument to busses 1 and 2. Monitor busses 1 and 2.

5. Find the knobs labeled Bus 1 IN and Bus 2 IN. They might be called "Aux Return" or "Effects Return." Turn them up to 0, about three-fourths of the way up.

6. Turn up the aux1 send knob, and there's your echo.

The delayed sound mixes with the dry sound in busses 1 and 2. You hear both sounds, which together make an echo. Each aux knob controls the amount of echo on each track, while the effect-return knobs control the overall amount of echo.

## Slap Echo

A delay from 50 to 200 msec is called a slap echo or slapback echo. It was often used in 1950's rock 'n' roll tunes, and still is used today.

## Repeating Echo

Most delay units can be made to feed the output signal back into the input, internally. Then the signal is re-delayed many times. This creates a repeating echo—several echoes that are evenly spaced in time (Figure 11.15). The regeneration control sets the number of repeats.

Repeating echo is most musical if you set the delay time to create an echo rhythm that fits the tempo of the song. A slow repeating echo—0.5 second between repeats, for example—gives an outer-space or haunted-house effect.

# *Doubling*

If you set the delay around 30 to 60 msec, the effect is called doubling or automatic double tracking (ADT). It gives an instrument or voice a fuller sound, especially if the dry and delayed signals are panned to opposite sides. The short delays used in doubling sound like early sound reflections in a studio, so they add some "air" or ambience.

Doubling a vocal can be done without a delay unit. Record a vocal part, then overdub another performance of the same vocal part. Mix the parts, pan them both to center, or pan them left and right.

# *Chorus*

This is a wavy or shimmering effect. The delay is 15 to 35 msec, and the delay varies at a slow rate. Sweeping the delay time causes the delayed signal to bend up and down in pitch, or to detune. When you combine the detuned signal with the original signal, you get chorusing.

**Figure 11.15** Repeating echo.

## Stereo Chorus

This is a beautiful effect. In one channel, the delayed signal is combined with the dry signal in the same polarity. In the other channel, the delayed signal is inverted in polarity, then combined with the dry signal. Thus, the right channel has a series of peaks in the frequency response where the left channel has dips, and vice versa. The delay is slowly varied or modulated.

## Bass Chorus

This is chorus with a high-pass filter so that low frequencies are not chorused, but higher harmonics are. It gives an ethereal quality to the bass guitar.

# *Flanging*

If you set the delay around 0 to 20 msec, you usually can't resolve the direct and delayed signals into two separate sounds. Instead, you hear a single sound with a strange frequency response. The direct and delayed signals combine and have phase interference, which puts a series of peaks and dips in the frequency response. This is called a **comb-filter effect** (Figure 11.16). It gives a very colored, filtered tone quality. The shorter the delay, the farther apart the peaks and dips are spaced in frequency.

The flanging effect varies or sweeps the delay between about 0 and 20 msec. This makes the comb-filter nulls sweep up and down the spectrum. As a result, the sound is hollow, swishing, and ethereal, as if the music were playing through a pipe. Flanging is easiest to hear with broadband signals such as cymbals but can be used on any instrument, even voices.

Some examples of flanging are on many Jimi Hendrix records, and on the oldies "Itchycoo Park" by the Small Faces and "Listen to the Music" by the Doobie Brothers.

**Positive flanging** refers to flanging in which the delayed signal is the same polarity as the direct signal (Figure 11.16). With **negative flanging**, the delayed signal is opposite in polarity to the direct signal, which makes a stronger effect. The low frequencies are cancelled (the bass rolls off), and the "knee" of the bass rolloff moves up and down the spectrum as the delay is varied. The high frequencies are still comb-filtered (Figure 11.17). Negative flanging makes the music sound like it's turning inside out.

**Figure 11.16** Flanging (or positive flanging).

**Figure 11.17** Negative flanging.

When the flanger feeds some of the output signal back into the input, the peaks and dips get bigger. It's a powerful "science fiction" effect called **resonant flanging**.

# Reverberation

This effect adds a sense of room acoustics, ambience, or space to instruments and voices. To know how it works, we need to understand how reverb happens in a real room. Natural reverberation in a room is a series of multiple sound reflections which make the original sound persist and gradually die away or decay. These reflections tell the ear that you're listening in a large or hard-surfaced room. For example, reverberation is the sound you hear just after you shout in an empty gymnasium.

A reverb effect simulates the sound of a room—a club, auditorium, or concert hall—by generating random multiple echoes that are too numerous and rapid for the ear to resolve (Figure 11.18).

Reverb and echo are not the same thing. Echo is a repetition of a sound ("HELLO hello hello"); reverb is a smooth decay of sound ("HELLO-OO-oo-oo").

Digital reverb is available either in a dedicated reverb unit, or as part of a multi-effects processor. A digital reverb has a lot of reverb patterns stored as programs or algorithms. You can get the sound of a small room, a big room, or a warm room (with more lows and fewer highs). Reverb

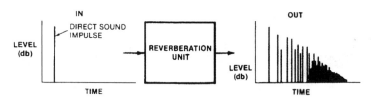

**Figure 11.18** Reverberation.

algorithms with high density of delayed signals sound smoother when they decay than low-density algorithms. Some reverbs let you roll off the top end (turn down the treble) around 5 kHz to get a more natural sound like real rooms.

A **plate reverb** setting duplicates the bright sound of a metal-foil plate, which used to be the most popular type of reverb in pro studios. Some units let you adjust tone quality, decay time, and other parameters. Unnatural effects are available, such as nonlinear decay, **reverse reverb** that builds up before decaying, or **gated reverb**. With gated reverb, the reverb cuts off suddenly shortly after a note is hit. It's often used on a snare drum. A good example is the oldie "You Can Call Me Al" on Paul Simon's album *Graceland*.

Another feature in some units is **pre-delay** (pre-reverb delay). This is a short delay (30 to 100 msec) before the reverb to simulate the delay that happens in real rooms before reverb starts. The longer the pre-delay, the bigger the room sounds. If your reverb unit does not have pre-delay built in, you can create it by connecting a delay unit between your mixer's aux-send and the reverb input.

To connect a reverb unit to your mixer, connect a cable from the mixer aux-send to the reverb input. Connect a cable (two for stereo) from the reverb outputs to the mixer aux returns (effects returns or bus inputs). Set the mix control on the reverb unit all the way to "wet" or "reverb." Turn the mixer's aux-return or bus-in knobs (if any) about two-thirds of the way up, and adjust the amount of reverb on each track with the aux-send knobs. Try to get an overall reverb-send level near 0 VU; then fine-tune the aux return level for the desired amount of reverb.

"Wet" lead vocals (with reverb) are the norm. But some recordings are made with totally dry vocals.

Multichannel digital reverbs are available for surround sound, both as hardware and software. Some examples are Eventide's Orville, Sony's DRE-S777, TC Electronics' System 6000, Lexicon's 960L, and Kind of Loud's RealVerb 5.1 Pro Tools plug-in. Surround reverb plug-ins for Steinberg's Nuendo platform include Steinberg's Surround Edition plug-in bundle and TC Works SurroundVerb plug-in.

# Enhancer

If a track or a mix sounds dull and muffled, you can run it through an enhancer to add brilliance and clarity. An enhancer works either by adding slight distortion (as in the Aphex Aural Exciter) or by boosting the treble when the signal has high-frequency content (as in the Alesis Micro Enhancer and the Barcus Berry 402 Sonic Maximizer).

This last device also divides the frequency range into three bands. The lows are delayed about 1.5 msec; the midrange is delayed about 0.5 msec; and the highs are delayed only a few microseconds. In this way, the Maximizer aligns the harmonics and fundamentals in time for added clarity.

# Octave Divider

This unit takes a signal from a bass guitar and provides deep, growling bass notes one or two octaves below the pitch of the bass guitar. It does this by dividing the incoming frequency by 2 or 4: If you put 82 Hz in, you get 41 Hz out. Some MIDI sound modules have bass patches with extra-deep sound, and some bass guitars have an extra string tuned especially low.

# Harmonizer

Basically a delay unit with time modulation, a harmonizer makes a variety of pitch-shifting effects. It can create harmonies, change pitch without changing the duration of the program, change duration without changing pitch, and many other oddities. You've heard harmonizers on radio station breaks when the announcer's voice sounds like a Munchkin or Darth Vader. The latest vocal formant-corrected pitch-shifters maintain the voice formant structure when they shift pitch; this prevents the "chipmunk" effect. Auto-Tune by Antares provides automatic pitch correction.

# Preverb

With this effect, you can make reverb precede the attack of each note. This can turn a snare hit into a whip—ssSSHHKK! Here's how to add preverb to a drum track recorded on an analog multitrack:

1. Reverse the reels so the tape plays backwards.
2. Add reverb to the drum track.

3. Record the reverb output on an open track.

4. Again reverse the reels and play the tape.

What if you're using an MDM recorder, which won't play backwards? You'll need a multitrack digital audio workstation (DAW) to create preverb.

1. Add reverb to a drum hit, and record the reverb on an open MDM track.

2. Using the DAW, copy the tape tracks to hard disk.

3. On your computer screen, find the drum hit, and find its reverb tail on the reverb track.

4. Define the reverb tail as a region or segment.

5. Reverse this segment so that it becomes preverb.

6. Slide the preverb segment earlier in time (to the left) until its timing sounds correct.

Some signal processors have a **reverse reverb** effect in which the reverb comes after the note that produced it, but builds up before it fades out. This is not quite the same as preverb. Reverse reverb can upset the musical timing; preverb doesn't.

# Tube Processor

This device uses a vacuum tube, or a transistor simulation of one, to add a warm sound, or to reduce digital harshness. Tubes have euphonic even-order harmonic distortion, which adds richness. There are tube mics, tube mic preamps, tube compressors, and standalone tube processors.

# Rotary Speaker Simulator

This effect simulates the sound of a Leslie organ speaker, which plays music through rotating horns. It's a complex sound effect of pitch shifting, tremolo, and phase shifting. The speed and depth of the effect are adjustable.

# Analog Tape Simulator

Analog tape saturation is mainly third-harmonic distortion and compression. An analog tape simulator adds this distortion to digital recordings in an attempt to smear or warm up the sound in a pleasant way.

# Spatial Processor

Spatial processors enhance the stereo imaging or spatial aspects of a mix heard over two speakers. Some units have joystick-type pan pots, which move the image of each track anywhere around the listener. Other units make the stereo stage wider, so that images can be placed to the left of the left speaker, and to the right of the right speaker. The listener might hear images toward the sides of the listening room. In 5.1 surround systems, this spatial processing is done by surround panning and surround reverbs.

# Microphone Simulator

Antares offers a microphone modeler or simulator. You tell it which mic you are using and which mic you want it to sound like. A wide variety of vintage and current mic simulations are available. Mic modeling comes in three forms: a standalone hardware unit, computer software, and firmware (programmed into a chip) in a recorder–mixer.

# Guitar Amplifier Simulator

Another simulator takes the sound of a direct-recorded guitar, and makes the guitar sound like it is played through a guitar amp. Several amp models can be simulated, as well as effects, tone, drive, the mic used to pick up the amp, and the mic's position. You can record a track of a clean, direct guitar signal, then process it during mixdown to sound like any amp you want.

Two hardware examples of amp modelers are the Line Six Pod and the Johnson J Station. Amp Farm is a guitar modeling plug-in for Pro Tools. Roland's digital workstations offer COSM mic modeling and guitar-amp modeling.

Guitar processors or guitar stomp boxes can be used on any instrument or vocal to add distortion, or to generally "shred" the sound for a low-fi effect.

# Multi-Effects Processor

This device provides several effects in a single chassis. Some units let you combine up to four effects in any order. Others have several channels, so you can put a different effect on different instruments. With most processors, you can edit the sounds and save them in memory as new programs.

An extension of the multi-effects processor is the vocal processor. It includes a high-quality mic preamp or two, plus EQ, compression, gating, de-esser, and perhaps some tube saturation distortion.

A multi-effects processor uses a digital signal processing (DSP) chip and RAM memory. The amount of memory is limited, so the more memory that one effect uses, the less is available for other effects. For example, suppose you're combining reverb and echo. If you use a reverb with a long decay time (which takes a lot of memory), you may have to settle for an echo with a short delay.

Most units have a frequency response up to 20 kHz and at least 16-bit resolution. They offer 100 or more programmable presets with MIDI control over any parameter. For example, with some units you can place an instrument in a simulated room, and use a MIDI controller to continuously change the size of that room.

Many signal processors can be controlled by MIDI program-change commands. You can quickly change the type of effect, or effect parameters, by entering certain program changes into a sequencer.

Suppose you want each tom-tom hit in a drum fill to have a different size room added to it. For example, put the high-rack tom in a small room; put the low-rack tom in a concert hall; and put the floor tom in a cave. To do this, first assign a different program number (patch or preset number) to each effects parameter. You do this with the effects device. Then, using the sequencer, punch in the appropriate program number for each note.

A MIDI program-change footswitch lets guitarists call up different effects on MIDI signal processors. By tapping a footswitch, they can get fuzz, flanging, wah-wah, spring reverb, and so on.

A MIDI mapper lets you control some effects parameters with any controller—for example, vary reverb decay time with a pitch wheel, or vary a filter with key velocity.

# Software (Plug-In) Effects

Most digital-editing software includes effects that you control on your computer screen. The software runs algorithms in the sound card's DSP to make effects. An **effects plug-in** is third-party software which you load into your digital-editing program (called the "host.") The plug-in becomes part of the host program, and can be called up from within the host. Some manufacturers make plug-in bundles, which are a variety of effects in a single package.

All the effects described earlier are available as plug-ins. Some plug-ins called **De-Click** and **De-Noise** can remove the clicks and pops from LP records, or remove hiss and hum from noisy recordings. Other plug-ins can vary the pitch of a sound without changing its duration, or change the duration without changing the pitch. The Auto-Tune plug-in by Antares offers automatic pitch correction. Recent plug-ins for surround sound are surround panning, surround reverb, and surround encoding/decoding.

# Looking Back

We've come a long way with effects. Looking back over the past few decades, each era had its own "sound" related to the effects used at the time. The '50s had tube distortion and slap echo; the '60s used fuzz, wah-wah, and flanging. Much of the early '70s sounded dry, and the early '90s emphasized synth, drum machines, and gated reverb. Now vacuum tubes and acoustic instruments are back, along with occasional low-fi (tinny, distorted, or noisy) sounds. Whatever effects you choose, they can enhance your music if used with taste.

# Sound-Quality Glossary

The sound of effects and EQ can be hard to translate into engineering terms. For example, what EQ should you use to get a "fat" sound or a "thin" sound? The glossary below may help. It's based on conversations with producers, musicians, and reviewers over many years. Not everyone agrees on these definitions, but they are common.

**AIRY**—Spacious. The instruments sound like they are surrounded by a large reflective space full of air. A pleasant amount of reverb. High-frequency response that extends to 15 or 20 kHz.

**BALLSY OR BASSY**—Emphasized low frequencies below about 200 Hz.

**BLOATED**—Excessive mid-bass around 250 Hz. Poorly damped low frequencies, low-frequency resonances.

**BLOOM**—Adequate low frequencies. Spacious. Good reproduction of dynamics and reverberation. Early reflections or a sense of "air" around each instrument in an orchestra.

**BOOMY**—Excessive bass around 125 Hz. Poorly damped low frequencies or low-frequency resonances.

**BOXY**—Having resonances as if the music were enclosed in a box. Speaker cabinet diffraction or vibration. Sometimes an emphasis around 250 Hz to 500 Hz.

**BREATHY**—Audible breath sounds in vocals, flute, or sax. Good high-frequency response.

**BRIGHT**—High-frequency emphasis. Harmonics are strong relative to fundamentals.

**BRITTLE**—High-frequency peaks, or weak fundamentals. Slightly distorted or harsh highs. Opposite of round or mellow. See **Thin**. Objects that are physically thin and brittle emphasize highs over lows when you crack them.

**CHESTY**—The vocalist sounds like his or her chest is too big. A bump in the low-frequency response around 125 to 250 Hz.

**CLEAN**—Free of noise, distortion, and leakage.

**CLEAR**—See **Transparent**.

**CLINICAL**—Too clean or analytical. Emphasized high-frequency response, sharp transient response. Not warm.

**COLORED**—Having timbres that are not true to life. Non-flat response, peaks or dips.

**CONSTRICTED**—Poor reproduction of dynamics. Dynamic compression. Distortion at high levels. Also see **Pinched**.

**CRISP**—Extended high-frequency response. Like a crispy potato chip, or crisp bacon frying. Often referring to cymbals.

**CRUNCH**—Pleasant guitar-amp distortion.

**DARK**—Opposite of bright. Weak high frequencies.

**DELICATE**—High frequencies extending to 15 or 20 kHz without peaks. A sweet, airy, open sound with strings or acoustic guitar.

**DEPTH**—A sense of closeness and farness of instruments, caused by miking them at different distances. Good transient response that reveals the direct/reflected sound ratio in the recording.

**DETAILED**—Easy to hear tiny details in the music; articulate. Adequate high-frequency response, sharp transient response.

**DRY**—Without effects. Not spacious. Reverb tends towards mono instead of spreading out. Overdamped transient response.

**DULL**—See **Dark**.

**EDGY**—Too much high frequencies. Trebley. Harmonics are too strong relative to the fundamentals. When you view the waveform on an oscilloscope, it even looks edgy or jagged, because of excessive high frequencies. Distorted, having unwanted harmonics that add an edge or raspiness to the sound.

**EFFORTLESS**—Low distortion, usually coupled with flat response.

**ETCHED**—Clear but verging on edgy. Emphasis around 10 kHz or higher.

**FAT**—See **Full** and **Warm**. Also, a diffuse spatial effect. Also, smeared out in time, with some reverberant decay.

**FOCUSED**—Referring to the image of a musical instrument which is easy to localize, pinpointed, having a small spatial spread.

**FORWARD**—Sounding close to the listener, projected. Emphasis around 2 kHz to 5 kHz.

**FULL**—Opposite of thin. Strong fundamentals relative to harmonics. Good low-frequency response, not necessarily extended, but with adequate level around 100 to 300 Hz.

**GENTLE**—Opposite of edgy. The harmonics—highs and upper mids—are not exaggerated, or may even be weak.

**GLARE, GLASSY**—A little less extreme than edgy. A little too bright or trebley.

**GRAINY**—The music sounds like it's segmented into little grains, rather than flowing in one continuous piece. Not liquid or fluid. Suffering from harmonic or I.M. distortion. Some early A/D converters sounded grainy, as do current ones of inferior design. "Powdery" is finer than "grainy"!

**GRUNGY**—Lots of harmonic or I.M. distortion.

**HARD**—Too much upper midrange, usually around 3 kHz. Or, good transient response, as if the sound is hitting you hard.

**HARSH**—Too much upper midrange. Peaks in the frequency response from 2 kHz to 6 kHz. Or, excessive phase shift.

**HEAVY**—Good low-frequency response below about 50 Hz. Suggesting an object of great weight or power, like a diesel locomotive or thunder.

**HOLLOW**—See **Honky**. Or, too much reverberation. Or, a mid-frequency dip.

**HONKY**—The music sounds the way your voice sounds when you cup your hands around your mouth. A bump in the response around 500 to 700 Hz.

**LIQUID**—Opposite of grainy. A sense of seamless flowing of the music. Flat response and low distortion. High frequencies are flat or reduced relative to mids and lows.

**LOW-FI (low fidelity)**—"Trashy" sounding. Tinny, distorted, noisy, or muddy.

**MELLOW**—Reduced high frequencies, not edgy.

**MUDDY**—Not clear. Weak harmonics, smeared time response, I.M. distortion. Too much reverb at low frequencies.

**MUFFLED**—The music sounds covered up. Weak highs or weak upper mids.

**MUSICAL**—Conveying emotion. Flat response, low distortion, no edginess.

**NASAL**—The vocalist sounds as if he or she is singing with the nose closed. Also applies to strings. Bump in the response around 300 to 1000 Hz. See **Honky**.

**NEUTRAL**—Accurate tonal reproduction. No obvious colorations. No serious peaks or dips in the frequency response.

**PAPERY**—Referring to a kick drum that has too much output around 400 to 600 Hz.

**PINCHED**—Narrowband. Midrange or upper-midrange peak in the frequency response. Pinched dynamics are overly compressed.

**PIERCING**—Strident, hard on the ears, screechy. Having sharp, narrow peaks in the response around 3 kHz to 10 kHz.

**PRESENT, PRESENCE**—Adequate or emphasized response around 5 kHz for most instruments, or around 2 to 5 kHz for kick drum and bass. Having some edge, punch, detail, closeness, and clarity.

**PUFFY**—Bump in the response around 500 to 700 Hz.

**PUNCHY**—Good reproduction of dynamics. Good transient response. Sometimes a bump around 5 kHz or 200 Hz.

**RASPY**—Harsh, like a rasp. Peaks in the response around 6 kHz which make vocals sound too sibilant or piercing.

**RICH**—See **Full**. Also, having euphonic distortion made of even-order harmonics.

**ROUND**—High-frequency rolloff or dip. Not edgy.

**SHARP**—See **Strident** and **Tight**.

**SIBILANT, ESSY**—Exaggerated "s" and "sh" sounds in singing, caused by a rise in the response around 4 to 7 kHz.

**SIZZLY**—See **Sibilant**. Also, too much highs on cymbals.

**SMEARED**—Lacking detail. Poor transient response. This may be a desirable effect in large-diameter mics. Also, poorly focused images.

**SMOOTH**—Easy on the ears, not harsh. Flat frequency response, especially in the midrange. Lack of peaks and dips in the response.

**SPACIOUS**—Conveying a sense of space, ambience, or room around the instruments. To get this effect, mike farther back, mix in an ambience mic, add reverb, or record in stereo. Components that have out-of-phase crosstalk between channels may add false spaciousness.

**SQUASHED**—Overly compressed.

**STEELY**—Emphasized upper mids around 3 to 6 kHz. Peaky, nonflat high-frequency response. See **Glassy**, **Harsh**, **Edgy**.

**STRAINED**—The component sounds like it's working too hard. Distorted. Inadequate headroom or insufficient power. Opposite of effortless.

**STRIDENT**—See **Harsh** and **Edgy**.

**SWEET**—Not strident or piercing. Flat high-frequency response, low distortion. Lack of peaks in the response. Highs are extended to 15 or 20 kHz, but they are not bumped up. Often used when referring to cymbals, percussion, strings, and sibilant sounds.

**THIN**—Fundamentals are weak relative to harmonics. Note that the fundamental frequencies of many instruments are not very low. For example, violin fundamentals are around 200 to 1000 Hz. So if the 300 Hz area is weak, the violin may sound thin—even if the mic's response goes down to 40 Hz.

**TIGHT**—Good low-frequency transient response. Absence of ringing or resonance when reproducing the kick drum or bass. Good low-frequency detail. Absence of leakage.

**TINNY, TELEPHONE-LIKE**—Narrowband, weak lows, peaky mids. The music sounds like it's coming through a telephone or tin can.

**TRANSPARENT**—Easy to hear into the music, detailed, clear, not muddy. Wide, flat frequency response, sharp time response, very low distortion and noise.

**TUBBY**—See **Bloated**. Having low-frequency resonances as if you're singing in a bathtub.

**VEILED**—The music sounds like you put a silk veil over the speakers. Slight noise or distortion, or slightly weak high frequencies.

**WARM**—Good bass, adequate low frequencies, adequate fundamentals relative to harmonics. Not thin. Or, excessive bass or midbass. Or, pleasantly spacious, with adequate reverberation at low frequencies. Or, gentle highs, like from a tube amplifier. See **Rich**.

**WOOLY, BLANKETED**—The music sounds like there's a wool blanket over the speakers. Weak high frequencies or boomy low frequencies. Sometimes, an emphasis around 250 to 600 Hz.

# 12

# RECORDER–MIXERS AND MIXING CONSOLES

In a recording studio, you do most of the work with a mixer and a multi-track recorder. The mixer accepts microphone or line-level signals and amplifies them up to the level needed by the recorder. The multitrack recorder records several tracks on tape, MiniDisc, or hard disk. One track might be a lead vocal, another track might be a saxophone, and so on. A mixing console (also called **board** or **desk**) is an elaborate mixer with extra controls.

A recorder–mixer combines a mixer and a multitrack recorder in a single portable chassis. This convenient unit is also called a **ministudio** or **portable studio**. Low-end recorder–mixers record 4 tracks, but high-end units record 8 to 24 tracks.

This chapter covers both mixers and mixing consoles. First we'll look at typical features of both, then at features found only in mixing consoles.

## Stages of Recording

This chapter will refer to the three stages in making a multitrack recording: recording, overdubbing, and mixdown.

- **Recording (tracking):** Record one or more instruments onto one or more tracks.
- **Overdubbing:** While listening to prerecorded tracks over headphones, the musician records new parts on open (unused) tracks.

- **Mixdown:** After all the tracks are recorded, mix or combine them into 2-track stereo or 6-channel surround. Add effects and any sequenced tracks of MIDI instruments.

  Record the stereo mix with a 2-track recorder, such as a cassette deck, open-reel deck, DAT machine, or CD-R burner. This recording is the master, which can be duplicated on cassettes, vinyl records, or compact discs.

# Mixer Functions

Although the knobs and meters on a mixer may appear intimidating, you can understand them if you read the manual and practice with the equipment. A mixer is rather complicated because it lets you control many aspects of sound:

- The loudness of each instrument (to control the balance among instruments in the mix)
- The tone quality of each instrument (bass, treble, midrange)
- The room that the instruments are in (reverberation)
- The left-to-right position of each instrument (panning)
- Special effects (flanging, echo, chorus, etc.)
- Track assignments (sometimes more than one instrument on each track)
- Recording level (to prevent distortion and noise)
- Monitor selection (what you want to listen to)

# Inputs and Outputs

A mixer can be specified by the number of inputs and outputs it has. For example, an 8-in, 2-out mixer (8 × 2 mixer) has 8 signal inputs, which can be mixed into 2 output channels (busses) for stereo recording. Similarly, a 16-in, 8-out (16 × 8) mixing board has 16 signal inputs and 8 output channels for multitrack recording. A 16 × 4 × 2 mixing board has 16 inputs, 4 submixes (explained later), and 2 main outputs. There also are connectors for external equipment, such as effects devices and a monitor power amplifier.

Most mixing boards are organized in three sections:

- Input modules
- Output section
- Monitor section

# Input Modules

A mixer is made of groups of controls called **modules**. An **input module** (Figure 12.1) affects a single input signal—from a microphone, for instance. The module is usually a narrow vertical strip, one per input. Several modules are lined up side-by-side. Each input module is the same, so if you know one, you know them all.

The more inputs your mixer has, the more instruments you can record at the same time. If you're recording only yourself, you may need only two inputs. Each input module typically has these parts:

- **Input connectors:** On the back of the module are connectors that accept the signal from a microphone, a direct box, an electric musical instrument, or a multitrack recorder.

- **Input selector:** Lets you choose which input signal you want to work with. Some consoles omit this control.

- **Preamp:** Inside the module, the preamp amplifies your input signal.

- **Gain** or **trim control:** Adjusts the level of the input signal for the best compromise between noise and distortion. Also can be used to set recording level.

- **Fader:** Adjusts the balance among tracks during mixdown.

- **Equalizer:** Adjusts the tone quality (bass, treble, and midrange).

- **Aux send (effects send):** Controls how many effects (reverb, chorus, etc.) are added to each input signal. Also might be used as a monitor-mix volume control.

**Figure 12.1**
A typical input module.

**Figure 12.2** Signal flow through a typical input module.

- **Assign switch:** Lets you select which tape track to send the signal to for recording (usually used in combination with the pan pot).
- **Pan pot:** Places various sounds where desired between your stereo speakers. In some mixers, the pan pot is also used with the assign switch to send signals to the desired tracks.

Figure 12.2 shows the signal flow from input to output through a typical input module.

## *Input Connectors*

Input connectors are for microphones, direct boxes, electric musical instruments, or an external multitrack recorder. The following are labels for each connector:

- MIC (for mic-level signals: microphones and direct boxes)
- LINE (for line-level signals: a synthesizer, drum machine, or electric guitar)
- TAPE (for line-level signals from an external multitrack recorder)

In some recorder–mixers, a single ¼-inch phone jack is used both for mic-level and line-level signals. A mic-level signal is typically about 1 to 2 millivolts. A line-level signal is about 0.3 to 1.23 volts. The two levels are handled either by a MIC/LINE switch or a TRIM control.

Some units have separate jacks for mic and line inputs. The mic input is either an unbalanced ¼-inch phone jack (a ¼-inch hole) or an XLR-type connector (with three small holes). The line input is a ¼-inch phone jack, an RCA (phono) jack (such as that on a stereo system), or an XLR-type connector. You can plug a synthesizer directly into a phone-jack input without using a direct box if the cable is under 10 feet; a longer cable may pick up hum. In some recorder–mixers, a phone-jack input is switchable between low impedance (for microphones) or high impedance (for electric guitar pickups). See Appendix D on impedance.

Some newer recorder–mixers also have a sync input. It goes into track 4 and is used for recording a special tape-sync tone from a computer running a sequencer program. The sync tone synchronizes tape tracks with MIDI sequencer tracks. It also lets you overdub two or more sequencer tracks onto tape by keeping them synchronized. On an 8-track cassette or open-reel machine, use track 8 as the sync track.

## *Phantom Power (P48, +48)*

The phantom power switch, found only in elaborate units, turns on phantom power to condenser microphones. This is 12 to 48 volts DC voltage applied through resistors equally to pins 2 and 3 of XLR-type mic-input connectors. The microphone receives phantom power and sends audio along the same two conductors. In some mixing consoles, each input module has its own phantom power switch.

## *Input Selector*

This switch selects the input you want to process: mic, line, or tape. The switch might be labeled in one of these ways:

Mic/line/tape
Mic/line/mix
Mic-line/off/tape
Input/off/tape
Input/mute/track
Input/off/line

The following list explains how each switch position works:

MIC: The mic signal enters the mixer.

LINE: The line or tape signal enters the mixer.

MIC-LINE or INPUT: Either the mic signal or the line signal enters the mixer, depending on what is plugged into that input.

TAPE, TRACK, or MIX: The recorder track signal enters the mixer (for overdubbing or mixdown).

OFF or MUTE: No signal is processed. During mixdown, it's a good idea to mute tracks that have nothing playing at the moment to reduce tape hiss.

Using the input selector is simple. If you plugged in a microphone or direct box to record its signal, set the input selector to "mic" or "input." If you plugged in a synth, drum machine, or electric guitar, set the selector to "line" or "input." When you're ready to mix, select "tape," "track," or "mix."

Some mixers have no input selector. The mixer processes whatever signal is plugged in.

## Mic Preamp

After entering the mic connector and input selector switch, a microphone signal goes into a mic preamplifier inside the mixer. The preamp boosts or amplifies the weak microphone signal up to a higher voltage, making it a line-level signal.

## Trim (Gain)

If the microphone is picking up a loud instrument or vocal, the mic signal is very strong. This signal can overload the mic preamp, causing distortion—a gritty sound. To prevent distortion, set the TRIM control as follows: First set the **master fader(s)** within the shaded portion of its travel (sometimes at 0, about ¾ up). Do the same for the **input fader** (discussed next). Assign the signal to a multitrack recorder track. Have the musician play the loudest part of the song, and adjust the TRIM control so that the meter peaks around 0.

In some mixers, in each input module is a tiny light (LED) labeled "clip" or "peak." It flashes when the mic preamp is distorting. If this light flashes when you're picking up an instrument or vocal, turn down the TRIM control just to the point where the light stays off, then turn it down another 10 dB for extra headroom.

Inexpensive recorder–mixers do not have an overload LED or a trim control. The input fader serves this function.

## Input Fader (Channel Fader)

After the preamp amplifies the mic signal, it goes to the input fader. This is a sliding volume control for each input signal. During recording, you either set the input fader to **design center** (at 0, about ¾ up) or set the fader to adjust the instrument's level in the monitor mix (depending on how your board is set up). During mixdown, you use the faders to set the loudness balance among instruments.

## Direct Out

Found only in fancier units, the direct out is an output connector following each input fader and equalizer. The signal at the direct-out jack is an amplified version of the input signal. The fader controls the level at the direct-out jack. Use the direct-out jack when you want to record one instrument per track (with EQ) on an external multitrack recorder. Connect the direct-out jack to a multitrack recorder track input. Since the direct output bypasses the mixing circuits farther down the chain, the result is a cleaner signal.

If a mixer has eight inputs with a direct-out jack for each input, you can use the mixer with an 8-track recorder—even if the mixer has only 2 or 4 outputs.

## EQ (Equalization)

The signal from the input fader goes to an equalizer, which is a tone control. With EQ you can make an instrument sound more or less bassy, and more or less trebley, by boosting or cutting certain frequencies. Equalizers cover two or three bands of the audible spectrum. Inexpensive units have a simple two-knob bass and treble control; you can boost or cut the treble or bass. Fancier models have a sweepable EQ (sometimes called semiparametric EQ) that lets you "tune in" the exact frequency range to work on. This feature adds cost and complexity, but gives you more control over the tone quality. We covered EQ in Chapter 11.

In some low-cost recorder–mixers, the EQ works on two tracks at a time during recording, and on the stereo mix during mixdown. This is less flexible than a unit with EQ on each input.

## Assign Switch

The equalized signal goes to the **assign switch** (sometimes called the **track selector switch**). It lets you send the signal of each instrument to the recorder track you want to record that instrument on.

Some units have an assign switch labeled 1, 2, 3, or 4. If you want to record bass on track 1, for instance, find the assign switch for the input module the bass is plugged into, and push switch 1. If you want to record four drum mics on track 2, push assign switch 2 for all those input

265

modules. Other recorder–mixers assign tracks with two controls: a selector switch and a pan pot (described next).

## Pan Pot

A pan pot is a device that sends a signal to two channels in adjustable amounts. By rotating the pan-pot knob, you control how much signal goes to each channel. Set the knob all the way left and the signal goes to one channel. Set it all the way right and the signal goes to the other channel. Set it in the middle and the signal goes to both channels. Here's how you might use a pan pot to assign an instrument to a track. The track-selector switch (assign switch) might have two positions labeled 1-2 and 3-4. If you turn the pan pot left, the signal goes to odd-numbered tracks (either 1 or 3, depending on how you set the assign switch). If you turn the pan pot right, the signal goes to even-numbered tracks (2 or 4). Suppose you want to assign the bass to track 1. Set the assign switch to 1-2, and turn the pan pot far left to choose the odd-numbered track (track 1).

During mixdown, the pan pot has a different function: It places images between your speakers. An **image** is an apparent source of sound, a point between your speakers where you hear each instrument or vocal. Set the pan pot to locate each instrument at the left speaker, right speaker, or anywhere in between. If you set the pan pot to center, the signal goes equally to both channels, and you hear an image in the center.

## Aux (Effects or FX)

The aux or aux-send feature (Figure 12.3) can be used in two ways:

- To set up a monitor mix—a balanced blend of input signals you hear over speakers or headphones
- To set the amount of effects (reverb, echo) heard on each instrument in a mix

Some recorder–mixers have no aux sends; some have one aux-send control per module; some have two or more (labeled aux 1, aux 2, etc.). The more aux sends you have, the more you can play with effects, but the greater the cost and complexity. The aux number (1 or 2) is not necessarily assigned a specific function; you decide what you want aux 1 and aux 2 to do.

During recording and overdubbing, the aux knobs of all the input modules are normally used to create a monitor mix. The monitor mix that you create with the aux knobs is independent of the levels going on tape. You use the gain-trims during recording to set recording levels, and you

**Figure 12.3** Auxiliary and output sections.

use the aux knobs to create an independent mix that is heard over your monitor system.

In Figure 12.3, the aux 1 send control is just before the fader. In this mixer, the signals from all the aux 1 knobs in the mixer combine at a connector jack labeled "aux 1 send" or "monitor." You can connect that jack to your power amplifier, which drives monitor speakers and headphones. In this mixer, the aux 2 send control is just after the fader. During mixdown, each aux 2 knob controls how much effects (reverb, echo) you hear on each track. The aux knob controls the level of each input signal sent to an external effects device, which adds echo, reverb, or some other effect. The effects signal returns to the mixer's aux return or bus in jacks. Inside the mixer, the effects signal blends with the original signal, adding spaciousness or ambience to an otherwise "dry" track.

A few recorder–mixers have an **aux return** control (also called **effects return** or **bus in**) that sets the overall effects level returning to the mixer. Follow these steps to use the aux controls to adjust the amount of effects heard on each track:

1. Patch an effects unit between your mixer's aux-send and aux-return (bus-in) jacks.

2. On the effects unit, set the dry/wet mix control all the way to "wet" or "effect."

3. If your mixer has aux-return (bus-in) knobs, turn them about ¾ up and pan their signals hard left and right.

4. Turn up the aux-send knob for each input, according to how much effect you want to hear on that input signal.

Suppose you're using reverb as an effect. You might turn it up by different amounts for the vocals, drums, and lead guitar, and leave it turned down for the bass and kick drum. As you're setting the aux levels, check the overload indicator on the reverb unit. If it's flashing, turn down the input level on the reverb unit just to the point where the overload light stops flashing. Then turn up the output level on the reverb unit (or turn up the aux return on the mixer) to achieve the same amount of reverb you heard before.

There might be a **pre/post switch** next to the aux-send knob. When an aux knob is set to pre (prefader), its level is not affected by the fader setting. You use the **pre** setting for a headphone mix during recording or overdubbing because you don't want the fader settings to affect the monitor mix. The **post** setting (postfader) is used for effects during mixdown. In this case, the aux level follows the setting of the fader. The higher you set the track volume with the fader, the higher the effects level is. But the dry/wet mix stays the same.

## Insert Jacks

These connectors on the mixer let you break the signal path in an input module, and insert an external device there, before the fader and EQ section. You might plug a compressor in series with an input module's signal for automatic volume control. Or insert any other signal processor (reverb/delay, for instance) into the signal path of one track. This way, if all your aux sends are tied up, you can add another signal processor. On the reverb/delay unit, set the dry/wet mix control for the desired amount of effect.

Another use for insert jacks is to send each input module's signal to a multitrack recorder track. The output of each track returns to the insert jack and continues through your mixer. In this case, you use the trim controls to set recording levels, and use the faders, EQ, and aux sends to set up a monitor mix.

Some insert jacks use a single connector for send and return. The tip connection is the send; the ring is the return; and the sleeve is the common ground or shield. Other insert jacks use a separate jack for send and another jack for return.

Inexpensive recorder–mixers omit insert jacks. Some units have insert jacks on only two inputs.

# Output Section

The output section is the final part of the signal path: the section that feeds mixed signals to the tape tracks. It includes mixing circuits, submaster faders (sometimes), master faders, and meters (Figure 12.4).

**Figure 12.4** Output section of a mixer.

# Mixing Circuits (Active Combining Networks)

The mixing circuits are near the right side of Figure 12.4. Recall that you use the assign switches to send each input signal to the desired channel or bus, and each bus feeds a different tape track. A bus is a channel in a mixer containing an independent mix of signals. The bus 1 mixing circuit accepts the signals from all the inputs you assigned to bus 1 and mixes them together to feed track 1 of the recorder. The bus 2 mixing circuit mixes all the bus 2 assignments, and so on.

Mixing circuits also accept the effects-return signals, such as the reverberated signal from an external digital reverb unit. A four-bus mixer provides four independent output channels or busses; each bus carries a signal which may contain the sounds from one or more musical instruments. The four busses feed a 4-track cassette recorder. A mixer with only two output busses can be used with a 4-track recorder by recording two tracks at a time.

# Master and Submaster Faders

Located toward the right side of your mixer, the **stereo master faders** are one or two sliding volume controls—or a knob—that affect the overall level of the stereo output channels or busses. Usually, you set the master fader(s) within **design center**, the shaded area about ¾ up on the scale. This setting minimizes mixer noise and distortion. You can **fade out** the end of a mix by turning down the master faders gradually.

Elaborate mixers also have faders that control the level of each bus independently, called **submaster**, **bus master**, or **group** faders. You might create a drum submix, or keyboard submix, and control the overall level of each submix with a submaster fader.

The submasters can serve double duty as master faders if you use only two of them. Then you can take your stereo mix from the bus 1 and 2 outputs. The noise is less there than after the master faders.

You feed the multitrack either from group outputs, direct outs, or insert sends. If you're mixing several instruments to track 5, for example, assign those instruments' signals to Group 5. Connect the Group 5 output to tape track 5 in. If you're recording *one* instrument on track 5, however, connect that instrument's direct out or insert send to track 5 in. The signal is cleaner at the direct out or insert send than at the group output.

## Meters

Meters are an important part of the output section. They measure the voltage or level of various signals. Usually, each output bus has a meter to measure its signal level. If these busses feed the tape tracks, you use the meters to set the recording level for each track. Your recorder–mixer will have one of three types of meters:

- **VU:** A voltmeter that shows approximately the relative loudness of various audio signals. Set the record level so that the meter needle reaches +3 VU maximum for most signals, and about −6 VU maximum for drums, percussion, and piano. That's necessary because the VU meter responds too slowly to show the true level of percussive sounds.
- **LED bargraph meter:** A column of lights (LEDs) that shows peak recording level. For all instruments, set the level to peak at 0 to +6 dB maximum, according to the manufacturer's recommendations.
- **LED peak indicator:** A light mounted in a VU meter. It flashes when peak recording levels are excessive. If you have this type of meter, set the level as high as possible, but not so high that the LED flashes.

## Tape-Out Jacks

Tape-out jacks are sometimes included in the output section of recorder–mixers. These are fed from the tape-track outputs and are used for copying your 4-track cassette recordings onto a multitrack studio recorder for further overdubs and processing.

# Monitor Section

The monitor section controls what you're listening to. It lets you select what you want to hear, and lets you create a mix over headphones or speakers to approximate the final product. The monitor mix has no effect on the levels going on tape.

During recording, you want to monitor a mix of the input signals. During playback or mixdown, you want to hear a mix of the recorded tracks. During overdubs, you want to hear a mix of the recorded tracks and the instrument that you're overdubbing. The monitor section lets you do this.

Your mixer might have a small group of knobs called a **monitor mixer** (**monmix** or **tape cue**). Or the monitor mixer might be a row of monitor knobs, aux knobs, or output knobs, one in each input module. In either case, these knobs control the mix you hear.

The monitor mixer is made of several **monitor gain** controls, plus mixing circuits that feed headphones or an external stereo amplifier and speakers. The gain knob controls how loud each live instrument or track is in the monitor mix. Some monitor mixers also have **monitor pan** and **monitor effects** controls. The pan knob controls the left–right position of the instrument or track between your stereo speakers or headphones.

The monitor mixer also is used to blend recorded tape tracks and live microphone signals into a **cue mix** that is sent to headphones. You overdub new parts while listening to the cue mix. In most recorder–mixers, the monitor mix and cue mix are identical.

Some recorder–mixers have several extra inputs for MIDI instruments, along with aux or monitor knobs for these instruments so you can add them to the monitor mix. Because of this feature, you can use the recorder–mixer to mix tape tracks and sequencer tracks; you don't need to purchase an extra mixer to do this. Remember that the auxiliary (aux) sends in the mixer can serve multiple duty as controls for a monitor mix, headphone mix, or effects sends.

## *Monitor Select Buttons*

Another feature of the monitor section is the monitor select buttons. They let you choose what signal you want to monitor or listen to. Since the configuration of these buttons varies widely among different recorder–mixers, they are not shown in Figure 12.4. The following are some of the monitor select buttons you may find:

- MONITOR TRACK 1, 2, 3, 4: You select which track or combination of tracks you want to hear.

- TAPE/BUS 1, 2, 3, 4: Signals from tape tracks 1, 2, 3, or 4 or from busses 1, 2, 3, or 4. Select "tape" to hear a playback, or to hear recorded tracks during an overdub. Select "bus" to hear the live signal that you're recording.
- STEREO or MIX: The 2-channel stereo mix at your mixer output.
- AUX: The aux-send signal (effects or headphone mix).
- CUE: The headphone cue mix.
- 2-TRACK: The playback from your 2-track recorder.

Some units have no monitor-select switches. Instead, you always monitor the 2-channel stereo monitor mix.

# Mixing-Console Styles: Split versus In-Line

In a **split console (side-by-side console)**, a separate monitor mixer is built into the control surface. This monitor mixer has level and pan controls for each track, and perhaps more functions. In an **in-line console (I/O console)**, the monitor mixer is a row of monitor knobs or aux knobs, one in each input module. This is the most common type of console. In either type, the monitor-mixer knobs are fed from the multitrack outputs.

An effective way to use an in-line console is to connect your multi-track recorder ins and outs to the insert jacks (Figure 12.5). Connect the insert-jack 1 tip (send) to track 1 in; connect track 1 out to the insert-jack ring (return). Make similar connections for the other tracks.

With this setup, use the trim controls to set recording levels. Use the faders to set up a monitor mix, cue mix, or mixdown with EQ and effects. Chapter 13 tells how to do this.

# Additional Features Found in Mixing Consoles

Mixing consoles have more features than recorder–mixers do. If you're working only with a recorder–mixer, you might want to skip this section.

**Figure 12.5**
Using insert jacks to send each input signal to a tape track. The track signal returns to the mixer, where you adjust level, panning, EQ, and effects.

PRE/POST SWITCH: When used with an aux send pot, the pre/post switch selects whether the aux send is derived prefader (before the fader) or postfader (following the fader). A prefader aux send is not affected by the fader level: If you turn down the input fader, the aux level is unaffected. A postfader aux send follows the fader action: If you turn down the fader, the aux send level goes down. Normally you use prefader for monitor sends and postfader for effects sends.

FOLDBACK (FB): Another name for cue, or headphone mix.

SOLO: The SOLO button in an input module lets you monitor only that input without affecting other console functions. More than one input can be soloed at one time. On British consoles, the SOLO function is called "PFL" or "AFL," which stand for Pre-Fader Listen and After-Fader Listen (postfader), respectively. You listen to or monitor the signal before or after the fader.

In consoles that have both PFL and SOLO, PFL is prefader and is used mainly to listen for distortion during recording; SOLO is postfader and is used for listening to one track during mixdown.

Suppose you hear a buzz in the audio and suspect it may be in the bass guitar signal. If you push the SOLO button in the bass guitar's input module, you'll monitor only the bass guitar. Then you can easily hear whether the buzz is in that input.

PHASE (POLARITY INVERT): Used only with balanced lines, this switch inverts the polarity of the input signal. That is, it switches pins 2 and 3 to flip the phase 180 degrees. You might use it to correct a miswired mic cable whose polarity is reversed. If you mic a snare drum top and bottom, you need to invert the polarity of the bottom mic.

AUTOMATED MIXING CONTROLS: These controls (Read, Write, Update, etc.) are beyond the scope of this book. Basically they control the functions of a sequencer-assisted mixing system. The sequencer circuit remembers and updates console settings so that a mix can be performed and refined in several stages. More on automated mixing at the end of Chapter 16.

EFFECTS PANNING: This feature places the images of the effects signals wherever desired between the monitor speakers. Some consoles let you pan effects in the monitor mix as well as in the final program mix.

FOLDBACK CONNECTORS: These connectors are in parallel with the TAPE IN jacks. The output of each tape track is connected to a

TAPE IN jack, so the FOLDBACK connector parallels, or "mults," the tape-machine output. The FOLDBACK jacks can be used to send the tape outputs to an outboard device in addition to the console, such as an external cue mixer.

BUS TRIM: This rotary pot lets you fine-tune the bus level, along with the bus master (submaster or group) fader.

EFFECTS RETURN TO CUE: This is an effects-return level control that adjusts the amount of effects heard in the studio headphone mix. These monitored effects are independent of any effects being recorded on tape.

EFFECTS RETURN TO MONITOR: This effects-return control adjusts the amount of effects heard in the monitor mix. These monitored effects are independent of any effects being recorded on tape.

BUS/MONITOR/CUE switch for effects return: A switch that feeds the effects-return signal to your choice of three destinations: program bus (for mixdown), monitor mix, cue mix, or any combination of the three.

METER SWITCHES: In many consoles, the meters can measure signal levels other than console output levels. Switches near the meters can be set so that the meters indicate bus level, aux-send level, aux-return level, monitor-mix level, etc.

Those readings help you set optimum levels for the outboard devices receiving those signals. Too low a level results in noise; too high a level causes distortion in the outboard unit. For example, if the aux-return signal sounds garbled or distorted, the cause may be an excessive aux-send level. Verify that condition by checking the meters switched to read the aux or effects bus.

DIM: A switch that reduces the monitor level by a preset amount (as in "Dim the lights").

TALKBACK: This function lets the people in the control room talk to the musicians in the studio. A small microphone often is built into the console for this purpose.

SLATE: This function routes the control-room microphone signal to all the busses for announcing on tape the name of the tune and take number. In some consoles, a low-frequency tone is recorded on tape during slating; then the beginning of the take can be quickly located by listening for tape tones during fast-forward or rewind.

OSCILLATOR or TONE GENERATOR: This is used to put alignment tones on tape, and to reference the tape recorder's meters to those on the console. You also can use it to check signal path, levels, and channel balance.

# Digital Mixers

A digital mixing console has an A/D converter on each analog input and a D/A converter on each analog output. There are also digital ins and outs. The signal stays in the digital domain for all mixer processing. Level changes, EQ, and so on are done by **digital signal processing** (computer calculations) rather than by analog circuits. Most digital consoles have fewer controls than analog consoles. One knob or switch can have several functions. This makes digital consoles harder to operate than analog ones—you have to press more buttons to access the features you want to adjust. Function parameters—such as EQ frequency and dB boost/cut—show up on an LCD screen. Digital consoles have built-in effects and automated mixing (explained in Chapter 16).

## *Digital Mixer Features*

Look for the following features in digital mixers when making a purchase decision:

- Number of mic inputs: 2 to 16 or more.
- Number and type of digital inputs and outputs (S/PDIF, AES/EBU, TDIF, ADAT)
- Number and type of option card slots (extra I/O, DSP, sync, effects)
- Number of effects processors
- Automation (scene, MIDI, dynamic; nonmoving or moving faders)
- Surround-sound monitoring

Now that you understand the typical features of mixers and mixing consoles, you are ready to learn how to use them.

# 13

# OPERATING THE MULTITRACK RECORDER AND MIXER

Get your hands on those knobs. You're going to operate a mixer as part of a recording session. This will be a basic run-through—detailed session procedures are described in Chapter 14.

First recall the stages in making a recording:

1. Session preparation
2. Recording
3. Punching in
4. Overdubbing
5. Bouncing tracks
6. Mixdown

This chapter considers each stage in turn.

## Session Preparation

If you're using an analog multitrack recorder, be sure to clean the tape path before you start recording. Dust or tape oxide can accumulate on the tape heads, making the sound dull. So clean the tape heads, tape guides, and rubber pinch roller with a cotton swab and the cleaner recommended by the manufacturer. A typical cleaner is denatured alcohol, available at hardware stores. Freon-based cleaners are also available. Don't use rubbing alcohol or isopropyl because they can leave a film on the heads, and they contain water.

When the heads are dry, thread on some blank recording tape or insert a cassette. Set the tape counter to zero.

Use high-quality blank tape. Chrome or metal cassette tape has better high-frequency response and better S/N ratio than ferric. C-60 or C-90 lengths record bass better than longer lengths. Use high-output, low-noise open-reel tape.

If you plan to use a tape-sync signal to synchronize your recorder with MIDI equipment, record it for the entire length of the song before recording any other tape tracks. Usually the sync tone is recorded on track 4 of a 4-track recorder or track 8 of an 8-track recorder. This procedure is detailed in Chapter 16.

If you're recording on a modular digital multitrack, fast-forward the tape to the end and rewind to the top. This loosens the tape pack, distributes the tape lubricants more evenly, and aligns the tape with the tape guides. Then format the tape from beginning to end. For efficiency, you might want to format an entire box of videocassettes at once.

Plan your track assignments. If you assign multiple instruments to the same track, you can't separate their images in the stereo stage. That is, you can't pan them to different positions; all the instruments on one track sound as if they're occupying the same point in space. If you're recording 4-track, you may want to do a stereo mix of the rhythm section on tracks 1 and 2; then overdub vocals and solos on tracks 3 and 4.

# Recording

To start the process, first zero or neutralize the mixer by setting all the controls to "off," "flat," or "zero." That's to establish a point of reference and avoid surprises later on. Set all faders down.

If you have a separate mixer and multitrack recorder, you need to make their meter readings match. To do this, play a steady tone into the mixer to get a 0 reading on the meters for all tracks. Then set the multitrack recorder's record level (if any) to get 0 readings on all the tracks.

Suppose you're ready to record a vocal or an acoustic instrument. Place the microphone and plug it into a mic input. If you want to record a synth or drum machine on tape, connect a cable between the instrument's output and a line input on the mixer.

Attach a strip of masking tape or white removable tape along the bottom of the faders, and label each fader according to what instrument you plugged into that input. Be sure that all the faders are down.

Set the input selector (if any) to "input," "mic," or "line" depending on what is plugged into each input. If there is no input selector, turn down the TRIM control for line-level signals.

Plug in headphones to hear what you're recording. Turn up the headphone volume control. Or, if you're in a control room and the musicians are in a studio, turn up the monitor level to listen over the monitor loudspeakers. Set the MONITOR SELECT switch to hear the signal you're recording, and turn up the musicians' cue mix.

Set the master faders about $\frac{3}{4}$ up, at 0, or within the shaded portion of fader travel. This is called **design center**. Do the same for the input fader(s) in use (Figure 13.1). These settings give the best compromise between noise and distortion.

## Assign Signals to Channels

Assign each input signal to the desired output channel (bus) as specified on your track sheet. Each bus is connected to the corresponding numbered track on the multitrack recorder.

If only one instrument is assigned to a track, you can eliminate the noise of the console combining amplifier by patching the instrument's signal directly to the tape track. To do this, locate the direct output jack (or the insert jack) of the input module for that instrument and patch it to the desired track. Some mixing boards also require pressing a direct button on the input module.

## Set Recording Levels

Now you're ready to "get a level." Have each instrument play the loudest part of the music, one at a time or all at once. Set the TRIM control so the recording level is as high as possible without causing distortion.

Below are suggested recording levels for analog multitrack:

- Peak-reading LED bargraph meter: 0 to +6 dB
- VU meter, drums and percussion: −6 to −8 VU
- VU meter, other instruments: +3 VU maximum
- Peak LED light in a VU meter: Occasional flashes

(A) Mixer.

DESIGN CENTER

INPUT FADERS

MASTER FADERS

(B) Recorder–mixer.

DESIGN CENTER

**Figure 13.1** Setting faders at design center.

While setting levels for a digital multitrack, peak each track around −5 dB. This allows some headroom for surprises. You don't want to exceed 0 dBFS (0 dB full scale).

If you have a separate mixer and multitrack recorder, which meters should you watch? Usually you watch the mixer meters to set levels, because you previously matched the recorder meters to the console meters. You have to watch the recorder meters for tracks that are patched direct.

If you are mixing several instruments to one or two groups (as in a drum submix), follow this procedure:

1. Monitor the group(s).

2. Set its submaster fader to design center.

3. Set the submix balances, panning, and recording level with the input faders.

4. Fine-tune each submix level with the submaster fader.

## Set EQ

You may want to apply equalization at this point to each instrument heard individually. Filter out frequencies above and below the range of the instrument. However, don't spend too much time on EQ until all the instruments are mixed together. The EQ that sounds right on a soloed instrument may not sound right when all the instruments are heard together. In creating the desired tonal balance, use EQ as a last resort after trying different mics and mic placements. You also can apply EQ during playback or mixdown. This may be preferable because EQ applied when recording cannot always be undone if you're unhappy with it.

# Recording

Next, set the track you want to record to "record ready" mode. Now start recording. Write down the tape-counter time for this take. "Slate" the tape: announce on tape the name of the tune and the take number. Then record a two-measure count-off. This is done to set the tempo for overdubs. For example, if the time signature is 4/4, you say, "1, 2, 3, 4, 1, 2, (rest) (rest)." The rests are silent beats. You need some silence before the song starts to make editing easier later on. If your recorder–mixer is part of a MIDI tape sync system, the count-off is unnecessary because your MIDI sequencer sets the song tempo.

After recording the track, rewind the tape to the beginning of the song using the return-to-zero or locate function. If necessary, set the monitor selector to "tape," "track," or "mix," and play back the recording to check the performance and sound quality. You can set a rough mix with the monitor mix (aux) knobs. If your multitrack is patched to the insert jacks, use the faders, pan pots, EQ, and aux knobs to set a rough mix.

# Overdubbing

After your first track is recorded, you might want to add more musical parts. This procedure is called **overdubbing**. When you overdub, the musician listens to tracks already recorded, and records a new part on an unused track.

Before you start, get or write a sheet of the song's arrangement. It shows the lyrics, verses, choruses, bridge, and so on. Play the song and write down the tape counter times at the start of each verse and chorus. That way, when the musician says "Let's fix that flat note at the end of the second chorus," you can wind the tape to the correct counter time.

Ready to overdub? Here's what to do:

1. Turn off the control room speakers and listen on headphones.

2. Set up a headphone monitor mix of the recorded tracks. Some mixers use the AUX knobs for this. If your multitrack recorder is connected to the mixer's INSERT jacks, monitor the stereo mix, and set up a mix with the channel faders.

3. Plug in the mic or direct box for the instrument or vocal you want to record. Assign it to an unused track. Turn up its fader to design center (the 0 point about ¾ up).

4. Set up your multitrack to monitor the tape playback of recorded tracks (in sync mode) and monitor the input signal of the instrument or vocal you want to record.

5. Have the musician play. Can you hear the signal in the phones? Set the recording level using the TRIM or GAIN control for that mic's channel.

6. Play the tape. As the musician plays or sings along, set up a good mix of the recorded tracks and the live instrument you're going to record. Ask the musician if he is hearing what he needs to hear. Change the mix if needed. Some musicians want to hear effects when they overdub; some want it dry. If you're overdubbing backup vocals one at a time, often it helps to remove certain other vocals from the headphone mix.

7. When you're ready to record the new part, wind the tape to a PREROLL point about 10 seconds before the part of the song where the musician plays. Set the recorded tracks to SAFE and set the track you're recording on to RECORD READY.

8. Before you hit that Record button, **stop**! Are you recording on the correct track(s)? Are you going to accidentally erase any tracks? Double-check your track sheet, and make sure the record-enable buttons are on **only** for the tracks that are safe to record over.

9. Start recording and have the musician play along with the tracks. If the musician makes a mistake, you can re-record or punch-in the new part without affecting the parts already on tape.

# Punching-In

**Punching-in** is used to fix mistakes in a recorded performance, or to record a musical part in segments. A punch is also called an **insert**. You play the multitrack recording, then "punch" or press the record button at the right spot, record a new part, then punch-out of record mode.

Some musicians record the same musical part over and over until the part is perfect. This process is tedious, but you have to pay attention. You need to be aware of where you are in the song at all times, and not erase anything you want to keep.

Some musicians like to record a performance a phrase at a time, perfecting each phrase as they go. Others record a complete take, then go back and fix the weak parts.

To do a punch-in, grab your song-arrangement sheet and follow these steps:

1. Wind the tape to a PREROLL point about 10 seconds before the point where you want to start recording. Note the tape-counter time and write it down. Also enter a memory location point there if your recorder can do that.

2. Play the song to the musician over headphones. The musician plays along to practice the part. Write down the tape counter times where to punch-in and punch-out. Otherwise you might erase a good take.

3. Finally you're ready to record. Before you hit that Record button, **stop**! Tell the musician what you're going to do so there's no chance of a mistake. Be very clear. For example, "I'm recording your keyboard part on two new tracks." Or, "I'm punching-in over your old performance—is that what you wanted?"

4. Okay, ready to go. Play the tape. During a rest or pause in the music just before the part needing correction, punch-in the record button (or use a footswitch). Have the musician record the new part, and punch-out right away. You don't want to erase the rest of the track!

5. Press LOCATE or rewind the tape to the preroll memory point you set, about 10 seconds before the punch. Play the tape to see if the punch was okay. If necessary, you can re-record the punch.

Some multitrack recorders have an **autopunch** function. You set the punch-in and punch-out points into the machine's memory. As the tape plays, the recorder automatically goes into and out of record mode at those points. Some recorders can loop repeatedly between those two points.

After you rewind to the preroll point, notice if the musician wants to practice the part with the tape stopped. Don't redo the punch until he or she is ready.

What if you want to overdub more parts, but all the tracks are full? With care, you can punch in more instruments on a completely full tape by recording them in the pauses on recorded tracks. For example, suppose all the tracks are full but you want to add a cymbal crash at the beginning of the chorus. Find a track that has a pause at that moment, and punch in the cymbal crash there.

Here's another way to free up tracks. Suppose that one track is mostly blank except for a short riff at certain points in the song. Using a patch cord, copy that riff to a blank area in another recorded track. Then you can erase the first track and record a new part on it.

# Composite Tracks

If several open tracks are available, you can record a solo performance in several takes, each on a separate track. This is called **recording composite tracks** or **comping**. Here's an example of its use:

1. Suppose you want to record four different takes of the lead vocal on tracks 5, 6, 7, and 8. Also suppose each mixer channel feeds a separate track. Set up channels 5, 6, 7, and 8 to have the same input gain, fader level, EQ, and effects.

2. Record a take on track 5. Turn down track 5; record another take on track 6, and so on.

3. When finished, play back each track by itself and note the tape-counter times (or lyrics) of the best parts. You might prefer the verse of track 5, the chorus of track 7, and so on.

4. Match the track levels. Play the tape, and switch between the tracks using the MUTE buttons on your mixer. You want to hear just the best parts of each track. Rather than muting unwanted parts of each take, you might erase them instead (be careful!). Then play a mix of tracks 5, 6, 7, and 8. You'll hear the best parts of all the takes in succession.

5. When you're ready, assign all those tracks to an open track set in record mode. Record the mix of the best parts to that composite track.

6. Finally, erase the original takes.

If you're recording on a hard-disk or MiniDisc recorder, those devices have virtual tracks (explained in Chapter 10). They let you comp a performance with virtual tracks rather than real tracks.

# Bouncing Tracks

If your recorder has too few tracks for all the parts you want to overdub, you can **bounce tracks**—mix several tracks to one or two open tracks, and record the mix on that track. Then you can erase the original tracks, freeing them for more overdubs.

Suppose you want to bounce tracks 1, 2, and 3 to track 4. Follow these steps:

1. Monitor only track 4.
2. Assign input modules 1, 2, and 3 to track 4.
3. Set all recorder tracks to "play" or "safe" mode.
4. Set the input selector switches for input modules 1, 2, and 3 to "tape."
5. Play the tape.
6. Using input faders 1, 2, and 3, mix the tracks as desired and set the recording level to peak around 0 on track 4.
7. When you're happy with the mix, rewind to the beginning of the song.
8. Set only recorder track 4 to "record ready" mode.
9. Start recording. The mix of tracks 1, 2, and 3 record on track 4.

To add live mic or instrument signals while you're bouncing, plug them into input 4 and assign input 4 to track 4. In this way, you can record up to 10 tracks on a 4-track machine while bouncing tracks. Table 13.1 shows this bouncing procedure. Each track with an asterisk is a live instrument or mic signal. Tracks without an asterisk are already recorded on tape.

Follow these steps to execute this bouncing procedure:

1. Record three instruments (A, B, C) on tracks 1, 2, and 3.
2. Mix these three tracks with a live instrument signal and record the result on track 4.
3. Record two more instruments on tracks 1 and 2.
4. Bounce tracks 1 and 2 onto track 3 while mixing in another live instrument.
5. Record one more instrument on track 1.
6. Bounce track 1 to track 2 while mixing in another live instrument.
7. Record one more instrument on track 1.

You can continue this process to add even more instruments, but every re-recording adds noise, distortion, and frequency-response errors.

**Table 13.1** Bouncing procedure for recording 10 tracks with a 4-track recorder

| Step 1 Track | Step 2 Track | Step 3 Track | Step 4 Track | Step 5 Track | Step 6 Track | Step 7 Track |
|---|---|---|---|---|---|---|
| 1 A* | 1 | 1 E* | 1 | 1 H* | 1 | 1 J* |
| 2 B* | 2 | 2 F* | 2 | 2 | 2 HI* | 2 HI |
| 3 C* | 3 | 3 | 3 EFG* | 3 EFG | 3 EFG | 3 EFG |
| 4 | 4 ABCD* | 4 ABCD | 4 ABCD | 4 ABCD | 4 ABCD | 4 ABCD |

This signal degradation is called **generation loss**. MiniDisc, hard-disk, and digital tape have less generation loss than analog tape.

Try a similar procedure for other track-bouncing combinations, setting up your recorder–mixer for the desired track assignments.

# Flying In

Suppose you have a multitrack recording of a pop song. One of the tracks is vocals. During the first chorus, the vocals sound great, but during the second chorus, the vocals are out of tune. You want to copy the vocal track from the first chorus to the second.

This can be done by a process called **flying in**. You copy the good vocal track to an external DAW or sampler, then fly-in (copy) the external recording back to the multitrack. The fly-in part must stay in sync with the other tracks.

Here's another use for a fly-in. You give a keyboard player a CDR, DAT, or MiniDisc of a song you recorded. The keyboardist takes the song home, figures out a keyboard part, and records it on another CDR, DAT, or MiniDisc while listening to the song. He or she sends the part to you, and you fly it into the multitrack recording.

Here are the steps to do a fly-in:

1. On the multitrack recorder, find the track you want to copy. Connect its output to a DAW or sampler.
2. Play the multitrack recording and copy the part to the DAW or sampler. If the part you want to fly-in is already on CDR, DAT, or MiniDisc, copy it to your DAW or sampler.
3. Connect the DAW or sampler output to the input of the track on which you want to record the fly-in.
4. Locate the multitrack recorder to a point a few seconds before where you want to fly-in the part.

5. Start recording on the correct track. While listening to the song play, press Play on the DAW, or trigger the sample, so that the flown-in part starts at the right time. Practice this until the timing is correct. The tempos should match if you recorded to a click track.

If you recorded your project on a multitrack DAW, use the copy and paste function to fly-in parts.

# Drum Replacement

Suppose you've recorded the drum tracks, but you don't like the sound of them. Maybe the kick drum is too flabby, and no amount of EQ or gating seems to help. You might try a technique called **drum replacement**. You take recorded drum tracks and replace them with drum samples generated by a drum machine, sampler, or sound module.

First, select the desired drum sound in the sampler. Feed the audio from a drum track into the sampler's trigger input. When each drum hit triggers the sampler, it instantly plays its internal drum sample. Feed the sampler's output signal to one channel of your mixer.

In this way you can replace individual drum tracks or an entire kit. You can also mix the samples with the original tracks to get a bigger drum sound.

# Mixdown

After all your tracks are recorded (maybe with some bouncing), it's time to mix or combine them to 2-track stereo. Use the mixer faders to control the relative volumes of the instruments, use panning to set their stereo position, use EQ to adjust their tone quality, and use the aux knobs to control effects.

If you're mixing only audio tracks (no live sequencer tracks), use the mixing console or recorder–mixer. But if you're synching a sequencer to your recorder, mix the audio tracks and sequencer tracks with an outboard mixer that is not part of the console or recorder–mixer. Some elaborate recorder–mixers have extra line inputs for MIDI instruments so that you can do the entire mix with the recorder–mixer.

## *Set Up the Mixer and Recorders*

To prepare for a mixdown, first locate the mixer jacks for output channels 1 and 2 (they might be called "Bus 1 and 2," or "Stereo mix bus"). Plug these outputs into the line inputs of your 2-track recorder (Figure 13.2).

**Figure 13.2**
Connections for mixdown.

Clean and demagnetize any analog tape machines. Set all the mixer controls to "off," "zero," or "flat." You should start from ground zero in building a mix.

Tape a strip of paper or masking tape along the front of the mixer to write which instrument(s) each fader affects. Keep this strip with the multitrack tape for use each time you play it.

If necessary, set the input-selector switches on the mixer to "tape" (or "track" or "mix") because you'll be mixing down the multitrack recording. Monitor the 2-track stereo mix bus.

For starters, put the master faders at design center (about $^3/_4$ up, at the shaded portion of fader travel). This sets the mixer gain structure for the best compromise between noise and headroom.

## Erase Unwanted Material

Mixing will be a lot easier if you first erase noises before and after each song, and within each track.

Play the multitrack recording and listen to each track alone. Erase unwanted sounds, outtakes, and entire segments that don't add to the song. To avoid mistakes, it's best to do this while the musicians are around.

What if a noise occurs just before the musician starts playing? When you erase the noise, you might erase the beginning of the performance. You can prevent this if you're using analog tape. Turn the cassette tape upside down or reverse the reels, then find the track of the desired instrument playing backwards. Play the tape section that came just after the noise. You hear it playing in reverse. Just after the reverse part ends, punch that track into record mode to erase the noise. It might be safer to mute the track during mixdown and then unmute it just before the musician plays.

If your multitrack is an MDM, set up an automatic punch-in/-out at the correct times to erase the noise.

# Panning

You need to pan the tracks before doing the mix, because the loudness of a track depends on where it's panned. Assign each track to busses 1 and 2 (or the stereo mix bus), and use the pan pots to place each track where desired between your stereo speakers. Typically the bass, snare, kick drum, and vocals go to center; keyboards and guitars can be panned left and right.

Pan tracks to many points between the monitors: left, half-left, center, half-right, right. Try to achieve a stereo stage that is well balanced either side of center. For clarity, pan to opposite sides any instruments that cover the same frequency range.

You may want some tracks to be unlocalized. Harmony singers and strings should be spread out rather than appearing as point sources. Stereo keyboard sounds can wander between speakers. You could fatten a lead-guitar solo by panning it left, and panning the solo delayed to the right. (This delay might come from a distant room mic you used while recording.)

Consider creating some front-to-back depth. Leave some instruments dry so they sound close; add reverb to others so they sound farther away.

If you want the stereo imaging to be realistic (say, for a jazz combo), then pan the instruments to simulate a band as viewed from the audience. If you're sitting in an audience listening to a jazz quartet, you might hear drums on the left, piano on the right, bass in the middle, and sax slightly right. The drums and piano are not point sources, but are somewhat spread out. If spatial realism is the goal, you should hear the same ensemble layout between your speakers. In most rock recordings, the piano and drums are spread all the way between speakers—interesting but unrealistic.

Pan-potted mono tracks often sound artificial; each instrument sounds isolated in its own little space. It helps to add some stereo reverb. It surrounds the instruments and "glues" them together.

When you monitor the mix in mono, you'll likely hear **center channel buildup**. Instruments in the center of the stereo stage will sound louder in mono than they did in stereo, so the mix balance will change in mono. To prevent this, note which tracks are panned hard left or right, and bring them a little toward the center.

# Compression

Sometimes the lead vocal track might be too loud or too quiet relative to the instruments because vocals have a wider dynamic range than instruments. You can control this by running the vocal track through a compressor. It will keep the loudness of the vocal more constant, making it easier to hear throughout the mix. Patch the compressor into the insert jack(s) of the vocal input module. Set it for the desired amount of compression (typically 2:1 ratio, −10 dB threshold). It's also common to compress the kick drum and bass. (For more information, see Chapter 11.)

## Set a Balance

Now comes the fun part. The mixdown is one of the most creative parts of recording. Here are some tips to help your mixes sound terrific.

Before doing a mix, tune up your ears. Play over your monitors some CDs whose sound you admire. This helps you get used to a commercial balance of the highs, mids, and lows.

Choose a CD with tunes like those you're recording. Check out the production. How is the balance set? How about EQ, effects, sonic surprises? Try to figure out what techniques were used to create those sounds, and duplicate them. Of course, you might prefer to break new ground.

Using the input faders, adjust the volume of each track for a pleasing balance among instruments and vocals. You should be able to hear each instrument clearly. In some units, you use the MONMIX controls for this function. Some mixing consoles have trim knobs that set the playback gain of the multitrack recorder tracks. In that case, set all faders in use to design center, and adjust the trims to get a rough mix.

Here's one way to build the mix. Make all the instruments and vocals equally loud. Then turn up the most important tracks and turn down background instruments. Or, bring up one track at a time and blend it with the other tracks. For example, first bring up the kick drum to about −10 VU, then add bass and balance the two together. Next add drums and set a balance. Then add guitars, keyboards, and finally vocals.

In a ballad, the lead vocal is usually on top. You might set the lead-vocal level to peak at −5 VU. Bring up the monitor level so that the vocal is as loud as you like to hear it, then leave the monitor level alone. Bring in the other tracks one at a time and mix them relative to the vocal track.

When the mix is right, everything can be heard clearly, yet nothing sticks out too much. The most important instruments or voices are loudest; less important parts are in the background. In a typical rock mix, the snare is loudest, and the kick is nearly as loud. The lead vocal is next in level. Note that there's a wide latitude for musical interpretation and personal taste in making a mix.

Sometimes you don't want everything to be clearly heard. Once in a while, you might mix in certain tracks very subtly for a subconscious effect.

It's a good idea to monitor around 85 dB SPL. If you monitor louder, the bass and treble will be weak when the mix is played softly.

To test your mix, occasionally play the monitors very quietly, and see if you can hear everything. Switch from large monitors to small, and make sure nothing is missing.

## Set EQ

Next, set EQ for the tonal balance you want on each track. If a track sounds too dull, turn up the highs or add an enhancer. If a track sounds too bassy, turn down the lows, and so on. Cymbals should sound crisp and distinct, but not sizzly or harsh; kick drum and bass should sound deep, but not overwhelming or muddy. Be sure the bass is recorded with enough edge or harmonics to be audible on small speakers.

You'll need to readjust the mix balances after adding EQ. The EQ that sounds right on a soloed track seldom sounds right when all the tracks are mixed together. So make EQ decisions when you have the complete mix happening.

In pop-music recordings, the tone quality or timbre of instruments does not have to be natural. Still, many listeners want to hear a realistic timbre from acoustic instruments, such as the guitar, flute, sax, or piano.

The overall tonal balance of the mix should be neither bassy nor trebly. That is, the perceived spectrum should not emphasize lows or highs. You should hear the low bass, mid-bass, midrange, upper midrange, and highs roughly in equal proportions. Too-loud frequency bands can tire your ears.

When your mix is almost done, switch between your mix and a commercial CD to see whether you're competitive. Play them through the same monitor speakers. If the tonal balance of your mix matches a commercial CD, you know your mix will translate to the real world. This works regardless of what monitors you use.

## Add Effects

With the balances and EQ roughed in, it's time to add effects. You might want to plug in an external reverb or delay unit to add spaciousness to the sound (see Chapter 11). This device connects between your mixer's aux-send and aux-return jacks (or aux-send and bus-in jacks).

Find the AUX RETURN or BUS IN controls (if any), set them ³/₄ up, and pan them hard left and right. Using the AUX knobs on the mixer, adjust the amount of delay or reverb for each track as desired. AUX might be labeled EFFECTS or FX on your mixer.

Too much effects and reverb can muddy the mix. You might turn up the reverb only on a few instruments or vocals. Once you have the reverb set, try turning it down gradually and see how little you can get by with.

The producer of a recording is the musical director and decides how the mix should sound. Ask to hear recordings having the kind of sounds the producer desires. Try to figure out what techniques were used to create those sounds.

Also try to translate the producer's sound-quality descriptions into control settings. If the producer asks for a "warmer" sound on a particular instrument, turn up the low frequencies. If the lead guitar needs to be "fatter," try a stereo chorus on the guitar track. If the producer wants the vocal to be more "spacious," try adding reverb, and so on.

## Set Levels

Set the overall recording level as you're mixing. To maintain the correct gain staging, keep the master faders at design center. Then adjust all the input faders by the same amount so your levels peak around 0. You can touch up the master faders a few dB if necessary. Don't exceed 0 dB if you're recording to a digital medium.

## Judging the Mix

When you mix, your attention scans the inputs. Listen briefly to each instrument in turn and to the mix as a whole. If you hear something you don't like, fix it. Is the vocal too tubby? Roll off the bass on the vocal track. Is the kick drum too quiet? Turn it up. Is the lead-guitar solo too dead? Turn up its effects send.

The mix must be appropriate for the style of music. For example, a mix that's right for rock music usually won't work for folk music or acoustic jazz. Rock mixes typically have lots of production EQ, compression, and effects; and the drums are way up front. In contrast, folk or acoustic jazz is usually mixed with no effects other than slight reverb, and the instruments and vocals sound natural. A rock guitar typically sounds bright and distorted; a straight-ahead jazz guitar usually sounds mellow and clean.

If you want a realistic, natural sound, adjust the controls to create the illusion of live musicians playing in front of you. To do this you must be familiar with the sound of real instruments. Manipulate the recorded tracks until they sound like your memory of the real thing.

Try to keep the mix clean and clear. A clean mix is uncluttered; not too many parts play at once. It helps to arrange the music so that similar parts don't overlap. Usually, the fewer the instruments, the clearer the sound. Mix selectively, so that not too many instruments are heard at the same time.

In a clear-sounding recording, instruments do not "crowd" or mask each other's sound. They are separate and distinct. Clarity arises when instruments occupy different areas of the frequency spectrum. For example, the bass provides lows; keyboards might emphasize midbass; lead guitar may provide upper mids, and cymbals fill in the highs.

Often the rhythm guitar occupies the same frequency range as the piano, so they tend to mask each other's sound. You can aid clarity by equalizing them differently. Boost the guitar at, say, 3 kHz, and boost the piano around 10 kHz. Or pan them to opposite sides.

## Changes during the Mix

It's rare to do a mix in which you set the faders and leave them there. Often you need to mute tracks, change fader levels, or change EQ during a mix.

To reduce tape and mixer noise, mute all tracks that have nothing playing at the moment. That is, if there is a long silence during a track, mute that silent portion. Unmute these tracks just before their instruments start playing. Mute unrecorded tracks as well.

Level changes during the mix should be subtle, or else instruments will "jump out" for a solo and "fall back in" afterwards. Set faders to preset positions during pauses in the music. Nothing sounds more amateurish than a solo that starts too quietly then comes up as it plays. You can hear the engineer working the fader.

If you need to change fader levels during the mix, you might mark these levels next to each fader, maybe on a thin piece of tape. Make a **cue sheet** that notes the mixer changes at various tape-counter times. For example:

| | |
|---|---|
| 0:15 | Unmute vocal |
| 1:10 | Lead solo −5 |
| 1:49 | Lead −10 |
| 2:42 | Synth EQ +6 at 12 K |
| 3:05 | Start fade, out by 3:15. |

What if you want the sound of an instrument to change drastically during a song, but there are too many mixer changes to handle at once? You can do this by multing and muting. Here's what to do:

Suppose you want a track to have a radically different level, EQ, and effects during the chorus. Using a Y-cord or a mult on a patch bay, connect that track to two mixer channels—say, channels 5 and 6. On channel 5, set the level, EQ, and aux sends as you want them to be for most of the song. On channel 6, set the level, EQ, and aux sends as you want them to be for the chorus.

When you're ready to mix, mute channel 6. Play the song and mix it. When the chorus comes up, unmute channel 6 and mute channel 5. The sound will change during the chorus.

## Calibration Tones

Before you record the mix, you should record calibration tones if your master tape is analog. Record the following tones on both channels simultaneously with noise reduction (20 seconds each):

- 1 kHz at 0 VU.
- Optionally, 15 kHz for azimuth alignment. Record at 0 VU for 15 or 30 ips; –10 VU for 7 ½ ips to prevent tape saturation.
- 1 kHz, 10 kHz, and 100 Hz (record at 0 VU for 15 or 30 ips; –10 VU for 7 ½ ips).
- If Dolby A is used, record an encoded Dolby tone at 0 VU, followed by an encoded 1 kHz tone at 0 VU. (Dolby A tones should be generated by each track's encoder.)

The duplicating engineer or CD-mastering engineer uses the 15 kHz tone to align the repro head, the 1 kHz 0 VU tone to set overall level and channel balance, and the other tones to set playback EQ. Then the engineer's tape machine plays back the same tonal balance and stereo balance that you recorded during mixdown.

If you don't have access to a multifrequency generator, just put on a 1 kHz tone or a sine-wave synthesizer note (two octaves above middle C) at 0 VU, both channels. DAT mixdown tapes and CD-Rs require no tones.

If you will record the mixes on DAT, put in a blank DAT tape and exercise it: fast-forward to the end and rewind to the top. You might want to clean the tape path with a cleaning cassette, but usually only if the DAT is producing errors. Another popular 2-channel recorder for mixes is CD-RW or CD-R.

## Record the Mix

When you're happy with the mix and recording levels, slate the tape and record the mix on your 2-track machine. Keep a log noting the 2-track start and stop times for each song. You'll use these times when you're ready to edit. If the mix is very difficult, you can record it a section at a time, and then edit the sections together.

To fade out the end of the tune, pull down the master faders slowly and smoothly. Try to have the music faded out by the end of a musical phrase. The slower the song, the slower the fade should be.

The mixdown is complete. Leave the 2-track recorder running for a few seconds—make a blank space so you don't accidentally erase the end of the mix you just did. Play back the mix to listen for dropouts and errors. You might record several different mixes of one song, then choose the best mix.

Repeat these mixdown procedures for the rest of the good takes, leaving about 20 seconds of silence between each recording. Give your ears a rest every few hours! Otherwise, your hearing loses highs and you can't make correct judgments.

After a few days, listen to the mix on a variety of systems—car speakers, a boom box, a home system. The time lapse between mixdown and listening will allow you to hear with fresh ears. Do you want to change anything? If so, make it right. You'll end up with a mix to be proud of.

# Summary

The following are summaries of the procedures for recording, overdubbing, and mixdown. Use these steps for easy reference.

## *Recording*

1. Turn up the headphone or monitor volume control. Monitor the aux bus you're using for the monitor mix. If your multitrack is wired to the insert jacks, monitor the stereo bus instead.

2. Assign instruments to tracks. To record one instrument per track, connect its direct-out (or insert send) to a track input.

3. Turn up the channel, submaster, and master faders to design center (the shaded portion of fader travel, about $3/4$ up).

4. Adjust the input attenuators (trim) to set submixes and recording levels.

5. Set the monitor/cue mix.

6. Record onto the multitrack recorder.

## *Overdubbing*

1. Assign the instruments or vocals to be recorded to open tracks. An open track is blank or has already been bounced.
2. Turn up the monitor/cue system.
3. Turn up the submasters and master to design center.
4. Play the multitrack tape (in sync mode, if necessary) and set up a cue mix of already-recorded tracks.
5. While a musician is playing, adjust the input attenuation and recording level.
6. Set the monitor/cue mix to include the sound of the instrument or vocal being added.
7. Record the new parts on open tracks.
8. Punch in and bounce as needed.

## *Mixdown*

1. If necessary, set the input selectors to accept the multitrack recorder output signals.
2. Monitor busses 1 and 2 (or the stereo mix bus).
3. Assign tracks to busses 1 and 2 (or the stereo mix bus).
4. Turn up the master fader to design center. In some mixers, the submasters should also be up.
5. Set preliminary panning.
6. Set a rough mix with the input faders.
7. Set equalization and effects.
8. Perfect the mix and set recording levels.
9. Record onto the 2-track recorder.

# Automated Mixing

A multitrack mixdown is often a complicated procedure. It can be difficult to change the mixer settings correctly at all the right times. So you might want to use **automated mixing**—have a sequencer remember and set the changes for you.

As you mix a song, you might adjust the mixer controls several times. For example, raise the piano's volume during a solo, then drop it back down. Mute a track to reduce noise during pauses in the performance. An automated mixing system can remember your mix moves, and later recall and reset them.

You can even overdub mix moves—for example, do the vocal-fader moves on the first pass, drum moves on the second pass, and so on. You also can punch-in fader moves to correct them. Effects changes can be automated as well in some units.

To understand automation, you need to know several terms related to MIDI. So more information on automation is given at the end of Chapter 16 on MIDI.

Here is a "poor man's" automation system suggested by producer/engineer Dave Aron. Suppose you are using a digital multitrack recorder—either tape or hard disk—and you have two empty tracks.

1. Connect your mixer's stereo outputs to the inputs of those two tracks.
2. Set up the mix at the beginning of the tune, and start recording the mix on the empty tracks, as if you were recording to a DAT.
3. When you come to a point in the song where the mix needs to be changed, stop recording.
4. Rewind a few seconds, hit Play, and reset the faders as desired.
5. Again, rewind the tape a few seconds and hit Play. On the two mix tracks, punch into record mode at the point where the mix changes.
6. Continue this process for all the changes in the mix, updating the mix as you go.

Now that you know how to run the mixer and recorders, you're ready to do an actual session—covered next.

# 14

# SESSION PROCEDURES, ASSEMBLY, AND MASTERING

"We're rolling. Take One." These words begin the recording session. It can be an exhilarating or an exasperating experience, depending on how smoothly you run it.

The musicians need an engineer who works quickly yet carefully. Otherwise, they may lose their creative inspiration while waiting for the engineer to get it together. And the client, paying by the hour, wastes money unless the engineer has prepared for the session in advance.

This chapter describes how to conduct a multitrack recording session. These procedures should help you keep track of things and run the session efficiently.

There are some spontaneous sessions—especially in home studios—that just "grow organically" without advance planning. The instrumentation is not known until the song is done! You just try out different musical ideas and instruments until you find a pleasing combination.

In this way, a band that has its own recording gear can afford to take the time to find out what works musically before going into a professional studio. In addition, if the band is recording itself where it practices, the microphone setup and some of the console settings can be more or less permanent. This chapter, however, describes procedures usually followed at professional studios, where time is money.

# Preproduction

Long before the session starts, you're involved in **preproduction**—planning what you're going to do at the session, in terms of overdubbing, track assignments, instrument layout, and mic selection.

## Instrumentation

The first step is to find out from the producer or the band what the instrumentation will be and how many tracks will be needed. Make a list of the instruments and vocals that will be used in each song. Include such details as the number of tom toms, whether acoustic or electric guitars will be used, and so on.

## Recording Order

Next, decide which of these instruments will be recorded at the same time and which will be overdubbed one at a time. It's common to record the instruments in the following order, but there are always exceptions:

1. Loud rhythm instruments—bass, drums, electric guitar, electric keyboards
2. Quiet rhythm instruments—acoustic guitar, piano
3. Lead vocal and doubled lead vocal (if desired)
4. Backup vocals (in stereo)
5. Overdubs—solos, percussion, synthesizer, sound effects
6. Sweetening—horns, strings

The lead vocalist usually sings a **reference vocal** or **scratch vocal** along with the rhythm section so that the musicians can get a feel for the tune and keep track of where they are in the song. The vocalist's performance in this case is recorded but probably is redone later.

In a MIDI studio, a typical order might be:

1. Drum machine (playing programmed patterns)
2. Synthesizer bass sound
3. Synthesizer chords
4. Synth melody
5. Synth solos, extra parts
6. Vocals and miked solos (recorded on tape or hard disk)

# Track Assignments

Now you can plan your track assignments. Decide what instruments will go on which tracks of the multitrack recorder. The producer may have a fixed plan already. The outer tracks of analog multitracks are most prone to dropouts at high frequencies, so they are usually reserved for bass, kick drum, or SMPTE time code.

What if you have more instruments than tracks? Decide what groups of instruments to put on each track. In a 4-track recording, for example, you might record a stereo mix of the rhythm section on tracks 1 and 2, then overdub vocals and solos on tracks 3 and 4. Or you might put guitars on track 1, bass and drums on track 2, vocals on track 3, and keyboards on track 4.

Remember that when several instruments are assigned to the same track, you can't separate their images in the stereo stage. That is, you can't pan them to different positions—all the instruments on one track sound as if they're occupying the same point in space. For this reason, you may want to do a stereo mix of the rhythm section on tracks 1 and 2, for instance, and then overdub vocals and solos on tracks 3 and 4.

It's possible to overdub more than four parts on a 4-track recorder. To do this, bounce or ping-pong several tracks onto one (see Chapter 13).

If you have many tracks available, leave several tracks open for experimentation. For example, you can record several takes of a vocal part using a separate track for each take, so that no take is lost. Then combine the best parts of each take into a single final performance on one track. It's also a good idea to record the monitor mix on one or two unused tracks. The recorded monitor mix can be used to make a work-print tape for the client to take home and evaluate, or for a cue mix for overdubs.

# Session Sheet

Once you know what you're going to record and when, you can fill out a session sheet (Figure 14.1). This simple document is adequate for home studios. "OD" indicates an overdub. Note the tape-counter time for each take, and circle the best take.

# Production Schedule

In a professional recording studio, the planned sequence of recording basic tracks and overdubs is listed on a **production schedule** (Figure 14.2).

```
SONG: Escape to Air Island

TRACK  INSTRUMENT       MICROPHONE
  1      Kick           AKG D-112
  2      Drums          Crown GLM-100
  3      Lead Voc  OD   Neumann U-87
  4      Harm Voc  OD   Neumann U-87
  5      Lead Guit OD   Shure SM-57
  6      Keys L         Direct
  7      Keys R         Direct
  8      Bass           Direct

TAKES:  1, 2, ③
```

**Figure 14.1**
A session sheet for a home studio.

```
Tape Speed:  15 ips                Artist:  Muffin
8 Track                            Producer:  B. Brauning
Noise Reduction:  Dolby c
```

1. Song:  "Mr. Potato Head."
   Instrumentation:  Bass, drums, electric rhythm guitar,
   electric lead guitar, acoustic piano, sax, lead vocal.
   Comments:  Record rhythm section together with reference
   vocal. Overdub sax, acoustic, piano, and lead vocal later.

2. Song:  "Sambatina."
   Instrumentation:  Bass, drums, acoustic guitar, percussion,
   synthesizer.
   Comments:  Record rhythm section with scratch acoustic
   guitar. Overdub acoustic guitar, percussion, and
   synthesizer.

3. Song:  "Mr. Potato Head."
   Overdubs:  (1) acoustic piano, (2) lead vocal, (3) sax.

4. Song:  "Sambatina."
   Overdubs:  (1) acoustic guitar, (2) synthesizer,
   (3) percussion.

5. Mix:  "Mr. Potato Head."
   Comments:  Add 80-msec delay to toms.
              Double lead guitar in stereo.
              Increase reverb on sax during solo.

6. Mix:  "Sambatina."
   Comments:  Add flanger to bass on intro only.
              Manually flange percussion.

**Figure 14.2**  A production schedule.

## Track Sheet

Another document used in a pro studio is the track sheet or multitrack log (Figure 14.3). Write down which instrument or vocal goes on which track. The track sheet also has blanks for other information.

**Figure 14.3** A track sheet (multitrack recorder log).

## Microphone Input List

Make up a microphone input list similar to the following:

| Input | Instrument | Microphone |
|-------|------------|------------|
| 1 | Bass | Direct |
| 2 | Kick | EV RE-20 |
| 3 | Snare/Hi-Hat | AKG C451 |
| 4 | Drums Overhead L | Shure SM81 |
| 5 | Drums Overhead R | Shure SM81 |
| 6 | Hi Toms | Sennheiser MD 421 |
| 7 | Low Toms | Sennheiser MD 421 |
| 8 | Electric Lead Guitar | Shure SM57 |
| 9 | Electric Lead Guitar | Direct |
| 10 | Piano L | Crown PZM-30D |
| 11 | Piano R | Crown PZM-30D |
| 12 | Scratch vocal | Beyer M500 |

Later you will place this list by the mic snake box and by the mixing console.

Be flexible in your microphone choices—you may need to experiment with various mics during the session to find one giving the best sound with the least console equalization. During lead-guitar overdubs, for example, you can set up a direct box, three close-up microphones, and one distant microphone—then find a combination that sounds best.

Find out what sound the producer wants—a "tight" sound; a "loose, live" sound; an accurate, realistic sound. Ask to hear recordings having the kind of sound the producer desires. Try to figure out what techniques were used to create those sounds, and plan your mic techniques and effects accordingly. Tips on choosing a microphone are given in Chapter 6.

## Instrument Layout Chart

Work out an instrument layout chart, indicating where each instrument will be located in the studio, and where baffles and isolation booths will be used (if any). In planning the layout, make sure that all the musicians can see each other and are close enough together to play as an ensemble.

# Setting Up the Studio

About an hour before the session starts, clean up the studio to promote a professional atmosphere. Lay down rugs and place AC power boxes according to your layout chart.

Now position the baffles on top of what has gone before. Put out chairs and stools according to the layout. Add music stands and music-stand lights. Run cue cables from each artist's location to the cue panel in the studio.

Place mic stands approximately where they will be used. Wrap one end of a microphone cable around each microphone-stand boom, leaving a few extra coils of cable near the mic-stand base to allow slack for moving. Run the rest of the cable back to the mic input panel or snake box. Plug each cable into the appropriate wall panel or snake box input, according to your mic input list.

Some engineers prefer to run cables in reverse order, connecting to the input panel first and running the cable out to the microphone stand. That procedure leaves less of a confusing tangle at the input panel where connections might be changed.

Now set up the microphones. Check each mic to make sure its switches are in the desired positions. Put the mics in their stand adapters, connect the cables, and balance the weight of the boom against the microphone.

Finally, connect the musicians' headphones for cueing. Set up a spare cue line and microphone for last-minute changes.

# Setting Up the Control Room

Having prepared the studio, run through this checklist to make sure the control room is ready for the session:

1. Pull all the patch cords from the patch panel.

2. If necessary, patch console bus 1 to recorder track 1, bus 2 to track 2, and so on.

3. Check out all the equipment to make sure it's working.

4. Clean and demagnetize the analog tape machines.

5. Label the blank tape with the artist, date, and reel number. If you're recording on hard disk or MiniDisc, type in this information on screen along with the file name.

6. Thread on or insert the blank tape.

7. Put calibration tones on analog tape.

8. Normalize or zero the console by setting all switches and knobs to "off," "zero," or "flat" so they have no effect.

9. If you're using a separate mixer and multitrack recorder, you might want to feed a 1 kHz tone to all the console outputs so that the console meters read 0 VU. Adjust the multitrack machine's record levels (if any) so the recorder meters also read 0 VU. This procedure matches the recorder meters to the console meters, so that you have to watch only the console meters while recording. If you're using noise-reduction equipment, refer to Chapter 9 for meter calibration and Dolby-tone recording.

10. Switch on phantom powering for condenser microphones.

11. Set the console input-selector switches (if any) to "mic" or "line" as needed.

12. Attach a **designation strip** of paper leader or masking tape across the front of the console. Referring to your mic input list, write on the strip the instrument each fader affects (bass, kick, guitar, etc.). Also label the submasters and monitor-mixer knobs according to what is assigned to them.

13. Turn up the monitor system. Carefully bring up each fader one at a time and listen to each microphone. You should hear normal studio noise. If you hear any problems such as dead or noisy microphones, hum, bad cables, or faulty power supplies, correct them before the session.

14. Verify the mic input list. Have an assistant scratch each mic grille with a fingernail and identify the instrument the microphone is intended to pick up. If you have no assistant, listen on headphones as you turn up one mic at a time and listen for background noise.

15. Check all the cue headphones by playing a tone or music through them and listening while wiggling the cable.

After the musicians arrive, allow them ½ hour to 1 hour free setup time for seating, tuning, and mic placement. Show them where to sit, and work out new seating arrangements if necessary to make them more comfortable.

Once the instruments are set up, you may want to listen to their live sound in the studio and do what you can to improve it. A dull-sounding guitar may need new strings, a noisy guitar amp may need new tubes, and so on. Adjust the studio lighting for the desired mood.

# Session Overview

This is the typical sequence of events:

1. For efficiency, record the basic rhythm tracks for several songs on the first session.
2. Do the overdubs for all the songs in a dubbing session.
3. Mix all the tunes.
4. Assemble and leader the analog mixdown tape, or edit the DAT mixdown tape.

# Recording

Follow the mixer recording procedures described in Chapter 13. Before you start recording, make connections to record a work-print tape of the studio monitor mix, either on two leftover tracks or on a cassette deck. This tape is for the producer to take home to evaluate the performance.

When you're ready to record the tune, briefly play a metronome to the group at the desired tempo, or play a click track (an electronic metronome) through the cue system. Or just let the drummer set the tempo with stick clicks.

Start the tape in record mode. Note the tape-counter time. Hit the slate button and announce the name of the tune and the take number.

Have someone play the keynote of the song (for tuning other instruments later). Then the group leader or the drummer counts off the beat, and the group starts playing.

The producer listens to the musical performance while the engineer watches levels and listens for audio problems. As the song progresses, you may need to make small level adjustments. As stated before, the recording levels are set as high as possible without causing distortion. Balancing the instruments at this time is done with the monitor mixer. The monitor mix affects only what is being heard, not what is going on tape.

The assistant engineer (if any) runs the multitrack recorder and keeps track of the takes on the track sheet, noting the name of the tune, the take number, and whether the take was complete (Figure 14.3). Use a code to indicate whether the take was a false start, nearly completed, a "keeper," and so on.

While the song is in progress, don't use the solo function, because the abrupt monitoring change may disturb the producer. The producer should stop the performance if a major fluff (mistake) occurs but should let the minor ones pass.

At the end of the song, the musicians should be silent for several seconds after the last note. Or, if the song ends in a fade-out, the musicians should continue playing for about a minute so there is enough material for a fade-out during mixdown.

After the tune is done, you can either play it back or go on to a second take. Set a rough mix with the aux or monitor-mix knobs. If you connected your multitrack to the insert jacks, use the faders to set a rough mix with EQ and effects. The musicians will catch their fluffed notes during playback; you just listen for audio quality.

Now record other takes or tunes. Pick the best takes. To protect your hearing, try to limit tracking sessions to four hours or less—five hours maximum.

# Overdubbing

After recording the basic or rhythm tracks for all the tunes, add overdubs. A musician listens to previously recorded tracks over headphones and records a new part on an open track. Follow the overdubbing and punching in/out procedures in Chapter 13.

## Composite Tracks

If several open tracks are available, you can record a solo overdub in several takes, each on a separate track. This is referred to as recording **composite tracks**. After recording all the takes, play back the solo (in sync mode) and assign all the overdubbed tracks to a remaining open track set in record mode. You bounce all the solo tracks to a composite track. Match the levels of the different takes. Then switch the overdubbed tracks on and off (using muting), recording just the best parts of each take. Finally, erase the old overdubbed tracks to free them up for other instruments. If you are recording on hard disk or MiniDisc, usually you can record several takes on virtual tracks, then comp those virtual tracks during mixdown.

## Drum Overdubs

Drum overdubs are usually done right after the rhythm session because the microphones are already set up, and the overdubbed sound will match the sound of the original drum track.

## *Overdubbing in the Control Room*

To aid communications among the engineer, producer, and musician, have the musician play in the control room while overdubbing. You can patch a synth or electric guitar into the console through a direct box, and feed the direct signal to a guitar amp in the studio via a cue line. Pick up the amp with a microphone, and record and monitor the mic signal.

# Breaking Down

When the session is over, tear down the microphones, mic stands, and cables. Put the microphones back in their protective boxes and bags. Wind the mic cables onto a power-cable spool, connecting one cable to the next. Wipe off the cables with a damp rag if necessary. Some engineers hang each cable in big loops on each mic stand. Others wrap the cable "lasso style" with every other loop reversed. You learn this on the job.

Put the labeled tape in its box (stored tail-out if it's analog tape). Also in the box, or in a file folder, put the designation strips, track sheet, and take sheet. Label the box and folder. Normally the studio keeps the multitrack master for possible future work unless the group wants to buy or rent it.

If you recorded analog, you may want to edit out the outtakes and splice them together on a separate reel. Then put one foot of paper leader between each of the master tape's keeper takes. Write new tape logs indicating the reels' contents.

Log the console settings by writing them in the track sheet or reading them slowly into a portable cassette recorder. At a future session you can play back the tape and reset the console the way it was for the original session. Consoles with automated mixing can store and recall the control settings.

# Mixdown

After all the parts are recorded, you're ready for mixdown. Prepare the console and recorders, record tones, erase noises, and play the multitrack tape through the console while adjusting balances, panning, equalization, reverberation, and effects. Once you've rehearsed the mix to perfection, record it onto a 2-track recorder (analog tape recorder, DAT, or computer hard disk). Follow the mixdown procedures in Chapter 13.

Record calibration tones on the analog 2-track master tape just before recording the mixes. (See Chapter 13 for more information.)

# Assembling Analog-Tape Master Reels

If you mixed to analog tape, now you're ready to assemble that tape into a finished format for cassette or CD duplication. It will contain the songs in the desired order, plus leader tape for separating the songs with silence. It also has calibration tones. The cassette/CD mastering engineer will use those tones to align the playback deck for flat response from your tape.

## *Sequencing the Songs*

Discuss the order of the songs on the recording. For the first song, use a strong, accessible, up-tempo tune. Follow it with something quieter. Alternate keys or tempos from song to song. The last tune should be as good as or better than the first to leave a good final impression.

If you intend cassette release, try to keep the total times for Side A and Side B about equal to conserve cassette tape. Side A should be slightly longer than Side B so that any blank cassette tape is at the end of Side B.

## *Leader Length*

The length of leader between songs depends on how long a pause you want between them. Two to four seconds is typical. Use longer leader if you want the listener to get out of the mood of the piece he or she just heard before going on to the next. Use shorter leader either to change the mood abruptly or to make similar songs flow together. Short leader also works well after a long fade-out because the fade-out itself acts like a long pause between songs. Each second of leader is 15 inches long (for 15 ips) or 30 inches long (for 30 ips).

What if you want to crossfade between two songs? Either use a digital audio workstation, or follow these steps:

1. Use two 2-track recorders. Put song 1 on one recorder and song 2 on another.

2. Feed both recorders into your mixer, and connect the mixer output to a third 2-track recorder. Match the levels and noise reduction on all the recorders.

3. Play song 1. Near the end of the song before the crossfade, start recording the mix on the third machine.

4. As song 1 fades out, start song 2 and fade it up.

5. After recording this crossfade on the third machine, edit the crossfade into the rest of the program.

## *Master-Reel Assembly*

If the recording is too long to fit on a single reel, make a separate reel for Side 1 and Side 2 of the cassette. To assemble the master tapes, wind onto the take-up reel the following material in this order:

1. At least 15 seconds of leader or blank recording tape
2. Tones
3. At least 10 seconds of leader
4. First song
5. Leader
6. Second song
7. Leader, etc.
8. Last song on Side 1 of album
9. At least 15 seconds of leader

Then rewind the tape. Play it and time it from the beginning of the first song to the end of the last song (including the leaders between songs). This is called the **running time**. Also note the start and stop time of each selection.

Using a piece of masking tape, fasten the leader tail to the reel and print "TAIL OUT" on the masking tape. Or use blue leader tape for tails out, red for heads out. Type or print a neat label for the tape reel including title, artist, "Side 1," and the running time.

Using another take-up reel, assemble Side 2 of the album (but without tones). Time Side 2 and label the reel.

Be sure to make a safety copy of the master before sending the master tape, in case it is lost or damaged. When copying the master, set the calibration tone from the playback machine to read the same level on the recording machine. There's no need to reset the program levels because you already set them while recording the master tape.

# Digitally Editing and Mastering Your Mixes

You can edit and re-sequence your mixes by using a personal computer, digital editing software, and a sound card. Chapter 10 describes how to edit with your computer. Basically, you edit out noises or false starts before the beginning of each song, put the songs in the desired order, and insert a few seconds of silence between each song. If the program will be duplicated on cassette, leave a minute of silence between the Side A songs and Side B songs.

Put $\frac{1}{10}$ second of silence at the beginning of each song, or set each Start ID about $\frac{1}{10}$ second before the beginning of each song. That is done so that CD players can find and play each song's beginning without missing any audio.

After doing this editing, you might want to **master** the program. In mastering you try to make each song the same loudness and the same tonal balance. The object is a consistent sound from track to track, so that everything flows better and the album sounds unified. You also might try to make the CD as loud or "hot" as possible.

Here are the basic steps in mastering:

1. Use the software, or a 20 Hz highpass filter, to remove any DC offset from the program. DC offset is a small DC voltage that may or may not be part of the audio signal. If not removed, this offset can reduce headroom and create clicks at transitions between two songs.

2. Find the song with the highest peaks, and normalize it—raise its gain, if possible, so that its maximum level reaches 0 dBFS.

3. Adjust the level of each other song by ear, relative to that song. Try to make the vocal equally loud in each song.

4. Add EQ to songs that sound different from the others. For example, if one song is thin in the bass, boost the bass on that song using the DAW's graphic equalizer.

5. You might want to make the CD as loud or hot as commercial CDs. To do that, you could add multiband compression to the entire program, then normalize the compressed program up to 0 dB. A compression ratio of 2 : 1 is common; 3 : 1 is maximum. Don't overdo the compression, because it can give a non-transparent, processed sound with no dynamic range.

As an alternative, or in addition, limit the highest signal peaks a few dB, then normalize. Limiting can create a loud CD without altering the dynamics. Try not to limit more than 3 dB or so; otherwise you might hear a "squeezed" or distorted sound, maybe with clicks on loud notes.

You might combine some compression, limiting, and normalization. These methods raise the average level of the program—which contributes to loudness—without raising the peak level beyond 0 dB.

You might prefer to send out your mixdown tape or CD-R for editing and mastering. A good mastering engineer can listen to your program with fresh ears, then suggest processing for your tape that will make it sound more commercial. He or she is likely to have a better monitor system than yours. If you plan to have your program mastered outside, do not apply any signal processing to your finished mixes such as level changes, compression, or EQ. Let the mastering house do it with their better equipment and software.

# Transferring the Edited Program to DAT or CD-R

Now you will copy the edited, mastered program from hard disk to a blank DAT or CD-R. Let's start with the DAT format.

After loading the DAT tape, fast-forward to the end and rewind to the top. This loosens the tape pack, distributes the tape lubricants more evenly, and aligns the tape with the tape guides. You might want to clean the DAT recorder with a cleaning tape (usually this is done only if the DAT machine is producing errors). Turn off "automatic start ID."

To prevent DAT drop-outs, record 2 minutes of silence at the head of the DAT tape. When the DAT ABS time reads 2:00 (2 minutes), play the edited program from the hard disk. The editing software has a view or window that tells the start and stop times of each song. Add 2 minutes to these times to get the song start/stop times on the DAT tape.

After the program has copied to DAT, rewind the DAT tape. Refer to your list of DAT start/stop times. Fast-forward to the beginning of each song, and write a manual Start ID there about ½ second before each song. When done, have the DAT machine renumber the program numbers.

Make a safety copy by doing another disk-to-tape transfer. Or run two DATs in parallel during the transfer. Hold onto the safety; you'll need it in case the master tape is lost or damaged.

You can copy your edited mixes to CD-R instead of a DAT tape. The CD-R becomes the master that can be duplicated. Here's what to do:

1. Some DAW software includes a feature called "Build mix to new soundfile" or something similar. After your program is edited, convert it to a new soundfile—a single WAV file.

2. Note the start time of each song in the editing software's Edit Decision List or playlist.

3. Write up a cue sheet, a text file that notes the start time of each song. Make each time about $\frac{1}{10}$ second early so that the CD player's laser has time to find the track before playing audio.

4. In your CD burning software, load in the cue sheet. Place a blank CD-R in your CD burner, and start recording. Burn the master CD for

```
                              DAT TAPE LOG

        PROJECT TITLE: Out of Your Head
        ARTIST: Hal Klee
        PROJECT NUMBER: 960716

        CLIENT: Hal Klee
                1061 College Ave.
                LaSuer, IN 46596
                Phone 219-555-1049

        RECORDING ENGINEER: Hal Klee
        EDITING ENGINEER: Bruce Bartlett, 56657 CR 40, Fenfen,IN 42596
                   219-555-1388 (work)  219-555-9366 (home)

        TAPE CONFIGURATION: TASCAM DA-P20 DAT, 44.1K

        MASTERING INSTRUCTIONS: Just cut flat, no EQ.  Add 6 dB of
        overall compression.  Make chrome cassettes, Dolby B.  Please
        send a proof DAT to Bruce Bartlett.

        There are lots of intentional noises, outtakes, etc.  Distortion
        at 08:32.

        Side A running time: 23:47    Side B running time: 23:08

        ABS times of highest level (0 dBFS):  03:38, 12:43

        Side A
        PGM NO.          TITLE                            START  STOP
             [HEAD OF TAPE]        ...................... 00:00
        1    David.................................        02:00  03:43
        2    Burl White In Manhattan..............        03:47  04:46
        3    Wake Up Samantha.....................        04:50  07:23
        4    Wrench and a Bad Man.................        07:27  09:39
        5    Down Rockaway........................        09:43  12:24
        6    Getting Up...........................        12:28  15:22
        7    Foont................................        15:26  17:06
        8    Lord of the Bytes....................        17:10  18:46
        9    Little Bummer Boy....................        18:50  24:33
        10   Jovian Boo Boos......................        24:37  25:47

        64 seconds of silence here separates Sides A and B.

        Side B
        PGM NO.          TITLE                            START  STOP
        11   Trumpechello.........................        26:51  29:42
        12   Climbin' Keds........................        29:46  31:12
        13   Rumble Machine.......................        31:16  34:45
        14   Ninety Hats..........................        34:49  37:24
        15   It Pays to Be Silent.................        37:28  39:50
        16   Ormes................................        39:54  42:31
        17   Frumplestein.........................        42:35  49:59
```

**Figure 14.4**  Example of a DAT tape log.

duplication at 1 × or 2 × speed to reduce errors. The software should create a series of tracks on the CD, each starting at the times you specified in your cue sheet.

**Note:** Some CD burning software does not create tracks on a CD from a single WAV file. Instead, you save each mixed song as a separate WAV file, then create a cue list of those WAV files. The CD burning software adds 2 seconds of silence between each song. See the CD-R section in Chapter 10 for more detail.

Another way to create master CDs is to use the Alesis MasterLink: a CD recorder with a built-in hard drive and mastering tools. With it you can record your stereo mixes, edit and master them, and burn a finished CD. Sample rates can be up to 96 kHz and word length can be 16-, 20-, or 24-bit. The MasterLink includes sample-rate conversion and noise shaping to alter sample rates and bit resolution as needed.

Several editing/mastering tools are offered with MasterLink, such as 16 different playlists, gain control, editing start and end points, joining or splitting song sections, EQ, compression, normalization, and peak limiting.

If you want to make a few cassette or CD-R copies of your master—say, for demo tapes—copy the DAT tape or CD-R several times with a stereo cassette deck or CD burner. For larger runs, you'll need an outside duplicating house.

# Log

Type or print a **log** describing the DAT master tape (Figure 14.4) or CD-R premaster. For analog tape, also include the tape-head format, stereo/mono, tape speed, playback equalization (usually NAB or IEC), noise reduction, tail-out designation, the location of the test tones (usually at the beginning of Reel 1), tone frequencies, and levels.

Also include the packaging text such as song lyrics, instrumentation, composers, arrangers, publishers, and artwork. Stay in contact with the duplication house, especially about artwork.

Note that the master tape or CD-R doesn't leave the studio until all studio time is paid for! When this is done, send the tape or CD-R to the duplication house.

It's amazing how the long hours of work with lots of complex equipment have been concentrated into that little tape—but it's been fun. You crafted a product you can be proud of. When played, it recreates a musical experience in the ears and mind of the listener—no small achievement.

# 15

# RECORDING THE SPOKEN WORD

Recording music is fun, but recording speech is the main income producer for many studios. Speech is the major sound element in commercials, promo videos, documentaries, drama, educational programs, and books on tape. In this chapter you'll learn ways to record the spoken word effectively.

## Be Consistent

One of the most important qualities of a speech recording is consistency. The tone quality, level, pitch, and tempo of the voice should not change throughout the recording (except for dramatic effect).

Why is this so important? Often, the voice track is assembled from takes recorded on different days, so the sound of the takes has to match. Otherwise, you hear jarring changes in the voice quality as the recording plays.

Typically, you record a complete script in a single session. Then you send a proof copy of the tape to the script's publisher for error checking. After you get the corrections back, you call the announcer back into your studio to record **inserts**—corrected sentences and paragraphs. You edit the inserts into the original recording. If the sound of the inserts doesn't match the sound of the original, the edited program doesn't sound like a single take. So you need to duplicate the recording setup exactly each time you record the announcer.

Several factors can vary from one session to the next: recording level, mic choice and placement, text position, announcer's position, EQ, noise reduction, and even the voice itself. You need to keep all these factors constant by documenting your setup.

Take notes on the mic used, its switch positions (if any), and its position and distance from the announcer. Also note any EQ or noise reduction used. To reduce the number of variables, you might record without EQ. Settle on a standard setup so you can record a predictable sound.

# Microphones

For voice recording, three types of mics are in common use:

- A flat-response cardioid condenser mic
- A "multiple-D" dynamic mic
- A top-quality lavalier condenser mic

A cardioid condenser mic provides a luxurious, big-budget sound—one with full lows and detailed highs. Unfortunately, the mic's bass response varies with the announcer's distance. The closer the announcer is to the mic, the bassier is the recording. Unless the announcer can remain a constant distance away, the voice tone quality will vary.

This close-up bass boost (proximity effect) occurs in **single-D** unidirectional mics. A **multiple-D** mic is designed to compensate for proximity effect: Its bass varies only a little with distance. A single-D mic has holes or slots only in the mic capsule; a multiple-D mic (such as the EV RE-20) has holes or slots in the handle. As an alternative, you might use an omni mic, which has no proximity effect.

A less popular choice is a **lavalier** microphone. It's a miniature unit (like the ones TV newscasters use) that clips onto the announcer's tie or shirt. There are excellent models in the $200 price range. Don't skimp on this microphone, or the sound quality will suffer. Even with a good mic, though, the sound is not as natural as with a conventional mic. Lavaliers work well for video shoots where the mic should be inconspicuous.

A lavalier has some advantages in script recording. Since the user wears the lavalier, it remains a constant distance from the mouth, which aids consistency. There are no breath pops unless the user exhales through the nose. If the announcer sits still, cable noise is not a problem. However, if the announcer's head tilts up and down, the voice gets brighter and duller.

# Mic Placement

Once you've chosen a mic, place it at various distances from the mouth until you hear the best sound quality. A typical distance is 8 to 12 inches. If the mic is too far away, you'll hear too much room reverb. Generally you don't want to hear room sound in a narration recording. If the mic is too close, you'll hear lip and tongue noises, and the voice level will vary when the announcer moves. Find a workable distance somewhere in the middle and stick with it.

Some studios set the miking distance with a spacer or ruler. The announcer can set the spacing with the hand. Ask announcers to spread their fingers, put their thumb on their mouth and their pinky on the mic.

In drama recording, mic distance is less critical. The actors often change their distance to the mic for special effect.

You need to place the mic to avoid breath popping. When a person says words with the letters "p," "t," or "b," a turbulent puff of air shoots out of the mouth. If this air puff hits a mic grille, you hear a thump or pop. Since a pop disturbance leaves the mouth within a narrow angle, you can prevent pops by putting the mic above the mouth at eye height. It also helps to put a foam pop filter on the mic, or use a disk-type pop screen on a gooseneck.

To prevent table thumps, mount the mic on a boom stand and place the stand on the floor. You might want to use a shock mount, too. Cover the script stand with felt or foam to absorb noises.

A typical placement for lavalier mics is 8 inches below the chin. Tape the cable to the shirt in order to prevent rubbing noises. Try not to cover the mic with clothing, or the sound will be muffled.

## *Minimizing Sound Reflections*

Angle the script so that the mic does not pick up sound reflections from the script. These reflections can combine at the mic with the direct sound from the announcer. This causes phase interference—a filtered, colored tone quality that changes as the announcer moves.

Figures 15.1 and 15.2 show some right and wrong ways to place scripts. In Figure 15.1A, sound reflects off the script stand into the mic. But in Figure 15.1B, the script is tilted more vertically so reflections bounce away from the mic. In Figure 15.2A, sound reflects off the script into the lavalier mic. But in Figure 15.2B, the script is tilted horizontally to prevent reflections.

If you record more than one announcer at once, seat them at least 4 feet apart to prevent phase interference between mics.

**Figure 15.1**
Angle the script stand to avoid reflections into the microphone.

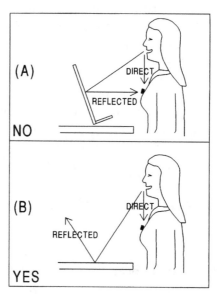

**Figure 15.2**
Angle the script to avoid reflections into the lavalier microphone.

# Reducing Sibilance

Another factor to keep under control is sibilance: the emphasis of "s" and "sh" sounds. These sounds have strong high frequencies around 5 to 10 kHz, which can saturate the tape of duplicated cassettes. If you need to reduce sibilance, use a flat-response mic, mike off-axis to the mouth, or cut EQ a little around 5 to 10 kHz.

A better solution is to use a **de-esser**. This signal processor removes sibilance without affecting tone quality. A de-esser is a compressor with a high-frequency boost before compression and a complementary cut after compression. With a de-esser, only excessive high frequencies (sibilant sounds) are compressed.

# At the Session

Give the announcer a comfortable fixed-frame chair with a back to prevent motion. Ask the announcer to move as little as possible, and not to slump over the table.

If the announcer's head moves, the tone quality will change. Why? Low frequencies radiate from the mouth in all directions, but high frequencies radiate mostly straight out. So, if an announcer's head moves while talking, the high frequencies ("s" sounds) will miss the mic sometimes.

Suppose you're ready to record a script. The announcer is seated the proper distance from the mic, and the script is on a music stand. The announcer has folded up the bottom corners of the script pages to form a handle for turning pages without noise. You have an identical script on which to mark **edit points**: spots where the announcer misreads a sentence.

After a level check, start recording. The announcer reads the script, and you follow along in your own script, marking edit points with a pen. Just leave the recorder rolling when mistakes occur.

If the announcer misreads a word, or makes a paper noise, have the announcer read the whole sentence over. The announcer should not try to correct the error in mid-sentence, because a mid-sentence edit tends to sound unnatural. If you edit between sentences, the edit will be undetectable.

Figure 15.3 shows a typical script with edit marks. Instead of marking the words that were misread, the producer marked the beginning of the sentences with errors. Those marks correspond to the edit points on tape. Two marks indicate a second retake.

# Digital Editing

After the recording is done, you're ready to edit out the mistakes with editing software. If you recorded the speech on DAT, copy it to your hard disk. (You could record directly to hard disk instead.) When the copy is done, follow this procedure:

EDITOR'S COPY

SCRIPT FOR "COSMIC ORDER" FILM

Client: Impossible Productions, Inc.

A branch consists of two or more radiations from a
common point. Its basic shape is the letter "Y."

Each branch has its own branches. For example, a tree
trunk branches into large limbs. Each limb branches into
smaller limbs. Each smaller limb branches into sticks.
Each stick branches into twigs. Each twig branches into
leaf veins. /If a tree were a symphony, you'd hear a basic
melody repeated with ever-increasing refinement and
complexity.

→ *remove cough*

Each small branch is a variation on the theme of
branching. That is, each part resembles the whole. /For
example, the veins in a leaf resemble a tree in shape;
capillaries resemble veins and arteries.

→ *noise?*

//Branches are also visible in tree roots, rivers, the
circulatory system, the nervous system, the lungs, roads,
audio systems, single-point grounding systems, organization
of knowledge, distribution of knowledge, and more.

Let's consider that last example.///Knowledge is
gathered and distributed like a tree: The research material
is the ground the tree is rooted in; the roots represent
research; the trunk represents the compilation of research
into a new synthesis, and the branches represent the
dissemination of the new knowledge to various students via
publishing, broadcasting, or education in classrooms.

To digress a bit, consider this: If life seems too
complicated, remember it's all happening to you here and
now. "Here" is small and "now" is short. You can handle
it.
                            ↖ *THUMP?*

/On the other hand, "here" follows you wherever you go,
and "now" is continuous. Never mind!

**Figure 15.3** A script with edit marks.

1. You'll see the waveform or the soundtrack of the narration on your
   computer monitor screen. Play the soundtrack and follow along in
   the marked-up script.

2. When you come to the beginning of a misread sentence, mark it on
   screen as the beginning of a region or sound segment.

3. Play the misread sentence up to the start of the corrected sentence. Mark that as the end point of the region. The region you marked will highlight.

4. Select EDIT and DELETE. The misread sentence will disappear, and the following audio will slide in to fill the gap.

Another method:

1. Mark the start and end points of sentences and paragraphs that you want to keep. Each start and stop point should be at the beginning of a sentence.

2. Define these sound segments as regions or zones.

3. Put them in order in a playlist, and play the playlist.

Check your edits. Are there any double-breaths between sentences? Are any sentences read twice? Do the pauses between sentences sound unnatural? If so, correct these problems by changing the segment start/end points.

# Proof CD-Rs and Inserts

You might want to make a proof CD-R or cassette of the edited tape to send to the script publisher for approval. The publisher may notice reading errors that you missed during the recording session. They'll send back a marked-up script showing the errors. The next time the announcer is back in your studio, rerecord the sentences or paragraphs needing corrections.

Be sure to match the recording level, mic position, and so on with those of the original tape. Otherwise the inserts may sound like another person talking. Play some of the original tape aloud so that the announcer can duplicate the pitch and tempo. You may need to equalize the inserts to match the original take.

After editing in the inserts, send another proof CD-R or cassette to the publisher. If it's error-free, you can add sound effects or music as needed.

# Sound Effects and Music

Many scripts call for sound effects or music to accompany the narration. Start with the edited speech on one track of a multitrack recorder (tape or DAW). On other tracks, record sound effects and music where noted in the script. Then mix the tracks.

Libraries of sound effects and mood music are advertised in recording magazines and audio-visual publications. Some publishers require royalty payments for each use of material. To avoid royalties, you can order sound-effects CDs from record stores, or record your own effects and music.

Sound effects can also be prerecorded and sequenced on a computer hard disk or a digital cart machine. You trigger the effects to play while you record the narration.

Many productions have a musical introduction, which you start and fade down just before the announcer starts talking. There's often an outro, too. An outro is music that begins near the end of the narration, then fades up and out to conclude the program.

## Backtiming a Musical Outro

You might want the outro to end when the narration ends. You'll perform a technique called **backtiming**. Follow these steps:

1. Find the spot in the script where you want the outro to start fading up. Play the speech starting from there, and time it to end of the narration. For this example, say it's 20 seconds from outro fade-up to end.

2. In your CD player, put in a CD of outro music and go to the end of the piece you want to use. Press Rewind on the CD player and go back 21 seconds. Press Pause. Now the outro is cued up 21 seconds from the end.

3. At the fade-up point in the script, press Play on the CD player and fade it up. The music should end just after the narration ends. You also can record the outro music on a separate DAW track, and slide the track left or right on-screen until its timing is correct.

This chapter gave some advice about recording the spoken word with a consistent, clean sound, and described how to add sound effects and music. Don't neglect this type of studio work, because it's a potential source of income. And it's another skill to add to your resumé.

# 16

# THE MIDI STUDIO: EQUIPMENT AND RECORDING PROCEDURES

Welcome to the computerized world of MIDI equipment—samplers, synthesizers, sampling keyboards, drum machines, and sequencers. Because other texts explain this equipment in detail, brief definitions serve the purpose here. See Appendix C for books on MIDI.

MIDI stands for Musical Instrument Digital Interface. It's a standard connection between electronic musical instruments and computers that allows them to communicate with each other. Some of the things you can do with MIDI are:

- Combine the sounds of two electronic musical instruments by playing them both with one keyboard.
- Create the effect of a band playing. To do this, you record keyboard performances into a computer memory, edit the recording note by note if you wish, and have the recording play through synthesizers and a drum machine in sync.
- Automate a mixdown, or automate effects changes.
- Make a keyboard, electric guitar, or breath controller produce a sound like any instrument.
- Automate the playback of sound effects and music for video productions.

The MIDI signal is a stream of digital data—not an audio signal—running at 31,250 bits per second. It sends information about the notes you play on a MIDI controller, such as a keyboard or drum pads. Up to 16 channels of information can be sent on a single MIDI cable.

There are three types of MIDI ports on MIDI devices:

- MIDI IN receives data going into the device.
- MIDI OUT sends out data generated by the device.
- MIDI THRU is like MIDI OUT, but duplicates the data that is at the MIDI IN port.

Connect MIDI OUT from the sending device to MIDI IN of the receiving device. For example, connect a keyboard controller's MIDI OUT to the MIDI IN connector of a sequencer or a sound module. Use MIDI THRU to connect two or more receiving devices in a row. For example, connect a keyboard controller's MIDI OUT to sequencer MIDI IN, and connect sequencer MIDI THRU to sound module MIDI IN.

# MIDI-Studio Components

The following equipment typically is used in a MIDI studio:

- Synthesizer
- Sampler
- Drum machine
- Sequencer
- Power amplifier and speakers
- Personal computer (optional)
- MIDI computer interface (optional)
- Recorder–mixer (optional)
- Tape synchronizer (optional)
- Mixer (optional)
- 2-track recorder
- Effects
- Audio cables
- MIDI cables
- Power outlet strip
- Equipment stand

You have learned about most of these in previous chapters, but a review might help at this point.

A **synthesizer** is a keyboard musical instrument that creates sounds electronically with oscillators (Figure 16.1). Your studio might have more than one of these.

A **multitimbral synthesizer** can play two or more patches at once. A **patch** is a sound preset (an instrumental timbre), such as a synthesized piano, bass, or snare drum. A **polyphonic synthesizer** can play several notes at once (chords) with a single patch.

A **sound module** is a synthesizer without a keyboard. It is triggered by a sequencer or a controller. A **sampler** is a device that records sound events, or samples, into computer memory. A **sample** is a digital recording of one note of a real sound source: a flute note, a bass pluck, a drum hit, etc. A sample also can be a digital recording of a short segment of another recording. The sampling process is described in Chapter 10.

Often a sampler is built into a sample-playing keyboard, which resembles an electronic piano. It contains samples of several different musical instruments. When you play on the keyboard, the sample notes are heard. The higher the key you press, the higher the pitch of the reproduced sample.

A **drum machine** is a device that plays built-in samples of all the sounds of a drum set and percussion (Figure 16.2). It also records and plays back drum patterns that you play or program with built-in keys or drum pads. Some units can sample sounds.

A **sequencer** is a device that records a MIDI signal—information about the notes you play—into computer memory. Unlike a tape recorder, a sequencer does not record audio. Instead, it records the key number of each note you play, note-on signals, note-off signals, and other parameters such as velocity, pitch-bend, and so on.

The sequencer can be a standalone unit (Figure 16.3), a circuit built into a keyboard instrument, or a computer running a sequencer program.

**Figure 16.1** A synthesizer.

**Figure 16.2**  A drum machine.

**Figure 16.3**  A sequencer.

Like a multitrack audio recorder, a sequencer can record 8 or more tracks, with each track containing a performance of a different instrument.

A **power amplifier and speakers** (or **powered speakers**) let you hear what you're performing and recording. Usually these are small monitor speakers set up in a Nearfield arrangement (about 3 feet apart and 3 feet from you).

You might want a computer system and perhaps a printer. The computer is used mainly to run a sequencer program, which replaces the sequencer. Compared to a standalone sequencer with an LCD screen, the computer monitor screen displays much more information at a glance, making editing easier and more intuitive (Figure 16.4).

The computer can run other useful programs. A **MIDI/digital audio program** records both MIDI sequences and digital audio tracks on your hard disk and keeps them in sync. A **librarian program** manipulates patches or samples and stores them on computer disks. A **voice editor**

**Figure 16.4** A monitor-screen shot of Passport Master Tracks Pro MIDI software. (Courtesy Passport Designs, Inc.)

**program** lets you create your own patches. A **notation program** converts your performance to standard musical notation and prints it. A **film-sound program** lets you enter a list of sound effects or music with the time each occurs, and runs through the list automatically, triggering the effects and music at the right times.

A **MIDI computer interface** plugs into a user port in your computer and converts MIDI signals into computer signals and vice versa. You need this only if you're using a computer in your system.

A combination **recorder and mixer** records vocals and acoustic instruments. A more elaborate studio might use a separate mixer and multitrack recorder.

An **FSK tape synchronizer** synchronizes tape tracks with sequencer tracks and makes the sequencer start at the same place in the song that you start the tape. Alternatives to FSK tape sync are SMPTE time code and MIDI time code (MTC).

If you have two or more synthesizers, or a synth and a drum machine, you need a **mixer** to blend their audio outputs into a single stereo signal.

A **2-track recorder** records the stereo mix of all your sound sources. The tape made on this recorder is the final product. The recorder can be open-reel, cassette, DAT, MiniDisc, or hard drive.

**Effects** include compression, reverb, gating, chorus, and so on.

**Audio cables** carry audio signals and typically have a $\frac{1}{4}$-inch phone plug on each end. They connect synths, sound modules, and drum machines to your mixer line inputs.

**MIDI cables** carry MIDI signals and are used to connect synths, drum machines, and computers together so that they can communicate with each other. A MIDI cable is a 2-conductor shielded cable with a 5-pin DIN plug on each end. Pins 4 and 5 are the MIDI signal, pin 2 is shield, and pins 1 and 3 are not connected.

A **power outlet strip** is a row of electrical outlets to power all your equipment. It's a good idea to have surge protection in the strip.

An **equipment stand** is a system of tubes, rods, and platforms that supports all your equipment in a convenient arrangement. It provides user comfort, shorter cable lengths, and more floor area for other activities.

## The Keyboard Workstation

A **keyboard workstation** includes several MIDI components in one chassis: a keyboard, a sample player, a sequencer, and perhaps a synthesizer and disk drive. That's everything you need to compose, perform, and record instrumental music. Some workstations include drum sounds so that you can get by without a separate drum machine.

If you want your songs to include vocals or miked instruments, you also need something to record them: a multitrack audio recorder, a recorder–mixer, a computer running multitrack recording software, or MIDI/digital audio software (explained later). You synchronize the MIDI equipment to the recorder with a tape synchronizer, SMPTE time code, or MIDI time code (MTC). To make a permanent copy of your stereo mixes, you also need a 2-track recorder.

# MIDI Recording Procedures

The rest of this chapter describes recording procedures for several different MIDI studio setups, from simple to complex. Read your instruction manuals thoroughly and simplify them into step-by-step procedures for various operations. Note that each piece of MIDI gear has its own idiosyncrasies, and the instructions may have errors or omissions. If you have questions, call the technical-service people at the manufacturer of your equipment.

# Recording with a Polyphonic Synthesizer

This is the simplest method of recording (Figure 16.5). You plug a MIDI interface into your computer, plug your synth into the interface, and run a sequencer program on the computer. You play chords and melody, record this MIDI data with your sequencer, and play back the sequence through your synthesizer. The basic steps follow:

1. Set your sequencer to record on one track.
2. Play a tune on your keyboard.
3. Play back the sequencer recording to hear it. Your performance will be duplicated by the synthesizer.
4. Quantize the track if desired.
5. Punch in/out to correct mistakes.
6. Arrange the song by combining various sequences.
7. Enter any program changes (changes in timbre).
8. Play the composition and set recording levels.
9. Start the sequencer playing, and record the synth output on a 2-track recorder. That recording is the final product.

Here are the details for each step.

## Set Your Sequencer to Record on One Track

Choose a tempo in your sequencer and choose the track you want to record on. Using your mouse, click on the RECORD key on-screen. You'll hear a metronome ticking at the tempo you set.

**Figure 16.5** A synthesizer connected via a MIDI interface to a computer running a sequencer program.

## Play Music on Your Keyboard

Listen to the sequencer's metronome and play along with its beat. The sequencer keeps track of the measures, beats, and pulses. When the song is done, click on STOP. The sequencer stops recording and should go to the beginning of the sequence (the top of the tune).

Another way to record your performance is in **step-time**, one note at a time. If the part is difficult to play rapidly, you also can set the sequencer tempo very slow, record while playing the synth at that tempo, and then play back the sequence at a faster tempo.

## Play Back the Sequencer Recording

Click on PLAY. You'll hear the sequence playing through your synthesizer.

## Quantize the Track

**Quantizing** is the process of correcting the timing of each note to the nearest note value (quarter note, eighth note, and so on). If you wish, quantize the performance by the desired amount.

## Punch In/Out to Correct Mistakes

To correct mistakes, you can punch in to record mode before the mistake, record a new performance, and then punch out of record mode. Here's one way to do it:

1. Go to a point in the song a few bars before the mistake.
2. Just before you get to the mistake, punch in to record mode and play a new, correct performance.
3. As soon as you finish the correction, punch out of record mode.

Alternatively, you can use **autopunch**. With this feature, the computer punches in and out automatically at preset measures; all you have to do is play the corrected musical part. Perform an autopunch as follows:

1. Using the computer keyboard or mouse, set the punch-out point (the measure, beat, and pulse where you want to go out of record mode).
2. Set the punch-in point (just before the part you want to correct).
3. Set the cue point (where you want the track to start playing before the punch).
4. Click on PLAY.
5. When the screen indicates punch-in mode, or when the appropriate measure comes up, play the corrected part.

6. The sequencer punches out automatically at the specified point in the song.

These punch-in routines were done in real-time. You can also punch-in/out in step-time:

1. Go to a point in the song just before the mistake.
2. Set the sequencer to step-time mode.
3. Step through the sequence pulse by pulse, and punch in to record mode at the proper point.
4. Record the proper note in step-time.
5. Punch out of record mode.

## Arrange the Song by Combining Sequences

Now your sequenced performance is perfect, so you can put together your composition. Many songs have repeated sections: The verse and chorus are each repeated several times. If you wish, you can play the verse and chorus once each and save them as a separate sequence, which you can copy for all the places each occurs in the song.

You can rearrange song sections, and append one section to another, by pressing a few keys on the computer. You can also have any section repeated. In this way, you might build a song by having the computer play sections A, A, B, A, C, A, B, B.

## Enter Program Changes

To add variety to the song, you might want to have the synth play different programs (patches) at different parts of the song. For example, play a piano on the first verse, organ on the second, and marimba on the chorus. One way is to press different presets (program numbers) as you record the sequence.

Another way is to record these program changes on another track, which is called the **controller track**. Be sure to set the controller track to the same channel as the performance track, and turn off any patch on the controller track. Enter the appropriate program numbers at the right time on your synthesizer. Putting the program changes on a separate track makes it easy to edit them. You can punch in new program changes just as you can punch in new performances. When all the program changes are correct, you can bounce them to the performance track if you wish.

Some sequencers do not record the program settings on your synth. They record only program **changes**. Consequently, when you play the sequence into a synth you just turned on, you might hear the wrong sounds. To prevent this problem, insert a few blank measures at the beginning of the tune and record your initial program changes there, according to the sounds you want to hear at the beginning of the tune. Follow this procedure:

1. Insert two or four blank measures at the beginning of your composition.

2. Set each track's patch to the wrong program number. If you want patch #17, for example, set it to #16. This way, you can key in a program change later.

3. Set your sequencer to punch-in mode so that you record only on the blank measures at the beginning of the tune.

4. When the punch-in starts, key in the correct program numbers. You can perform these program changes in several passes, one track at a time.

5. When the sequence plays back, it sets the synth automatically to the correct patches at the beginning of the tune.

An alternative to this procedure is to record a **system exclusive** or **sysex** dump—data about patch settings and so forth—into the sequencer. This works only if your synth and sequencer implement the sysex dump.

## Play the Composition and Set Recording Levels

Plug your synthesizer's audio output (mono or stereo) into the line inputs of your 2-track recorder. Hit the play key on your computer keyboard, and set the recording level for your recorder according to these guidelines: cassette, +3 dB maximum; open-reel, +3 VU maximum; DAT or hard drive, 0 dB maximum.

## Record the Synth Output

Once your levels are set, put your 2-track recorder in record mode, and start the sequencer. This produces the finished product—a stereo recording of your song.

# *Recording with a Multitimbral Synthesizer*

With this method, you play the parts for several different instruments (patches) on the same keyboard, and record each performance on a separate track of a sequencer. During playback, the sequencer plays the desired patches (instruments) in your synth. It sounds like a band playing. You record the synthesizer's output, and that recording is the final product.

Each track and patch is set to corresponding MIDI channels. For example, suppose both track 1 and the bass patch are set to channel 1. Then track 1's performance in the sequencer plays the bass patch in the synthesizer. Track 2 will play another patch (piano, flute, or whatever).

Some sequencers are designed so that, on power-up, track 1 goes to channel 1, track 2 goes to channel 2, and so on. You simply select a track to record on and select a patch for that track. The channel assignments are already taken care of.

Refer back to Figure 16.5 to see the connections. Here is an outline of the steps for recording:

1. Start recording on the first sequencer track.
2. Play music on your keyboard.
3. Play back the recording.
4. Punch in/out to correct mistakes.
5. Record overdubs on other tracks.
6. Bounce tracks.
7. Edit the composition.
8. Mix the tracks.
9. Record the mix.

Again, these steps require a closer look. The following sections present details for each one.

## Record the First Sequencer Track

Adjust the metronome tempo on your sequencer as desired. Set the sequencer to record on track 1. If necessary, set sequencer track 1 to MIDI channel 1.

Select the first patch you want to hear on your synthesizer (in this case, bass guitar). You might want to adjust the timbre of the patch with the parameter controls on the synthesizer in order to create unusual sounds. If necessary, set the synthesizer patch to MIDI channel 1.

Click on RECORD on your computer screen.

## Play Music on Your Keyboard

Listen to the sequencer's metronome and play along with its beat, or record in step-time. The sequencer keeps track of the measures, beats, and pulses. When you click on STOP, the sequencer stops recording and goes to the beginning of the sequence (the top of the tune).

## Play Back the Recording

Click on PLAY on the computer screen. You'll hear the sequence playing through your synthesizer.

## Punch In/Out to Correct Mistakes

As described in the previous section, you can correct mistakes by punching into record mode before the mistake, recording a new performance, and then punching out of record mode. You can also quantize the track to make it correct rhythmically.

## Record Overdubs on Other Tracks

With your first track recorded and corrected, you're ready to record other tracks. Set the sequencer to record on track 2. If necessary, set sequencer track 2 to MIDI channel 2.

On your synthesizer, select the next patch (instrument timbre) you want to use (in this case, piano). If necessary, set it to MIDI channel 2.

Then click on RECORD on your computer screen. Play the piano on the synthesizer while listening to your prerecorded bass on track 1. This track is played by the synthesizer.

Another example may help. Imagine you just recorded a drum part into the sequencer on track 1. You can go back to the start of the sequence, play the drum part, and add a bass line on track 2 in sync with the drums. Then you can go back to the top and add a piano on track 3.

In short, you record the performance of a different patch on each track in the sequencer, and play back the recording through the multitimbral synthesizer, which plays all the patches simultaneously. Or you can use several synths, one for each part, if necessary. Set each track to a different MIDI channel, and set each instrument or patch to the same channel that its track is set to.

## Bounce Tracks

What if your sequencer records 8 tracks, but you want to play 10 patches at once with several synths? You can make more tracks available by bouncing tracks. If you bounce track 5 into track 4, for example, track 5 can be erased, so that you can record a new instrument on track 5.

To do this, click on BOUNCE on your computer screen. Type in the source track and destination track (indicate to which track you want to bounce). In a few seconds, the bounce is accomplished.

You can bounce only one track at a time. You can bounce a track into a prerecorded track, however, without erasing the prerecorded track. The prerecorded track and bounced track then merge. Unlike bouncing with a tape deck, there is no generation loss (no loss of sound quality) when you bounce with a sequencer.

You can record program changes on a separate track set to the same channel as the performance track. Later, bounce the program-change track to the performance track. The performance track and program-change track merge into one. Be sure both tracks are set to the same channel, and that the program-change track has its patch turned off.

## Edit the Composition

Now your sequenced performance is satisfactory, so you can put together your composition. As described in the previous section, you can rearrange song sections and append one section to another by making selections on your computer screen. You also can have any section replayed. Key in program changes at the beginning of the song and anywhere else you want the sounds to change.

## Mix the Tracks

Now that your song is recorded and arranged, you want to adjust the relative volumes of the tracks to achieve a pleasing balance.

If your multitimbral synthesizer doesn't have separate outputs for each patch, you have to adjust the mix at the sequencer. To do this, adjust the volume (key-velocity scaling) of each track with your computer. This only works if your keyboard is velocity-sensitive.

After you adjust the volume of each track in this way, click on PLAY on your computer screen to play the sequence. The desired mix of patches plays on your synth. Some synths let you add internal effects to the overall mix.

If your synth has several individual outputs—one for each patch—connect them to a mixer and set up a stereo mix with panning and effects.

## Record the Mix

If your synth has a single output (mono or stereo), use your 2-track recorder to record the mix off that output. Plug your synthesizer's audio output into the line inputs of your 2-track recorder. Or, if your synth has several individual outputs connected to a mixer, record off the mixer stereo outputs.

Click PLAY on your computer screen and set the recording level for your recorder. Then put your 2-track recorder in record mode and start the sequencer. This produces the finished product—a stereo recording of your song.

337

# *Recording with a Keyboard Workstation*

Each workstation operates in a different way, but here is a typical recording procedure:

1. Set up for recording a song.
2. Record the first musical part.
3. Do step recording (optional).
4. Overdub more parts.
5. Punch in.
6. Set effects.
7. Store the song.

The following sections present more detailed instructions for each step.

## Set Up for Recording a Song

1. Press SEQ (for SEQUENCER) on the front panel.
2. A sequencer menu appears on the LCD screen. You can move a cursor to select various parameters, and press the up or down buttons to set the value of each parameter.
3. Set the time signature (in the Initialize menu).
4. Select the song number.
5. Set the tempo (in the sequencer play/real-time record menu).
6. Select the track number (track 1 to start).
7. Select the program number for the desired sound (for example, a drum set).

## Record the First Musical Part

1. Press REC (record) and START. Listen to two measures of metronome clicks and then start playing.
2. When you finish, press STOP.
3. To hear what you just played, press START.
4. If you want to re-record the part, press REC and START, and play the part again. You also could edit the performance, do punch-ins, and so on.

## Step Recording

Instead of performing a musical part in real-time, you might prefer to enter the notes one at a time, in step-time. Here's the basic procedure:

1. Select the track number and the measure number where you want to start.
2. Press REC and START.
3. Set the length of the first note (1/32 to 1/1).
4. If necessary, specify triplets, dotted notes, key dynamics, style of playing, and rests.
5. Press the desired note or chords on the keyboard.
6. Release all the keys; the recording proceeds to the next step.
7. After entering all the notes, press STOP.

## Overdub More Parts

1. To record the next track, set the track number to the desired track (in this case, track 2).
2. Select the program number for the desired sound (for example, a bass).
3. Press REC and START. As you listen to track 1 playing the drum part, play a bass part on track 2.
4. Continue this procedure (steps 1–3) up to 8 tracks, adding a new instrument each time.

## Punch In

You can correct mistakes easily in each track by punching in, either manually or automatically. The procedure follows:

1. Play the song to find the measures needing correction.
2. Select punch-in mode.
3. Page up one page; set the punch-in measure and the punch-out measure; page down one page.
4. Set the measure number to a point a few bars before the punch-in.
5. Press REC and START. You'll hear the song playing.
6. When the punch-in measure comes up, play the corrected part.
7. Press STOP when done.

## Set Effects

You can page up to the effects menus to set overall effects: hall reverb, chorus, flanging, echo, distortion, and so on. Press the correct number on the numeric keypad to get to the effects menus. (Note that these are built-in keyboard effects, not outboard studio effects.)

## Save the Song File

Save the completed song in multitrack form to a plug-in RAM card or to an external sequencer and disk drive. To prevent data overload, you might have to do the external sequencer recording one track at a time with other tracks muted. If you're satisfied with the final results, record the stereo output signals of the workstation to a 2-track recorder. In addition to these basic operations, you can:

- Bounce tracks
- Edit each note event
- Create and copy patterns—for a drum or bass part, for example
- Modify track and song parameters
- Insert/delete/erase measures
- Modify sounds and effects (in great detail)
- Change the instrument (patch) that each track plays

# *Recording with a Drum Machine and a Synthesizer*

This system combines a synthesizer with a drum machine. Figure 16.6 shows how to connect the cables. Figure 16.7 shows a preferred setup if your synth has a MIDI THRU port.

## Understanding Synchronization

The drum machine has a built-in sequencer that records what you tap on its pads. Suppose you record a drum pattern with its built-in sequencer,

**Figure 16.6** Connections to make a sequencer drive a drum machine and a synthesizer.

**Figure 16.7**
Connections to make a
sequencer drive a drum
machine if your synth has
a MIDI THRU port.

and you record a synthesizer melody with an external sequencer. How do you synchronize the drum patterns in the drum machine with the synthesizer melody in the sequencer? In other words, how do you get the two devices to play in sync, when both have different patterns recorded in different memories?

To synchronize the machines, use a single **MIDI clock** (timing reference) that sets a common tempo for all the equipment. The MIDI clock is a series of bytes in the MIDI data stream that conveys timing information. The clock is like a conductor's baton movements, keeping all the performers in sync at the same tempo. The clock bytes are added to the MIDI performance information in the MIDI signal. The clock signal is 24, 48, or 96 pulses per quarter note (ppq). That is, for every quarter note of the performance, 24 or more clock pulses (bytes) are sent in the MIDI data stream.

Decide which device you want to be your master timing reference—the sequencer or the drum machine. Set the master device to internal clock and set the slave device to external clock or MIDI clock. Then the slave will follow the tempo of the master.

To make this happen, the master sends clock pulses from its MIDI OUT connector. The slave receives those clock pulses at its MIDI IN connector. The slave also passes clock pulses through its MIDI THRU connector to other slave devices down the chain.

If a slave device lacks a MIDI THRU, enable "Echo MIDI in" in the slave device. Then the incoming pulses are duplicated at the MIDI OUT connector.

In the setups shown in Figures 16.6 and 16.7, the sequencer's clock drives both the drum machine and the synthesizer. In other words, the sequencer is the master tempo setter, and the drum machine and synth follow along. The drum machine's internally recorded patterns play in sync with the synthesizer's sequencer-recorded melody.

## Basic Recording Procedure

Once you work out the synchronization problem, you are ready to begin recording with this system. There are two basic methods. The first uses the following steps:

1. Record drum patterns into the drum machine.
2. While listening to the drum patterns, record a synth part with your sequencer.
3. Sync the drums and synth by setting MIDI clocks and channels.
4. Press the play key on the sequencer.

   Use these steps for the second method:

1. Record drum patterns into the drum machine.
2. Copy these patterns onto one track of your sequencer.
3. While listening to the drum track, record a synth part on another track.
4. Play both sequencer tracks.

   Detailed explanations follow for recording drum patterns and synchronizing the drums with the synth.

## Recording Drum Patterns

The first step in composing a song is to record a drum pattern. There are many ways to do this; the following is one suggested procedure:

1. On the drum machine, set the tempo, time signature, and pattern length in measures. For this example, the pattern is 2 bars long.
2. Start recording, and play the hi-hat key in time with the metronome beat.
3. At the end of 2 bars, the hi-hat pattern you tapped repeats over and over (loops).
4. While this is happening, you can add a kick drum beat.
5. While the hi-hat and kick drum are looping, add a snare drum back beat, and so on.
6. Mix the recording by adjusting the faders on the drum machine for each instrument.

   Next, you repeat the process for a different rhythmic pattern—say, a drum fill—and store this as Pattern 2. Then develop other patterns. Finally, you make a song by repeating patterns and chaining them together as described in the drum machine's instruction manual. A song is a list of patterns in order.

It's a good idea to add a count-off (a few measures of clicks) at the beginning so that later overdubs can start at the correct time.

Some musicians like to program a simple repeating drum groove first. While listening to this, they improvise a synth part. After recording the synth part, they redo the drum part in detail, adding hand claps, tom-tom fills, accents, and so on.

## Synching Drums and Synth

Now you're ready to add a synth part and synchronize it with the drum track. The following procedure refers to a sequencer; it could also be a computer running a sequencer program.

1. Record a synth part with the sequencer.
2. Set the drum machine to external clock or MIDI clock.
3. Set the sequencer to internal clock.
4. Set MIDI channels: set the drum machine to channel 1; set the sequencer synth track and the synthesizer to channel 2. In this way, the sequencer's recorded performance will play only the synthesizer. The MIDI clock still controls both devices, even though they are set to different channels.
5. Press the PLAY key on the sequencer. As the sequencer plays its recorded synth melody, the sequencer's clock pulses drive the drum machine and synthesizer at the same tempo. The drum machine plays its internally recorded patterns, while the synth plays the sequencer track.

Another way to synchronize a drum machine and a synthesizer is to record the drum patterns on one track of your sequencer. The advantage is that, whenever you rearrange parts of the music in the sequencer, you also rearrange the drum part. So you don't have to change drum patterns each time you repeat or delete a verse or a chorus. Follow this procedure to record the drum patterns into your sequencer:

1. Record a drum pattern with the drum machine's internal sequencer.
2. Enable the drum machine's clock out and MIDI data out.
3. On your sequencer, turn off the MIDI-THRU feature (if it has one).
4. Set the sequencer to external clock or MIDI clock mode, and set an open track in record mode.
5. Hit the play key on the drum machine. The sequencer records the drum pattern on the open track.

To play back the drum patterns you just recorded, follow this procedure:

1. Set the drum machine to external clock mode.
2. Set the sequencer to internal clock.
3. Set the drum machine's track and the drum machine to the same MIDI channel.
4. Load an empty pattern into the drum machine so that the machine plays only the sequencer track.
5. Put the sequencer in play mode. The drum machine plays its sequencer track at the sequencer's tempo, and other synths connected to the sequencer play their tracks on their channels.

## Recording with a MIDI System plus Tape Sync

You might have a complete MIDI workstation: a synthesizer, sound module, drum machine, sequencer, and recorder–mixer. Here is a suggested procedure for recording, overdubbing, and mixdown with this system:

1. Connect the system.
2. Record drum patterns; record synth tracks into your sequencer.
3. Record the sync tone.
4. Check the sync-tone playback.
5. Overdub acoustic parts.
6. Mix down all the tracks.

These six steps are the basic outline of the procedure. Detailed explanations follow.

### Connect the System

Figure 16.8 shows the hookup. Connect the tape-sync output connector of the sequencer (or MIDI computer interface) to your tape recorder's sync-track input connector. This is an outside track—track 4 of a 4-track recorder, or track 8 of an 8-track recorder. Connect the sync track's output to the tape-sync input of the sequencer or interface. Plug the MIDI equipment audio outputs and the tape-track outputs into a mixer (not shown), and monitor the mixer's output. If your recorder–mixer has enough inputs, you can use it as the mixer.

If your sequencer lacks a tape-sync connector, you need a smart tape-sync box (converter). Connect this system as shown in Figure 16.9.

**Figure 16.8** Connections for a complete MIDI workstation with tape sync.

**Figure 16.9** Connections for a complete MIDI workstation with smart tape sync.

## Compose and Record MIDI Tracks

Now that the system is set up, record drum and synth tracks. Here is a suggested procedure:

1. Set the sequencer, drum machine, and/or converter to internal sync mode.

2. Program the drum tracks into the drum machine. Be sure to set the tempo as desired, because once you record the sync tone, you can't change the tempo. Also consider programming the drum part longer than you need, since the sync tone can be made shorter but not longer.

3. Develop your instrumental arrangement using the synthesizer and its sequencer, set to the same tempo as the drum machine. You can have tempo changes during the song if you enter them before recording the sync track. You might want to record the drum sequence into your sequencer so that changes in the main sequence (new arrangements, tempo changes) affect the drum track as well.

## Record the Sync Tone

Either the drum machine or the sequencer can be used to generate the sync tone. In this example, use the sequencer.

1. Clean and demagnetize the tape heads.

2. Start playing the sequence. A sync tone is generated from the sync output jack.

3. Put the recorder in record-ready mode and set the recording level of the sync tone. Use a level that produces correct synchronization on playback (usually around –4 VU).

4. If you can switch off the noise reduction for the sync track, do so. Dolby is rarely a problem, but dbx can make the sync tone unreadable.

5. Stop the sequencer and reset it to the top of the tune.

6. Tape sync works best if you record the sync track before you record any other tape tracks. Start the tape recorder in record mode. A few seconds later, press PLAY on your sequencer. You'll be recording (**striping**) the FSK or SMPTE tape-sync tone on track 4 of the recorder–mixer. This will be your master clock. **Note:** Some recorders sync to MIDI devices with MIDI time code (MTC).

7. Let the sequencer run for the duration of the song. While striping the tone, do not record any musical material because it may not sync with material recorded later.

## Check the Sync-Tone Playback

Now you play the sync tone you just recorded on tape, and it activates the drum machine and sequencer. First, reset the drum machine and sequencer to the top of the tune, and set them and the converter to external clock mode:

1. Rewind the recorder a little before the beginning of the sync tone and take the sync track out of record-ready mode.

2. Start playing the tape. (You may need to press the play key on the drum machine or sequencer first.) The sequencer should start playing when the tone starts. The tone drives the sequencer, which in turn plays the synth and drives the drum machine—all at the same tempo. They stop when the tone stops.

3. If you have sync problems, try re-recording the tone at a different level. If a tape drop-out causes loss of sync, re-record the tone on a different section of tape or on a new tape or track. You can re-record the sync track before recording other tracks, but not after—you'll lose sync.

## Overdub Acoustic Parts

Now you're ready to overdub vocals and acoustic instruments on tape.

1. Plug a mic into your recorder and assign it to an open track. If possible, don't assign percussive or bass parts to a track adjacent to the sync track because they can interfere with the sync tone.

2. Set the microphone input trim and recording level as described in Chapter 13 on recorder–mixer operation.

3. Rewind the tape to just before the beginning of the sync tone, and hit Play. The drum machine and sequencer should start playing. (You may need to press the PLAY key on the drum machine or sequencer first.)

4. While listening to the synth and drum machine playing through headphones, record any vocals and non-MIDI instruments onto tape. Because you have three tracks available, you could record, for example, lead vocal on track 1, harmony vocal on track 2, and sax on track 3.

## Mix Down All the Tracks

After all your tracks are recorded, use the mixer to set up a mix of the tape tracks and MIDI instruments. If your mixer doesn't have enough inputs for all the tape tracks, you can set a stereo mix of the tape tracks with the recorder–mixer, and combine this stereo mix with the audio signals from your MIDI instruments.

1. Adjust levels, panning, and effects. You'll have three tape tracks, probably eight tracks from the synth and sound module, plus stereo drum tracks, with stereo effects—all first generation!

2. Play the song several times to perfect the mix.

3. When you're satisfied with the mix, rewind the tape just before the beginning of the sync tone and hit play. Record the mix onto the 2-track recorder.

Refer to these chapters for more detail: Chapter 13, the section on mixing procedures; Chapter 14, the section on master-tape assembly; and later in this chapter, the section on automated mixing.

## Recording with a MIDI/Digital Audio Recording System

The tape-sync system just described can be cumbersome. Instead, you can record MIDI sequences and digital audio tracks, edit them, and mix them, all with your computer. You need MIDI/Digital Audio software, a sound card and a MIDI interface. Some examples of software are Cakewalk Pro Audio, Cakewalk Sonar, and Cubase VST. Many sound cards have MIDI connectors built in.

This system lets you add several tracks of vocals, sax, guitar, or any audio signal to your MIDI sequences. While playing MIDI tracks, you record the audio digitally to a hard disk. The software synchronizes the sequencer's MIDI data with the audio tracks.

The sound quality is at least as good as that of a compact disc (16-bit quantization, 44.1 kHz sampling rate or better). Plus, you can edit the digital audio performances—cut and paste, copy, rearrange, and so on. Because the disk drive is random access, you don't have to wait for shuttling tape.

Be sure your hard drive has enough capacity for digital recording. One track of 1 minute of CD-quality audio consumes about 5 megabytes. So a 1.2-gigabyte drive can record 60 minutes of 4 audio tracks. Some software removes data created during silent portions of tracks. In this way, one track-minute of audio might use only 1 megabyte instead of 5.

Here's how such a system might work (Figure 16.10):

1. Use the sequencer part of the software to record the MIDI parts, which might play a synth, sound module, sampler, or drum machine.

2. Set up a microphone to record a vocal.

3. While listening to the MIDI tracks, record the vocal onto hard disk as digital audio.

4. You might record a few takes of the vocal part and then cut and paste selected portions to create a perfect take. Record one good chorus and copy it in each chorus section in your song.

**Figure 16.10**  Connections for a MIDI/digital audio recording system (mixer not shown).

5.  Add effects to various tracks by using plug-ins, or by using the program's effects.

Several things happen when you play back what you recorded:

1.  The sequence's MIDI signal comes from the MIDI OUT connector in the MIDI interface.
2.  The sequence's MIDI signal plays notes through a synth, sound module, and/or drum machine.
3.  The digital audio—a multitrack mix—plays from the sound-card output.
4.  A mixer combines the MIDI-equipment audio with the sound-card audio, and you record the mix on a 2-track recorder (using the software's automated-mixing feature).

## Using Effects

No matter how you record with MIDI, effects are an important part of the mix. To keep the sound lively, try to vary the effects throughout the song, or use several types of effects at once.

For example, suppose you have a multitimbral synth, and you want to add a different effect to each patch. Whether or not you can do this depends on your synth. If it has a separate output for each patch, you can use a different effect on each patch. But if your synth has only a single output (mono or stereo) and you run it through an effects device, the same effect is on all the patches.

If your song includes program changes (patch changes), you can have the effects change when the patch changes. Set up a MIDI multi-effects processor so that each synth program change corresponds to the desired effect. When the synth program changes, the effect changes also.

What if you want the effect, but not the synth patch, to change during a mix? Reserve a track and channel just for effects program changes. You don't hear these program changes in your synth, but you do hear the effects change. During a mixdown, it's usually easier to change effects automatically with your sequencer, rather than manually.

If your synth is a sampling keyboard, each sample could have reverberation or some other effect already on it; in that case each sample can have a different effect. The effect is not recorded in the sequencer; rather, the effect is part of the sampled sound. Note that the sampled reverberation cuts off every time you play a new note. Although this sounds unnatural, you can use it for special effect.

Because effects are audio signals, audio recorders can record effects but sequencers can't. If an effect is an integral part of the sound of an instrument, it's probably best to record it with the instrument on the multitrack audio recorder. If the effect is overall ambience or reverb (to put the band in a concert hall), however, then it's best to add it to almost everything during mixdown.

# Automated Mixing

Chapter 13 began a discussion of automated mixing, which uses a sequencer circuit to store and reset your mix changes. Automated mixing has many advantages. With it you can:

- Perform complicated mixes without errors
- Fine-tune the mix moves
- Recall mixes weeks or months after storing them
- Listen to the mix without the distraction of having to adjust faders

Many types of automation use MIDI devices. Now that you understand these devices, we can explain automation in more detail.

## *Types of Automation Systems*

Four types of automation systems are:

- Automated mixer with non-moving faders
- Automated mixer with moving faders

- Automated fader/VCA unit
- Digital editing software with automated mixing

Each of these is worth a closer look.

## Automated Mixer with Non-Moving Faders

An automated mixer has a built-in circuit that remembers your mix moves and control settings. In the mixer, volume levels and mutes are controlled either by Voltage Controlled Amplifiers (VCAs) or by Digitally Controlled Amplifiers (DCAs). Control signals are MIDI, FSK, or SMPTE. All digital mixers, and many hard-disk recorder–mixers, can do automated mixes.

During playback of the automated mix, the signal levels for each channel are set according to what is stored in memory, but the faders do not move. This can be confusing because the fader positions do not represent the mix you are hearing.

## Automated Mixer with Moving Faders

With this sophisticated system, SMPTE time code is used to control motorized faders. They move up and down as if controlled by a ghost. There are no VCAs to degrade the signal. In some systems, all control settings can be remembered and recalled.

## Automated Fader/VCA Unit

You also can automate a standard mixer by adding an external **automated fader/VCA unit**, a box with several faders that control VCAs or DCAs. The VCAs/DCAs plug into your mixer's insert jacks (Figure 16.11). These are in series with the signal of each channel. One VCA or DCA is needed for each channel (input, master, or return) you want to automate. Some boxes have one fader or mute button per channel; others have a single fader that you set to the desired channel. MIDI controls this type of system.

## Digital Editing Software with Automated Mixing

As we said in Chapter 10, a Digital Audio Workstation (DAW) is a personal computer running digital editing software. A sound card or I/O box plugged into the computer has connectors to get audio into and out of the computer.

To do automated mixing with this software, first you need to get the multiple tracks of music onto your hard drive. There are two ways to do this:

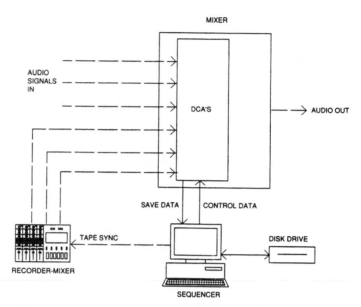

**Figure 16.11** Typical connections for MIDI-automated mixing.

1. Record music on a multitrack tape recorder. Connect the recorder outputs to the I/O box inputs. Then use the software to copy the tape tracks to virtual tracks on your hard drive. In other words, do all your recording on a multitrack tape unit, then dump the tracks to your computer's hard drive for editing and mixing.

2. Amplify mic signals with a mic preamp or mixer. Connect the preamp or mixer output to the I/O box line inputs (some I/O boxes have mic preamps built in). Then use the software to record the music tracks onto the hard drive. In other words, record directly onto your computer's hard drive, one or more tracks at a time.

Once the tracks are in the computer, you're ready to edit and mix. The monitor screen shows **virtual faders** that you adjust with a mouse or with a controller surface. The computer remembers your mix moves, EQ settings, and so on, and does an automated mix during playback.

As we said earlier, a MIDI/digital audio program includes both digital audio tracks and sequencer tracks. The audio track levels are controlled by adjusting their gain; the MIDI tracks are controlled by adjusting their MIDI volume or key velocity.

Lower-cost programs let you control volume only; higher-cost programs let you control all parameters (EQ, panning, and effects). Some or all of these parameters can be automated.

# Storing Mix Moves

A MIDI sequencer can record your mix moves via MIDI program changes. The sequencer is either built into the automated mixer or is external (stand-alone or computer program). When you play the sequencer recording, MIDI program changes control the DCAs to mix the tracks as you did manually. Or the program changes move motorized faders.

# Snapshot versus Continuous Automation

Two types of automation are **snapshot** and **continuous** (**dynamic**). With snapshot automation, a computer memory in the mixer takes a "snapshot" or "scene" of the mixer settings and stores them as MIDI program changes. To reset the mixer to any of these stored settings, you punch up the appropriate number (MIDI program change). Alternatively, your sequencer recording can reset the mixer at the correct times as a song plays.

With continuous or dynamic automation, the motion of the mixer controls is recorded. Continuous automation costs more than snapshot and consumes more memory, but permits finer resolution of mix moves. Some digital mixers do both snapshot and continuous automation with their internal memory. Other mixers require an external MIDI sequencer to record continuous automation moves.

Some snapshot units let you program fade times so that you can fade between snapshots to simulate continuous control.

# Controls

Some automated-mixing systems have several knobs and faders: one per parameter. Others have just a few "soft" controls: You assign the control one function at a time and adjust its value on a screen.

# Automated Mixing Procedure

Here is a suggested order of steps in doing an automated mix:

1. Set up a rough mix manually, with effects.
2. Program the mutes or cuts. Mute tracks that aren't being used, or that don't add to the arrangement. For example, a chorus might sound better without the horns.
3. Program the fader rides. Examples: Turn up the guitar during the solo, turn up the toms during the fills, turn down the background vocals when they get too loud. Save your changes often.

4. Program the effects changes. You might bring up the chorusing on the acoustic guitar during the bridge, and so on.

5. Sit back and listen to the mix. Is there anything you want to change?

Suppose you want a track's sound to change radically during the song. Maybe you want the lead guitar to change level, EQ, and reverb during the chorus. Here's a slick way to do it: Using a Y-cable or patchbay mult, split the guitar track's signal to two adjacent channels on your mixer—say, channels 5 and 6. Channel 5 is set up the way you want it for most of the song. Channel 6 is set up with the EQ, level, and reverb you want during the chorus. Mute channel 6 and start playing the song. When the chorus comes up in the song, mute channel 5 and unmute channel 6. Save this mute change. (This technique also works on non-automated mixers.)

## Simulating Automatic Mixing with MIDI

If you lack an automated-mixer system, you can simulate one by recording MIDI controller data as volume changes on an open sequencer track. This lets you vary the balance among sequencer tracks, but not tape tracks. You might proceed as follows:

1. Choose a continuous controller on your master keyboard, such as a pitch-bend wheel.

2. Set the keyboard to transmit on the MIDI channel of the track you want to automate.

3. In your sound module, assign or map the controller to affect MIDI volume for level changes.

4. Set your sequencer to record on a new track, called the controller track. Set the controller track to the same channel as your master keyboard. Be sure to turn off any patch on the controller track.

5. Start recording. While listening to the music, move the controller to adjust the volume of the track. Later, you can edit the controller track, and perhaps bounce it to the musical track.

6. Repeat this procedure for all the tracks you want to automate. (You can assign the controller to affect filtering or panning as well, but this takes up a lot of sequencer memory.)

MIDI studio equipment, keyboard workstations, and digital audio workstations bring new procedures into the studio with them. Typical recording procedures for MIDI can range from simple to complex. This technology has changed the way recordings are made.

# ON-LOCATION RECORDING OF POPULAR MUSIC

Sooner or later you'll want to record a band—maybe your own—playing in a club or concert hall. Many bands want to be recorded in concert because they feel that's when they play best. Your job is to capture that performance on tape and bring it back alive.

There are several ways to record live:

- Record with two mics out front into a 2-track recorder.
- Using the PA mixer, record off a spare MAIN output.
- Place a stereo mic at the FOH (Front Of House) position. Plug into a spare PA mixer output. Record these signals on a 4-track recorder–mixer.
- Feed the PA mixer INSERT jacks to a multitrack.
- Feed the PA mixer DIRECT OUTS or INSERT jacks to a recording mixer, and from there to a 2-track or a multitrack recorder.
- Use a mic splitter on stage to feed the PA snake and recording snake. Record to multitrack or 2-track.

We'll start by explaining simple two-microphone techniques and work our way up to elaborate multitrack setups.

# Two Mics Out Front

Let's start with the simplest, cheapest technique—two mics and a 2-track recorder. The sound will be distant and muddy compared to using a mic on each instrument and vocal. Not exactly CD quality! But you'll hear how your band sounds to an audience.

Recording this way is much simpler, faster, and cheaper than multi-mic, multitrack recording. Still, if time and budget permit, you'll get better sound with a more elaborate setup.

## *Equipment*

Here's what you need for 2-mic recording:

- A stereo mic, or two mics of the same model number. Your first choice might be cardioid condenser mics. The cardioid pickup pattern cuts down on room reverb and noise. The condenser type generally sounds more natural than the dynamic type. Another option is a pair of boundary mics such as PZMs. Simply put them on the floor or on the ceiling in front of your group.

- A DAT recorder, MiniDisc recorder, 2-track open-reel recorder, or cassette deck. DAT has the least distortion and hiss, and lets you record up to 2 hours nonstop. Either use a unit with mic inputs, or use a separate mic preamp.

- Blank recording tape. Buy the best you can afford. Bring enough tape to cover the duration of the recording.

- Two long mic cables.

- Two mic stands.

- Headphones. You could use speakers in a separate room, but headphones are more portable and sound consistent in any environment. Closed-cup headphones partly block out the live sound of the band so you can better hear what's going on tape. Ideally you'd set up in a different room than the band is in, so you can clearly hear what you're recording.

## *Mic Placement*

Use a pair of mic stands or hang the mics out of the reach of the audience.

Aim the two mics at the group about 12 feet away, and space them about 5 to 15 feet apart (Figure 17.1). Place the mics far apart (that is, close

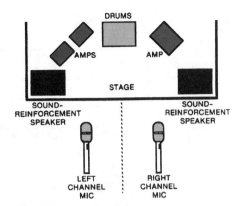

**Figure 17.1**
Recording a musical group
with two spaced
microphones.

to the PA speakers) to make the vocals louder in the recording. Do the opposite to make them quieter. The stereo imaging will be pretty vague, but at least you can control the balance between instruments and vocals.

To record a small folk group or acoustic jazz group, set up two mics of the same model number in a stereo arrangement of your choice. Place the mics about 3 to 10 feet from the group. The balance may not be the best, but the method is simple.

## *Recording*

After setting the recording level, leave it alone as much as possible. If you must change the level, do so slowly and try to follow the dynamics of the music. Switch tapes during pauses or intermissions.

If the playback sounds distorted—even though you did not exceed a normal recording level—the mics probably overloaded the mic preamps in the tape deck. A mic preamp is a circuit in the tape recorder that amplifies a weak mic signal up to a useable level. With loud sound sources such as rock groups, a mic can put out a signal strong enough to cause distortion in the mic preamp.

Some recorders have a **pad** or **input attenuator**. It reduces the mic signal level before it reaches the preamp, and so prevents distortion. You can build a pad (Figure 17.2), or buy some plug-in pads from your mic dealer. Some condenser mics have a switchable internal pad that reduces distortion in the mic itself. If you have to set your record-level knobs very low (less than $\frac{1}{3}$ up) to get a 0 recording level, that shows you probably need to use a pad.

357

ASSEMBLY SHOULD BE SHIELDED.
MATCH 470-Ω RESISTORS WITHIN 1%

**Figure 17.2** Balanced and unbalanced microphone pads.

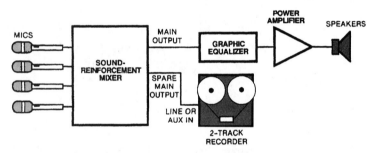

**Figure 17.3** Recording from the sound-reinforcement mixer.

# Recording from the PA Mixer

You can get a fairly good recording by plugging into the main output of the band's PA mixer. (PA stands for public address, but here it means sound reinforcement.) Connect the main output(s) of the mixer to the line input(s) of a 2-track recorder. Use the mixer output that is ahead of any graphic equalizer that is used to correct the speakers' frequency response (Figure 17.3).

Mixers with balanced +4 dBu outputs can produce a signal that is too high in level for the recorder's line input, causing distortion. This is probably occurring if your record-level controls have to be set very low. To reduce the output level of the mixer, turn it down so that its signal peaks around −12 VU on the mixer meters, and turn up the PA power amplifier to compensate. That practice, however, degrades the mixer's S/N.

**Figure 17.4** 12 dB pad for matching a balanced output to an unbalanced input.

A better solution is to make a 12 dB pad (Figure 17.4). The output level of a balanced-output mixer is 12 dB higher than the normal input level of a recorder with an unbalanced input.

## *Drawbacks*

The recorded mix off the PA might be poor. The operator of the band's mixer hears a combination of the band's live sound and the reinforced sound through the house system, and tries to get a good mix of both these elements. That means the signal is mixed to augment the live sound—not to sound good by itself. A recording made from the band's mixer is likely to sound too strong in the vocals and too weak in the bass.

## Taping with a 4-Tracker

A 4-track portable studio can do a good job of capturing a band's live sound. With this method, you place a stereo mic (or a pair of mics) at the FOH position (front of house—the PA mixer location). Record the mic on tracks 1 and 2. Also plug into a spare main output on the PA mixer, and record it on tracks 3 and 4 (Figure 17.5). After the concert, mix the four tracks together.

The FOH mics pick up the band as the audience hears it: lots of room acoustics, lots of bass, but rather muddy or distant. The PA mixer output sounds close and clear, but typically is thin in the bass. When you mix the FOH mics with the PA-mixer signal, the combination has both warmth and clarity.

Consider using a stereo mic at the FOH position. Good stereo mics cost more than $500, but they provide great stereo in a portable, conve-

**Figure 17.5**

Recording two mics and a PA mix on a 4-track recorder–mixer.

nient package. You can also set up two mics of the same model number in a stereo arrangement. For example, angle two cardioid mics 90 degrees apart and space them 1 foot apart horizontally. Or place two omni mics 2 feet apart.

Plug the mics into your 4-track's mic inputs 1 and 2. Adjust the trim to prevent distortion, and set the recording level. Find a spare main output on the PA mixer, and plug it into your 4-track's line inputs 3 and 4. You may need to use the 12 dB pad described earlier. Set recording levels and record the gig.

Back home, mix the four tracks to stereo. Tracks 1 and 2 provide ambience and bass; tracks 3 and 4 provide definition and clarity.

You might hear an echo because the FOH mics pick up the band with a delay (sound takes time to travel to the mics). A typical delay is 20 to 100 msec. To remove the echo, delay the PA mix by the same amount. Patch a delay unit into the insert jacks for tracks 3 and 4. As you adjust the delay time up from zero, the echo will get shorter until the signals are aligned in time. You may be surprised at the quality you get with this simple method.

# Recording off the PA Mixer Aux Outputs

On the PA mixer, find an unused aux send output. Plug in a Y-cord: One end fits the PA mixer connector; the other end has two connectors that mate with your 2-track recorder's line inputs (Figure 17.6). If you have two spare aux busses, you could plug a cable into both of them, and set up a stereo mix.

Put on some good closed-cup headphones and plug them into your 2-track recorder to monitor the recording. Adjust the aux-send knob for each instrument and vocal to create a good recording mix. Record the gig.

The advantages of this method are:

**Figure 17.6**
Recording off the PA mixer
aux outputs.

- It's simple. All you need is a recorder, a cable, and headphones.
- The recorded sound is close-up and clear.
- If the mix is done well, the sound quality can be very good.

The disadvantages are:

- It's hard to hear what you're mixing. You may need to do several trial recordings. Set up a mix, record, play back, and evaluate. Redo the mix and try another recording.
- As you adjust the aux knobs, you might get in the way of the PA operator.
- The recording will be dry (without effects or room ambience). However, you could plug two room mics into the PA mixer and add them to the recording mix. Do not assign these mics to the PA output channels.
- If the aux send is pre-EQ, there will be no EQ on the mics. If the aux send is post-EQ, there will be EQ on the mics, but it may not be appropriate for recording.

Recording an aux mix works best where the setup is permanent and you have time to experiment. Some examples are recording a church service, and recording a regularly scheduled show in a fixed venue.

# Feeding the PA Mixer Insert Sends to a Modular Digital Multitrack

This is an easy way to record, and it offers excellent sound quality. Plug one or more MDMs into the insert-send jacks on the back of the PA mixer. Set levels with the PA mixer input trims. After the concert, mix the tape tracks back in your studio.

# Connections

Suppose you want to record one instrument or vocal on each track. In each PA mixer input channel, locate the INSERT or ACCESS jacks. Connect that jack to a tape track input (Figure 17.7). INSERT jacks are usually pre-fader, pre-EQ. So any fader or EQ changes that the PA operator does will not show up on your tape.

If the PA mixer has separate Send and Return INSERT jacks, connect the Send to the tape track input, and connect the tape track output to the Return. Some boards use a single stereo INSERT jack with TRS (tip/ring/sleeve) connections. Usually the tip is send and the ring is return. In the stereo phone plug that you plug into the INSERT jack, wire tip and ring together, and also to the cable hot conductor.

On some PA mixers with a tip/ring/sleeve insert jack, you can use a mono (tip/sleeve) phone plug. Plug it in halfway to the first click so you don't break the signal path—the signal still goes through the PA mixer. If you plug in all the way to the second click, the signal does not go through the PA mixer—just to your multitrack recorder.

What if you want to record several instruments on one track, such as a drum mix? Assign all the drum mics to one or two output busses in the PA mixer. Plug the BUS OUT insert jack to the tape track input. Use two busses for stereo.

# Monitor Mix

You may want to set up a monitor mix over headphones so you can hear what you're recording. Here are some ways to do this:

- Connect all the MDM outputs to unused line inputs on your mixer. Use those faders to set up a monitor mix. Assign them to an unused bus, and monitor that bus with headphones.

- Use the aux 1 or aux 2 knobs to set up a monitor mix. Monitor the aux send bus over headphones.

**Figure 17.7**
Feeding an MDM from the
PA mixer insert jacks.

## *Setting Levels*

Set recording levels with the PA mixer's TRIM or INPUT ATTEN knobs. This affects the levels in the PA mix, so be sure to discuss your trim adjustment in advance with the PA mixer operator. If you turn down an input trim, the PA operator must compensate by turning up that channel's fader and monitor send.

Set recording levels before the concert during the sound check (if any!). It's better to set the levels a little too low than too high because during mixdown you can reduce noise but not distortion. A suggested starting level is −10dBFS, which allows for surprises. You don't want to exceed 0dBFS.

Keep a tape log as you record, noting the counter times of tunes, sonic problems, and so on. Refer to this log when you mix.

## *Mixdown*

After the recording is finished, mix down the tracks back in the studio, spending as much time as you need to perfect the mix. You even can overdub parts that were flubbed during the live performance, taking care to match the overdubbed sound to the original recording.

# Feeding PA Mixer Direct Outs or Insert Sends to a Recording Mixer

The previous method has a drawback: You have to adjust the PA mixer's trim controls, and this changes the PA mix slightly. A way around this is to connect the PA mixer direct outs or insert sends to the line inputs of a separate recording mixer. Connect the recording mixer insert sends to the MDM(s) (Figure 17.8). Set MDM recording levels with the recording mixer.

**Figure 17.8**
Connecting PA mixer to
recording mixer to MDM.

This method has some compromises. You need more cables and another mixer. Also, the signal goes through more electronics, so it is not quite as clean as connecting straight to the MDM.

Using the recording mixer's faders, you can set up a monitor mix. If you can hear the monitor mix well enough over headphones, you can even omit the multitracks, and attempt a live mix to 2-track.

In a live mix, never turn off a mic completely unless you know for sure that it's not going to be used. Otherwise, you'll invariably miss cues. Turn down unused mics about 10dB.

# Splitting the Microphones

With this method, you plug each mic into a microphone splitter on stage. The mic splitter sends each mic's signal to two paths: the PA mixer snake and the recording mixer snake. Some splitters have a third output to feed a stage monitor mixer. Back at the recording mixer where the snake is plugged in, assign each mic to a different track.

In most mic splitters, the signals are transformer isolated to prevent ground loops and interaction between the mixers. There is a ground-lift switch on each channel (Figure 17.9). Set it to the position where you monitor the least hum. Usually the mic-cable shields are grounded only to

**Figure 17.9**
Transformer-isolated
microphone splitter.

one console that provides phantom power. The cable shields going to the other mixer are floated (disconnected) at the splitter with ground-lift switches.

# Multitrack Recording in a Van

Here's the ultimate setup. Each mic is split three ways to feed the snake boxes for the recording, reinforcement, and monitor consoles. A long multiconductor snake is run to a recording truck or van parked outside the concert hall or club.

In the van, the snake connects to a mixing console, which is used to submix groups of mics and route their signals to a multitrack tape machine. Sometimes two tape machines are run in parallel to provide a backup in case one fails. Or two analog machines can be synchronized with SMPTE time code to increase the number of tracks available. SMPTE time code is explained in Appendix B.

# Preparing for the Session

So far this chapter gave an overview of several on-location recording methods. The rest of this chapter explores the details of on-location pre-session procedures.

Ready to record a live gig? The recording will go a lot smoother if you plan what you're going to do. So sit down, grab a pen, and make some lists and diagrams as described here. We'll go over the steps to plan a recording.

## *Preproduction Meeting*

Call or meet with the PA company and the production company putting on the event. Find out the date of the event, location, phone numbers of everyone involved, when the job starts, when you can get into the hall, when the second set starts, and other pertinent information. Decide who will provide the split, which system will be plugged in first, second, and so on. Draw block diagrams for the audio system and communications (comm) system. Determine who will provide the comm headphones.

If you're using a mic splitter, work out the splitter feeds. The mixer getting the direct side of the split provides phantom power for condenser mics that are not powered on stage. If the house system has been in use for a long time, give them the direct side of the split.

Overloud stage monitors can ruin a recording, so work with the sound-reinforcement people toward a workable compromise. Ask them to start with the monitors quiet because the musicians always want them turned up louder.

Make copies of the meeting notes for all participants. Don't leave things unresolved. Know who is responsible for supplying what equipment.

Figure 17.10 shows a typical equipment layout worked out at a pre-production meeting. There are three systems in use: sound reinforcement, recording, and monitor mixing. The mic signals are split three ways to feed these systems.

## Site Survey

If possible, visit the recording site in advance and go through the following checklist:

**Figure 17.10** Typical layout for an on-location recording of a live concert.

- Check the AC power to make sure the voltage is adequate, the third pin is grounded, and the waveform is clean.

- Listen for ambient noises—ice machines, coolers, 400-Hz generators, heating pipes, air conditioning, nearby discos, etc. Try to have these noise sources under control by the day of the concert.

- Sketch dimensions of all rooms related to the job. Estimate distances for cable runs.

- Turn on the sound-reinforcement system to see if it functions okay by itself (no hum, and so on). Turn the lighting on at various levels with the sound system on. Listen for buzzes. Try to correct any problem so that you don't document bad PA sound on your tape.

- Determine locations for any audience/ambience mics. Keep them away from air-conditioning ducts and noisy machinery.

- Plan your cable runs from stage to recording mixer.

- If you plan to hang mic cables, feel the supports for vibration. You may need microphone shock mounts. If there's a breeze in the room, plan on taking windscreens.

- Make a file on each recording venue including the dimensions and the location of the circuit breakers.

- Determine where the control room will be. Find out what surrounds it—any noisy machinery?

- Visit the site when a crowd is there to see where there may be traffic problems.

## Mic List

Now write down all the instruments and vocals in the band. If you want to put several mics on the drum kit, list each drum that you want to mike. As for keyboards, decide whether you want to record off each keyboard's output, or off the keyboard mixer (if any).

Next, write down the mic or direct box you want to use on each instrument:

### Mic List (Example)

| | |
|---|---|
| 1. Bass | DI |
| 2. Kick | AKG-D112 |
| 3. Snare | Shure Beta 57 |

| | |
|---|---|
| 4. Hi-hat | Crown CM-700 |
| 5. Small rack tom | 57 |
| 6. Big rack tom | 57 |
| 7. Small floor tom | Sennheiser MD421 |
| 8. Big floor tom | 421 |
| 9. Cymbals overhead left | Shure SM81 |
| 10. Cymbals overhead right | SM81 |
| 11. Lead guitar | 57 |
| 12. Rhythm guitar | 57 |
| 13. Keyboard mixer | DI |
| 14. Lead vocal | Beyer M88 |
| 15. Harmony vocal | Crown CM-311A |

Make two copies of this mic list. At the gig, you'll place one list by the stage box, and the other by the PA mixer. Each list will act as a guide to keep things organized.

## Track Sheet

Next, decide what will go on each track of your multitrack tape recorder. If you have enough tracks, your job is easy: Just assign each instrument or vocal to its own track. Bass to track 1, kick to track 2, and so on.

What if you have more instruments than tracks? Suppose you have an 8-track recorder, but you have 15 instruments and vocals (including each part of the drum set). You'll need to assign several instruments or vocals to the same track. That is, you will set up a submix.

Let's say the drum kit includes a snare, kick drum, two rack toms, two floor toms, a hi-hat, and cymbals. If you want to mike everything individually, that's nine mics. But you don't need to use up nine tracks. Assign or group those mics to busses 1 and 2 to create a stereo drum mix. Connect busses 1 and 2 to tape tracks 1 and 2. At the sound check, you set up a submix of all the drum mics, and assign them to busses 1 and 2. You control the overall level of the drum mix with submaster faders 1 and 2 (also called bus faders or group faders).

Use tracks 3 through 8 for amps and vocals (as shown below). Feed tracks 3–8 from insert sends.

## Track Sheet (Example)

| Track | Instrument |
| --- | --- |
| 1 | Drum mix L |
| 2 | Drum mix R |
| 3 | Bass |
| 4 | Lead guitar |
| 5 | Rhythm guitar |
| 6 | Keys mix |
| 7 | Lead vocal |
| 8 | Harmony vocal |

## *Block Diagram*

Now that your track assignments are planned, you can figure out what equipment you'll need. Draw a block diagram of your recording setup from input to output (such as Figure 17.11). Include mics, mic cables, mic

**Figure 17.11** Example block diagram of recording setup.

stands and booms, DI boxes, insert cables, multitrack tape recorder(s), outlet strip and extension cord, and recording tape. You might bring your own mixer and snake, or use those from the PA system. On your diagram, label the cable connectors on each end so you'll know what kinds of cables to bring. It's a good idea to keep a file of system block diagrams for various recording venues.

In Figure 17.11, the block diagram shows a typical recording method: feeding PA-console insert jacks to a Modular Digital Multitrack. We'll use this example in the rest of this chapter.

## Equipment List

Generate a list of recording equipment from your block diagram. Based on Figure 17.11, you'd need the following recording gear:

- Direct boxes, mics, mic cables, mic stands, and booms (unless these are part of the PA system)
- Insert cables (for example, 8 stereo phone plugs to 8 RCA connectors)
- Multitrack recorder
- Outlet strip and extension cord
- Recording tapes (bring enough for the duration of the gig)

Don't forget the incidentals: a cleaning tape or alcohol/cotton swab, pen, notebook, flashlight, guitar picks, heavy-duty guitar cords, drum keys, spare tape, mic pop filters, gaffer's tape, tuner, ear plugs, audio-connector adapters, electrical 3-to-2 AC adapters, ground-lift adapters, in-line pads, in-line polarity reversers, spare cables, gooseneck lights for the console, spare batteries—and aspirin!

Bring a tool kit with screwdrivers, pliers, soldering iron and solder, AC-outlet checkers, fuses, a pocket radio to listen for interference, ferrite beads of various sizes for RFI suppression, canned air to shoot out dirt, cotton swabs and pipe cleaners, and De-Oxit from Caig Labs to remove oxide from connectors.

Check off each item on the list as you pack it. After the gig, you can check the list to see whether you reclaimed all your gear.

# Preparing for Easier Setup

You want to make your setup as fast and easy as possible. Here are some tips to help this process.

## Protective Cases

Mount your console and recorders in protective carrying cases. Install casters or swivel wheels under racks and carrying cases so you can roll them in. Rolling is so much easier than lifting and carrying.

You might permanently install the MDMs in SKB carrying cases that act as racks. When a remote job comes up, just grab them and go.

A very helpful item is a dolly or wheeled cart to transport heavy equipment into the venue. Consider getting some lightweight tubular carts. Being collapsible, they store easily in your car or truck. One maker of equipment carts is Rock 'n' Roller, who advertises in the Musician's Friend catalog, www.musiciansfriend.com. Another cart is the Remin Kart-a-Bag, www.kart-a-bag.com.

Pack mics, headphones, and other small pieces in trunks or milk crates.

> CAUTION: Keep tapes separated from magnets, such as in head-phones, monitor speakers, and dynamic mics. (However, tape erasure is much less of a problem with digital media such as DAT than it is with analog tapes.)

You might want to build a mic container: a big box full of foam rubber with cutouts for all the mics. Or construct a wheeled cabinet with drawers for mics, DIs, and speaker cables.

In an article in the Sept./Oct. 1985 issue of *db* magazine, remote recording engineer Ron Streicher offers these suggestions:

> Especially for international travel, make sure your documentation is up to date and matches the equipment you're carrying. Make a list of everything you take: all the details, such as each pencil, razor blade, connector, etc.
>
> Also make sure your insurance is up to date. You need insurance for enroute as well as at the destination.
>
> I organize my cases so I know where every item is. They're ready to go anytime and make setup much faster. The cables are packed with their associated equipment, not in a cables case. I check everything coming and going, and try to have 100% redundancy, such as a small mixer to substitute for the large console.

## Mic Mounts

If you'll be recording a singer/guitarist, take a short mic mount that clamps onto the singer's mic stand. Put the guitar mic in the mount. Also bring some short mounts to clamp onto drum rims and guitar amps. By using these mounts, you eliminate the weight and clutter of several mic stands.

Some examples of short mounts are the Mic-Eze units by Ac-cetera. They have standard ⅝-27 threads and mic clamps that either spring shut or are screw-tightened. Flex-Eze is two clamps joined by a short goose-neck. Max-Eze is two clamps joined by a rod; Min-Eze is two clamps joined by a swivel. Ac-cetera, Inc. is at 3120 Banksville Road, Pittsburgh, PA 15216, phone 800-537-3491, e-mail aaps@pgh.nauticom.net.

## Snakes and Cables

You can store mic cables on a cable spool, available in the electrical department of a hardware store. Wrap one mic cable around the spool, plug it into the next cable and wrap it, etc. No more tangled cables!

A snake can be wrapped around a garden-hose spool. Commercial snake reels are made by such companies as Whirlwind, ProCo, and Hannay (www.hannay.com).

Use wire ties to join cables that you normally run together, such as PA sends and returns.

Snake hookup is quicker if the snake has a multipin twist-lock connector (such as Whirlwind W1 or W2). This connector plugs into a mating connector that divides into several male XLRs. Those XLRs plug into the mixing console. Leave the XLRs in the console carrying case. You'll find that the snake is easier to handle without the XLR pigtails on it.

For a clean, rapid hookup of drum mics, put a small snake near the drum kit, and run it to the main stage box. Or, put the main stage box by the drum kit. Snakes are made by such companies as Whirlwind, ProCo, and Horizon.

Check that your mic cables are wired in the same polarity—pin 2 hot.

You might want to use 3-conductor shielded mic cables. Connect the shield to ground only at the male XLR end. Also use cables with 100% shielding. Those measures enhance the shielding capability of the shield and reduce pickup of lighting buzzes.

In XLR-type cable connectors, do not connect pin 1 to the shell, or you may get ground loops when the shell contacts a metallic surface.

Label all your cables on both ends according to what they plug into—for example, DSP-9 effects in, track 12 out, power amp in, snake aux 3 out. Or you might prefer to number the cables near their connectors. Cover these labels with clear heat-shrink tubing.

Label both ends of each mic cable with the cable length. Put a drop of glue on each connector screw to temporarily lock it in place.

# Rack Wiring

You can speed the console wiring by using a small snake between the rack and the console, and between the multitrack tape recorders and the console. When packing, plug the snakes into the rack gear and multitracks, and coil the snake inside the rack and the multitrack carrying case. In other words, have all your equipment prewired. At the gig, pull out a bundled harness and plug it into the console jacks.

You might be feeding your multitrack from the insert jacks of a PA company's console. If so, use a snake with tip-ring-sleeve stereo phone plugs at the console end. Carry some TRS-to-dual-mono phone adapters to handle consoles that have separate jacks for insert send and return.

Some engineers prefer to make a clearly marked interface panel on the rear of the racks, and plug into the panels. This is easier than trying to find the right connectors on each piece of equipment.

Small bands might get by with all their equipment in a single, tall rack. Mount a small mixer on top, wired to effects in the middle, with a coiled snake and power cord on the bottom.

Small snakes for rack and multitrack connections are made by Hosa, Horizon, and ProCo, among others.

# Other Tips

Here are some more helpful hints for successful on-location recordings.

- Plan to use a talk-back mic from the board to the stage monitors during sound checks. You might bring a small instrument amp for talkback so that you can always be heard.
- Hook up and use unfamiliar equipment before going on the road. Don't experiment on the job!
- Consider recording with redundant (double) systems so you have a backup if one fails.
- If a concert will be longer than the running time of a reel of tape, switch reels at intermissions. Another method is to feed two identical tape machines the same signal in parallel. Record on one machine. As the reel of tape nears the end, start recording on the second machine so that none of the performance is lost. Edit the two tapes together back in the studio.
- Walkie-talkies are okay for preshow use, but don't use them during the performance because they cause RF interference. Use hard-wired communications headsets. Assistants can relay messages to and from the stage crew while you're mixing.

- During short set changes, use a closed-circuit TV system and light table (or fax machines) to show what set changes and mic-layout changes are coming up next; transmit this information to the monitor mixer and sound-reinforcement mixer.

- Don't put tapes through airport X-ray machines because the transformer in these machines is not always well shielded. Have the tapes inspected by hand.

- Hand carry your mics on airplanes. Arrange to load and unload your own freight containers, rather than trusting them to airline freight loaders. Expect delays here and at security checkpoints.

- Get a public-liability insurance policy to protect yourself against lawsuits.

- Call the venue and ask directions to the load-in door. Make sure that someone will be there at setup time to let you in. Ask the custodian not to lock the circuit-breaker box the day of the recording.

- A few days before the session, check out the parking situation.

- Just before you go, check out all your equipment to make sure it's working.

- Arrive several hours ahead of time for parking and setup. Expect failures—there's always something going wrong, something unexpected. Allow 50% more time for troubleshooting than you think you'll need. Have backup plans if equipment fails.

- In general, plan everything in advance so you can relax at the gig and have fun!

# At the Session: Setup

Okay! You've arrived at the venue. After parking, offload your gear to a holding area, rather than onstage, because gear on stage will likely need to be moved.

Learn the names of the PA company crew members, and be friendly. These people can be your assets or your enemies. Think before you comment to them! Try to remain in the background and do not interfere with their normal way of doing things (for example, take the secondary side of the split).

At the job, you need to take special precautions with power distribution, interconnecting multiple sound systems, and electric guitar grounding.

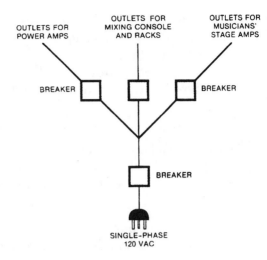

**Figure 17.12**
An AC power distribution system for a touring sound system.

## Power Distribution System

Consider buying, renting, or making your own single-phase power distribution system (distro). It will greatly reduce ground loops and increase reliability. Figure 17.12 shows a suggested AC power distribution system.

The amp rating of the distro's main breaker box should exceed the current drain of all the equipment that will be plugged into the distro system.

Furman makes a model ACD-100 AC Power Distro. It distributes a 100-amp feed (which you get from a breaker box) to five 20 amp, 120 V circuits. The unit works on 120 V, 240 V, or 208 V three-phase circuits. Furman's Web site is at http://www.furmansound.com.

## Power Source

If you're using a remote truck, find a source of power that can handle the truck's power requirements, usually at a breaker panel. Some newer clubs have separate breaker boxes for sound, lights, and a remote truck. Find out whether you'll need a union electrician to make those connections. Label your breakers.

Check that your AC power source is not shared with lighting dimmers or heavy machinery; these devices can cause noises or buzzes in the audio.

The industry-standard power connector for high-current applications is the Cam-lok, a large cylindrical connector. Male and female Cam-loks join together and lock when you twist the connector ring. Distro systems and power cables with Cam-lok connectors can be rented from rental houses for film, lighting, electrical equipment, or entertainment equipment. One such rental house is Mole-Richardson, 213-851-0111, http://www.mole.com.

Use an adapter from Cam-lok to bare wires. Pull the panel off the breaker box, insert the bare wires, and connect the Cam-lok to your truck's power.

> CAUTION: Have an electrician do the wiring if you don't know what you're doing. A union electrician might be required anyway. Some breaker boxes have Cam-loks already built in.

To reduce ground-loop problems, get on the same power that the PA is using. From that point, run your distribution system, or at least run one or two thick (14 or 16 gauge) extension cords, to your recording system. These cords may need to be 100 to 200 feet long. Plug AC outlet strips into the extension cord; then plug all your equipment into the outlet strips.

If your recording system is one or two multitrack tape recorders that will connect to the PA mixer, simply plug into the same outlet strip that the PA is using.

Measure the AC line voltage. If the AC voltage varies widely, use a line voltage regulator (power conditioner) for your recording equipment. If the AC power is noisy, you might need a power isolation transformer.

Check AC power on stage with a circuit checker. Are grounded outlets actually grounded? Is there low resistance to ground? Are the outlets correct polarity? There should be a substantial voltage between hot and ground, and no voltage between neutral and ground.

Some recording companies have a gasoline-powered generator ready to switch to if the house power fails. If there are a lot of lighting and dimmer racks at the gig, you might want to put the truck on a generator to keep it isolated from the lighting power.

## Interconnecting Multiple Sound Systems

If you encounter an unknown system where balanced audio cables are grounded at both ends, you might want to use some cable ground-lift adapters (Figure 17.13) to float (remove) the extra pin-1 ground connection at equipment inputs.

If you hear hum or buzz when the systems are connected, first make sure that the signal source is clean. You might be hearing a broken snake shield or an unused bass-guitar input.

**Figure 17.13** A ground-lift adapter for balanced line-level cables.

If hum persists, experiment with flipping the ground-lift switches on the splitter and on the direct boxes. On some jobs you need to lift almost every ground. On others you need to tie all the grounds. The correct ground-lift setting can change from day to day because of a change in the lighting. Expect to do some trial-and-error adjustments.

If the PA has serious hum and buzz problems, offer help. You can hear buzzes in your quiet truck that they can't hear over the main system with noise in the background.

Often, a radio station or video crew will take an audio feed from your mixing console. In this case, you can prevent a hum problem by using a console with transformer-isolated inputs and outputs. Or you can use a 1:1 audio isolation transformer between the console and the feeds. For best isolation, use a distribution amp with several transformer-isolated feeds. Lift the cable shield at the input of the system you're feeding. Some excellent isolation transformers are made by Jensen (213-876-0059, http://www.jensen-transformers.com).

John Fasarano, owner of Studio on Wheels in Glendale, California, describes how he prevents ground loops and hum: "I usually don't connect ground on the AC power. This solves 80 percent of the hum problems. I also flip the ground lifts or run AC into the house, and have them plug into that."

Guy Charbonneau, owner of Le Mobile, Hollywood, has this to say: "The truck uses 3-phase, filtered 240 V power with a 25 kVA transformer having six different taps. I don't use the neutral; it carries a lot of current from lighting systems. The truck chassis is grounded. I use no ground lifts 99 percent of the time; I carry through the shield with the sound company. In some clubs, I bring 50 amps to the stage on a 220 V line with a distribution box. All the musicians' instruments and the club console plug in there. This prevents ground loops and AC line noises from coffee machines and dishwashers. When working with a big P.A. company, I just ask for their split. Often a Y-adapter works." Source: "AES Workshop: The State of the Art of Remote Recording," *db* magazine, Sept./Oct. 1989.

# Connections

After unpacking, place one mic list by the stage box so you know what to plug in where. Place a duplicate list by the PA mixer. Attach a strip of white tape just below the mixer faders. Use this strip to write down the instrument that each fader affects.

Based on the mic list you wrote, you might plug the bass DI into snake input 1, plug the kick mic into snake input 2, and so on. Label fader 1 "BASS," label fader 2 "KICK," etc. Also plug in equipment cables according to your block diagram.

Have an extra microphone and cable offstage ready to use if a mic fails.

Don't unplug mics plugged into phantom power because this will make a popping noise in the sound-reinforcement system.

# Running Cables

To reduce hum pickup and ground-loop problems associated with cable connectors, try to use a single mic cable between each mic and its snake-box connector.

Avoid bundling mic cables, line-level cables, and power cables together. If you must cross mic cables and power cables, do so at right angles and space them vertically.

Plug each mic cable into the stage box; then run the cable out to the each mic and plug it in. This leaves less of a mess at the stage box. Leave the excess cable at each mic stand so you can move the mics. Don't tape the mic cables down until the musicians are settled.

It's important that audience members do not trip over your cables. In high-traffic areas, cover cables with rubber floor mats or cable crossovers (metal ramps). At least tape them down with gaffer's tape.

It helps to set up a closed-circuit TV camera and TV monitor to see what's happening on stage. You need to know when mics get moved accidentally, or when singers use the wrong mic, etc.

# Recording-Console Setup

Here's a suggested procedure for setting up the recording system efficiently:

1. If the console is set up in a dressing room or locker room, add some acoustic absorption to deaden the room reflections. You might bring a carpet for the floor, plus fiberglass insulation and packing blankets for the walls.

2. Turn up the recording monitor system and verify that it is clean.

3. Plug in one mic at a time and monitor it to check for hums and buzzes. Troubleshooting is easier if you listen to each mic as you connect it, rather than plugging them all in, and trying to find a hum or buzz.

4. Check and clean up one system at a time: first the sound-reinforcement system, then the stage-monitor system, then the recording system. Again, this makes troubleshooting easier because you have only one system to troubleshoot.

5. Use as many designation strips as you need for complex consoles. Label the input faders bottom and top. Also label the monitor-mix knobs and the meters.

6. Monitor the reverb returns (if any) and check for a clean signal.

7. Make a short test recording and listen to the playback.

8. Verify that left and right channels are correct, and that the pan-pot action is not reversed audibly.

9. If you are setting up a separate recording monitor mix, do a preliminary pan-pot setup. Panning similar instruments to different locations helps you identify them.

# Mic Techniques

Usually the miking is left up to the PA company. But there are some mic-related problems you should know about, such as feedback, leakage, room acoustics, and noise. Here are some ways to control these problems:

- Use directional microphones, such as cardioid, supercardioid, or hypercardioid. These mics pick up less feedback, leakage, and noise than omnidirectional mics at the same miking distance.

- With vocal mics, aim the null of the polar pattern at the floor monitors. The null (area of least pickup) of a cardioid is at the rear of the mic—180 degrees off-axis. The null of a supercardioid is 125 degrees off-axis; hypercardioid is 110 degrees.

- Mike close. Place each mic within a few inches of its instrument. Ask vocalists to sing with lips touching the mic's foam pop filter.

- Use direct boxes. Bass guitar and electric guitar can be recorded direct to eliminate leakage and noise in their signals. However, you might prefer the sound of a miked guitar amp. You could record the guitar direct from its effects boxes. Then use a guitar-amp emulator during mixdown. Note that sequencers and some keyboards have high-level outputs, so their DI boxes need transformers that can handle line level.

- Use contact pickups. On acoustic guitar, acoustic bass, and violin, you can avoid leakage by using a contact pickup. Such a pickup is sensitive only to the instrument's vibration, not so much to sound waves. The sound of a pickup is not as natural as a microphone, but a pickup may be your only choice. Consider using both a pickup and a microphone on the instrument. Feed the pickup to the PA and monitor speakers, and feed the mic to the recording mixer.

To reduce breath pops with vocal mics, be sure to use foam pop filters. Allow a little spacing between the pop filter and the mic grille. It also helps to switch in a low-cut filter (100 Hz highpass filter).

When you're recording a band that has been on tour, should you use their PA mics or your own mics? In general, go with their mics. The artists and PA company have been using their mics for a while and may not want to change anything. Most mics currently used in PA are good quality anyway, unless they are dirty or defective.

If you're not happy with their choice, you could add your own instrument mics. Let the PA people listen to the sound in the recording truck, or in headphones. If it sounds bad because of their mic choice, ask "Would it be okay if we tried a different mic (or mic placement)?" Usually it's all right with them—it's a team effort.

## Electric Guitar Grounding

While setting up mics, you need to be aware of a safety issue with the electric guitar. Electric-guitar players can receive a shock when they touch their guitar and a mic simultaneously. This occurs when the guitar amp is plugged into an electrical outlet on stage, and the mixing console (to which the mics are grounded) is plugged into a separate outlet across the room. If you're not using a power distro, these two power points may be at widely different ground voltages. So a current can flow between the grounded mic housing and the grounded guitar strings.

> CAUTION: Electric guitar shock is especially dangerous when the guitar amp and the console are on different phases of the AC mains.

It helps to power all instrument amps and audio gear from the same AC distribution outlets. If you lack a power distro, run a heavy extension cord from a stage outlet back to the mixing console (or vice versa). Plug all the power-cord ground pins into grounded outlets. That way, you prevent shocks and hum at the same time.

If you're picking up the electric guitar direct, use a transformer-isolated direct box and set the ground-lift switch to the minimum-hum position.

Using a neon tester or voltmeter, measure the voltage between the electric-guitar strings and the metal grille of the microphones. If there is a voltage, flip the polarity switch on the amp. Use foam windscreens for additional protection against shocks.

## Audience Microphones

If you have enough mic inputs, you can use two audience mics to pick up the room acoustics and audience sounds. This helps the recording to sound "live." Without audience mics, the recording may sound too dry, as if it were done in a studio.

One easy technique is to tape two boundary mics about 4 feet apart on the front face of the stage (Figure 17.14). You don't have to hang any microphones, but the mics may pick up conversation in the first few rows of seating. You might try a pair of PZMs on the side walls.

Another method is to aim two cardioid mics at the audience. Hang them high over the front row of the audience aiming at the back row (Figure 17.14). You might be able to set up a stereo pair on a mic stand, and tape off the seats around the stand so that it doesn't get bumped.

Some engineers pick up the audience and hall with two mics placed at the FOH mix position. That's an easy, effective way to capture the crowd. But the signal from these mics is delayed relative to the on-stage mics. If the FOH mix position is far from the stage (say, 50 feet or more), this delay will cause an echo when the audience mics are mixed with the stage mics. Prevent this by placing the audience mics fairly near the stage. Or, during mixdown, delay the stage-mics' signals so that they coincide with the

**Figure 17.14**
Some audience miking techniques.

audience-mics' signals. If you're using the audience mics only to capture applause, the delay is not an issue.

Here is another way to prevent this echo: Record the stage-mic mix on two tracks of a digital editor. Record the audience mics on two other tracks. Slide the stage-mic tracks to the right in time (that is, delay them) so that they coincide with the audience-mic tracks.

What if you don't have enough tracks for the audience mics? Record them on a 2-track DAT. Load this recording into your digital editor along with the stage-mic mix. Align the two recordings in time as described above.

If the audience mics are run through the PA mixer, leave the audience mics unassigned in that mixer to prevent feedback.

To get more isolation from the house speakers in the audience mics, use several mics close to the audience. Some engineers put up four audience mics maximum; some use eight to ten. Use directional mics and aim the rear null at the PA speakers.

Another option is *not* miking the audience, or not using the audience tracks. Instead, during mixdown, you could simulate an audience with audience-reaction CDs. Simulate room reverb with an effects unit.

# Setting Levels and Submixes

Now that the mics are set up, you might have time for a sound check. That's when you set recording levels. Have the band play a loud song. Locate a mixer input module that is directly feeding a tape track. Set the input trim (mic preamp gain) to get the desired recording level on each track. On an MDM recorder, you might set each track's level to peak around −10 dB, which allows for surprises if someone plays louder during the live gig.

Most of the mixer channels feed tape tracks directly from the insert sends. On those channels, any fader moves during the gig will not affect the levels going on tape. Why? In most mixers, the insert send is pre-fader. That is, the signal at the insert-send jack is not affected by the fader. However, you may encounter PA consoles where some insert sends are tied up with signal processors. You must use those channels' direct-out jacks instead, which are usually post-fader (unless they can be switched to pre-fader).

Now let's set up the drum submix. (Ideally, you would do this with the PA turned down, and monitor over headphones or Nearfield monitors in a separate room.) Assign each drum mic to busses 1 and 2, and pan each mic as desired. Put the faders for busses 1 and 2 at design center—the shaded area about $\frac{1}{2}$ to $\frac{3}{4}$ up. Set each drum-mic fader to about −10. Set a rough drum-kit mix with the input trims while keeping the mixer meters around 0. Fine-tune the drum mix with the faders, and set the recording level with the drum-mix bus faders.

Here's another way to create the drum submix. Have the drummer hit each drum repeatedly, one at a time, as you adjust the input trims to prevent clipping. For example, ask the drummer to bang on the kick drum. Turn down the kick drum's input trim all the way. Slowly bring it up until the clip LED (overload light) flashes. Then turn down the input trim about 10 dB to allow some headroom.

When all the drum trims are set, set a drum mix with the faders, and set the recording level with the bus 1 and 2 faders.

CAUTION: Any changes to the drum mix or drum-mix level will show up on your tape.

# Recording

If your recording will be synched later with a video tape, record their SMPTE time-code feed on a spare track or two.

A few minutes before the band starts playing, roll tape. Keep a close eye on recording levels. If a track is going into the red, slowly turn down its input trim and note the tape-counter time where this change occurred.

CAUTION: If you are recording off the PA mixer, turning down its input trim will affect the PA levels. The PA operator will need to turn up the corresponding monitor send and channel fader.

This is a touchy situation that demands cooperation. Ideally, you set enough headroom during the sound check so you won't have to change levels. But be sure the PA operator knows in advance that you might need to make changes. Ask the operator whether she wants to adjust the gain trims for you, so she can adjust corresponding levels at the same time. Thank the operator for helping you get a good recording.

If you are recording with a splitter and mic preamps on stage, assign someone to watch the levels and adjust them during the concert. Preamps with meters allow more precise level setting than preamps with clip LEDs.

Keep a track sheet and tape log as you record. For each song in the set list, note the tape-counter time when the song starts. Later, during mixdown, you can fast-wind to those counter times to find songs you want to mix. Also note where any level changes occurred so you can compensate during mixdown. It helps to note a counter time when the signal level was very high. When you mix the tape you can start at that point in setting your overall mix levels.

# Teardown

After the gig, pack your mics away first because they may be stolen or damaged. Refer to your equipment list as you repack everything. Note equipment failures and fix broken equipment as soon as possible.

After you haul your gear back to the studio, it's time for mixing and editing.

Some of the information this chapter was derived from two workshops presented at the 79th convention of the Audio Engineering Society in October 1985. These workshops were titled "On the Repeal of Murphy's Law—Interfacing Problem Solving, Planning, and General Efficiency On-Location," given by Paul Blakemore, Neil Muncy, and Skip Pizzi; and "Popular Music Recording Techniques," given by Paul Blakemore, Dave Moulton, Neil Muncy, Skip Pizzi, and Curt Wittig.   ·

# 18

# ON-LOCATION RECORDING OF CLASSICAL MUSIC

Perhaps your civic orchestra or high school band is giving a concert, and you would like to make a professional recording. Or maybe there's an organist or string quartet playing at the local college, and they want you to record them.

This chapter explains how to make professional-quality recordings of these ensembles. It describes the necessary equipment, microphone techniques, and session procedures.

Incidentally, recording classical-music ensembles is a great way for the beginning recording engineer to gain experience. With just two microphones and a 2-track recorder, much can be learned about acoustics, microphone placement, level setting, and editing—all essential skills in the studio.

## Equipment:

You need the following equipment to record classical music on-location:

- 2-track recorder
- Microphones
- Cables
- Mic stands and stand adapters

- Headphones (or powered speakers)
- Mic preamps (optional)
- Mixer (optional)

If you plan to record overseas, you may need a power converter that converts 50 Hz, 220V AC power to 60 Hz, 110V. Or power your equipment from batteries, and recharge DAT batteries overnight with a 220V/110V converter. You also need some AC power outlet adapters.

## The 2-Track Recorder

A good cassette, MiniDisc, or open-reel recorder can be used for live recording, but for highest quality a DAT recorder is preferred. Chapter 10 covers DAT machines in detail.

DAT tapes can record up to 2 hours nonstop, making them ideal for recording live concerts. DAT tape cannot be edited unless you copy from one DAT recorder to another, or edit the tape with a digital audio workstation.

## Microphones

Next on your list of equipment are some quality microphones. You need two or three of the same model number, or a stereo mic. Good mics are essential, for the microphones—and their placement—determine the sound of your recording. You should spend at least $250 per microphone, or rent some good ones, for professional-quality sound.

For classical-music recording, the preferred microphones are condenser types with a wide, flat frequency response and very low self-noise (less than 21 dB equivalent SPL, A-weighted). (Self-noise is explained in Chapter 6.)

These mics are available with an omnidirectional or unidirectional pickup pattern. An omnidirectional mic is equally sensitive to sounds arriving from any direction, so it helps to add liveness (reverberation) to a recording made in an acoustically dead hall. Omni condenser mics have excellent low-frequency response, so they are a good choice for recording pipe organ or bass drum.

A unidirectional microphone (such as a cardioid) is most sensitive to sounds approaching the front of the microphone, and partly rejects sounds approaching the sides and rear. It helps reduce excessive reverberation in the recording. You need a pair of unidirectional mics if you want to do coincident or near-coincident stereo miking (see Chapter 7).

### Stands versus Hanging

You can mount the microphones on stands or hang them from the ceiling with nylon fishing line. Stands are much easier to set up, but are more visually distracting at live concerts. Stands are more suitable for recording rehearsals or sessions with no audience present.

The mic stands should have a tripod folding base and should extend at least 14 feet high. You can purchase "baby booms" to extend the height of regular mic stands. Many camera stores have telescoping photographic stands that are lightweight and compact.

A useful accessory is a **stereo bar** or **stereo microphone adapter**. This device mounts two microphones on a single stand for stereo recording.

### Hiding Microphones

In some live concerts—especially those that are videotaped—the microphones must not be seen. You might be able to hang some miniature condenser mics, or place boundary mics on the stage floor. If the musical ensemble is large (e.g., an orchestra), and you lay the mics on the stage floor, this placement usually overemphasizes the front row of the ensemble and results in a muffled sound. But if the ensemble is small (a string quartet or small choir, e.g.), floor placement can work very well. You can also mount boundary mics on the ceiling or on the front edge of a balcony. These placements tend to sound too distant, but they may be your only option.

## *Monitors*

For monitoring, you can use either high-quality loudspeakers or headphones. The headphones should be closed-cup, circumaural (around the ear) types to block out the sound of the musicians. You want to hear only what's being recorded. Of course, the headphones should have a wide-range, smooth response for accurate monitoring.

Loudspeakers give more accurate stereo imaging than headphones. So you might want to set up monitor speakers in a control room separate from the concert hall. Place a pair of Nearfield monitors about 3 feet apart and 3 feet from you, on stands behind the mixer. An alternative is to use high-end consumer or professional loudspeakers placed several feet from the walls to weaken early reflections. You could add absorptive material such as acoustic foam to the walls behind and to the side of the speakers. For the best stereo imaging, sit exactly between the speakers, and as far from them as they are spaced apart.

## Mic Cables

You have to sit far from the musicians to clearly monitor what you're recording. To do that, you need a pair of 50-foot mic cables. Longer extensions are needed if the mics are hung from the ceiling, or if you want to monitor in a separate room.

## Mic Preamp or Mixer

You need a mixer when you want to record more than one source—an orchestra and a choir, for instance, or a band and a soloist. You might put a pair of microphones on the orchestra and another pair on the choir. The mixer blends the signals of all four mics into a composite stereo signal. It also lets you control the balance (relative loudness) among microphones. You also need a mixer if you want to use **spot microphones** (**accent microphones**) placed close to each orchestra section or soloist.

For the cleanest sound, consider using some high-quality standalone mic preamps instead of the preamps built into recorders and mixers. Place each preamp on stage; then run its line-level output signal back to your recording gear.

Other miscellaneous equipment you may need includes a power extension cord, an outlet strip, DAT dry cleaning tape, spare mic cables, pen and notebook, and duct tape or vinyl mats to keep cables in place.

# Stereo Microphone Techniques

As a starting point, you place two or three mics several feet in front of the group, raised up high (Figure 18.1). The mic placement controls the acoustic perspective or sense of distance to the ensemble, the balance among instruments, and the stereo imaging.

Recall from Chapter 7 that there are four mic techniques commonly used for stereo recording: coincident pair, near-coincident pair, spaced-pair, and baffled omni techniques. Below is a review:

- **Coincident-pair:** Two directional mics angled apart with their grilles nearly touching and their diaphragms aligned vertically

- **Near-coincident pair:** Two directional mics angled apart and spaced a few inches apart horizontally

- **Spaced pair:** Two or three matched microphones of any pattern aiming straight ahead toward the ensemble and spaced several feet apart horizontally

*(A) Top view.*

*(B) Side view.*

**Figure 18.1** Typical microphone placement for on-location recording of a classical-music ensemble.

- **Baffled omni:** Two omnidirectional mics that are ear spaced and separated by a padded baffle or a hard-surface sphere

Recall from Chapter 6 that boundary microphones can be mounted on clear plastic panels about 2 feet square. You can space these panels apart for spaced-pair stereo, or place them with one edge touching to form a "V." Aim the point of the V at the ensemble. This near-coincident arrangement provides excellent stereo imaging. Also available is a stereo boundary microphone that is smaller than the two panels and provides excellent stereo imaging, extended low-frequency response, and mono compatibility.

# Preparing for the Session

Once you have the equipment, you are ready to go on-location. First, ask the musical director what groups and soloists will be playing, where they will be located, and how long the program is.

If possible, plan to record in a venue with good acoustics. It should have low background noise and adequate reverberation time for the music being performed. This is very important, because it can make the difference between an amateur-sounding recording and a commercial-sounding one. Try to record in an auditorium or spacious church rather than in a band room or gymnasium. If you're forced to record in a hall that is relatively dead, you might want to add artificial reverberation.

Next, get all your equipment ready. Fast-forward and rewind the blank DAT tape and clean the heads with a dry cleaning tape. Label the tape with the name of the artist, location, and date of the session. Check all cables and equipment for proper operation.

Keep your equipment inside your home or studio until you're ready to leave. A DAT recorder left outside in a cold car may become sluggish if the lubricant stiffens, and batteries may lose some voltage.

# Session Setup

Allow an extra hour or so for setup and for fixing broken cables, etc. There's always something unexpected in any new recording situation.

When you first arrive at the recording venue, locate some AC power outlets where you want to set up. Check that these outlets are "live." If not, ask the custodian to turn on the appropriate circuit breaker. Always check in with union technicians if the venue is a union one.

Find a table or folding chairs on which to set your equipment. You might even sit in an audience seat with a portable DAT recorder on your lap. Plug into the AC outlets and let your equipment warm up. Leave a few turns of AC cord near the outlet, and tape down the cord so that it isn't pulled out accidentally.

Then take out your microphones and place them in the desired stereo miking arrangement. As an example, suppose you are recording an orchestra rehearsal with two crossed cardioids on a stereo bar (the near-coincident method). Screw the stereo bar onto a mic stand, and mount two cardioid microphones on the stereo bar. For starters, angle them 110 degrees apart and space them 7 inches apart horizontally. Aim them down so that they point at the orchestra when raised.

You may want to mount the microphones in shock mounts or put the stands on sponges to isolate the mics from floor vibration.

As a starting position, place the mic stand behind the conductor's podium, about 12 feet in front of the front-row musicians. Connect mic cables. Raise the microphones about 14 feet off the floor. This prevents overly loud pickup of the front row relative to the back row of the orchestra.

Mic techniques for piano recitals and other solo instruments are covered in Chapter 8.

Leave some extra turns of mic cable at the base of each stand so you can reposition the stands. This slack also allows for people pulling on the cables accidentally. Try to route the mic cables where they won't be stepped on, or cover them with mats.

Make connections in one of the following ways:

- If you are using two mics, and your DAT recorder has high-quality mic preamps, plug the mics directly into the recorder mic inputs.
- If you prefer to use an outboard mic preamp, plug the mics into the preamp, and plug the preamp output into the recorder line inputs.
- If you're using multiple mics and a mixer, plug the mics into the mixer mic inputs, and plug the mixer stereo outputs into the recorder line inputs.

Now put on your headphones, turn up the recording-level controls, and monitor the signal. When the orchestra starts to play, set the recording levels to peak around −12 dBFS.

# Microphone Placement

Nothing has more effect on the production style of a classical-music recording than microphone placement. Miking distance, stereo positioning, and spot miking all influence the recorded sound character.

## Distance

The microphones must be placed closer to the musicians than a good live listening position would be. If you place the mics out in the audience where the live sound is good, the recording probably will sound muddy and distant when played over speakers. That's because the recorded reverberation is condensed into the space between the playback speakers, along with the direct sound of the orchestra. Close miking (5 to 20 feet from the front row) compensates for this effect by increasing the ratio of direct sound to reverberant sound.

The closer the mics are to the orchestra, the closer it sounds in the recording. If the instruments sound too close, too edgy, too detailed—if the recording lacks hall ambience—the mics are too close to the ensemble. Move the mic stand 1 or 2 feet farther from the orchestra and listen again.

If the orchestra sounds too distant, muddy, or reverberant, the mics are too far from the ensemble. Move the mic stand a little closer to the musicians and listen again.

Eventually you'll find a "sweet spot" where the direct sound of the orchestra is in a pleasing balance with the ambience of the concert hall. Then the reproduced orchestra will sound neither too close nor too far.

## Stereo-Spread Control

Now concentrate on the stereo spread. If the spread heard over headphones is too narrow, that means the mics are angled or spaced too close together. Increase the angle or spacing between mics until localization is accurate. Angling the mics farther apart makes the instruments sound farther away; spacing the mics farther apart does not, but may make the images less focused.

If the instruments that are slightly off-center are heard far-left or far-right in your headphones, your mics are angled or spaced too far apart. Move them closer together until localization is accurate.

You localize sounds differently with headphones than with speakers. For this reason, coincident-pair recordings have less stereo spread over headphones than over loudspeakers. Take this into account when monitoring.

You can test the stereo localization accuracy of your chosen stereo miking method. If you have time, record yourself speaking from various positions on stage while announcing your position: far-left, half-left, center, half-right, and far-right. Listen to the monitor system to check whether the image of your voice is reproduced in corresponding positions. Generally, the far-left and far-right positions should be reproduced at the left and right loudspeakers, respectively.

## Soloist Pickup and Spot Microphones

Sometimes a soloist plays in front of the orchestra. By raising or lowering the stereo mic pair, you can control the balance between soloist and ensemble. If the soloist is too loud relative to the orchestra (as monitored), raise the mics. If the soloist is too quiet, lower the mics. You may want to add a spot mic about 3 feet from the soloist and mix it with the other microphones.

Many recording companies prefer to use several spot mics and a multitrack recorder when taping classical music. Such a method gives more control of balance and definition and is necessary in many situations. If you use spot or accent mics on various instruments or instrumental sections, mix them at a low level relative to the main pair—just loud enough to add definition, but not loud enough to destroy depth. Operate the spot-mic faders subtly or leave them untouched. Otherwise the close-miked instruments may "jump forward" when you bring up the fader, and then "fall back in" when you bring down the fader.

Spot mics sound more natural if you delay their signals to match the acoustic delay of the main pair. Typical delays are 15 to 25 msec.

Solo the main stereo pair, and note the image locations of instruments that you are spot-miking. Pan the spot mics so their image locations coincide with those of the main mic pair.

# Recording

Now that the mics are positioned properly, you're ready to record. At a live concert, you might want to set your recording levels to read about −15 dBFS with the opening applause. This procedure should result in approximately correct recording levels when the musicians start playing. Or set the record-level controls where they were at previous sessions.

Start recording a few seconds before the music starts. Once the recording is in progress, let the recording-level meters peak at −3 dB maximum for a DAT recorder. This allows a little headroom for surprises. Leave the recording level alone as much as possible. If you must adjust the level, do so slowly and try to follow the dynamics of the music.

If there is applause at the end of a musical piece, you can fade it out over 3 to 5 seconds by slowly turning down the recording-level controls or the mixer master volume control. Or leave it alone and do the fade-out while editing the program.

Most classical recording sessions are done in several takes. Write down the DAT ABS times for these takes, and slate each one. Mark the keeper takes for later editing.

After the concert, pack the mics away first; otherwise, they may be stolen or damaged.

# Editing

Once you have your tapes home, you may want to edit them to make a tight presentation. Currently most editing is done with a digital audio workstation, described in Chapter 10.

Put about 4 seconds of silence between each selection. Or you may want to insert an interval of recorded "room sound" or "room tone," especially between movements of a symphony.

Some on-location recordings have a fair amount of background noise. If you insert silence between pieces, there will be an abrupt cutoff of this noise at the end of each piece. To prevent that, either fade the noise down to silence, or replace the silence with room tone.

If you recorded a live concert with applause, fade down the applause over several seconds. At the point where the applause fades to silence, edit that to a point a few seconds before the start of the next piece, and fade up there.

After copying the edited program to another blank DAT, add Start IDs as described in Chapter 14. Or copy the program to a CD-R using CD-R recording software.

Congratulations! You now have your finished product—a realistic, professional recording of a classical-music ensemble.

# 19

# JUDGING SOUND QUALITY

Seat an engineer behind a mixing console and ask him or her to do a mix. It sounds great. Then seat another engineer behind the same console and again ask for a mix. It sounds terrible. What happened?

The difference lies mainly in their **ears**—their critical listening ability. Some engineers have a clear idea of what they want to hear and how to get it. Others haven't acquired the essential ability to recognize good sound. By knowing what to listen for, you can improve your artistic judgements during recording and mixdown. You are able to hear errors in microphone placement, equalization, and so on, and correct them.

To train your hearing, try to analyze recorded sound into its components—such as frequency response, noise, reverberation—and concentrate on each one in turn. It's easier to hear sonic flaws if you focus on a single aspect of sound reproduction at a time. This chapter is a guide to help you do this.

## Classical versus Popular Recording

Classical and popular music have different standards of "good sound." One goal in recording classical music (and often folk music or jazz) is to accurately reproduce the live performance. This is a worthy aim because the sound of an orchestra in a good hall can be quite beautiful. The music was composed and the instruments were designed to sound best when heard live in the concert hall. The recording engineer, out of respect for the music, should always try to translate that sound to tape with as little technical intrusion as possible.

By contrast, the accurate translation of sound to tape is not always the goal in recording popular music. Although the aim may be to reproduce the original sound, the producer or engineer may also want to play with that sound to create a new sonic experience, or to do some of both.

In fact, the artistic manipulation of sounds through studio techniques has become an end in itself. Creating an interesting new sound is as valid a goal as re-creating the original sound. There are two games to play, each with its own measures of success.

If the aim of a recording is realism or accurate reproduction, the recording is successful when it matches the live performance heard in the best seat in the concert hall. The sound of musical instruments is the standard by which such recordings are judged.

When the goal is to enhance the sound or produce special effects (as in most pop-music recordings), the desired sonic effect is less defined. The live sound of a pop group could be a reference, but pop-music recordings generally sound better than live performances. Recorded vocals are clearer and less harsh, the bass is cleaner and tighter, and so on. The sound of pop music reproduced over speakers has developed its own standards of quality apart from accurate reproduction.

# Good Sound in a Pop-Music Recording

Currently, a good-sounding pop recording might be described as follows (there are always exceptions):

- Well-mixed
- Wide-range
- Tonally balanced
- Clean
- Clear
- Smooth
- Spacious

    It also has:

- Presence
- Sharp transients
- Tight bass and drums
- Wide and detailed stereo imaging
- Wide but controlled dynamic range

- Interesting sounds
- Suitable production

The next sections explore each one of these qualities in detail so that you know what to listen for. Assume that the monitor system is accurate, so that any colorations heard are in the recording and not in the monitors.

# A Good Mix

In a good mix, the loudness of instruments and vocals is in a pleasing balance. Everything can be clearly heard, yet nothing is obtrusive. The most important instruments or voices are loudest; less important parts are in the background.

A successful mix goes unnoticed. When all the tracks are balanced correctly, nothing sticks out and nothing is hidden. Of course, there's a wide latitude for musical interpretation and personal taste in making a mix. Dance mixes, for example, can be very severe sonically.

Sometimes you don't want everything to be clearly heard. On rare occasions you may want to mix in certain tracks very subtly for a sub-conscious effect.

The mix must be appropriate for the style of music. For example, a mix that's right for loud rock music usually won't work for a pop ballad. A rock mix typically has the drums way up front and the vocals only slightly louder than the accompaniment. In contrast, a pop ballad has the vocals loudest, with the drums used just as "seasoning" in the background.

Level changes during the mix should be subtle, or should make sense. Otherwise, instruments jump out for a solo and fall back in afterwards. Move faders slowly, or set them to preset positions during pauses in the music. Nothing sounds more amateurish than a solo that starts too quietly and then comes up as it plays. You can hear the engineer working the fader.

# Wide Range

Wide range means extended low-frequency and high-frequency response. Cymbals should sound crisp and distinct, but not sizzly or harsh; kick drum and bass should sound deep, but not overwhelming or muddy. Wide-range sound results from using high-quality microphones and adequate EQ. Analog tape recorders need proper alignment, good tape, high tape speed, and clean tape heads.

Recently, it's become popular to combine "hi-fi" and "low-fi" sounds in a single mix. The low-fi sounds generally cover a narrow frequency range and might be distorted.

## Good Tonal Balance

The overall tonal balance of a recording should be neither bassy nor trebley. That is, the perceived spectrum should not emphasize low frequencies or high frequencies. Low bass, midbass, midrange, upper midrange, and highs should be heard in equal proportions (Figure 19.1). Emphasis of any one frequency band over the other eventually causes listening fatigue. Dance club mixes, however, are heavy on the bass end to get the crowd moving.

Recorded tonal balance is inversely related to the frequency response of the studio's monitor system. If the monitors have a high-frequency rolloff, the engineer will compensate by boosting highs in the recording to make the monitors sound right. The result is a bright recording.

Before doing a mix, it helps to play over the monitors some commercial recordings whose sound you admire. This helps you become accustomed to a commercial spectral balance. After your mix is recorded, play it back and alternately switch between your mix and a commercial recording. This comparison indicates how well you matched a commercial spectral balance. Of course, you may not care to duplicate what others are doing.

In pop-music recordings, the tonal balance or timbre of individual instruments does not necessarily have to be natural. Still, many listeners want to hear a realistic timbre from acoustic instruments, such as the guitar, flute, sax, or piano. The reproduced timbre depends on microphone frequency response, microphone placement, the musical instruments themselves, and equalization.

**Figure 19.1**
Loudness versus frequency of a good-sounding pop recording.

# Clean Sound

Clean means free of noise and distortion. Tape hiss, hum, and distortion are inaudible in a good recording. Distortion in this case means distortion added by the recording process, not distortion already present in the sound of electric-guitar amps or Leslie speakers. There are exceptions to this guideline; some popular recordings have noise or distortion added intentionally.

Clean also means "not muddy"—free of low-frequency overhang and leakage. A clean mix is one that is uncluttered, free of excess instrumentation. This is achieved by arranging the music so that similar parts don't overlap, and not too many instruments play at once in the same frequency range. Usually, the fewer the instruments, the cleaner the sound. Too many overdubs can muddy the mix.

# Clarity

In a clear-sounding recording, instruments do not crowd or mask each other's sound. They are separate and distinct, and blend well. As with a clean sound, clarity arises when instrumentation is sparse, or when instruments occupy different areas of the frequency spectrum. For example, the bass provides low frequencies; keyboards might emphasize midbass; lead guitar provides upper midrange; and cymbals fill in the highs.

In addition, a clear recording has adequate reproduction of each instrument's harmonics. That is, the high-frequency response is not rolled off.

# Smoothness

Smooth means easy on the ears, not harsh, uncolored. Sibilant sounds are clear but not piercing. A smooth, effortless sound allows relaxation; a strained or irritating sound causes muscle tension in the ears or body. Smoothness is a lack of sharp peaks or dips in the frequency response, as well as a lack of excessive boost in the midrange or upper midrange.

# Presence

Presence is the apparent sense of closeness of the instruments—a feeling that they are present in the listening room. Synonyms are clarity, detail, and punch.

Presence is achieved by close miking, overdubbing, and using microphones with a presence peak or emphasis around 5 kHz. Using less reverb and effects can help. Upper-midrange boost helps, too. Most instruments have a frequency range that, if boosted, makes the instrument stand out more clearly or become better defined. Presence sometimes conflicts with smoothness because presence often involves an upper-midrange boost, while a smooth sound is free of such emphasis. You have to find a tasteful compromise between the two.

## Spaciousness

When the sound is spacious or airy, there is a sense of air around the instruments. Without air or ambience, instruments sound as if they are isolated in stuffed closets. (Sometimes, though, this is the desired effect.) You achieve spaciousness by adding reverb, recording instruments in stereo, using room mics, or miking farther away.

## Sharp Transients

The attack of cymbals and drums generally should be sharp and clear. A bass guitar and piano may or may not require sharp attacks, depending on the song.

## Tight Bass and Drums

The kick drum and bass guitar should "lock" together so that they sound like a single instrument—a bass with a percussive attack. The drummer and bassist should work out their parts together so as to hit accents simultaneously, if this is desired.

To further tighten the sound, damp the kick drum and record the bass direct. Equalize them for presence and clarity. Rap music, however, has its own sound—the kick drum usually is undamped and boomy, sometimes with short reverb added.

## Wide and Detailed Stereo Imaging

Stereo means more than just left and right. Usually, tracks should be panned to many points across the stereo stage between the monitor speakers. Some instruments should be hard-left or hard-right; some should be in the center; others should be half-left or half-right. Try to achieve a stereo stage that is well balanced between left and right (Figure 19.2). Instruments occupying the same frequency range might be panned to opposite sides of center.

**Figure 19.2** An example of image placement between speakers.

You may want some tracks to be unlocalized. Backup choruses and strings should be spread out rather than appearing as point sources. Stereo keyboard sounds can wander between speakers. A lead-guitar solo can have a fat, spacious sound.

There should also be some front-to-back depth. Some instruments should sound close or up front; others should sound farther away.

If you want the stereo imaging to be realistic (for a jazz combo, for example), the reproduced ensemble should simulate the spatial layout of the live ensemble. If you're sitting in an audience listening to a jazz quartet, you might hear drums on the left, piano on the right, bass in the middle, and sax slightly right. The drums and piano are not point sources, but are somewhat spread out. If spatial realism is the goal, you should hear the same ensemble layout between your speakers. On some commercial CDs, the piano and drums are spread all the way between speakers—an interesting effect, but unrealistic.

Pan-potted mono tracks often sound artificial in that each instrument sounds isolated in its own little space. It helps to add some stereo reverberation around the instruments to "glue" them together.

Often, TV mixes are heard in mono. Hard-panned signals sound weak in mono relative to center-panned signals. So pan sound sources to 3 and 9 o'clock, not hard-right and hard-left.

## *Wide but Controlled Dynamic Range*

**Dynamic range** is the range of volume levels from softest to loudest. A recording with a wide dynamic range becomes noticeably louder and softer, adding excitement to the music. To achieve this, don't add too much compression (automatic volume control). An overly compressed recording sounds squashed—crescendos and quiet interludes lose their impact.

Vocals often need some compression or gain-riding because they have more dynamic range than the instrumental backup. A vocalist may sing too loudly and blast the listener, or sing too softly and become buried in the mix. A compressor can even out these extreme level variations, keeping the vocals at a constant loudness. Bass guitar also can benefit from compression.

## Interesting Sounds

The recorded sound may be too flat or neutral—lacking character or color. In contrast, a recording with creative production has unique musical instrument sounds, and typically uses special effects. Some of these are equalization, echo, reverberation, doubling, chorus, flanging, compression, distortion, and stereo effects.

Making sounds interesting or colorful can conflict with accuracy or fidelity. That's okay, but you should know the trade-off.

## Suitable Production

The way a recording sounds should imply the same message as the musical style or lyrics. In other words, the sound should be appropriate for the particular tune being recorded.

For example, some rock music is rough and raw. The sound should be, too. A clean, polished production doesn't always work for high-energy rock 'n' roll. There might even be a lot of leakage or ambience to suggest a garage studio or nightclub environment. The role of the drums is important, so they should be loud in the mix. The toms should ring, if that is desired.

New Age, disco, rhythm and blues, contemporary Christian, or pop music is slickly produced. The sound is usually tight, smooth, and spacious.

Actually, each style of music is not locked into a particular style of production. You tailor the sound to complement the music of each individual tune. Doing this may break some of the guidelines of good sound, but that's usually okay as long as the song is enhanced by its sonic presentation.

# Good Sound in a Classical-Music Recording

As with pop music, classical music should sound clean, wide-range, and tonally balanced. But since classical recordings are meant to sound realistic—like a live performance—they also require good acoustics, a natural balance, tonal accuracy, suitable perspective, and accurate stereo imaging (see Chapter 18).

## Good Acoustics

The acoustics of the concert hall or recital hall should be appropriate for the style of music to be performed. Specifically, the reverberation time should be neither too short (dry) nor too long (cavernous). Too short a reverberation time results in a recording without spaciousness or grandeur. Too long a reverberation time blurs notes together, giving a muddy, washed-out effect. Ideal reverberation times are around 1.2 seconds for chamber music or soloists, 1.5 seconds for symphonic works, and 2 seconds for organ recitals. To get a rough idea of the reverb time of a room, clap your hands once, loudly, and count the seconds it takes for the reverb to fade to silence.

## A Natural Balance

When a recording is well balanced, the relative loudness of instruments is similar to that heard in an ideal seat in the audience area. For example, violins are not too loud or soft compared to the rest of the orchestra; harmonizing or contrapuntal melody lines are in proportion.

Generally, the conductor, composer, and musicians balance the music acoustically, and you capture that balance with your stereo mic pair. But sometimes you need to mike certain instruments or sections to enhance definition or balance. Then you mix all the mics. In either case, consult the conductor for proper balances.

## Tonal Accuracy

The reproduced timbre or tone quality should match that of live instruments. Fundamentals and harmonics should be reproduced in their original proportion.

## Suitable Perspective

Perspective is the sense of distance of the performers from the listener—how far away the stage sounds. Do the performers sound like they're eight rows in front of you, in your lap, or in another room?

The style of music suggests a suitable perspective. Incisive, rhythmically motivated works (such as Stravinsky's "Rite of Spring") sound best with closer miking; lush, romantic pieces (a Bruckner symphony) are best served by more distant miking. The chosen perspective depends on the taste of the producer.

Closely related to perspective is the amount of recorded ambience or reverberation. A good miking distance yields a pleasing balance of direct sound from the orchestra and ambience from the concert hall.

## *Accurate Imaging*

Reproduced instruments should appear in the same relative locations as they were in the live performance. Instruments in the center of the ensemble should be heard in the center between the speakers; instruments at the left or right side of the ensemble should be heard from the left or right speaker. Instruments halfway to one side should be heard halfway off center, and so on. A large ensemble should spread from speaker to speaker, while a quartet or soloist can have a narrower spread.

It's important to sit equidistant from the speakers when judging stereo imaging, otherwise the images shift toward the side on which you're sitting. Sit as far from the speakers as they are spaced apart. Then the speakers appear to be 60 degrees apart, which is about the same angle an orchestra fills when viewed from the typical ideal seat in the audience (tenth row center, for example).

The reproduced size of an instrument or instrumental section should match its size in real life. A guitar should be a point source; a piano or string section should have some stereo spread. Each instrument's location should be as clearly defined as it was heard from the ideal seat in the concert hall.

Reproduced reverberation (concert-hall ambience) should surround the listener, or at least it should spread evenly between the speakers. Surround-sound technology is needed to make the recorded ambience surround the listener, although spaced-microphone recordings have some of this effect.

There should be a sense of stage depth, with front-row instruments sounding closer than back-row instruments. Accurate imaging is illustrated in Figure 19.3.

# Training Your Hearing

The critical process is easier if you focus on one aspect of sound reproduction at a time. You might concentrate first on the tonal balance—try to pinpoint what frequency ranges are being emphasized or slighted. Next listen to the mix, the clarity, and so on. Soon you have a lengthy description of the sound quality of your recording.

**Figure 19.3** With accurate imaging, the sound-source location and size are reproduced during playback, as well as the reverberant field.

Developing an analytical ear is a continuing learning process. Train your hearing by listening carefully to recordings—both good and bad. Make a checklist of all the qualities mentioned in this chapter. Compare your own recordings to live instruments, and to commercial recordings.

A pop-music record that excels in all the attributes of good sound is *The Sheffield Track Record* (Sheffield Labs, Lab 20), engineered and produced by Bill Schnee. In effect, it's a course in state-of-the-art sound—required listening for any recording engineer or producer.

Another record with brilliant production is *The Nightfly* by Donald Fagen (Warner Brothers 23696-2), engineered by Roger Nichols, Daniel Lazerus, and Elliot Scheiner, produced by Gary Katz, and mastered by Bob Ludwig. This recording, and Steely Dan recordings by Roger Nichols, sound razor sharp, very tight and clear, elegant, and tasteful; and the music just pops out of the speakers.

The following listings are more examples of outstanding rock production, and set high standards:

Songs:

*I Need Somebody*, by Bryan Adams; producer, Bob Clearmountain

*The Power of Love*, by Huey Lewis & The News; producer, Huey Lewis & The News

Albums:

*90125*, by Yes; producer, Trevor Horn

*Synchronicity*, by The Police; producer, Hugh Padgham and The Police

*Dark Side of the Moon*, by Pink Floyd; producer, Alan Parsons

*Thriller*, by Michael Jackson; engineer, Bruce Swedien; producer, Quincy Jones

*Avalon*, by Roxy Music; engineer, Bob Clearmountain; producer, Roxy Music

Then there are the incredibly clean recordings of Tom Jung (with DMP records) and George Massenberg. You can learn a lot by emulating these superb recordings, and many others.

Once you're making recordings that are competent technically—clean, natural, and well mixed—the next stage is to produce imaginative sounds. You're in command; you can tailor the mix to sound any way that pleases you or the band you're recording. The supreme achievement is to produce a recording that is a sonic knockout—beautiful, thrilling, and/or overwhelming.

# Troubleshooting Bad Sound

Now you know how to recognize good sound, but can you recognize bad sound? Suppose you're monitoring a recording in progress, or listening to a recording you've already made. Something doesn't sound right. How can you pinpoint what's wrong, and how can you fix it?

The rest of this chapter includes step-by-step procedures to solve audio-related problems. Read down the list of "bad sound" descriptions until you find one matching what you hear. Then try the solutions until your problem disappears. Only the most common symptoms and cures are mentioned; console maintenance is not covered.

This troubleshooting guide is divided into four main sections:

- Bad sound on all recordings (including those from other studios)
- Bad sound on playback only (mixer output sounds all right)
- Bad sound in a pop-music recording
- Bad sound in a classical-music recording

Before you start, check for faulty cables and connectors. Also check all control positions; rotate knobs and flip switches to clean the contacts, and clean connectors with De-Oxit from Caig Labs.

# Bad Sound on All Recordings

If you have bad sound on all your recordings, including those from other studios, follow this checklist to find the problem:

- Upgrade your monitor system.
- Adjust tweeter and woofer controls on speakers.
- Adjust the relative gains of tweeter and woofer amplifiers in a bi-amped system.
- Relocate speakers.
- Improve room acoustics.
- Equalize the monitor system.
- Try different speakers.
- Upgrade the power amp and speaker cables.

# Bad Sound on Playback Only

You might have bad sound on your playback only, but your mixer output sounds okay. If cassette or open-reel playback has a dull sound or drop-outs, follow these steps:

- Check that the oxide side of the tape is against the heads.
- Clean and demagnetize the tape path.
- Try another brand of tape.
- Align tape heads; calibrate the electronics.
- Do maintenance on the tape transport.
- Check and replace tape heads if necessary.

If your tape playback is plagued with distortion, try the following:

- Reduce the recording level.
- Increase the bias level.
- Check for bad cables.

If your tape playback has tape hiss, follow these steps:

- Increase the recording level.
- Use Dolby or dbx noise reduction.
- Use better tape.
- Align the tape recorder.

If DAT tape playback has glitches or drop-outs, try these steps:

- Clean the recorder with a dry cleaning tape.
- Before recording, fast-forward the tape to the end and rewind it to the top.
- Use better tape.
- Format videocassettes nonstop from start to finish.

# Bad Sound in a Pop-Music Recording Session

Sometimes you have bad sound in a pop-music recording session.

### Muddiness (Leakage)

If the sound is muddy from excessive leakage, try the following:

- Place the microphones closer to their sound sources.
- Spread the instruments farther apart to reduce the level of the leakage.
- Place the instruments closer together to reduce the delay of the leakage.
- Use directional microphones (such as cardioids).
- Overdub the instruments.
- Record the electric instruments direct.
- Use baffles (goboes) between instruments.
- Deaden the room acoustics (add absorptive material, flexible panels, or slot absorbers).
- Filter out frequencies above and below the spectral range of each instrument. Be careful or you'll change the sound of the instrument.
- Turn down the bass amp in the studio, or monitor the bass with headphones instead.

### Muddiness (Excessive Reverberation)

If the sound is muddy due to excessive reverberation, try these steps:

- Reduce the effects-send levels or effects-return levels. Or don't use effects until you figure out what the real problem is.
- Place the microphones closer to their sound sources.
- Use directional microphones (such as cardioids).
- Deaden the room acoustics.

- Filter out frequencies below the fundamental frequency of each instrument.

## Muddiness (Lacks Highs)

If your sound is muddy and lacks highs, or has a dull or muffled sound, try the following:

- Use microphones with better high-frequency response, or use condenser mics instead of dynamics.
- Change the mic placement. Put the mic in a spot where there are sufficient high frequencies. Keep the high-frequency sources (such as cymbals) on-axis to the microphones.
- Use small-diameter microphones, which generally have a flatter response off-axis.
- Boost the high-frequency equalization or cut slightly around 300 Hz.
- Change musical instruments; replace guitar strings; replace drum heads. (Ask the musicians first!)
- When bouncing tracks, record bright-sounding instruments last to reduce generation loss.
- Avoid excessive recording levels with bright-sounding instruments. The high-frequency response of cassettes and open-reel gradually rolls off as the recording level is increased.
- Use an enhancer signal processor, but watch out for noise.
- Use a direct box on the electric bass. Have the bassist play percussively or use a pick if the music requires it. When compressing the bass, use a long attack time to allow the note's attack to come through. (Some songs don't require sharp bass attacks—do whatever's right for the song.)
- Damp the kick drum with a pillow or blanket, and mike it next to the center of the head near the beater. Use a wooden beater if the song and the drummer allow it.
- Don't plug an electric guitar directly into a mic input. Use a direct box or a high-impedance input.

## Muddiness (Lacks Clarity)

If your sound is muddy because it lacks clarity, try these steps:

- Consider using fewer instruments in the musical arrangement.
- Equalize instruments differently so that their spectra don't overlap.

- Try less reverberation.
- Using equalizers, boost the presence range of instruments that lack clarity. Or cut 1 to 2 dB around 300 Hz.
- In a reverb unit, add about 30 to 100 msec of predelay.

## Distortion

If you have distortion in a pop-music recording, try the following:

- Increase input attenuation (reduce input gain), or plug in a pad between the microphone and mic input.
- Readjust gain-staging: Set faders and pots to their design centers (shaded areas).
- If you still hear distortion, switch in the pad built into the microphone (if any).
- Check connectors for stray wires and bad solder joints.
- Unplug and plug-in connectors. Clean them with Caig Labs De-Oxit or Pro Gold.

## Tonal Imbalance

If you have bad tonal balance—the sound is boomy, dull, or shrill, for example—follow these steps:

- Change musical instruments; change guitar strings; change reeds, etc.
- Change mic placement. If the sound is too bassy with a directional microphone, you may be getting proximity effect. Mike farther away or roll off the excess bass.
- Use the 3:1 rule of mic placement to avoid phase cancellations. When you mix two or more mics to the same channel, the distance between mics should be at least three times the mic-to-source distance.
- Try another microphone. If a cardioid mic's proximity effect is causing a bass boost, try an omnidirectional mic instead.
- If you must place a microphone near a hard, reflective surface, try a boundary microphone on the surface to prevent phase cancellations.
- If you're recording a singer/guitarist, delay the vocal mic signal by about 1 msec.
- Change the equalization. Avoid excessive boost. Maybe cut slightly around 300 Hz if the sound is muddy, or cut around 3 kHz if the sound is harsh.

- Use equalizers with a broad bandwidth, rather than a narrow, peaked response.

## Lifelessness

If your pop-music recording has a lifeless sound and is unexciting, these steps might help you solve it:

- Work on the live sound of the instruments in the studio to come up with unique effects.
- Add special effects—reverberation, echo, exciter, doubling, equalization, etc.
- Use and combine recording equipment in unusual ways.
- Try overdubbing little vocal licks or synthesized sound effects.

If your sound seems lifeless due to dry or dead acoustics, try these:

- If leakage is not a problem, put microphones far enough from instruments to pick up wall reflections. If you don't like the sound this produces, try the next suggestion.
- Add reverb or echo to dry tracks. (Not all tracks require reverberation. Also, some songs may need very little reverberation so that they sound intimate.)
- Use omnidirectional microphones.
- Add hard, reflective surfaces in the studio, or record in a hard-walled room.
- Allow a little leakage between microphones. Put mics far enough from instruments to pick up off-mic sounds from other instruments. Don't overdo it, though, or the sound becomes muddy and track separation becomes poor.

## Noise (Hiss)

Sometimes your pop-music recording has extra noise on it. If your sound has hiss, try these:

- Check for noisy guitar amps or keyboards.
- Switch out the pad built into the microphone (if any).
- Reduce mixer input attenuation (increase input gain).
- Use a more sensitive microphone.
- Use an impedance-matching adapter (a low-Z to high-Z step-up transformer) between microphones and phone-jack mic inputs.

- Use a quieter microphone (one with low self-noise).
- Increase the sound pressure level at the microphone by miking closer. If you're using PZMs, mount them on a large surface or in a corner.
- Apply any high-frequency boost during recording, rather than during mixdown.
- If possible, feed tape tracks from mixer direct outs or insert sends instead of group or bus outputs.
- Use a lowpass filter (high-cut filter).
- As a last resort, use a noise gate.

## Noise (Rumble)

If the noise is a low-frequency rumble, follow these steps:

- Reduce air-conditioning noise or shut off the air conditioning temporarily.
- Use a highpass filter (low-cut filter) that is set around 40 to 80 Hz.
- Use microphones with limited low-frequency response.
- See Noise (Thumps) below.

## Noise (Thumps)

- Change the microphone position.
- Change the musical instrument.
- Use a highpass filter set around 40 to 80 Hz.
- If the cause is mechanical vibration traveling up the mic stand, put the mic in a shock-mount stand adapter. Or place the mic stand on some carpet padding. Or use a microphone that is less susceptible to mechanical vibration, such as an omnidirectional mic, or a unidirectional mic with a good internal shock mount.
- Use a microphone with a limited low-frequency response.
- If the cause is piano pedal thumps, also try working on the pedal mechanism.

## Hum

Hum is a subject in itself. See Chapter 5 for causes and cures of hum. A noise gate can remove guitar-amp buzz between notes.

## Pop

Pops are explosive breath sounds in a vocalist's microphone. If your pop-music recording has pops, try these solutions:

- Place the microphone above or to the side of the mouth.
- Place a foam windscreen (pop filter) on the microphone.
- Stretch a silk stocking over a crochet hoop, and mount it on a mic stand a few inches from the microphone (or use an equivalent commercial product).
- Place the microphone farther from the vocalist.
- Use a microphone with a built-in pop filter (ball grille).
- Use an omnidirectional microphone, because it is likely to pop less than a directional (cardioid) microphone.
- Switch in a highpass filter (low-cut filter) set around 80 Hz.

## Sibilance

Sibilance is an overemphasis of "s" and "sh" sounds. If you are getting sibilance on your pop-music recording, try these steps:

- Use a de-esser.
- Place the microphone farther from the vocalist.
- Place the microphone toward one side of the vocalist, rather than directly in front.
- Cut equalization in the range from 5 to 10 kHz.
- Change to a duller-sounding microphone.

## Bad Mix

If you get a bad mix on your recording, some instruments or voices are too loud or too quiet. To improve a bad mix, try the following:

- Change the mix. (Maybe change the mix engineer!)
- Compress vocals or instruments that occasionally get buried.
- Change the equalization on certain instruments to help them stand out.
- During mixdown, continuously change the mix to highlight certain instruments according to the demands of the music.

## Unnatural Dynamics

When your pop-music recording has unnatural dynamics, loud sounds don't get loud enough or soft sounds disappear. If this happens, try these steps:

- Check the tracking of noise-reduction units. For example, a 10-dB level increase at the input of the encode unit should appear as a 10-dB level increase at the output of the decode unit.
- Use the same type of noise reduction during playback that was used during recording.
- Use less compression or limiting.
- Avoid overall compression.
- Use multiband compression on the stereo mix instead of wideband (full-range) compression.

## Isolated Sound

If some of the instruments on your recording sound too isolated, as if they are not in the same room as the others, follow these steps:

- In general, allow a little crosstalk between the left and right channels. If tracks are totally isolated, it's hard to achieve the illusion that all the instruments are playing in the same room at the same time. You need some crosstalk or correlation between channels. Some right-channel information should leak into the left channel, and vice versa.
- Place microphones farther from their sound sources to increase leakage.
- Use omnidirectional mics to increase leakage.
- Use stereo reverberation or echo.
- Pan effects returns to the channel opposite the channel of the dry sound source.
- Pan extreme left-and-right tracks slightly toward center.
- Make the effects-send levels more similar for various tracks.
- To give a lead-guitar solo a fat, spacious sound, use a stereo chorus. Or send its signal through a delay unit, pan the direct sound hard left, and pan the delayed sound hard right.

## Lack of Depth

If the mix lacks depth, try these steps:

- Achieve depth by miking instruments at different distances.
- Use varied amounts of reverberation on each instrument. The higher the ratio of reverberant sound to direct sound, the more distant the track sounds.

# Bad Sound in a Classical-Music Recording

Check the following procedures if you have problems recording classical music:

## Too Dead

If the sound in your classical recording is too dead—there is not enough ambience or reverberation—try these measures to solve the problem:

- Place the microphones farther from the performers.
- Use omnidirectional microphones.
- Record in a concert hall with better acoustics (longer reverberation time).
- Add artificial reverberation.

## Too Close

If the sound is too detailed, too close, or too edgy, follow these steps:

- Place the microphones farther from the performers.
- Place the microphones lower or on the floor (as with a boundary microphone).
- Roll off the high frequencies.
- Use mellow-sounding microphones (many ribbon mics have this quality).

## Too Distant

If the sound is distant and there is too much reverberation, these steps might help:

- Place the microphones closer to the performers.
- Use directional microphones (such as cardioids).
- Record in a concert hall that is less live (reverberant).

## Stereo Spread Too Narrow or Too Wide

If your classical-music recording has a narrow stereo spread, try these steps:

- Angle or space the main microphone pair farther apart.
- If you're doing midside stereo recording, turn up the side output of the stereo microphone.
- Place the main microphone pair closer to the ensemble.

If the sound has excessive stereo spread (or "hole-in-the-middle"), try the following:

- Angle or space the main microphone pair closer together.
- If you're doing midside stereo recording, turn down the side output of the stereo microphone.
- In spaced-pair recording, add a microphone midway between the outer pair, and pan its signal to the center.
- Place the microphones farther from the performers.

## Lack of Depth

Try the following to bring more depth into your classical-music recording:

- Use only a single pair of microphones out front. Avoid multimiking.
- If you must use spot mics, keep their level low in the mix.
- Add more artificial reverberation to the distant instruments than to the close instruments.

## Bad Balance

If your classical-music recording has bad balance, try the following:

- Place the microphones higher or farther from the performers.
- Ask the conductor or performers to change the instruments' written dynamics. Be tactful!
- Add spot microphones close to instruments or sections needing reinforcement. Mix them in subtly with the main microphones' signals.

## Muddy Bass

If your recording has a muddy bass sound, follow these steps:

- Aim the bass-drum head at the microphones.

- Put the microphone stands and bass-drum stand on resilient isolation mounts (such as a carpet pad), or place the microphones in shock-mount stand adapters.
- Roll off the low frequencies or use a highpass filter set around 40 to 80 Hz.
- Record in a concert hall with less low-frequency reverberation.

## Rumble

Sometimes your classical-music recording picks up rumble from air conditioning, trucks, and other sources. Try the following to clear this up:

- Check the hall for background rumble problems.
- Temporarily shut off the air conditioning.
- Record in a quieter location.
- Use a highpass filter set around 40 to 80 Hz.
- Use microphones with limited low-frequency response.

## Distortion

If your classical-music recording has distortion, try the following:

- Switch in the pads built into the microphones (if any).
- Increase the mixer input attenuation (turn down the input trim).
- Check connectors for stray wires or bad solder joints.

## Bad Tonal Balance

Bad tonal balance expresses itself in a sound that is too dull, too bright, or colored. If your recording has this problem, follow these steps:

- Change the microphones. Generally, use flat-response microphones with minimal off-axis coloration.
- Follow the 3:1 rule mentioned in Chapter 7.
- If a microphone must be placed near a hard, reflective surface, use a boundary microphone to prevent phase cancellations between direct and reflected sounds.
- Adjust equalization.
- Place the mics at a reasonable distance from the ensemble (too-close miking sounds shrill).
- Avoid mic positions that pick up standing waves or room modes. Experiment with small changes in mic position.

This chapter described a set of standards for good sound quality in both popular-music and classical-music recordings. These standards are somewhat arbitrary, but the engineer and producer need guidelines to judge the effectiveness of the recording. The next time you hear something you don't like in a recording, the lists in this chapter will help you define the problem and find a solution.

# 20

# SURROUND SOUND: TECHNIQUES AND MEDIA

So far we've covered techniques that result in a 2-channel stereo recording. With stereo, you hear all the instruments and reverb in front of you, in the area between the two loudspeakers. But with surround sound, you hear audio images in every direction. For example, the musical ensemble could be up front, while the hall ambience envelops you from the sides and rear.

Stereo uses two channels feeding two loudspeakers in front of you. Surround sound uses multiple channels feeding multiple speakers placed all around you. A disadvantage of stereo is that you must sit in a tiny "sweet spot" to hear correct localization. In contrast, surround sound can be heard correctly in a wide area between the speakers.

Surround gives a wonderfully spacious effect. It puts you inside the concert hall with the musicians. You and the music occupy the same space—you're part of the performance. For this reason, surround is more musically involving, more emotionally intense, than regular stereo. There's a sense of envelopment. Surround mixing is fast becoming a valuable new tool to offer your customers. Since many listeners have home theater systems with multiple speakers, they are already set up to play surround audio recordings.

A magazine devoted to multichannel sound production is *Surround Professional*, 6 Manhasset Ave., Port Washington, NY 11050, fax 516-767-1745.

# Surround Speaker Arrangement

Inherited from the film industry, surround-sound uses six channels feeding six speakers placed around the listener. This forms a 5.1 surround system, where the "point 1" is the subwoofer or Low-Frequency Effects channel. The LFE channel is band-limited to 125 Hz and below, while the other channels are full bandwidth (20 Hz to 20 kHz). "5.1" is a channel format— a surround-sound standard that states the number of channels, their frequency response, and the speaker placement.

The six speakers are:

- Left-front
- Center
- Right-front
- Left-surround
- Right-surround
- Subwoofer

Figure 20.1 shows the recommended placement of monitor speakers for 5.1 surround sound. It is the standard setup proposed by the International Telecommunication Union (ITU). From the center speaker, the left and right speakers should be placed at ±30 degrees, and the surrounds at ±110 degrees. (Some engineers prefer 120 to 125 degrees for the surround

**Figure 20.1**
Recommended placement
of monitor speakers for
5.1 surround sound.

speakers.) If you are mixing movie soundtracks, use dipole speakers for the surrounds, and place them to the sides (±90 degrees).

The left-front and right-front speakers provide regular stereo. The surrounds provide a sense of envelopment due to room ambience. They also allow sound images to appear behind the listener. Deep bass is filled in by the subwoofer. Because we do not localize low frequencies below about 120 Hz, the sub can be placed almost anywhere without degrading localization.

Originally developed for theaters, the center-channel speaker is mounted directly in front of the listener. In a home-theater system, it is placed just above the TV screen, or just below and in front of the TV screen. This speaker plays center-channel information in mono, such as dialog.

Why use a center speaker, when two stereo speakers create a phantom center image? If you use only two speakers and you sit off-center, the phantom image shifts toward the side on which you're sitting. But a center-channel speaker produces a real image, which does not shift as you move around the listening area. The center speaker keeps the actors' dialog on-screen, regardless of where the listener sits.

Also, the phantom center image does not have a flat frequency response, but a center speaker does. Why is this? Remember that a center image results when you feed identical signals to both stereo speakers. The right-speaker signal reaches your right ear, but so does the left-speaker signal after a delay around your head. The same thing occurs symmetrically at your left ear. Each ear receives direct and delayed signals, which interfere and cause phase cancellations at 2 kHz and above. A center-channel speaker does not have this response anomaly.

With a phantom center image, the response is weak at 2 kHz because of the phase cancellation just mentioned. To compensate, recording engineers often choose mics with a presence peak in the upper midrange for vocal recording. The center-channel speaker does not need this compensation.

For sharpest imaging and continuity of the soundfield, all the speakers should be:

- The same distance from the listener
- The same model (except the sub)
- The same polarity
- Direct-radiator types
- Driven with identical power amps
- Matched in sound pressure level with pink noise (the sub is 10 dB louder)

If you are mixing movie soundtracks, the surround speakers should be dipole designs rather than direct-radiator types. The dipole speakers project sound forward and backward to create a diffuse effect.

Typically the speakers are 4 to 8 feet from the listener and 4 feet high. Use a length of string to place the monitors the same distance from your head. The sub can go along the front wall on the floor. Be sure that all the speakers sound the same so there is no change in tonal balance as you pan images around.

A DSP algorithm to reproduce surround sound on headphones has been developed by Lake Technology. It is licensed to Dolby Labs under the name "Dolby Headphone." This feature is beginning to appear in consumer receivers and surround processors.

# Setting Up a Surround Monitoring System

Working in surround, of course, requires more equipment than working in stereo. You'll need a console or editing software with extra outputs, a multitrack recorder instead of a stereo recorder, five monitors and a sub-woofer, and six channels of power amplification with a common volume control and a sub/satellite crossover (a bass management system). Once the monitoring system is set up, it needs to be carefully calibrated. Let's look at these requirements in detail.

## Surround Mixing Equipment

Here's what you need:

- Multitrack recordings in any format—analog tape, digital tape, hard disk, etc.

- A mixing console with at least six output channels (also called busses or subgroups). Most digital consoles have a surround matrix, a section set up for mixing and monitoring in surround.

- An alternative to a mixing console is a Digital Audio Workstation (DAW): multitrack recording and editing software than runs on a computer. For example, Minnetonka's Mx51 software DAW includes a surround sound panner, LFE sends, and a 6-channel monitor section. MOTU's Digital Performer 3.0 offers surround panning as well.

- An 8-track recorder to record the surround mix—such as a TASCAM DA-88/DA-78 or ADAT. Tracks 1–6 record the surround channels, while tracks 7 and 8 record a separate stereo mix.

- Five monitor speakers and a subwoofer, set up as described before.
- Six channels of power amplification. You could use a home-theater surround receiver for this purpose. It has a single volume control that simultaneously adjusts the level of all the tracks. Most home-theater receivers have five amp channels and a line output that feeds a powered subwoofer. The sub's power amp should be at least 100 watts, and the receiver should have six analog inputs for your surround mix. An alternative to a receiver is a standalone surround sound processor and six channels of power amplification.

A feature to look for in surround sound receivers is Dolby Digital and DTS decoders (explained later). Receivers labeled "5.1 ready" or "Dolby Digital ready" are not Dolby Digital compatible. The receiver must have Dolby Digital and DTS decoders to play those formats. However, you don't need those decoders to do surround mixes.

## Bass Management

In the surround receiver is a "bass management" circuit. Bass management is nothing more than a subwoofer/satellite crossover filter. It sends the deep lows to the sub, and sends other frequencies to the five "satellite" speakers that surround you.

A bass management circuit routes frequencies above about 100 Hz to the five full-range speakers, and routes frequencies below about 100 Hz from all six channels to the subwoofer. In other words, the bass management circuit routes low-frequency signals from all the five channels—and the LFE channel—to your sub. By keeping the deep lows out of the full-range speakers, bass management reduces their low-frequency distortion and lets them be made relatively small for home use. Note that bass management affects only what you monitor, not what goes on tape.

Bass management can be done by a surround-receiver circuit, a standalone box, a special circuit in a subwoofer, or a software plug-in.

You set the bass management crossover frequency as low as possible to remove the directionality of the bass, and to extend the headroom of the sub. Typically you'd set the crossover frequency to the frequency where your full-range speakers are down 3 dB on the low end. If your five main speakers extend down to 20 or 30 Hz, you don't need bass management. In some receivers, the bass management crossover frequency is adjustable among 120/100/80 Hz—whatever your system needs for flattest response.

The crossover frequency is 120 Hz with the Dolby Digital standard and 80 Hz with the DTS standard. However, the Dolby Digital, DTS, and THX standard crossover frequencies are irrelevant to the frequency of the bass-management filter for the mixing work in your studio. And the upper-frequency limit of the LFE track (125 Hz) has nothing to do with the crossover frequencies of the bass management (120 to 40 Hz). As mentioned above, you set the crossover frequency according to the response of your monitor speakers.

### LFE Channel Filtering

The LFE channel lowpass filter used in bass management is a very steep filter (48 dB/octave) so it causes a lot of phase shift. But you can turn off the LFE filter in the encoder, and use your own gentler filter instead. Try 80 Hz, 24 dB/octave. Use any filter you like, as long as it removes all the energy at 125 Hz. Insert this filter between your console's LFE channel output and the input of the mixdown deck's LFE track. In other words, record the LFE track prefiltered, and turn off filtering in the encoder.

## *Connections*

Now that you know the necessary equipment for surround mixing (including bass management), you can wire the system together. Basically you connect line-level signals from six busses to the associated tracks on your mixdown recorder. To monitor those six tracks, connect that recorder's outputs either to a surround receiver, or to a bass-management filter that feeds six channels of power amps. The receiver or amplifiers drive the five small speakers and the sub.

Figure 20.2 shows the connections. Patch the multitrack recorder as usual to your console or DAW. Patch the console's or DAW's surround matrix outputs, or bus outputs, to the 8-track mixdown deck. On the back of this deck, connect track outputs 1–6 to the inputs of the surround receiver or power amp inputs. On the receiver or power amps, connect the speaker outputs to the speakers. If your subwoofer is self-powered, connect the LFE channel line output to the sub line input. If your speakers are self-powered, connect them to outputs 1–6 of your bass manager.

When you connect your mixer or DAW to the 8-track mixdown deck, which signal goes on which track? Currently there is no standard assignment of surround tracks. So be sure to label your tapes with the track assignment. The most common track assignment (the Dolby Digital standard and the SMPTE standard) is given below:

1. Left-front
2. Right-front

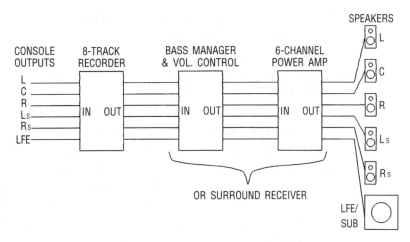

**Figure 20.2** Monitoring system for 5.1 surround with bass management.

3. Center

4. LFE (Low Frequency Effects) or subwoofer channel

5. Left-surround

6. Right-surround

7. Stereo mix left

8. Stereo mix right

Be sure to include a subwoofer in your monitor system. If you don't, you might not hear low-frequency noises that a home listener with a sub will hear. These noises include breath pops, mic-stand thumps, air-conditioning rumble, and excessively heavy deep-bass notes.

## Calibration

It's essential to calibrate your speakers so that their levels match. You need a sound level meter (a low-cost one from Radio Shack is adequate). Here's a suggested procedure:

1. Turn on the LFE channel and disable bass management.

2. Set each power amp channel to the same volume setting.

3. Get a pink noise signal from a console noise generator, receiver, or CD. Connect the signal to a console input. Another option is a surround calibration tape, such as the one available from http://www.tmhlabs.com.

4. Assign that input channel to one surround channel (output bus or group fader). For example, start with the front-left channel.

5. Set the console's bus faders and master faders to unity gain (the shaded portion of fader travel).

6. Adjust the input fader so the level on the mixing deck's meter is −20 dBFS, the standard level for surround mixes. This level allows for some headroom.

7. Hold the sound level meter at your mixing position and set it to C-weighting, slow response. Aim the meter's mic at the speaker. Set the level of the power-amp channel so you read 85 dB SPL on the meter.

8. Repeat steps 4–7 for each channel and its speaker, one at a time, so that all speakers are putting out the same level. (In most home-theater receivers is a menu that lets you set the level of each channel.) If you are mixing for theater sound with dipole speakers, set their level to 82 dB SPL instead.

9. Assign pink noise to just the LFE channel so that you hear the noise coming from the subwoofer. The playback level of the LFE channel is set 10 dB higher than the main speaker levels because that's done in consumer surround systems. Using the receiver's LFE gain control, or the sub's level control, set the sub's SPL to 95 dB SPL if you're using an RTA, or to 89 dB SPL if you're using a sound level meter.

Why the difference? Unlike an RTA, an SPL meter integrates the energy of all the octaves it is measuring to come up with a single reading. The main speakers produce 8–10 octaves, but the sub produces 2 octaves. The sub's 2-octave energy reads lower on the SPL meter than the main speakers' 8- to 10-octave energy. So, instead of setting the sub's SPL to 95 dB, you set it to 89 dB to allow for this energy difference.

It's important to phase-align the subwoofer's signal with the full-range speakers' signals. Improper alignment can cause a dip in the system's frequency response at the crossover frequency. If your sub has a phase-matching control, send a sine wave to all speakers at the crossover frequency. Adjust the phase control to get the loudest sound at the mix position. If the sub has a polarity switch, try it both ways, and use the position that gives the loudest bass when all the speakers are playing.

10. After calibration, record your mixes at 0 dBFS maximum, and set your monitor level as desired.

Here's another calibration method developed by Lorr Kramer of DTS and surround-sound expert Mike Sokol: Use bandwidth-limited pink noise (20 to 80 Hz) for the woofer and 500 to 2000 Hz for the main speakers. Set each speaker to the same SPL, one at a time. Using 500 Hz to 2 kHz pink noise for the main speakers keeps the signal out of the LFE channel and avoids exciting room modes. And limiting the top end to 2 kHz helps avoid directionality effects of the mic in the SPL meter.

Now that your monitors are calibrated, do the same for your mixing console:

1. Feed pink noise into one channel strip.
2. Route or patch that strip's signal equally to all six surround output busses.
3. Set each output bus fader to unity gain.
4. At the input strip, set the trim to make the output level –20 dB on the console's meters.
5. Trim the console's ADAT or TDIF outputs, or the mixdown deck's input levels, so that all six tracks read –20 dBFS. (The LFE channel does not get 10 dB extra gain in the recording path, only in the monitoring path.)
6. On your surround receiver, set the small/large speaker switch to small, and enable bass management.

# Recording and Mixing Pop Music for Surround

Doing a multitrack recording for later mixdown in surround is almost identical to recording for mixdown to stereo. Some engineers add a few ambience mics to pick up the studio acoustics. These ambience tracks are panned to the rear speakers during mixdown.

Many producers like to monitor the original recording session in stereo, not surround, to reduce the technical issues that can slow down the session. They wait until mixdown to monitor in surround.

Earlier in this book we showed some ways to mix multitrack tapes to 2-track stereo. Now let's look at mixing those same tapes to 5.1 surround.

## *Panning*

To place the image of each track in space around you, some consoles include a pair of pan controls (left/right and front/rear) for each channel. Others use a trackball, mouse, or joystick. Some digital audio editing programs, or plug-ins for those programs, permit surround panning as well. For example, SmartPan Pro by Kind of Loud Technologies is a surround panner plug-in for Digidesign's Pro Tools. Minnetonka's Mx51 is a program to mix 5.1 surround sound, including a "Build your own mixer" GUI and automated surround panners.

Suppose your console or recording software has 8 output busses, and you want to pan or move a track between front-left and rear-right. Assign the track to the front-left and rear-right busses. They should be odd-even numbered. When you turn the pan knob from left to right, the sound image should move as desired.

Where should you pan tracks in a surround mix? There are no set rules. Some producers like to put all the musicians up front, and put the hall ambience and applause in the rear. This works especially well for live concerts and recordings of classical music. This ambience can be created artificially with a digital reverb, or recorded with mics in the concert hall. Stereo reverb returns are typically sent to the rear channels. Several multichannel digital reverbs are available, both as hardware and as software.

Some producers use the rear speakers for background vocals, percussion, horn stabs, or strings, leaving the lead vocal and rhythm instruments in front. A group of five singers could be panned to place one singer in each speaker, so that the listener is in the middle of the group. You might put the lead vocal in the center speaker, and also partly in the surrounds to pull the vocal out toward the listener. Spreading instruments between left-front and left-surround, and right-front and right-surround, gives a greater sense of envelopment.

You can place instruments in fixed positions (static panning), or move them around in space (dynamic panning). Some consoles let you move a sound by drawing its path in space on your monitor screen. You might move a sound along a circle, arc, or line. Then save these pans as part of your automated mix.

## Using the Center Speaker

Some engineers prefer to send center tracks equally to the left and right speakers—not the center speaker. This creates a phantom center image. However, sending a track to the center speaker gives a better tonal balance and more stable imaging than the center phantom image.

It's not recommended to send a track only to the center speaker. Some listeners don't have a center speaker. So if you send, say, a vocal to just the center speaker, those listeners without a center speaker won't hear it. Also, home listeners can solo the center channel and hear punch-ins on that channel. So many producers route center tracks mainly to the left and right speakers, and also feed a little signal to the center speaker (maybe 6 dB down).

## Using the LFE Channel

With music mixes you seldom need to send anything to the LFE subwoofer track—it gets deep bass from the bass management circuit in the listener's playback system, and at the proper level. Since the five main channels of 5.1 surround encoders reproduce from 20 Hz to 20 kHz, there's no need to put anything musical in the LFE channel. The consumer's bass management filter will redirect any sub-80-Hz energy to their own subwoofer anyway, whether or not you put this bass signal in the LFE track. On the other hand, suppose the end listener has a subwoofer/satellite system with six channels, but no bass management system. In that case, the sound they hear will be thin in the bass if there is no signal in the LFE channel.

With film mixes, you typically send low-frequency sound effects (explosions, tornadoes, crashes) to the LFE channel. The LFE track also helps with DJ mixes and synth mixes that have lots of lows. Even if you mix only music, you need a subwoofer to hear the very deep noises (breath pops, room rumble) that a home listener will hear with a sub.

## Downmixing

Downmixing is making a stereo mix from a 5.1 surround mix. It is done in the consumer's home theater receiver. In the downmixing circuit, the left and right surround channels are blended with the left and right front channels. The center channel is blended equally with the left and right channels. The LFE channel is either mixed with the front signals or not used.

Downmixes made this way seldom create a well-balanced stereo mix, so be sure to check your 5.1 mix for stereo compatibility. Surround monitoring systems should have a downmix button so you can hear how your surround mixes will sound when downmixed to stereo by consumer receivers.

It's best to do a separate stereo mix and record it on tracks 7 and 8 of your 8-track mixdown deck. This stereo mix can be put on DVD-Audio discs or Super Audio CDs (explained later) along with the surround mix.

# Surround-Sound Mic Techniques

So far we've talked about mixing multitrack recordings to surround—a method intended mainly for pop music. But for classical music, you can record in surround using five microphones, which capture the spatial character of the concert hall in which the musical ensemble is playing. Each mic feeds a separate track of an 8-track recorder.

Surround mic techniques are somewhat different from stereo mic techniques. In addition to the usual front-left and front-right mics, you need two surround mics to pick up the hall ambience, and a center mic to feed to the center channel. Note that listening in surround reduces the stereo separation (stage width) because of the center speaker, but mic techniques for surround are optimized to counteract this effect.

A number of mic techniques have been developed for recording in surround. Let's take a look at them.

## Soundfield 5.1 Microphone System

This system is a single, multiple-capsule microphone (Soundfield ST250 or MKV) and Soundfield Surround Decoder for recording in surround. The decoder translates the mic's B-format signals (X, Y, Z, and W) into L, C, R, LR, RR, and mono subwoofer outputs.

## Delos VR² Surround Miking Method

John Eargle, Delos' director of recording, developed their $VR^2$ (Virtual Reality Recording) format. Recordings made with this method offer discrete surround. They also are claimed to sound good in stereo and very good with "steered" analog decoding, such as Dolby Pro Logic.

In making these recordings, Eargle typically uses the mic placement shown in Figure 20.3. This method employs a coincident-stereo mic in the center, flanked by two spaced omni's typically 4 feet apart. Two house mics (to pick up hall reverb) are placed 30 to 40 feet behind the main pair. (Greater spacing creates an undesirable echo.) These house mics are omnis or cardioids aiming at the rear of the hall, spaced about 12 feet apart. There also might be spot mics (accent mics) placed within the orchestra.

The mics are assigned to various tracks of a digital 8-track recorder:

- 1 and 2: A mix of the coincident-pair mics, flanking mics, house mics, and spot mics
- 3 and 4: Coincident-pair stereo mic
- 5 and 6: Flanking mics
- 7 and 8: House mics (surround mics)

## NHK Method

The Japanese NHK Broadcast Center has worked out another surround miking method. They found that, for surround recording, cardioid mics

430

**Figure 20.3**
A Delos surround miking method.

record a more natural amount of reverb than omni mics. The mics are placed as described below:

- A center-aiming mic feeds the center channel.
- A near-coincident pair feeds front-left and front-right.
- Widely spaced flanking mics add expansiveness.
- Up to three pairs of ambience mics aim toward the rear.

Figure 20.4 shows the mic placement. The front mics are placed at the critical distance from the orchestra, where the direct-sound level matches the reverberant-sound level. Typically, this point is 12 to 15 feet from the front of the musical ensemble and 15 feet above the floor.

NHK engineers make this a recommendation: When you're monitoring the surround program, the reverb volume in stereo listening should match the reverb volume in multichannel listening. That is, when you fold down or collapse the monitoring from 5.1 to stereo, the direct/reverb ratio should stay the same.

## *The KFM 360 Surround System*

Jerry Bruck of Posthorn Recordings developed this elegant surround-miking method. It is a form of the mid-side (MS) stereo technique.

Bruck starts with a modified Schoeps KFM 6U stereo microphone, which is a pair of omni mics mounted on opposite sides of a 7-inch hard

**Figure 20.4**
An NHK surround-sound
miking method.

**Figure 20.5**
KFM 360 surround-sound
miking method.

sphere. Next to those mics, nearly touching, are two figure-8 mics, one on each side of the sphere, each aiming front and back (Figure 20.5). This array creates two MS mic arrays aimed sideways in opposite directions. The mics do not seriously degrade each other's frequency response.

In the left channel, the omni and figure-8 mic signals are summed to give a front-facing cardioid pattern. They are also differenced to give a rear-facing cardioid pattern. The same thing happens symmetrically in the right channel. The sphere, acting as a boundary and a baffle, "steers" the cardioid patterns off to either side of center, and makes their polar patterns irregular.

By adjusting the relative levels of the front and back signals, the user can control the front/back separation. As a result, the mic sounds like it is moving closer to or farther from the musical ensemble.

According to Bruck:

The system is revelatory in its ability to recreate a live event. Perhaps most remarkable is the freedom a listener has to move around and select a favored position, as one might move around in a concert hall to select a preferred seat. The image remains stable, without a discernible "sweet spot." The reproduction is unobtrusively natural and convincing in its sense of "being there."

The four mic signals can be recorded on a 4-track recorder for later matrixing. The figure-8 mics need some equalization to compensate for their low-frequency rolloff and loss in the extreme highs. To maintain a good signal-to-noise ratio, this EQ can be applied after the signal is digitized.

## Five-Channel Microphone Array with Binaural Head

This method was developed by John Klepko of McGill University. It combines an array of three directional mics with a 2-channel dummy head (Figure 20.6):

- For the front left and right channels: identical supercardioid mics
- For the center channel: a cardioid mic
- For the surround channels: a dummy head with two pressure-type omni mics fitted into the ear molds

**Figure 20.6**
The Klepko surround-sound miking method.

The mics are shock mounted and have equal sensitivity and equal gains. Supercardioids are used for the front left/right pair to reduce center-channel buildup. Although the dummy head's diffraction causes peaks and dips in the response, it can be equalized to compensate. During playback, the listener's head reduces the acoustical crosstalk that would normally occur between the surround speakers.

According to Klepko:

> The walkaround tests form an image of a complete circle of points surrounding the listening position. Of particular interest is the imaging between ±30 degrees and ±90 degrees. The array produces continuous, clear images here where other (surround) techniques fail.
>
> The proposed approach is downward compatible to stereo although there will be no surround effect. However, stereo headphone reproduction will resolve a full surround effect due to the included binaural head-related signals. Downsizing to matrix multichannel (5-2-4 in this case) is feasible except that it will not properly reproduce binaural signals to the rear because of the mono surrounds. As well, some of the spatial detail recorded by the dummy-head microphone would be lost due to the usual bandpass filtering scheme (100 Hz–7 kHz) of the surround channel in such matrix systems.

## DMP Method

DMP engineer Tom Jung has recorded in surround using a Decca Tree stereo array for the band and a rear-aiming stereo pair for the surround ambience (Figure 20.7). Spot mics in the band complete the miking. The Decca Tree uses three mics spaced a few feet apart, with the center mic placed slightly closer to the performers. It feeds the center channel in the 5.1 system.

The rear-aiming mics are either a coincident stereo mic, another Decca tree, or a spaced pair whose spacing matches that of the Decca tree outer pair. Jung tries to aim the rear mics at irregular surfaces to pick up diffuse sound reflections.

## Woszcyk Technique (PZM Wedge plus Opposite-Polarity, 180-Degree Coincident-Cardioid Surround Mics)

A recording instructor at McGill University, Wieslaw Woszcyk developed an effective method for recording in surround that also works well in

MUSICAL
ENSEMBLE
(SPOT MICS NOT SHOWN)

CARDIOIDS

STEREO MIC
FOR SURROUND
CHANNELS

**Figure 20.7**
A DMP surround miking
method.

HALL OR RPG DIFFUSOR

stereo. The orchestra is picked up by a PZM wedge made of two 18-inch
× 29-inch hard baffle boards angled 45 degrees. A mini omni mic is
mounted on or flush with each board. At least 20 feet behind the wedge
are the surround mics: two coincident cardioids angled 180 degrees apart,
aiming left and right, and in opposite polarity (Figure 20.8).

According to Woszcyk, his method has several advantages:

- Imaging is very sharp and accurate, and spaciousness is excellent due
  to strong pickup of lateral reflections.
- The out-of-phase impression of the surround pair disappears when a
  center coherent signal is added.
- The system is compatible in surround, stereo, and mono. In other
  words, the surround signals do not phase-interfere with the front-pair
  signals. That is because (1) the surround signals are delayed more
  than 20 msec, (2) the two mic pairs operate in separate sound fields,
  and (3) the surround mics form a bidirectional pattern in mono, with
  its null aiming at the sound source.

If a PZM wedge is not acceptable because of its size and weight, other
arrays with wide stereo separation may be substituted.

18"X29"
BAFFLE

OMNI MIC

PZM WEDGE
FRONT MICS

45°

>20 FT

SURROUND MICS

**Figure 20.8**
Woszcyk surround miking
method.

COINCIDENT CARDIOIDS
IN OPPOSITE POLARITY

## Williams Five Cardioid Mic Array

Michael Williams, an independent audio consultant, worked out the math
to determine the best cardioid microphone arrangement for realistic reproduction of surround-sound fields. His method is shown in Figure 20.9.

## Double MS Technique

Developed by Curt Wittig and Neil Muncy, the double MS technique uses
a front-facing mid-side mic pair for direct sound pickup and a rear MS pair
facing away from the front (Figure 20.10). The rear pair is placed at or just
beyond the critical distance of the room—where the reverberant sound
level equals the direct sound level. The matrixed outputs feed front-left,
front-right, rear-left, and rear-right speakers. No center channel mic is
specified, but you could use the front-facing cardioid mic of the front MS
pair for this purpose.

## Surround Ambience Microphone (SAM) Array

This array was developed by Gunther Theile of the Institute für Rund-
funktechnik (IRT). Four cardioid mics are placed 90 degrees to each other
and 21 to 25 cm apart. No center channel is described.

**Figure 20.9**
Williams Five Cardioid Mic Array (MMA, or Multichannel Microphone Array).

**Figure 20.10**
Double MS technique.

# SPL Atmos 5.1/ASM 5 Surround Recording System

This system uses a special mic mount with five arms that radiate out from a center point, like a star. At the end of each arm is a Brauner condenser mic aiming outward from the center. The five mics feed a five-channel mixing console, which adjusts the mic polar patterns and offers panning, bass management, and surround monitoring. SPL's website is www.spl-electronics.com. The SPL system uses the Ideal Cardioid Arrangement (ICA 5, Figure 20.11) developed by Volker Henkels and Ulf Herrmann.

# The Holophone

This is a surround microphone using several omni mic capsules flush-mounted in a football-shaped surface. Web site: www.theholophone.com.

**Figure 20.11**
Ideal Cardioid
Arrangement (ICA) used
in Brauner SPL Atmos
5.1/ASM5 Adjustable
Surround Microphone.

## Stereo Pair plus Surround Pair

In this method, the center-channel mic is omitted. You use a standard stereo pair of your choice to pick up the musical ensemble, plus another stereo pair of your choice to pick up the hall ambience. The hall mics feed the left-surround and right-surround channels. For example, two Crown SASS-P MKII microphones can be placed back-to-back, separated by several feet.

You might try a hybrid approach for a pop-music concert: Feed the front speakers a mix of multiple close-up mics on stage, and feed the rear speakers the signals from a rear-aiming stereo mic.

# Surround Media

So far we've discussed surround recordings, and their creation either by multitrack mixdown or by surround mic techniques. Now let's turn our attention to the media that will play those surround recordings. They can be distributed to the public on CD, Super Audio CD (SACD), or DVD (Digital Versatile Disc). Two DVD formats for surround sound are DVD-Audio and DVD-Video. Let's examine all these formats in detail.

## Compact Disc

The compact disc is a 2-channel format that uses linear PCM (pulse code modulation) encoding. The CD's bit depth is fixed at 16 bits, and the sampling rate is fixed at 44.1 kHz. Storage capacity is 640 MB, or about 74 minutes of stereo audio. To fit the six channels of surround into the CD's two channels, two data-reduction encoding schemes are used: Dolby Digital or Digital Theater Systems (DTS). We'll explain them later.

# Digital Versatile Disc (DVD)

Another medium for playing surround recordings is the Digital Versatile Disc or DVD. It is a high-capacity optical storage medium the size of a compact disc (4.73 inches diameter). DVD can store digital data in three formats: audio, video, and computer.

## DVD Compatibility

The DVD player reads:

- CD
- CD-R (in some units)
- CD-ROM
- DVD-Video disc (video plus audio)

A DVD-Video player can play a DVD-Audio disc if the latter has a Dolby digital version of the audio in the DVD-Video zone on the disc.

## DVD Capacity

Compared to a CD, DVD has much greater capacity due to its smaller pits and closer tracks. The scanning laser has a shorter wavelength than in a CD player, which lets it read DVD's denser data stream. In addition, MPEG-2 data compression of the video data increases the data density on the DVD.

Some DVDs have a single layer of pits; others have a dual layer at different depths. The laser automatically focuses on the required layer.

Listed below are the storage capacities of various media:

- A compact disc holds 640 MB.
- A single-sided, single-layer DVD holds 4.7 GB (7 times CD capacity).
- A single-sided, dual-layer DVD holds 8.5 GB.
- A double-sided, single-layer DVD holds 9.4 GB.
- A double-sided, dual-layer DVD holds 17 GB.

The single-sided, single-layer disc was the main DVD format when this book went to print. Its 4.7 GB capacity is enough to hold a 2-hour and 10-minute movie plus subtitles.

## DVD Players

Most DVD players have these outputs:

- 2-channel analog outputs playing a Dolby-Surround-encoded stereo signal
- A digital output that can be connected to an external decoder for 5.1-channel surround sound (either Dolby Digital or DTS)
- 6 analog outputs fed from built-in Dolby Digital or DTS decoders (in some units)

## DVD Data Rate

The DVD data transfer rate is 10.1 megabits per second (mps). A 6-channel surround track, with data compression, consumes 384 or 448 kilobits per second (kps). Linear PCM stereo, at 16 bits and 48 kHz sampling rate, takes 1.5 mps. A 96 kHz sample rate doubles the transfer rate to 3 mps. A 24-bit resolution increases the rate to 4.5 mps.

Two forms of DVD are DVD-Video and DVD-Audio, and we'll look at them now.

## DVD-Video

DVD-Video is a DVD format for videos: movies with a surround-audio soundtrack. The audio tracks can be Dolby Digital (AC-3) surround, 5.1 channels, with MPEG-1 compressed audio, or they can be 2 channels, 16 to 24 bit, 48 or 96 kHz, linear PCM audio. In other words, you can have surround sound with compromised fidelity, or 2-channel sound with excellent fidelity. A DVD disc can be encoded with both formats, and listeners can choose which one they want to hear.

Although the spec provides for multichannel PCM audio, current players have only 2 channels of PCM audio. All players support Dolby Digital (AC-3) surround.

## DVD-Audio

DVD-Audio is a DVD format that features audio programs. It also can have optional still pictures (slide shows), Internet links, visual interactive menus, on-screen text and lyrics, and video clips.

DVD-Audio discs use PCM encoding. This encoding can be linear, as on CDs, or "packed" using Meridian Lossless Packing. MLP reduces the data rate up to 50%, but without any data loss: The reproduced signal is identical, bit for bit, with the original signal. While a standard CD is a 2-channel format fixed at 16-bit/44.1 kHz resolution, DVD-Audio is a multichannel surround format with higher resolutions. Compared to a standard CD, DVD-Audio permits:

- Better fidelity due to higher sampling rate and higher quantization (up to 24 bit, 96 kHz with six channels, or 176.4 and 192 kHz with two channels).

- Longer playing time in some formats (up to 6 hours of 16-bit, 44.1K stereo).

- More channels (up to six in the 5.1 scheme, allowing surround sound).

- Optional formats in addition to PCM, such as MPEG-2 BC, DTS, Dolby Digital, or DSD (Direct Stream Digital—the format used in the Super Audio CD).

- Option for different sampling rate and bit depth on different channels. DVD-Audio allows a wide range of sampling rates, number of channels, and quantizations. For example, a 4.7 GB single-layer disc can hold a 75-minute program in which the left-center-right signals are 88.2 kHz/24 bit and the two surround channels are 44.1 kHz/20 bit.

- Option for different formats on different tracks. One track might be 16-bit/96 kHz surround, while another could be 24-bit/192 kHz stereo.

- Other optional media formats besides audio.

DVD-Audio content is stored in a separate **DVD-Audio zone** on the disc (the AUDIO_TS directory). The program can be copy protected by a digital **signature signal** and digital **watermarking**.

Most DVD-Audio players will also play DVD-Videos and CDs, and some will play Super Audio CDs. A DVD-Video player can play a DVD-Audio disc if the latter has a Dolby digital version of the audio in the **DVD-Video zone** on the disc. The digital outputs on a DVD-Audio player include PCM and Dolby Digital. Some units have DTS and DSD outputs, and all have multichannel analog outputs. Future players might have Firewire (IEEE 1394) connections.

You compile and record a DVD-Audio disc as you do a CD-R disc: with software, a hardware disc recorder, and blank discs. Specifically, you need DVD-Audio authoring software, a DVD-R recorder or DLT tape backup drive, and blank DVD discs. The write-once discs have dye on one side like a CD-R. Handling up to 4.7 GB on a single-sided disc, they can record DVD-Video, DVD-Audio, or DVD-ROM files.

One major title of authoring software is Sonic Solutions Studio HD and DVD Creator for Macintosh G3 or G4. If you want to make pure audio DVD-Audio discs, Sonic HD will do the job. Just click the mouse to assemble a playlist of surround-sound tracks. If you want to include video, etc.,

Sonic DVD Creator can handle it. In that case, compiling the DVD-Audio disc can become complex, with a variety of sampling rates, bit depths, channels, video, interactive menus, and so on. Sonic Solutions' Web site is www.sonic.com.

Another major DVD-authoring package is MASS 5.1 for Windows, a bundled product containing three items:

- Minnetonka's Mx5—a program to mix 5.1 surround sound, including a "Build Your Own Mixer" GUI and automated surround panners.
- Minnetonka's MASS 5.1—a program to compile those mixes for DVD-Audio. You drag-and-drop soundfiles from one window to another to create your playlist. Then you press the Record button and burn the DVD-Audio disc.
- A Pioneer S201 DVD-R recorder. This drive connects to your computer via a SCSI port. It can make data DVDs and audio DVDs. Minnetonka's Web site is at www.minnetonkaaudio.com.

## Super Audio CD

An alternative to DVD-Audio is the Super Audio CD developed by Sony and Philips. It uses the Direct Stream Digital (DSD) process, which encodes a digital signal in a 1-bit (bitstream) format at a 2.8224MHz sampling rate. This system offers a frequency response from DC to 100kHz with 120dB dynamic range.

The Super Audio CD has two layers that are read from one side of the disc. On one layer is a 2-channel stereo DSD program followed by the same program in six channels for surround sound. On the other layer is a Red-Book 16-bit/44.1K program, which makes dual inventories unnecessary. The 16/44.1K signal is derived from Sony's Super Bit Mapping Direct processing, which downconverts the bitstream signal with minimal loss of DSD quality. Standard CD players can play the 16/44.1K layer, and future players would be able to play the 2- or 6-channel DSD layer for even better sound quality.

# Encoding Surround for Release on Various Formats

As we said, surround mixes can be released on CD, DVD-Video, DVD-Audio, or Super Audio CD (SACD). We need to consider how to get six channels of surround audio onto those formats.

In the past, DVD-Video discs and videocassettes used Dolby Surround: a matrix encoding system that combined four channels (left, center, right, surround) into two channels. The Dolby Pro Logic decoder in the consumer playback system unfolded the two channels back into four. The surround channel, which was mono and limited bandwidth, was reproduced over left and right surround speakers. Unfortunately, matrixing reduced the separation between channels because it mixed the channels together.

Recent encoding schemes let us encode six channels of surround audio onto disc, while keeping the channels discrete, not matrixed together. Let's look at how this is done for CD, DVD-Video, and DVD-Audio.

## Surround Encoding for CD

A compact disc has only enough capacity for two channels of audio. So to get six channels of surround audio onto CD, data reduction is needed. Two data-reduction schemes are Dolby Digital and Digital Theater Systems (DTS).

### Dolby Digital and DTS

Dolby Digital and DTS each use a different lossy encoding process to reduce the bit rate needed to transmit the six channels via a 2-channel bitstream. "Lossy" means that the reproduced signal is missing some data that appeared in the original signal, so there is a slight loss in sound quality.

Why is this data reduction necessary? Audio at 44.1 kHz sampling frequency and 16-bit word length flows at a rate of about 700 kilobits per second (kbps) for each channel. The rate for six channels is 4.2 Mbps. In order to handle this huge data flow, data reduction is needed. The data-reduction encoder in Dolby Digital is AC-3. It can be used on any number of channels.

First used in movie theaters, Dolby Digital and DTS are perceptual coding methods. They use data reduction (data compression) to remove sounds deemed inaudible due to masking. Dolby Digital's AC-3 encoder compresses the data about 12:1, while DTS compresses about 3:1. Both formats offer six discrete channels of digital surround sound. DTS resolution is 20-bit, while Dolby Digital is 16, 18, or 20 bits (perhaps 24 bits in the future). Dolby's AC-3 encoder accepts data at sample rates of 32, 44.1, or 48 kHz; DTS accepts 44.1 kHz. Compared to Dolby Digital, DTS uses less data compression and needs more data storage space and bandwidth. But some listeners say that DTS sounds more transparent—more like the original discrete tracks that were fed into the DTS encoder. Still, Dolby is the most common format.

To play a Dolby Digital or DTS recording, you need a newer DVD player or a CD player with a digital output. Plug the digital output into a decoder, which extracts the six channels of digital audio and converts them to analog. The decoder has a DSP chip that can decode both the DTS and Dolby Digital formats. Some surround receivers have DTS and Dolby Digital decoders built in.

## Surround Encoding for DVD-Video

In a DVD-Video disc, much of the disc's capacity is taken up by video signals. So this format also can handle only two channels of audio. DVD-Video uses Dolby Digital's AC-3 scheme to encode (data-reduce) the six channels of surround into two channels. During playback, the two channels are decoded to recover the six channels. As we said, those six channels are separate or discrete—not matrixed.

## Surround Encoding for DVD-Audio

A DVD-Audio disc has lots of capacity for audio signals, so the six channels can be encoded without any data loss by using Meridian Lossless Packing (MLP).

## Summary of Media Formats

Let's summarize the surround encoding schemes used in different media:

- CD uses DTS or Dolby Digital. Both are lossy systems.
- DVD-Video uses Dolby Digital, a lossy system.
- DVD-Audio uses Meridian Lossless Packing, a lossless system. However, a DVD-Audio disc also can include Dolby Digital mixes so that it will play on CD players and DVD-Video players.

Table 20.1 summarizes the sample rate, the resolution (bit depth), and the stereo or surround systems associated with various media formats.

## Encoding Hardware and Software for CD and DVD-Video

With the CD and DVD-Video formats, the surround encoding can be done either by you or by the mastering house that manufactures the disc. To do it yourself you need a hardware encoder or software encoder. Some exam-

**Table 20.1**

| Format | Sample rate | Resolution | Stereo/surround systems |
|---|---|---|---|
| CD | 44.1 kHz | 16-bit | Stereo PCM. 16-, 20-, or 24 bit DTS (6 channels) |
| SACD | 2.82 MHz | 1-bit | Direct Stream Digital (DSD) (2 or 6 channels) |
| DVD-V | 48 kHz | 16- or 24-bit | Stereo PCM, Stereo MPEG-2, Dolby Digital, or DTS (2 to 6 channels) |
| DVD-A | 48 kHz | 16-bit | Dolby Digital (6 channels) |
| | 96 kHz | 24-bit | PCM encoded with MLP (6 channels) |
| | 192 kHz | 24-bit | PCM encoded with MLP (stereo) |

ples of software encoders are Minnetonka Audio's SurCode CD Pro DTS and SurCode Dolby Digital, Sonic Foundry's SoftEncode 5.1 Channel, or Kind of Loud's SmartCode Pro/DTS plug-in for the Pro Tools platform. If you're using a hardware encoder, connect its inputs to the outputs of your 8-track mixdown deck, in parallel with the connections to the monitor system.

Surround-sound expert Mike Sokol suggested a way to put Dolby Digital or DTS encoded surround mixes on a CD-R. Load the six audio tracks as WAV files into your computer and feed them to the encoding software. Select an AC-3 WAV file output or DTS WAV file output. Encode the tracks. Finally, burn the resulting WAV file onto a CD-R. To hear the surround mix, connect the CD player's digital output to a surround decoder, such as the one in a surround receiver. Commercially released CDs must use only DTS.

# DVD Premastering Formats

You don't necessarily have to buy an encoder; the encoding can be done by a mastering house or DVD manufacturer. Simply send them your 8-track tape. But you might want to put an encoder in your monitor system in order to hear the effect of the encoder as the end listener will hear it.

445

Here are acceptable media formats to send to a DVD manufacturer. For 2-channel stereo, use one of these formats:

- A removable hard drive with SMPTE time code
- DAT with SMPTE
- The digital audio tracks on the video master tape (D-1, D-5, Digital Betacam, DCT, or D-2)

For 5.1 channel surround, you can use one of these formats:

- 20-bit Alesis ADAT with time code.
- Genex magneto-optical 8-track 20-bit machine.
- DLT, DVD-R, or Sonic Solutions 24- or 20-bit Exabyte.
- TASCAM DTRS (DA-38/88/78/98). Record the six audio channels on tracks 1 through 6. Put SMPTE on track 8. Or put a stereo mix on tracks 7 and 8. For Dolby Digital, track assignments are 1, left; 2, center; 3, right; 4, LFE (low-frequency effects or subwoofer); 5, left surround; 6, right surround; 7, data channel; 8, data channel. For DTS the track assignment is 1, left; 2, right; 3, left surround; 4, right surround; 5, center; 6, LFE; 7, data; 8, data.
- Or use all eight TASCAM DA-88 tracks to simulate six tracks with 20-bit resolution. This is done with a Prism MR-2024T processor.
- Pro Tools 24 with Jaz drives.
- Nagra-D is fine for four-channel surround.

If you want to create the LFE or 5.1 channel, you can mix the five other channels and feed them through a 120 Hz lowpass filter. Note that most music-only surround mixes don't use the LFE channel.

You might have video slide-show data that accompanies the audio. Store the video on a removable hard drive or send the file by modem on the Internet. TIFF and bitmap (BMP) formats are acceptable.

# Dolby Units for DVD Mastering

This information is for those who produce the actual DVD. DVD mastering requires MPEG-2 video and Dolby Digital encoders. You can use either one for multichannel audio on DVD titles. Dolby Digital soundtracks are compatible with mono, stereo, or Dolby Pro Logic systems.

Some Dolby encoders and decoders include:

- DP561B: A free-standing 5.1-channel AC-3 audio encoder with data compression

- DP569: 5.1-channel Dolby digital encoder
- DP567: 2-channel audio encoder
- DP562: Multichannel Dolby Digital and Dolby Surround decoder—up to 5.1 channels decoding (for monitoring) and 4-channel Dolby Pro Logic decoding
- SEU4 and SDU4 Dolby Surround Encoder/Decoder units
- Dolby Surround tools TDM Plug-ins for Digidesign Pro Tools Workstations

Thanks to Mike Sokol for his generous technical help with this chapter.

# 21

# PUTTING YOUR MUSIC ON THE WEB

You've recorded a new song and you can't wait for people to hear it. You might want to distribute it on the World Wide Web, in addition to (or instead of) CDs and cassettes.

Why put your music online? Web excerpts of your songs can entice listeners to buy your CDs. Making songs available on the Web costs less than duplicating CDs and selling them in stores. Also, distributing online can be done much more quickly than distributing CDs. Keep in mind, though, that it's hard to get your songs noticed among the millions of other titles that are online.

## Streaming versus Downloading

There are two basic ways to transmit music on the Internet: streaming files and downloading files. A streaming file plays as soon as you click on its title. A downloaded file doesn't play until you copy the entire file to your hard disk. Streaming audio is heard almost instantly (after the buffer memory fills), but usually sounds muffled and can be interrupted by net congestion.

The sound quality of streaming audio depends on the speed of the modem and ranges from funky AM radio (with a 56K modem) to near-CD quality (with a cable modem). With downloaded audio you must wait up to several minutes to download the song. But when it plays, the sound is high-fidelity and continuous.

# Data Compression

Audio files that you record on your computer are usually WAV or AIFF files. They have no data reduction or data compression, so they take up lots of memory. A 3-minute song recorded at 16-bits, 44.1 kHz consumes about 32 MB. Downloading a 32-MB WAV file on the Web would take several hours using a 56K modem. So, audio files intended for Web download are generally data-reduced or data-compressed. For example, if you compressed a 3-minute song by 10:1 (as in an MP3 file), it would consume about 3.2 MB and would download 10 times faster than the equivalent WAV file.

Most types of data compression tend to degrade sound quality. The sound quality of a compressed-data format depends on its **bitrate**, measured in kilobits per second (kbps). The higher the bitrate, the better the sound, but the greater the file size. A bitrate of 128 kbps for MP3 files is considered "near-CD" quality. At low bitrates (below 128 kbps), you can hear artifacts such as "swirly" cymbals, smeared transients such as drum hits, a general "phasey" effect, and less treble. At higher bitrates above 200 kbps, the artifacts start to disappear, and to most listeners the sound is CD quality.

Table 21.1 relates MP3 bitrate to sound quality. Mono files consume half the file space of stereo files.

# Web-Related Audio Files

You can put audio on the Web in several file formats. Let's look at some of the file types in current use.

- **WAV:** A standard PC format for audio files. It encodes sound without any data reduction, using pulse code modulation. Audio CD resolution is 16-bit, 44.1 kHz. Since WAV files consume a lot of memory

**Table 21.1**

| Bitrate | Compression | Sound quality |
| --- | --- | --- |
| 8 kbps | 176:1 | CB radio quality |
| 64 kbps | 20:1 | AM radio quality |
| 128 kbps | 10:1 | Near-CD quality (22 kHz bandwidth) |
| 320 kbps | 4.4:1 | CD quality |

(about 32 MB for a 3-minute song in stereo), they are seldom used on the Internet because they take so long to download. This may change when we start using the much faster Internet 2, which employs fiber-optic cables.

- **AIFF (Audio Interchange File Format):** A standard Mac format for audio files. Like WAV files, AIFF files are not data-compressed.

- **MP3 (MPEG Level-1 Layer-3):** A format that stores audio in a small space with high quality. In an MP3 file (.mp3), the data has been compressed or reduced to $\frac{1}{10}$ its original size or less. Compressed files take up less memory, so they download faster. You download MP3 files to your hard drive, then listen to them. MP3 audio quality at a 128-kbps rate is nearly the same as that of CDs (depending on the source material).

- **MP3Pro:** An improvement over MP3. Songs encoded at 64 kbps with MP3Pro are said to sound as good as songs encoded at 128 kbps with MP3. MP3Pro offers faster downloads and nearly doubles the amount of music you can put on a flash-memory player. MP3 and MP3Pro files are compatible with each others' players, but an MP3Pro player is needed to hear MP3Pro's improvement in sound quality.

- **MP3 with VBR:** MP3 encoding done with variable bitrate, which depends on the requirements of the signal from one instant to the next. VBR reduces file size but keeps the audio quality high.

- **RealAudio G2:** A highly compressed audio file format used for streaming audio. Generally, RealAudio G2 has lower fidelity (less treble) than MP3, but the fidelity depends on modem speed and the current Internet bandwidth. RealAudio files (.ra or .rm) are often used as short excerpts or previews of songs.

- **WMA (Windows Media Audio):** Another popular compressed audio file format for streaming audio and for downloads. Windows Media 8 promises performance similar to MP3Pro: near-CD quality at 48 kbps and CD quality at 64 kbps.

- **AAC (MPEG Advanced Audio Coding):** A relatively new compressed audio file format, AAC is intended to replace MP3. AAC offers better sound quality than MP3 at the same bitrate. What's more, AAC supports multichannel audio and a wide range of sample rates and bit depths. It's also used with Digital Rights Management technology by helping to control the copying and distributing of music.

- **MID (MIDI, or Musical Instrument Digital Interface):** A string of numbers that represent performance gestures, such as note on/off, which note is played, key velocity, and so on. See Chapter

451

16 on MIDI. Since MIDI files do not include audio, they are very compact.

- **.RMF (Rich Music Format):** A MIDI file that might have digital audio embedded. It's used with the Beatnik browser plug-in, which plays RMF files using sampled instruments or custom samples triggered by the MIDI data. Beatnik features interactive control of the music.

There are many other formats—some of which include video—but MP3, Windows Media, and RealAudio are currently the most popular audio formats on the Internet. For more information on using Windows Media, see http://www.microsoft.com/windows/windowsmedia/. This chapter focuses on MP3 and RealAudio.

Currently, Windows Media and RealAudio are the most popular streaming types, and MP3 and Windows Media are the most popular download types.

# What You Need

To put your music on the Web, you need to download a few pieces of software, which are low-cost or free:

- **Audio editing software:** A program that takes an audio signal through a sound card and records the audio on your hard drive. Most programs let you edit the audio on-screen with a mouse, then save the edited program as a WAV or AIFF file. Examples: Windows Sound Recorder, MusicMatch Jukebox from musicmatch.com, Cool Edit from Syntrillium.com, Cakewalk, SAW Plus, Pro Tools.

- **Ripper:** A program that converts audio from a CD or CD-R to a WAV file. Examples: MusicMatch Jukebox from musicmatch.com or from mp3.com, Windows Media Player. Not all CD-ROM drives support ripping.

- **MP3 Encoder:** A program that converts a WAV or AIFF file to an MP3 file. Example: Xingmp3 encoder from xingtech.com. Some other sites for encoders are mp3.com, team-mp3.com, realaudio.com, and liquidaudio.com. Some audio editing software includes an MP3 encoder.

- **RealAudio Encoder (optional):** A program that converts a WAV or AIFF file to a RealAudio file for streaming. Examples: Basic RealProducer G2 or Premium RealProducer Plus G2 from real.com/products/tools/producer/index.html.

- **Windows Media Encoder (optional):** Converts WAV files to Windows Media files. Windows Media Technologies has Digital Rights Management, which limits who can hear your music.

To listen to your music that you put on the Web, you need:

- **MP3 Player:** A program or a device that plays MP3 files. Some software player examples: MusicMatch Jukebox from musicmatch.com, Winamp from winamp.com, Windows Media Player from microsoft.com/windows/mediaplayer, RealPlayer from real.com, MacAMP from www.macamp.net, and QuickTime-4 in Apple's OS. Diamond Rio is a portable hardware player that plays MP3 files downloaded from the Web. Others are Creative Labs' Nomad and RCA's Lyra.
- **RealAudio Player:** A free program that plays RealAudio streaming files. Example: RealNetwork's RealPlayer from real.com.
- **Windows Media Player:** Although intended to play mainly Windows Media files, this free program plays many file types: .avi, .asf, .asc, .rmf, .wav, .wma, .wax, .mpg, .mpeg, .m1v, .mp2, .mp3, .mpa, .mpe, .ra, .mid, .rmi, .qt, .aif, .aifc, .aiff, .mov, .au, .snd, .vod. This player, and other information on Windows Media, is available from http://www.windowsmedia.com.

All-in-one software combines several of these functions in one program. Examples: RealJukebox Plus from real.com and MusicMatch Jukebox from musicmatch.com are MP3 player/ripper/encoders. Audio-Catalyst from xingtech.com is a ripper/encoder that converts CD data directly to MP3. Some digital audio editing programs, such as Pro Tools, can output MP3 files directly. Cool Edit can output RealMedia G2 files with the RealMedia G2 plug-in, and can output MP3 files with the MP3 plug-in. One source for players, rippers, and encoders is team-mp3.com.

# How to Upload MP3 Files

Got everything you need? Let's go. Basically, here's what you will be doing:

1. Convert your song from a cassette or DAT to a WAV file by using audio editing software. Or convert your song from a CD to a WAV file by using a ripper.
2. Edit and process the WAV file to optimize it for the Internet.
3. Then use an encoder to convert the WAV file to an MP3 file.

4. Finally, send (upload) the MP3 file to a Web site that features music in the MP3 format.

Let's go over the procedure in more detail.

1. Start with a cassette, DAT, or CD recording of a song.

2. If you have a cassette, plug your cassette-deck line outputs into your sound card's line input. If you have a DAT, plug your DAT recorder analog outputs into your sound card's line input. If your sound card has a digital input, connect it to your DAT recorder's digital output.

3. If your source is a cassette or DAT, use the editing software to copy the recording to your hard disk. If the source is a CD or CD-R, put it in your CD-ROM drive. Turn off all other programs. Then use a ripper to convert the CD audio file to a WAV file on your hard drive. (Not all CD-ROM drives support ripping.)

4. Edit the start and stop points of the song. You might want to edit a 30-second excerpt of a song to use as a preview of your music. If so, add a fade-in and fade-out to the preview.

5. Next, you might want to process the audio so that it will sound louder and clearer when played on the Web. To do this, reduce the bandwidth: apply low cut below 40 Hz and high cut above 15 kHz. You might want to try a higher-frequency low cut and a lower-frequency high cut. Apply compression or multiband compression, then normalize the song to maximize its level.

6. Save the edited, processed song as a WAV file (PC) or AIFF file (Mac) on your hard drive.

7. Use an MP3 encoder to convert the song's WAV or AIFF file to an MP3 file on your hard drive. You might want to use a bitrate of 128 kbps, which many Web sites require. It's a good compromise between file size and sound quality. A 3-minute MP3 song encoded at 128 kbps typically is 3 MB in size. Higher bitrates give better sound but longer download times. A file encoded at 256 kbps sounds the same as CD but is one-sixth the file size.

   You might want to convert the excerpt's WAV or AIFF file to a RealAudio file by using a RealAudio encoder. **Note:** Some Web sites—such as iuma.com and mp3.com—automatically create a RealAudio file from your uploaded MP3 file.

8. If your band has a Web site, you could upload the MP3 and Real-Audio files to that site. Later in this chapter I'll cover how to set up those files to play on your own Web site.

9. Another option: send your MP3 files to an MP3 server—a Web site that accepts MP3 files for distribution on the Web. Examples: mp3.com, eMusic.com, iuma.com, peoplesound.com, AMP3.com, AWAL.com, or eptitonic.com/contact.html. (Also see the MP3 Links page at team-mp3.com.) Some sites offer free downloads of their music files; others charge the listener so that you make some income.

   Here's how to put your MP3 files on an MP3 server. Point your Web browser to the desired site. Then click on the button labeled "Artists Only," "Submit your music," or something similar. This is where you upload your MP3 files.

10. Once you sign up and fill out some forms, click on "Upload" (or whatever). With a 56K modem, an upload of one 3-minute song might take up to 30 minutes. You can also upload scanned photos of your band, your album cover, and text describing your band and its music. Some sites take a few days to approve your songs.

   Congratulations—you're on the Web!

# Putting Your Music on Your Web Site

Does your band have a personal Web site? You'll want to put samples of your music there. So far I've covered how to upload your songs to an MP3 server such as mp3.com. Now I'll explain how to put your songs on your own Web site. People visiting your site can click on a song title to hear a streaming song preview, or to download an entire song.

Let's start by creating Web-page links to MP3 files.

## Putting MP3 Files on Your Site

1. Download an MP3 encoder (such as the Xing MP3 Encoder from http://www.xingtech.com). **Note:** Some audio editing software has an MP3 encoder built in. Also download an MP3 player (such as WinAmp from winamp.com or RealPlayer from real.com).

2. Suppose you have a song on DAT called "Blues Bash." Using digital editing software, record that song onto your hard drive as a WAV file (PC) or AIFF file (Mac). In this example, we'll call the file BLUES.WAV.

3. Use the MP3 encoder to convert the WAV file to an MP3 file. I recommend a setting of 128 kbps bitrate, stereo. This setting gives hi-fi sound with a relatively small file, so it's fairly quick to download. You now have an MP3 file called BLUES.MP3.

4. Go to your Web page and type in the title of the song. In this example it's "Blues Bash." Using Web-page design software, link that title to BLUES.MP3. In HTML it would look something like this:

<A HREF="blues.mp3">Blues Bash </A>

5. Let's say your Web page is called PAGE1.HTML. Upload (send) PAGE1.HTML and BLUES.MP3 to your Web site. Make sure that both files go to the same directory. Some Web servers have an upload page for this purpose. If yours doesn't, you can upload the files using ftp (file transfer protocol) client software. Do a Web search for ftp freeware, such as http://www.davecentral.com/ftp.html. **Note:** Some Web servers do not allow MP3 files. Find the page on the Web server site that tells what files they permit.

6. Now start your Web browser and go to PAGE1.HTML on your site. Click "Reload" in your browser so that you see the PAGE1.HTML that you just uploaded.

7. Right-click the song title (in this case, "Blues Bash") and select "Save link as." The song should download over a few minutes. Then you can play it with your MP3 player in glorious hi-fi stereo.

## Putting RealAudio Files on Your Site

Now let's consider streaming audio. If you are running your own Web site from your own computer, you need RealAudio server software, such as RealAudio Basic Server at http://real.com/products. Setting up your own server is beyond the scope of this book.

If your Web site is hosted on someone else's computer, you don't need server software. For example, if you have a free Web site at Geocities.com, they already have a RealAudio server, so you don't need one.

Download the free RealProducer G2 software from http://www. realnetworks.com/developers/index.html. RealProducer Plus is another option. Also download the latest free RealAudio player (RealPlayer) from http://www.real.com.

Now decide what music you want to stream. Generally, you'll want your streaming audio files to be short samples or "clips" of your music, but they can be entire songs. Let's start by creating a short sample.

1. Suppose you have a song on DAT called "Blues Bash." Using digital editing software, record your song onto your hard drive as a WAV file (PC) or AIFF file (Mac). In this example, we'll call the file BLUES.WAV.

2. Load BLUES.WAV into your digital editing software. Trim it to about 30 seconds long. Fade out the music toward the end. In this example, let's save the edited song as BLUES2.WAV.

3. Use RealProducer to convert BLUES2.WAV into BLUES2.RM, which is a RealMedia file.

4. Next, use a word processor or text editor (such as Notepad) to create a small text file that points to the location of your RealMedia file. For example: http://www.webserver.com/mywebsite/blues2.rm. Fill in your own Web server and the URL of your Web site. Save this line as a plain ASCII text file with a .RAM extension. In this case, you'd call it BLUES2.RAM. This type of file is called a metafile.

5. Go to your Web page and type the title of the song, such as "Blues Bash." Using Web-page design software, link that title to the location of BLUES2.RAM. In HTML it would look something like this:

   <AHREF="blues2.ram">Blues Bash </A>

   **Important:** Don't link your song title directly to the sound file BLUES2.RM. Instead, link it to the text file (metafile) called BLUES2.RAM. This metafile makes the RealPlayer pop up and play the streaming audio. If you incorrectly link your song to BLUES2.RM, and a listener clicks on "Blues Bash," that file will download instead of streaming.

6. Suppose your Web page is called PAGE1.HTML. It contains the song title linked to BLUES2.RAM. Upload (send) PAGE1.HTML, BLUES2.RAM, and BLUES2.RM to your Web site. Be sure they all go to the same directory. As we said before, some Web servers have an upload page. If yours doesn't, try uploading the files with ftp software. You might want to search for ftp freeware on the Web.

7. Now start your Web browser and go to your site. Open PAGE1.HTML. Then click "Reload" in your browser so that you see the current page, not the one in your cache.

8. Click on the song title. In a few seconds RealPlayer should pop up, fill the buffer memory, and play the tune. If not, recheck everything you typed. Then try real.com for tech support.

An important part of this process is providing the right bitrate for your target audience. When you use RealPublisher, you might create one file suited for a 28K modem, and another file for a 56K modem. Why use both formats? The faster the modem speed, the better the sound quality (more extended highs). So a file optimized for a 56K modem sounds better than a file made for a 28K modem. However, a 28K modem can't play 56K-

Play low-fi "Tango" sample (28K modem)

Play low-fi "Tango" sample (56K modem)

Download hi-fi "Tango" sample

**Figure 21.1**   Sample Web page with three song formats: RealAudio for 28K modem, RealAudio for 56K modem, and MP3.

modem files without skipping, so you need both formats. If you are working in RealPublisher's Advanced mode, select "mono" because it gives brighter sound than "stereo" for the same bitrate.

Figure 21.1 shows a sample Web page with three song formats: RealAudio for 28K modem, RealAudio for 56K modem, and MP3. Figure 21.2 shows the HTML code for that page.

The methods described here will provide streaming audio from any HTTP server. Now we'll look at ways to stream audio from a RealServer (RTSP) site, which has some advantages.

## Streaming Audio from a RealServer Site

In your Web surfing, have you ever clicked on a song title to hear the music, only to have it interrupted? You try to play a streaming audio file, but it skips instead of playing continuously. One cause is too much traffic on the Internet. Your connection speed to the Net changes continuously depending on how many folks are using it the same time you are. If your connection speed is too slow to keep up with the streaming file's bitrate, the sound skips. Is there a way to play streaming files that adapts to changing connection speeds? There is, and it's called SureStream. Developed by RealNetworks, SureStream is a file format for streaming audio files that varies the bitrate to match what your modem can handle at the moment. The sound quality varies with the bitrate—sometimes bright, sometimes dull. But at least the stream is continuous. No skipping—unless traffic is really bad. With SureStream, you don't need to offer several audio files at

```
<HTML>
<BODY>
<CENTER>
<P ALIGN=Left>
<P ALIGN=Left>
<A HREF="http://www.yourweburl.com/tango28.ram">
<IMG SRC="ra.gif" WIDTH="65" HEIGHT="65" ALIGN="Left">
<FONT COLOR="Yellow"> Play low-fi "Tango" sample (28K modem)
</FONT></A>
<P ALIGN=Left>
<P ALIGN=Left>
<P ALIGN=Left>
<A HREF="http://www.yourweburl.com/tango56.ram">
<IMG SRC="ra.gif" WIDTH="65" HEIGHT="65" ALIGN="Left">
<FONT COLOR="Yellow"> Play low-fi "Tango" sample (56K modem)
</FONT></A>
<P ALIGN=Left>
<P ALIGN=Left>
<P ALIGN=Left>
<A HREF="http://www.yourweburl.com/tango.mp3">
<FONT COLOR="Yellow"> Download hi-fi "Tango" sample
</FONT></A>
</BODY></HTML>
```

**Figure 21.2** HTML code for Web page shown in Figure 21.1.

different bitrates to handle different modem speeds. One SureStream file can work for any modem.

If you'd like to have SureStream ability on your Web site, have your Web page hosted by a server who has RealServer software. Geocities.com is one example. If you are a member of Geocities, and you are a member of their Geomedia group, you can access their RealServer and play Sure-Stream files from your Web site.

There are two ways to stream RealAudio files: via HTTP (Hyper Text Transfer Protocol) or RTSP (Real Time Streaming Protocol). Any standard Web server is HTTP format. Earlier in this chapter we looked at ways to stream your music from any Web-site host using HTTP. Now we'll cover streaming from a Web-site host that has RealServer.

## Setting Up RealServer Files with RealProducer

Imagine that your band's Web page is on a RealServer host, and you want to add SureStream RealAudio files to your page. Here's how to go about it.

First, download the free RealProducer software from http://www.realnetworks.com/developers/index.html. RealProducer Plus is another option. Also download the free RealAudio player, RealPlayer 7.0 or later, from http://www.real.com.

**Note:** Your Web server might require a special version of RealProducer that you download from the server. For example, Geocities says that you must download and use the Geomedia-optimized RealProducer—otherwise your files won't play correctly. You might need to become a RealMedia member in your Web server. For instance, the Geocities Web server has a RealMedia option called Geomedia. Once you've subscribed, you can use their RealServer to play SureStream files.

Now decide what music you want to stream. Generally, you'll want your streaming audio files to be short samples or "clips" of your music, but they can be entire songs. Let's start by creating a short sample.

1. Suppose you have a song called "Blues Bash" recorded on your hard drive as BLUES.WAV. Load the file BLUES.WAV into your digital editing software. Trim it to about 30 seconds long. Fade out the music toward the end. In this example, let's save the edited song as BLUES2.WAV.

2. Use RealPublisher to convert BLUES2.WAV into BLUES2.RM, which is a RealMedia file. In this process, select "SureStream" file rather than "Fixed Rate" file. If you are working in RealPublisher's Advanced mode, select "mono" because it gives brighter sound than "stereo" for the same bitrate.

3. Use RealPublisher's Web Page Wizard to create a Web page, such as PAGE1.HTML. This page includes the song title, such as "Blues Bash." You can add more text and graphics to the page. The Web Wizard will also create a short text file called a **metafile**. Its filename is BLUES2.RAM (for a pop-up player) or BLUES2.RPM (for an embedded player). A pop-up player appears only when you click on a song title. An embedded player is part of a Web page. In working with the Web Page Wizard, try to use the default settings. Be sure that BLUES2.RM, BLUES2.RAM, and PAGE1.HTML are all saved in the same directory on your hard drive.

4. Use RealPublisher's Publishing Wizard to upload those three files to your Web site. If for some reason it doesn't work, go to your Web site and upload those three files from there. They should all go to the same directory (your Web page directory).

5. At your Web site, open PAGE1.HTML (or whatever). Click "Reload" so that you see the current version, not the one in your cache.

6. Click on the song title. The RealPlayer should pop up and play the song. If you selected "Embedded Player" when you created the song file, you should see a RealPlayer on your Web page. Click the "Play" button to hear the song. **Note:** If Internet traffic is high, you might get an error message saying "Requested file not found" even though the file is there. You might have to wait for a less busy time.

## Setting Up RealServer Files with HTML Code

You can do all the above without RealPublisher if you're willing to write your own HTML code.

1. Using a word processor or text editor (such as Notepad), create a small text file that points to the location of your RealMedia file. For example: rtsp://real.webserver.com/your Web site address/blues2.rm

Replace "webserver.com" with your own Web server—for example, geocities.com. Save this line as a plain ASCII text file with a .RAM extension. In this case, you'd call it BLUES2.RAM. This type of file is called a metafile. The URL above has three parts:

- The protocol
- The server
- The address

The protocol part is rtsp:, which stands for Real Time Streaming Protocol—used by the RealNetworks G2 server. The server part is real.webserver.com, which points to the Web server's address. The "real" at the beginning directs your request to the RealNetworks G2 servers. The address part includes your entire Web server and Web site address, along with the audio filename.

2. Now go to your Web page and type the title of the song, such as "Blues Bash". Using Web-page design software, link that title to the metafile you just wrote and saved. In HTML it would look something like this:

<A HREF="blues2.ram">Blues Bash </A>

**Important:** Don't link your song title directly to the sound file BLUES2. RM. Instead, link it to the text file (metafile) called BLUES2.RAM. This metafile makes the RealPlayer pop up and play the streaming audio. If you incorrectly linked your song to BLUES2.RM, and a listener clicks on "Blues Bash," that file will download instead of streaming.

3. Suppose your Web page is called PAGE1.HTML. It contains the song title linked to BLUES2.RAM. Upload (send) PAGE1.HTML, BLUES2.RAM, and BLUES2.RM to your Web site. Be sure they all go to the same directory (your Web site directory).

4. Now start your Web browser and go to your site. Open PAGE1.HTML. Then click "Reload" in your browser so that you see the current page, not the one in your cache.

5. Click on the song title. In a few seconds RealPlayer should pop up, fill the buffer memory, and play the tune. If not, re-check everything you typed. Also, net congestion or Web-server glitches can cause false error messages. Try again when the Net is not so busy. If all else fails, contact tech support at your Web server and at http://www.real.com.

The methods described here will provide streaming audio from any Web host that offers RealServer. I hope to hear your music on the Web!

# Sample Web Page

A song title in a sample Web page is shown below:
PLAY BLUES BASH (LO-FI)
The HTML code for that song title is: <A HREF="blues2.ram">PLAY BLUES BASH (LO-FI)</A>
The text of BLUES2.RAM is: [Web site URL address goes here]/blues2.rm

# Liquid Audio (www.liquidaudio.com)

An online music service you should know about is Liquid Audio. This server company provides music retailers and record labels a secure way to sell and distribute high-quality audio tracks on the Internet, with Digital Rights Management. Once you open an account with Liquid Audio, you have access to Liquefier Pro software. It encodes your music to the high-quality AAC format and uploads it to the Liquid Audio server. The encoder adds to the file an inaudible digital "watermark," which tracks the song owner and controls copies.

To hear your music, listeners download the free Liquid Player. It plays free preview clips and handles a variety of file types. It also lets the user purchase full-length tracks online. In addition, the player displays graphics, liner notes, lyrics, and promotional material, and includes CD burning software.

# 22

# MUSIC: WHY YOU RECORD

This book focuses on techniques for recording music, without paying much attention to the music itself. Occasionally it's wise to remember that music is the main reason for recording!

Music can be exalting, exciting, soothing, sensuous, and fulfilling. It's wonderful that recordings can preserve it. As a recording engineer, it's to your advantage to better understand what music is all about.

Music starts as musical ideas or feelings in the mind and heart of its composer. Musical instruments are used to translate these ideas and feelings into sound waves. Somehow, the emotion contained in the music—the message—is coded in the vibrations of air molecules. Those sounds are converted to electricity and stored magnetically. The composer's message manages to survive the trip through the mixing console and tape machines; the signal is transferred to disc or tape. Finally, the original sound waves are reproduced in the listening room, and miraculously the original emotion is reproduced in the listener as well.

Of course, not everyone reacts to a piece of music the same way, so the listener may not perceive the composer's intent. Still, it's amazing that anything as intangible as a thought or feeling can be conveyed by tiny magnetic patterns on a cassette tape, or by pits on a compact disc.

The point of music lies in what it's doing now, in the present. In other words, the meaning of "Doo wop she bop" is "Doo wop she bop." The meaning of an Am7 chord followed by a Fmaj7 chord is the *experience* of Am7 followed by Fmaj7.

# Increasing Your Involvement in Music

Sometimes, to get involved in music, you must relax enough to lie back and listen. You have to feel unhurried, to be content to sit between your stereo speakers or wear headphones, and listen with undivided attention. Actively analyze or feel what the musicians are playing.

Music affects people much more when they are already feeling the emotion expressed in the song. For example, hearing a fast Irish reel when you're in a party mood, or hearing a piece by Debussy when you're feeling sensuous, is more moving because your feelings resonate with those in the music. When you're falling in love, any music that is meaningful to you is enhanced.

If you identify strongly with a particular song, that tells you something about yourself and your current mood. And the songs that other people identify with tell you something about them. You can understand individuals better by listening to their favorite music.

# Different Ways of Listening

There are so many levels on which to listen to music—so many ways to focus attention. Try this. Play one of your favorite records several times while listening for these different aspects:

- Overall mood and rhythm
- Lyrics
- Vocal technique
- Bass line
- Drum fills
- Sound quality
- Technical proficiency of musicians
- Musical arrangement or structure
- Reaction of one musician to another's playing
- Surprises versus predictable patterns

By listening to a piece of music from several perspectives, you'll get much more out of it than if you just hear it as background. There's a lot going on in any song that usually goes unnoticed. Sometimes you play an old familiar record and listen to the lyrics for the first time. The whole meaning of the song changes for you.

Most people react to music on the basic level of mood and rhythmic motivation. But as a recording enthusiast, you hear much more detail because your focus demands sustained critical listening. The same is true of trained musicians focusing on the musical aspects of a performance.

It's all there for anyone to hear, but you must train yourself to hear selectively, to focus attention on a particular level of the multidimensional musical event. For example, instead of just feeling excited while listening to an impressive lead-guitar solo, listen to what the guitarist is actually playing. You may hear some amazing things.

Here's one secret of really involving yourself in recorded music: Imagine yourself playing it! For example, if you're a bass player, listen to the bass line in a particular record, and imagine that you're playing the bass line. You'll hear the part as never before. Or respond to the music visually—see it as you do in the movie *Fantasia*.

Follow the melody line and see its shape. Hear where it reaches up, strains, relaxes. Hear how one note leads into the next. How does the musical expression change from moment to moment?

There are times when you can almost touch music. Some music has a prickly texture (many transients, emphasized high frequencies); some music is soft and sinuous (sine-wave synthesizer notes, soaring vocal harmonies); some music is airy and spacious (much reverberation).

# Two Different Production Styles

Suppose you are in the control room working on a pop music mix, and you're aiming for a realistic, natural sound. Listen to the reproduced instruments and try to make them sound as if they're really playing in front of you. That is, instead of trying to make a pleasant mix or a sonically interesting recording, try to control the sound you hear to simulate real instruments—to make them believable.

It's like an artist trying to draw a still-life as realistically as possible. The artist compares the drawing to the real object, notes the difference, and then modifies the drawing to reduce the difference.

When you're striving for a natural sound, compare the recorded instrument with your memory of the real thing. How does it sound different? Turn the appropriate knob on the console that reduces the difference.

Alternatively, when you're mixing, imagine you're creating a sonic experience between the monitor speakers, rather than just reproducing instruments. Sometimes you don't want a recording to sound too realistic. If a recording is very accurate, it sounds like musical instruments, rather than just music itself.

This approach contradicts the basic edict of high fidelity—to reproduce the original performance as it sounded in the original environment. Some songs seem to require unreal sounds. That way, you don't connect the sounds you hear with physical instruments, but with the music behind the instruments—the composer's dream or vision.

Here's one way to reproduce pure music rather than reproducing instruments playing in a room: Mike closely or record direct to avoid picking up studio ambience and then add reverb. Also add EQ, double-tracking, sampling, and special effects to make the instrument or voice slightly unreal. The idea is to make a production, rather than a documentation—a record, rather than a recording.

Try to convey the musician's intentions through the recorded sound quality. If the musician has a loving, soft message, translate that into a warm, smooth tone quality. Add a little mid-bass or slightly reduce the highs. If the musical composition suggests grandeur or space, add reverberation with a long decay time. Ask the musicians what they are trying to express through the music, and try to express that through the sound production as well.

# Why Record?

Recording is a real service. Without it, people would be exposed to much less music, limited to the occasional live concert or to their own live music, played once and forever gone.

With recordings, you can preserve a performance for thousands of listeners. You can hear an enormous variety of musical expressions whenever you want. Unlike a live concert, a record can be played over and over for analysis. Tapes or discs are also a way to achieve a sort of immortality. The Beatles may be gone, but their music lives on.

Records can even reveal your evolving consciousness as you grow and change. A tape or disc stays the same physically, but you hear it differently over the years as your perception changes. Recordings are a constant against which you measure change in yourself.

Be proud that you are contributing to the recording art—it is done in the service of music.

# A

# dB OR NOT dB

In the studio, you must know how to set and measure signal levels and match equipment levels. You also need to evaluate microphones by their sensitivity specs. To learn these skills, you must understand the decibel, the unit of measurement of audio level.

## Definitions

In a recording studio, **level** originally meant power, and amplitude referred to voltage. Nowadays, many audio people also define "level" in terms of voltage or sound pressure, even though this terminology is not strictly correct. You should know both definitions in order to communicate.

**Audio level** is measured in decibels (dB). One dB is the smallest change in level that most people can hear—the just-noticeable difference. Actually, the just-noticeable-difference varies from 0.1 dB to about 5 dB, depending on bandwidth, frequency, program material, and the individual. But 1 dB is generally accepted as the smallest change in level that most people can detect. A 6- to 10-dB increase in level is considered by most listeners to be "twice as loud." Sound pressure level, signal level, and change in signal level all are measured in dB.

## Sound Pressure Level

**Sound pressure level** (SPL) is the pressure of sound vibration measured at a point. It's usually measured with a sound level meter in dB SPL (decibels of sound pressure level).

The higher the sound pressure level, the louder the sound (Figure A.1). The quietest sound you can hear, the threshold of hearing, is 0 dB SPL. Average conversation at 1 foot is 70 dB SPL. Average home-stereo listening level is around 85 dB SPL. The threshold of pain—so loud that the ears hurt and can be damaged—is 125 to 130 dB SPL.

Sound pressure level in decibels is 20 times the logarithm of the ratio of two sound pressures:

$$\text{dB SPL} = 20 \log \frac{P}{P_{ref}}$$

where P is the measured sound pressure in dynes/cm², and $P_{ref}$ is a reference sound pressure: 0.0002 dyne/cm² (the threshold of hearing).

# Signal Level

**Signal level** also is measured in dB. The level in decibels is 10 times the logarithm of the ratio of two power levels:

$$\text{dB} = 10 \log \frac{P}{P_{ref}}$$

where P is the measured power in watts, and $P_{ref}$ is a reference power in watts.

**Figure A.1**

A chart of sound pressure levels.

Recently it's become common to use the decibel to refer to voltage ratios as well:

$$dB = 20\log\frac{V}{V_{ref}}$$

where V is the measured voltage, and $V_{ref}$ is a reference voltage.

This expression is mathematically equivalent to the previous one, because power equals the square of the voltage divided by the circuit resistance:

$$dB = 10\log\frac{P_1}{P_2}$$

$$= 10\log\left(\frac{V_1^2/R}{V_2^2/R}\right)$$

$$= 10\log\left(\frac{V_1^2}{V_2^2}\right)$$

$$= 20\log\frac{V_1}{V_2}$$

The resistance R (or impedance) in this equation is assumed to be the same for both measurements, and thus divides out.

Signal level in decibels can be expressed in various ways, using various units of measurement:

- dBm: decibels referenced to 1 milliwatt
- dBu or dBv: decibels referenced to 0.775 volt (dBu is preferred)
- dBV: decibels referenced to 1 volt

## *dBm*

If you're measuring **signal power**, the decibel unit to use is dBm, expressed in the equation

$$dBm = 10\log\frac{P}{P_{ref}}$$

where P is the measured power, and $P_{ref}$ is the reference power (1 milliwatt).

469

For an example of signal power, use this equation to convert 0.01 watt to dBm:

$$dBm = 10 \log \frac{P}{P_{ref}}$$

$$= 10 \log \frac{0.01}{0.001}$$

$$= 10$$

So, 0.01 watt is 10 dBm (10 decibels above 1 milliwatt). Now convert 0.001 watt (1 milliwatt) into dBm:

$$dBm = 10 \log \frac{P}{P_{ref}}$$

$$= 10 \log \frac{0.001}{0.001}$$

$$= 0$$

So, 0 dBm = 1 milliwatt. This has a bearing on voltage measurement as well.

Any voltage across any resistance that results in 1 milliwatt is 0 dBm. This relationship can be expressed in the equation

$$0 dBm = \frac{V^2}{R} = 1 \text{ milliwatt}$$

where V = the voltage in volts, and R is the circuit resistance in ohms.

For example, 0.775 volt across 600 ohms is 0 dBm. One volt across 1000 ohms is 0 dBm. Each results in 1 milliwatt.

Some voltmeters are calibrated in dBm. The meter reading in dBm is accurate only when you're measuring across 600 ohms. For an accurate dBm measurement, measure the voltage and circuit resistance, then calculate:

$$dBm = 10 \log \frac{(V^2/R)}{0.001}$$

## *dBv or dBu*

Another unit of measurement expressing the relationship of decibels to voltage is dBv or dBu. This means decibels referenced to 0.775 volt. This figure comes from 0 dBm, which equals 0.775 volt across 600 ohms (because 600 ohms used to be a standard impedance for audio connections):

$$dBu = 20\log\frac{V}{V_{ref}}$$

where $V_{ref}$ is 0.775 volt.

## *dBV*

Signal level also is measured in dBV (with a capital V), or decibels referenced to 1 volt:

$$dBV = 20\log\frac{V}{V_{ref}}$$

where $V_{ref}$ is 1 volt.

For example, use this equation to convert 1 millivolt (0.001 volt) to dBV:

$$dBV = 20\log\frac{V}{V_{ref}}$$
$$= 20\log\frac{0.001}{1}$$
$$= -60$$

So, 1 millivolt = –60 dBV (60 decibels below 1 volt).
Now convert 1 volt to dBV:

$$dBV = 20\log\frac{1}{1}$$
$$= 0$$

So, 1 volt = 0 dBV.
To convert dBV to voltage, use the formula

$$Volts = 10^{(dBV/20)}$$

## *Change in Signal Level*

Decibels also are used to measure the change in power or voltage across a fixed resistance. The formula is

$$dB = 10 \log \frac{P_1}{P_2}$$

or

$$dB = 20 \log \frac{V_1}{V_2}$$

where $P_1$ is the new power level, $P_2$ is the old power level, $V_1$ is the new voltage level, and $V_2$ is the old voltage level.

For example, if the voltage across a resistor is 0.01 volt, and it changes to 1 volt, the change in dB is

$$dB = 20 \log \frac{V_1}{V_2}$$

$$= 20 \log \frac{1}{0.01}$$

$$= 40 \, dB$$

Doubling the **power** results in an increase of 3 dB; doubling the **voltage** results in an increase of 6 dB.

# The VU Meter, Zero VU, and Peak Indicators

A **VU meter** is a voltmeter of specified transient response, calibrated in volume units or VU. It shows approximately the relative volume or loudness of the measured audio signal.

The VU-meter scale is divided into volume units, which are not necessarily the same as dB. The volume unit corresponds to the decibel only when measuring a steady sine-wave tone. In other words, a change of 1 VU is the same as a change of 1 dB only when a steady tone is applied.

Most recording engineers use 0 VU to define a convenient "zero reference level" on the VU meter. When the meter on your mixer or recorder reads "0" on a steady tone, your equipment is producing a certain level at its output. Different types of equipment produce different levels when the meter reads 0 (Figure A.2). Zero VU corresponds to:

- +8 dBm in older broadcast and telephone equipment
- +4 dBm in balanced recording equipment
- −10 dBV in unbalanced recording equipment

**Figure A.2**  VU-meter scale.

When a tape operator says to a mixing engineer, "Send me a 0 VU tone," it means, "Send me a tone that reads 0 on your VU meter." The signal level itself isn't too important because the tape operator receiving the tone just wants to match the tape-deck meters to those on the console.

A **0 VU recording level** (0 on the record level meter) is the normal operating level of an analog tape recorder; it produces the desired recorded flux on tape. A "0 VU recording level" does not mean a "0 VU signal level."

With a VU meter, 0 VU corresponds to a recording level 8 dB below the level that produces 3% third-harmonic distortion on tape at 400 Hz. Distortion at 0 VU typically is below 1%.

The response of a VU meter is not fast enough to track rapid transients accurately. In addition, when a complex waveform is applied to a VU meter, the meter reads less than the peak voltage of the waveform. (This means you must allow for undisplayed peaks above 0 VU that use up headroom.)

In contrast, a **peak indicator** responds quickly to peak program levels, making it a more accurate indicator of recording levels. One type of peak indicator is an LED that flashes on peak overloads. Another is the LED bargraph meter commonly seen on cassette decks. Yet another is the PPM (peak program meter). It is calibrated in dB, rather than VU. Unlike the VU meter reading, the PPM reading does not correlate with perceived volume.

In a 16-bit digital recorder, the meter is an LED or LCD bargraph meter that reads up to 0 dBFS (FS means full scale). In theory, 0 dBFS means all 16 bits are ON. The OVER indication means that the input level exceeded the voltage needed to produce 0 dBFS, and there is some short-duration clipping of the output analog waveform. Some manufacturers calibrate their meters so that 0 dBFS is less than 16 bits ON; this allows a little headroom.

# Balanced versus Unbalanced Equipment Levels

Generally, audio equipment with balanced (3-pin) connectors works at a higher nominal line level than equipment with unbalanced (phono) connectors. There's nothing inherent in balanced or unbalanced connections that makes them operate at different levels; they're just standardized at different levels.

These are the nominal (normal) input and output levels for the two types of equipment:

- Balanced: +4 dBu (1.23 volts)
- Unbalanced: −10 dBV (0.316 volt)

In other words, when a balanced-output recorder reads 0 VU on its meter with a steady tone, it is producing 1.23 volts at its output connector. This voltage is called +4 dBu when referenced to 1 milliwatt. When an unbalanced-output recorder reads 0 on its meter with a steady tone, it is usually producing 0.316 volt at its output connector. This voltage is called −10 dBV when referenced to 1 volt.

# Interfacing Balanced and Unbalanced Equipment

There's a difference of 11.8 dB between +4 dBu and −10 dBV. To find this, convert both levels to voltages:

$$dB = 20 \log \left( \frac{1.23}{0.316} \right)$$
$$= 11.8$$

So, +4 dBu is 11.8 dB higher in voltage than −10 dBV (assuming the resistances are the same).

A cable carrying a nominal +4 dBu signal has a signal-to-noise ratio (S/N) 11.8 dB better than the same cable carrying a −10 dBV signal. This is an advantage in environments with strong radio-frequency

**Figure A.3**  Use a pad of 12 dB to match a balanced +4 dBu output to an unbalanced −10 dBV input.

or hum fields. But in most studios with short cables, the difference is negligible.

Connecting a +4 dBu output to a −10 dBV input might cause distortion if the signal peaks of the +4 equipment exceed the headroom of the −10 equipment. If this happens, use a pad to attenuate the level 12 dB (Figure A.3). The pad converts from balanced to unbalanced as well as reducing the level 12 dB. You may have to substitute a stereo phone plug for the 3-pin connector.

You don't always need that pad. Many pieces of equipment have a **+4/−10 level switch**. Set the switch to the nominal level of the connected equipment.

# Microphone Sensitivity

Decibels are an important concern in another area: microphone sensitivity. A high-sensitivity mic puts out a stronger signal (higher voltage) than a low-sensitivity mic when both are exposed to the same sound pressure level.

A **microphone-sensitivity specification** tells how much output (in volts) a microphone produces for a certain input (in SPL). The standard is millivolts per pascal, where one pascal (Pa) is 94 dB SPL.

A typical "open-circuit sensitivity" spec is 5.5 mV/Pa for a condenser mic and 1.8 mV/Pa for a dynamic mic. "Open-circuit" means that the mic is unloaded (not connected to a load, or connected to a mic preamp with a very high input impedance). If the spec is 5.5 mV/Pa, that means the mic produces 5.5 mV when the SPL at the mic is 94 dB SPL.

If you put a microphone in a 20 dB louder sound field, it produces 20 dB more signal voltage. For example, if 74 dB SPL in gives 0.18 mV out (−75 dBV), then 94 dB SPL in gives 1.8 mV out (−55 dBV); 150 dB SPL in gives 1.1 volt out (+1 dBV), which is approximately line level! That's why you need so much input padding when you record a kick drum or other loud source.

# B

# INTRODUCTION TO SMPTE TIME CODE

Have you ever wished you had more tracks? Suppose you've filled up all the tracks of a 16-track recorder, the band you're recording wants to overdub several more instruments, and you don't have a 24-track machine.

There is a solution: Synchronize the 16-track machine with an 8-track machine by using SMPTE time code. This is a special signal recorded on tape that can sync together two multitrack recorders so that they operate as one. Time code also can synchronize an audio recorder with a video recorder, or even an automated mixing system to a multitrack recorder.

SMPTE stands for the Society of Motion Picture and Television Engineers. The SMPTE standardized the time-code signal for use in video production, and you can use it in audio recording as well. SMPTE time code is something like a digital tape counter, where the counter time is recorded as a signal on tape.

## How the Time Code Works

A **time-code generator** creates the time-code signal (a 1200 Hz modulated square wave). You record—or stripe—this signal onto one track of both recorders. A **time-code reader** reads the code off the two tapes. Then a **time-code synchronizer** compares the codes from the two transports and locks them together in time by varying the motor speed of one of the transports.

FRAME
START

0   4   8   12   16   20   24   28   32   36

F | U | F | U | S | U | S | U | M

F = FRAMES      M = MINUTES    U = USER BITS
S = SECONDS     H = HOURS

**Figure B.1**   An 80-bit time-code word.

The counter time is recorded as a signal on tape. Pictures on a video screen are updated approximately 30 frames per second, where a frame is a still picture made of 525 lines on the screen. SMPTE time code assigns a unique number (address) to each video frame—8 digits that specify HOURS:MINUTES:SECONDS:FRAMES.

Each video frame is identified with its own time-code address; for example, 01:26:13:07 means "1 hour, 26 minutes, 13 seconds, and 7 frames." These addresses are recorded sequentially: for each successive video frame, the time-code number increases by one frame count. There are approximately 30 frames per second in the American TV system, so the time code counts frames from 0 to 29 each second.

# Time-Code Signal Details

The SMPTE time code is a data stream that is divided into **code words**. Each code word includes 80 binary digits (or **bits**) that identify each video frame (Figure B.1).

The 80-bit time-code word is synchronized to the start of each video frame. The code uses binary 1's and 0's. During each half-cycle of the square wave, the voltage may be constant (signifying a 0) or changing (signifying a 1). That is, a voltage transition in the middle of a half-cycle of the square wave equals a 1. No transition signifies a 0. This is called **biphase modulation** (Figure B.2). It can be read forward or reverse, at almost any tape speed. A time-code reader detects the binary 1's and 0's and converts them to decimal numbers to form the time-code addresses.

SMPTE words also can include user information. There are 32 multi-purpose bits (8 digits or 4 characters) reserved for the user's data—for example, the take number.

**Figure B.1**  Continued.

**Figure B.2**
Biphase modulation used
in SMPTE time code.

The last 16 bits in the word are a fixed number of 1's and 0's called **sync bits**. These bits indicate the end of the time-code word, so that the time-code reader can tell whether the code is being read forward or in reverse.

## Drop-Frame Mode

SMPTE code can run in various modes depending on the application. One of these, Drop-Frame mode, is needed for specific reasons.

Black-and-white video runs at 30 frames/second. A time-code signal also running at 30 frames/second will agree with the clock on the wall. Color video, on the other hand, runs at 29.97 frames/second. If a color program is clocked at 30 frames/second for 1 hour, the actual show length will run 3.6 seconds (108 frames) longer than an hour.

The **Drop-Frame mode** causes the time code to count at a rate to match the clock on the wall. Each minute, frame numbers 00 and 01 are dropped, except every 10th minute. (Instead of seeing frames . . . 27, 28, 29, 00 on the counter; you see frames . . . 27, 28, 29, 02.) This speeds up the time-code counter to match the rate of the video frames. The video frames still progress at 29.97 frames/second, and the time code progresses at 30 frames/second, but it drops every few frames—so the effective time-code frame rate is 29.97 frames/second.

You program the time-code generator to operate in **Drop** (Drop-Frame) or **Non-Drop** (Non-Drop-Frame) mode. Non-Drop can be used for audio-only synchronizing, but Drop mode should be used if the audio will be synced to a video tape later on.

# Setting Up a Time-Code System

To use the SMPTE time code, you need a time-code generator, reader, and synchronizer. These may be all-in-one or separate units. Figure B.3 shows a typical system hookup, in which the generator, reader, and synchronizer are combined in one unit.

Set the generator to Time-of-Day code, or any other convenient starting time. If you are syncing to video, feed the generator a sync signal from the video source being recorded. This will lock the generator together in time with the video source. For audio-only applications, use the internal crystal sync.

Select Drop-Frame or Non-Drop-Frame mode, and stay with it for the entire production. Use Drop-Frame mode if you anticipate syncing audio to video in the future.

Next, set the frame rate: 29.97, 30, 24, or 25 frames/second, using the following guidelines:

- Color video productions require 29.97 frames/second.
- Black-and-white video or audio-only productions use 30 frames/second.

**Figure B.3**
Typical hookup for synchronizing two tape transports with SMPTE time code.

- Film usually runs at 24 frames/second.
- European TV—using EBU (European Broadcast Union) time code—requires 25 frames/second.

The time-code signal appears at the generator output, which is a standard 3-pin audio connector. Signal level is +4 dBm. The signal is fed through a standard 2-conductor shielded audio cable. To avoid crosstalk of time code into audio channels, separate the time-code cables from audio cables. Patch the time-code signal into an outside track of the recorders you want to lock together. Then, patch the outputs of those time-code tracks to the inputs of the time-code reader.

The reader decodes the information recorded on tape and, in some models, displays the time-code data in HOURS:MINUTES:SECONDS:FRAMES format. Some readers have an **error bypass** feature that corrects for missing data.

The time-code synchronizer matches bits between two time-code signals to synchronize them. The synchronizer compares tape direction, address, and phase to synchronize two SMPTE tracks via servo control of the transport motors. The two tape machines to be synced are called "master" and "slave." The synchronizer controls the slave by making its tape position and speed follow that of the master.

Connect the shielded multipin interface cable between the synchronizer and slave machine to control the slave's tape transport and motors. This interface cable has channels for controlling the capstan motor, tape direction, shuttle modes, and tachometer (more on the tach later).

Because the time-code signal becomes very high in frequency when the tape is shuttled rapidly, special playback amplifier cards with extended high-frequency response may be needed to reproduce the SMPTE signal accurately. These cards are available from the recorder manufacturer.

Unfortunately, when the tape is in shuttle mode (fast forward or rewind), the tape usually is lifted from the heads—losing the SMPTE signal. In this case, the recorders are synchronized using tach pulses from the recorders as a replacement for the SMPTE time code. Some synchronizers are fed tach pulses from the slave only.

If **chase mode** is available, the slave follows the shuttle motions of the master. If the master is put in fast-forward, the slave goes into fast-forward, and so on. Without chase mode, the synchronizer notes the address of the master tape when it is stopped and cues the slave to match that location. Chase mode is useful for repetitive overdubs.

# How to Use SMPTE Time Code

Suppose you want to synchronize two multitrack recorders. Follow this procedure:

1. Clean the heads and the tape path.

2. Record the SMPTE time code on an outside track of both recorders at −5 to −10 VU, leaving the adjacent track blank, if possible, to avoid time-code crosstalk. Don't put high-transient sounds (such as drums) on that adjacent track; they can cause sync problems in analog tape machines.

3. Start recording, or striping, the code about 20 seconds before the music starts, and continue nonstop with no breaks in the signal. Stripe the two tapes simultaneously. If that is not possible, you need a **time-code editor** to correct or insert an offset.

4. During playback, manually cue the slave to approximately the same point as the master tape, using time-code address information as a reference.

5. Engage the synchronizer in Lock and Chase mode, and enable it.

6. Put both recorders in Play mode.

7. Adjust the slave's tape speed to gradually reduce the error between transports to less than one time-code frame.

With some synchronizers, this operation is automatic. You set the slave tape to approximately the same point as the master tape. Then put the master in Play. When the synchronizer detects master time code, it sets the slave machine in Play mode and, in a few seconds, adjusts the slave's speed to synchronize the two recorders. This condition is called **locked up**.

When you record on two synchronized transports, try not to split stereo pairs between two tapes. The slight time differences between machines can degrade stereo imaging. Keep all stereo pairs on the same tape, copying them if necessary onto the other tape.

# Restriping Defective Code

You may encounter degraded or erased sections on a time-code track. This lost code must be replaced with good code in proper sequence. If you need to re-record (restripe) a defective SMPTE track, use the **Jam Sync** mode on the time-code generator. This feature produces new code that matches the original addresses and frame count.

For example, suppose the slave tape needs to be restriped. Follow this procedure:

1. Patch the slave's time-code track into the generator set to Jam Sync mode.

2. Patch the generator output into the time-code track input on the slave machine (or into another track).

3. Play the tape. The time-code reader built into the generator detects a section of good code and initializes the generator with that information.

4. Start recording the new, regenerated code over the bad data (or on a new track).

Jam Sync also should be used when you copy a tape containing time code. With Jam Sync in operation, the code is regenerated to create a clean copy. This procedure is preferable to copying the time-code track directly because each generation can distort the code signal.

# Audio-for-Video SMPTE Applications

With the advent of music videos and other audio/video combinations, there's a widespread need to sync audio to video. Studios doing soundtrack work for film or video can use SMPTE time code to synchronize sound and picture for overdubbing narration, dialog, lip-sync, music, environmental sounds, or sound effects.

## Synchronizing to Video

Running audio and video tapes in synchronization for TV audio editing is a typical postproduction method. You can edit the audio and video portions of a program independently even though they are locked together in time.

When you sync audio and video, select **Longitudinal Time Code** (LTC) or **Vertical Interval Time Code** (VITC). Longitudinal code records along the length of an audio track on the video tape. Vertical Interval code is combined with the video signal and is placed in the vertical blanking interval—the black bar seen over the TV picture when it is rolling vertically. VITC frees up an audio track for other purposes.

If you record the time-code signal on an audio or cue track of the videotape, do not use automatic level control because it may distort the SMPTE waveform. Instead, adjust the time-code signal level manually.

483

When you play an audio tape synced to video, the time-code track on the audio tape will be delayed with respect to the video's code because of the spacing between the record and playback heads in the audio recorder. This delay (about 5 frames) can be corrected by the offset function in the synchronizer.

Some time-code systems include a character inserter that displays the address on the video monitor. If desired, these addresses can be recorded with (burned into) the picture, a feature called window dub.

## The Audio-Tape Synchronization Procedure

At a typical on-location video shoot, the video from the camera(s) is recorded on a videocassette recorder, while the audio from the microphones is recorded on a separate high-quality tape recorder (such as a Nagra) or a portable DAT with SMPTE time-code capability. Both video and audio tapes are prestriped with SMPTE time code so that they can be synchronized later in postproduction.

Back at the studio, you connect the audio and video decks for SMPTE sync as described earlier. When you play the video tape, the SMPTE time code locks the picture and sound together. You can equalize the audio tape or change levels, and then lay it back (copy it) to the video cassette.

If you sync video to a multitrack tape recorder, you can run the video over and over as you refine the mix. Update your mix moves with an automated mixer or automated mixing program. Finally, when the mix is satisfactory, record the mixer output signal onto the video tape.

This procedure eliminates the dubbing step when transferring the audio soundtrack to video tape. That is, you can mix the multitrack tape master directly to the video tape (keeping sync), rather than mixing down to 2-track and dubbing that to video tape.

## The Film/Video Soundtrack Program

SMPTE can be used with a film/video soundtrack program you run on a computer. This software package automates the playback of music and sound-effects cues for motion-picture and video postproductions. Using SMPTE time code, you can synchronize audio events, such as sound effects, to film or video tape. You create a **cue list** (also known as an **edit decision list** or **EDL**) of audio events, each with its own time-code address. These events are played by MIDI instruments, or are played from recordings on a computer hard disk.

Some programs let you record the video and audio onto hard disk. The video shows up in a window on your computer screen. While watching the video, you note the SMPTE times where you want sound effects or music to occur. In this way you create the sound track and sync it to video, all in your computer. Then dump the edited soundtrack to a pre-striped videocassette.

### Soundtrack Program Features

The following are some of the many tasks that are offered in a soundtrack program.

1. Spot and lay back sound effects (turn them on at the proper times and record them onto the video tape).
2. Do an automated mix.
3. Backtime events.
4. Repeat events.
5. Name events.
6. Print cue lists, libraries, and recording logs.
7. Map keyboards (show each effect's location on a piano-style keyboard).
8. Cut/copy/paste, insert, and delete events.
9. Enter cue locations by tapping on the space bar as the program progresses.
10. Display sound-effect cues graphically along with the music.
11. Convert sequencer files to a cue sheet (hit list).
12. Indicate both SMPTE time code and bar/beat for each event.
13. Expand or compress the duration of a soundtrack.
14. Enter subtle tempo variations, or introduce time offsets, to make cues fall exactly on the beat.
15. Write standard MIDI files with meter, beat, tempo, and event data for use in a sequencer.
16. Lock to MIDI Time Code and SMPTE.

You also can perform various other tasks found in sequencer programs, such as quantization, tap-in tempo, and so on.

## *Digital Audio Editing*

It's becoming common to record the elements of a soundtrack—dialog, ambience, music, and sound effects—into a digital audio workstation, then edit the soundtrack with that. Either SMPTE or MIDI time code keeps the soundtrack and video in sync. With MIDI time code, you can cue MIDI devices to play music and effects at various SMPTE times relative to the video program. This process can go through various steps.

1. First, you're handed a **work tape**, which is a video tape of the program you're working on. It has SMPTE time code already striped on tape, and the SMPTE time code appears in a window on-screen called a window dub. As stated before, some programs let you copy the video onto your hard disk.

2. Watch the picture. Using a MIDI keyboard workstation, compose musical parts related to the video scenes and their SMPTE start/stop times. These times indicate how long the music needs to be for each musical segment. This music can be recorded with a MIDI sequencer or multitrack recorder synced to the video recorder.

3. Dialog and wild sound are often recorded on a portable 2-track recorder with a center track for time code. (Wild sound is ambient noise recorded on the set while shooting, not synced with the video.) Sync the dialog tape to the video tape.

4. Missing or poorly recorded dialog is replaced during a process called looping or **ADR (Automatic Dialog Replacement)**. Have actors watch the work tape and lip-sync their lines onto a synced multitrack audio recorder.

5. Record sound effects so that they line up with corresponding events in the video. Audition several sound effects from CD libraries, pick the ones you like, and sample them into the digital audio workstation.

6. Using slow motion or freeze frame, go through the video and note the SMPTE times where each sound effect should occur.

7. Using a sequencer program, enter the cue point (SMPTE time) for each sound effect. This creates the EDL.

8. Play the video. The sequencer runs down the cue list. Each cue point (SMPTE time-code address) triggers the sampler to play a corresponding sound effect or music at the correct time.

9. If you wish, you can redo the SMPTE time cues or change the effects independently.

# Other Time-Code Applications

SMPTE time code allows video editing under computer control. In editing a video program, you copy program segments from two or more video tapes onto a third recorder. On a computer you specify the edit points (time-code addresses) where you want to switch from one video source to another. You can rehearse edits as often as required.

Time code is used also as an index for locating cue points on tape. During a mixdown, you can use these cue points to indicate where to make changes in the mix.

Time code also can be used as a reference for console automation and MIDI instruments. With this latter application, MIDI synthesizers can be cued to any point within a sequence, rather than having to start at the beginning. By using SMPTE time code to lock together multiple audio or video transports, you can greatly expand your operating flexibility.

# FURTHER EDUCATION

The following books, magazines, and literature are recommended to anyone desiring further education in recording technology.

## Books

### Music Books Plus

A catalog that offers many audio-related books. Their Web site is http://www.musicbooksplus.com. Address: P.O. Box 670, 240 Portage Road, Lewiston, NY 14092, phone 800-265-8481.

### Music Maker Publications

Offers several books on recording. Web site: http://www.recordingmag.com/mumak/catalog.

### Focal Press

Another major audio books catalog is http://www.focalpress.com. They also offer workshops and discussions. For a detailed explanation of stereo theory and stereo mic techniques, see *Stereo Microphone Techniques* or *On-Location Recording Techniques* by Bruce Bartlett, published by Focal Press.

## Recording Magazines

*Recording* (home and project studio recording)
5412 Idylwild Trail

Suite 100
Boulder, CO 80301
Phone 303-516-9118
http://www.recordingmag.com
E-mail: info@recordingmag.com

*Mix* (pro recording and concert sound)
Subscriptions:
*Mix*
P.O. Box 1939
Marion, OH 43306
800-532-8190
http://mixmag.com

*Mix* also offers a master directory of the pro audio industry, and a quarterly magazine called *Internet Audio*. http://www.mixonline.com/internetaudio/intaud.cfm.

*EQ* (home, project, and pro recording)
Subscriptions:
P.O. Box 0532
Baldwin, NY 11510
212-378-0400
http://www.eqmag.com

*EQ* also offers a recording and sound buyer's guide.

*Electronic Musician* (home and project studio recording)
6400 Hollis Street, #12
Emeryville, CA 94608
510-653-3307
http://www.emusician.com
Subscriptions and customer service:
P.O. Box 1939
Marion, OH, 43306
800-532-8190

*Electronic Musician* offers a supplement called "Desktop Music Production Guide."

*Gig* (a musician's magazine with some recording and live sound columns)
P.O. Box 51070
Boulder, CO 80322-1070
800-678-8066
http://www.gigmag.com

*Tape Op* (home and project studio creative recording)
P.O. Box 14517

Portland, OR 97293
503-239-5389
E-mail: info@tapeop.com
http://www.tapeop.com

In the back of those magazines are ads related to recording products and services.

# Pro Audio Magazines

*Journal of the Audio Engineering Society* (*JAES*; pro audio engineering—scholarly and academic, mostly theoretical)
60 E. 42nd Street
New York, NY 10165-2520
212-661-8528
http://www.aes.org
E-mail: HQ@aes.org

*Pro Audio Review* (reviews of pro audio equipment)
IMAS Publishing
P.O. Box 1214
Falls Church, VA 22041
703-998-7600

*Live Sound* (concert sound reinforcement)
4741 Central #2222
Kansas City, MO 64112
913-568-6980
http://www.livesoundint.com
E-mail: livesoundinternational@compuserve.com

*Church Production* (audio for houses of worship)
Production Media Inc.
25799 Hunt Trail
South Bend, IN 46628
877-241-7461
For subscriptions see http://www.churchproduction.com.

*Technologies for Worship* (audio for houses of worship)
Box 35
20 Wellington Street
E. Aurora, Ontario, Canada L4G 3KA
905-830-4300 (Canada)
http://www.tfwm.com

*Netmedia* (magazine for Internet streaming content and delivery)

913-341-1300

http://www.netmedia-online.com

*Internet Audio* (magazine for professionals involved in Web-based audio production)
http://www.internet_audio@intertec.com or mixonline.com

# Consumer Audio Magazines

*Sound and Vision* (consumer audio and video)
1633 Broadway
New York, NY 10019
212-767-6000 or 800-876-9011
http://www.soundandvisionmag.com

*Stereophile* (high-end audio)
800-666-3746
http://www.stereophile.com

*The Absolute Sound* (high-end audio)
*The Absolute Sound*, Subscription Services
Box 3000
Denville, NJ 07834
888-732-1625

# Guides, Brochures, and Other Literature

**Careers in Audio Engineering, Directory of Educational Programs,** and the **Journal of the Audio Engineering Society,** from The Audio Engineering Society, 60 E. 42nd Street, New York, NY 10165.

Microphone application guides are available from Crown International, 1718 W. Mishawaka Road, Elkhart, IN 46517; Shure Brothers Inc., 222 Hartrey Avenue, Evanston, IL 60202; Countryman Associates Inc., 417 Stanford Avenue, Redwood City, CA 94063; AKG Acoustics Inc., 77 Selleck Street, Stamford, CT 06902; Sennheiser Electronic Corp., 6 Vista Drive, P.O. Box 987, Old Lyme, CT 06371; and Audio-Technica U.S. Inc., 1221 Commerce Drive, Stow, Ohio 44224.

You can find a lot of valuable information in user manuals and free sales literature provided by manufacturers of recording equipment. Ask your equipment dealer for manufacturer's phone numbers.

The International MIDI Association has MIDI technical information for sale, such as the MIDI 1.0 specification and a 50-page detailed explanation of MIDI. International MIDI Association, 5316 W. 57th St., Los Angeles, CA 90056, 213-649-MIDI.

# Guides to Recording Schools

Each July issue of *Mix* magazine contains a comprehensive directory of recording schools, seminars, and programs. Universities and colleges in most major cities have recording-engineering courses. Investigate them thoroughly, however, before making a decision.

A complete reference guide to audio education is the book *New Ears: A Guide to Education in Audio and the Recording Sciences*, 2nd ed., edited by Mark Drews, and published by New Ear Productions of Syracuse, New York (1992). It's all here: course descriptions of all the known recording schools; directories of industry-related magazines, journals, and textbooks; professional audio, music, and broadcasting associations; audio research facilities, nonprofit studios, and other helpful resources. The book is available from New Ear Productions, 1033 Euclid Ave., Syracuse, NY 13210.

# The Internet

A great place to ask questions, besides magazines, is on the Internet. Check out the newsgroup rec.audio.pro. You can ask questions and get answers from pro engineers. You may get conflicting answers, because often there are many ways to do the same thing. Also, some who reply are more expert than others. But you'll often find stimulating debates. Some other valuable Web sites are homerecording.com, prorec.com, microphones.com, tape.com, digido.com, musicplayer.com, artistpro.com, and solorb.com/dat-heads/.

Do an Internet Web search with the keywords audio, recording, audio recording links, DAT, digital audio, and so on. Also search for the name and model number of equipment you have, or are interested in. You'll discover hundreds of audio-related Web sites and links.

# Recording Equipment Catalogs

Here are but a few catalogs from which to order recording gear:

American Musical Supply
600 Industrial Avenue
Paramus, NJ 07652

800-458-4076

http://www.americanmusical.com

Guitar Center

http://www.guitarcenter.com

Music Emporium
12401 Twinbrook Parkway
Rockville, MD 20852
800-648-8460

Musician's Friend
P.O. Box 4520
Medford, OR 97501
800-776-5173
http://www.musiciansfriend.com

Sam Ash
7726 Cheri Court
Tampa, FL 33634
800-4-SAMASH
http://www.samash.com

Sweetwater Sound
5335 Bass Road
Ft. Wayne, IN 46808
219-432-8176
http://www.sweetwater.com

The Woodwind and the Brasswind
19880 State Line Road
South Bend, IN 46637
800-348-5003

# D

# IMPEDANCE

Impedance is one of audio's more confusing concepts. To clarify this topic, I'll present a few questions and answers about impedance.

## What is impedance?

**Impedance** (Z) is the resistance of a circuit to alternating current, such as an audio signal. Technically, impedance is the total opposition (including resistance and reactance) that a circuit has to passing alternating current.

A high-impedance circuit tends to have high voltage and low current. A low-impedance circuit tends to have relatively low voltage and high current.

## I'm connecting two audio devices. Is it important to match their impedances? What if I don't?

First some definitions. When you connect two devices, one is the **source** and one is the **load**. The source is the device that puts out a signal. The load is the device you are feeding the signal into. The source has a certain output impedance, and the load has a certain input impedance.

A few decades ago in the vacuum-tube era, it was important to match the output impedance of the source to the input impedance of the load. Usually the source and load impedances were both 600 ohms. If the source impedance equals the load impedance, this is called "matching" impedances. It results in maximum *power* transfer from the source to the load.

In contrast, suppose the source is low Z and the load is high Z. If the load impedance is 10 times or more the source impedance, it is called a "bridging" impedance. Bridging results in maximum *voltage* transfer from the source to the load. Nowadays, nearly all devices are connected bridging—low-Z out to high-Z in—because we want the most voltage transferred between components.

If you connect a low-Z source to a high-Z load, there is no distortion or frequency-response change caused by this connection. But if you connect a high-Z source to a low-Z load, you might get distortion or altered response. For example, suppose you connect an electric bass guitar (a high-Z device) into an XLR-type mic input (a low-Z load). The low frequencies in the signal will roll off, so the bass will sound thin. And the highs might roll off, making the sound dull.

We want the bass guitar to be loaded by a high impedance, and we want the mic input to be fed by a low-impedance signal. A direct box or impedance-matching adapter does this (Figure D.1). Such adapters are available from Radio Shack.

The adapter is a tube with a phone jack on one end and a male XLR connector on the other. Inside the tube is a transformer. Its primary winding is high Z, wired to the phone jack. The transformer's secondary winding is low Z, wired to the XLR. You plug the guitar cord into the phone jack, and plug the XLR into a mic input in a snake or mixer. Use it with a bass guitar, electric guitar, or synth.

This impedance-matching adapter works, but is not ideal. The load it presents to the bass guitar might be 12 kilohms, which will slightly load down the high-Z guitar pickup, causing thin bass.

An active direct box solves this problem. In place of a transformer, the active DI usually has an FET (field effect transistor). The FET has a very high input impedance that does not load down the bass guitar.

**Figure D.1**
High-to-low impedance matching adapter.

# How do I know what a microphone's impedance is?

Check the impedance spec on the mic's data sheet. A microphone rated at 150 to 300 ohms is considered low impedance. About 600 to 2000 ohms is medium impedance, and 10,000 ohms or more is high impedance. Most mics are low Z, and all mics with XLR (3-pin) connectors are low Z.

A low-Z mic can be used with hundreds of feet of cable without picking up hum or losing high frequencies. A medium-Z mic cable is limited to about 40 feet without losses. A high-Z mic will lose highs and pick up hum if the cable exceeds about 10 feet. This high-frequency loss depends on the capacitance of the cable as well as the mic impedance.

# I'm connecting a mic to a mixer. Is impedance a consideration?

Yes. If your mixer has phone-jack inputs, they are probably high Z. But most mics are low Z. When you plug a low-Z mic into a high-Z input you get a weak signal. That's because a high-Z mic input is designed to receive a relatively high voltage from a high-Z mic, and so the input is designed to have low gain. So you don't get much signal amplification.

Solution: Between the mic cable and the input jack, connect an impedance matching adapter (Figure D.2). It steps up the voltage of the mic, giving it a stronger signal.

The adapter is a tube with a female XLR input and a phone-plug output. Inside the tube is a transformer. Its primary winding is low Z, wired to the XLR. It secondary winding is high Z, wired to the phone plug. Connect the mic to the XLR; connect the phone plug to the mixer's phone jack. Then the mixer will receive a strong signal from the mic.

If your mixer has XLR inputs, they are low-Z balanced. In this case, simply connect the mic to the mixer using a mic cable with a female XLR on the mic end and a male XLR on the mixer end. A low-Z mic input is

**Figure D.2**
Low-to-high impedance
matching adapter.

typically about 1500 ohms, so it provides a bridging load to a mic that is 150 to 300 ohms.

# How about speaker impedance?

Most loudspeakers are 4 or 8 ohms nominal. Actually the impedance varies with frequency. A speaker rated at 8 ohms impedance might range between 4 and 50 ohms, depending on the frequency of the signal.

If you connect two identical speakers in parallel, the total impedance is half. For example, two 8-ohm speakers in parallel present a 4-ohm load to a power amplifier. If you connect two identical speakers in series, the total impedance is doubled. Two 8-ohm speakers in series present a 16-ohm load to a power amplifier.

Suppose you have a speaker connected to a power amplifier. Generally, the lower the speaker impedance, the more power you get from the power amp. Some amps can handle a 2-ohm load, but many will overheat. Try to keep the load 4 ohms or higher.

# Should I consider impedance when I connect two line-level devices?

This is seldom a problem. In most audio devices, the impedance of the line output is low—about 100 to 1000 ohms. The impedance of the line input is high—about 10 kilohms to 1 megohm. So every connection is bridging, and you get maximum voltage transfer. Some audio devices, such as passive equalizers, require a terminating resistor at the input or output for best performance.

# Can I connect one source to two or more loads?

Usually yes. You can connect several devices in parallel across one line output. Suppose you connect a mixer output simultaneously to a recorder input, an amplifier input, and another mixer's input in parallel. The combined input impedance of those three loads might be 4000 ohms, which still presents a bridging load to the mixer's 100-ohm output impedance.

Mics are a different story. If you connect one mic to two or more mixers with a Y cable, the combined input impedance will be about 700 ohms or less. This can load down some microphones, reducing the bass in dynamic mics or causing distortion in condenser mics. One solution is to use a transformer mic splitter.

# Can I connect two or more sources to one input?

Not recommended. If you combine two or more sources into a single load, the low-output impedance of one source will load down the output of the other source, and vice versa. This can cause level loss and distortion.

If you want to combine the signals from two devices into one input, you need to put a series resistor in line with each device before combining them. That prevents each device from loading down the other. A minimum resistor value might be 470 ohms per source. If the source is balanced, use one resistor on pin 2 and one on pin 3—two resistors per source.

# Summary

- Impedance (Z) is the opposition to alternating current, measured in ohms.
- Microphones and line outputs are usually low Z.
- Electric guitars, synthesizers, and line inputs are usually high Z.
- XLR mic inputs are low impedance; phone jack mic inputs are high impedance.
- Speakers are usually 4 to 8 ohms.
- Equal impedances in parallel result in half the impedance.
- Equal impedances in series result in twice the impedance.
- Connect low-Z sources to low-Z inputs. (A low-Z input is usually 7 to 10 times the source impedance, but it's still called a low-Z input.)
- Connect high-Z sources to high-Z inputs.
- Connect a low-Z source to a high-Z input through a step-up transformer (impedance matching adapter).
- Connect a high-Z source to a low-Z input through a step-down transformer (impedance matching adapter, or direct box).

# Impedance technical details

Impedance includes both resistance and reactance. The reactance parts are inductive reactance and capacitive reactance. Both vary with frequency. The resistive part is constant with frequency.

Impedance is measured in magnitude (ohms) and phase (degrees) at a certain frequency. Usually the magnitude part is all we are concerned with. The magnitude part of impedance is:

$$Z = SQR\left(R^2 + (XL - XC)^2\right)$$

where SQR means "square root," R is resistance, XL is inductive reactance, and XC is capacitive reactance, all in ohms. Many devices don't have much reactance, so we often consider impedance to be the same as resistance.

# GLOSSARY

**A WEIGHTING**—*See* Weighted.

**AAC (Advanced Audio Codec)**—A relatively new compressed audio file format, AAC offers better sound quality than MP3, but with less storage space and bandwidth. It's also used with Digital Rights Management technology to help control the copying and distributing of music.

**A–B**—A listening comparison between two audio programs, or between two components playing the same program, performed by switching immediately from one to the other. The levels of the two signals are matched. *See also* Spaced-Pair.

**AC-3**—Same as Dolby Digital, a perceptual encoding scheme that data-reduces the six surround channels of a 5.1 system to two channels.

**ACCENT MICROPHONE**—*See* Spot Microphone.

**ACCESS JACKS (INSERT JACKS)**—Two jacks (send and return) in a console input module or output module that allow access to points in the signal path, usually for connecting a compressor. Plugging into the access jacks breaks the signal flow and allows you to insert a signal processor or recorder in series with the signal. In many mixers, a single insert jack has both send and return terminals.

**ACTIVE COMBINING NETWORK**—A combining network with gain. *See* Combining Network.

**AES**—Audio Engineering Society.

**AES/EBU**—Also called IEC 988 Tape 1. An interface format for digital signals, using a balanced 110 ohm mic cable terminated with XLR-type connectors. *See also* S/PDIF.

**AIFF (Audio Interchange File Format)**—A standard Mac format for uncompressed digital audio files.

**ALIGNMENT**—The adjustment of tape-head azimuth and of tape-recorder circuitry to achieve optimum performance from the particular type of tape being used.

**ALIGNMENT TAPE**—A prerecorded tape with calibrated tones for alignment of a tape recorder.

**AMBIENCE**—Room acoustics, early reflections, and reverberation. Also, the audible sense of a room or environment surrounding a recorded instrument.

**AMBIENCE MICROPHONE**—A microphone placed relatively far from its sound source to pick up ambience.

**AMPLITUDE, PEAK**—On a graph of a sound wave, the sound pressure of the waveform peak. On a graph of an electrical signal, the voltage of the waveform peak. The amplitude of a sound wave or signal as measured on a meter is 0.707 times the peak amplitude.

**ANALOG-TO-DIGITAL (A/D) CONVERTER**—A circuit that converts an analog audio signal into a stream of digital data (bitstream).

**ASIO**—Audio Stream Input/Output, Steinberg's computer audio driver spec for Mac and Windows. ASIO has low latency because it interfaces directly between a sound card and the audio application software.

**ASSIGN**—To route or send an audio signal to one or more selected channels.

**ATRAC**—Adaptive Transform Acoustic Coding. A data compression scheme (used in the MiniDisc) that reduces by 5:1 the storage needed for digital audio. ATRAC is a perceptual coding method, which omits data deemed inaudible due to masking.

**ATTACK**—The beginning of a note. The first portion of a note's envelope in which a note rises from silence to its maximum volume.

**ATTACK TIME**—In a compressor, the time it takes for gain reduction to occur in response to a musical attack.

**ATTENUATE**—To reduce the level of a signal.

**ATTENUATOR**—In a mixer (or mixing console) input module, an adjustable resistive network that reduces the microphone signal level to prevent overloading of the input transformer and mic preamplifier.

**AUDIO INTERFACE**—*See* Breakout Box.

**AUTOLOCATE**—A recorder function that makes the tape or disk go to a program address (counter time) at the press of a button.

**AUTOMATED MIXING**—A system of mixing in which a computer remembers and updates console settings. With this system, a mix can be performed and refined in several stages and played back at a later date exactly as set up previously.

**AUXILIARY BUS (AUX-BUS)**—*See* Effects Bus.

**AUXILIARY SEND (AUX-SEND)**—*See* Effects Send.

**A/V DRIVE**—A hard-disk drive meant for audio/video use. It postpones thermal recalibration until the disk is inactive, preventing data errors.

**AZIMUTH**—In a tape recorder, the angular relationship between the head gap and the tape path.

**AZIMUTH ALIGNMENT**—The mechanical adjustment of the record or playback head to bring it into proper alignment (90 degrees) with the tape path.

**BACK-TIMING**—A technique of cueing up the musical background or a sound effect to a narration track so that the music or effect ends simultaneously with the narration.

**BAFFLED-OMNI**—A stereo miking arrangement that uses two ear-spaced omnidirectional microphones separated by a hard padded baffle.

**BALANCE**—The relative volume levels of various tracks or instruments.

**BALANCED AC POWER**—AC power from a center-tapped power transformer. Instead of one 120 V line and one 0 V line, it has two 60 V lines. They are in phase with each other and sum to 120 V. But they are connected to the center-tap ground out of phase (one is +60 V; the other is −60 V). Any hum and noise on the grounding system cancel out.

**BALANCED LINE**—A cable with two conductors surrounded by a shield, in which each conductor is at equal impedance to ground. With respect to ground, the conductors are at equal potential but opposite polarity; the signal flows through both conductors.

**BANDPASS FILTER**—In a crossover, a filter that passes a band or range of frequencies but sharply attenuates or rejects frequencies outside the band.

**BASIC TRACKS**—Recorded tracks of rhythm instruments (bass, guitar, drums, and sometimes keyboard).

**BASS MANAGEMENT**—A subwoofer/satellite crossover, usually part of a surround receiver. Bass management routes frequencies above about 100 Hz to the five full-range speakers, and routes frequencies below about 100 Hz from all six channels to the subwoofer. It affects only what you monitor, not what goes on tape. Bass management can be done by a surround-receiver circuit, a standalone box, a special circuit in a sub-woofer, or a software plug-in.

**BASS TRAP**—An assembly that absorbs low-frequency sound waves in the studio.

**BIAMPLIFICATION (BIAMPING)**—Driving a woofer and tweeter with separate power amplifiers. An active crossover is connected ahead of these power amplifiers.

**BIAS**—In tape-recorder electronics, an ultrasonic signal that drives the erase head. This signal is also mixed with the audio signal applied to the record head to reduce distortion.

**BIDIRECTIONAL MICROPHONE**—A microphone that is most sensitive to sounds arriving from two directions—in front of and behind the microphone. It rejects sounds approaching either side of the microphone. Sometimes called a cosine or figure-eight microphone because of the shape of its polar pattern.

**BINAURAL RECORDING**—A 2-channel recording made with an omni-directional microphone mounted near each ear of a human or a dummy head, for playback over headphones. The object is to duplicate the acoustic signal appearing at each ear.

**BIT DEPTH**—In a digital signal, the number of bits in each word. Each word (binary number) represents the amplitude of the analog signal from one instant to the next. High bit depth = long word length = high resolution of the analog signal amplitude.

**BLUMLEIN ARRAY**—A stereo microphone technique in which two coincident bidirectional microphones are angled 90 degrees apart (45 degrees to the left and right of center).

**BOARD**—*See* Mixing Console.

**BOUNCING TRACKS**—A process in which two or more tracks are mixed, and the mixed tracks are recorded on an unused track or tracks. Then the original tracks can be erased, which frees them up for recording more instruments.

**BOUNDARY MICROPHONE**—A microphone designed to be used on a boundary (a hard reflective surface). The microphone capsule is mounted very close to the boundary so that direct and reflected sounds arrive at the microphone diaphragm in phase (or nearly so) for all frequencies in the audible band.

**BREAKOUT BOX (I/O BOX)**—A group of audio input and output connectors in a chassis, which is wired to a sound card or USB port in a computer. Used to interface analog audio signals (and often MIDI and digital signals) with a computer.

**BREATHING**—The unwanted audible rise and fall of background noise that may occur with a compressor. Also called pumping.

**BULK TAPE ERASER**—A large electromagnet used to erase a whole reel of recording tape at once.

**BUS**—A common connection of many different signals. An output of a mixer or submixer. A channel that feeds a tape track, signal processor, or power amplifier.

**BUS IN**—An input to a program bus, usually used for effects returns.

**BUS MASTER**—In the output section of a mixing console, a potentiometer (fader or volume control) that controls the output level of a bus.

**BUS OUT**—The output connector of a bus.

**BUS TRIM**—A control in the output section of a mixing console that provides variable gain control of a bus, used in addition to the bus master for fine adjustment.

**BUS MASTER**—In the output section of a mixing console, a potentiometer (fader or volume control) that controls the output level of a bus.

**BUZZ**—An unwanted edgy tone that sometimes accompanies audio, containing high harmonics of 60 Hz.

**CALIBRATION**—*See* Alignment.

**CAPACITOR**—An electronic component that stores an electric charge. It is formed of two conductive plates separated by an insulator called a dielectric. A capacitor passes AC but blocks DC.

**CAPACITOR MICROPHONE**—*See* Condenser Microphone.

**CAPSTAN**—In a tape-recorder transport, a rotating post that contacts the tape (along with the pinch roller) and pulls the tape past the heads at a constant speed during recording and playback.

**CARDIOID MICROPHONE**—A unidirectional microphone with side attenuation of 6 dB and maximum rejection of sound at the rear of the microphone (180 degrees off-axis). A microphone with a heart-shaped directional pattern.

**CD**—*See* Compact Disc.

**CD-R**—CD-Recordable, a recordable compact disc that cannot be rewritten. Once recorded, it cannot be erased and reused.

**CD-ROM**—A computer disk drive that plays computer data from CD-ROM disks. The disks are read optically by a laser, as in a compact disc player.

**CD-RW**—CD-Rewritable, a recordable compact disc that can be rewritten. Once recorded it can be erased and reused.

**CHANNEL**—A single path of an audio signal. Usually, each channel contains a different signal.

**CHANNEL ASSIGN**—*See* Assign.

**CHORUS**—1. A special effect in which a signal is delayed by 15 to 35 msec, the delayed signal is combined with the original signal, and the delay is varied randomly or periodically. This creates a wavy, shimmering effect. 2. The main portion of a song that is repeated several times throughout the song with the same lyrics.

**CLEAN**—Free of noise, distortion, overhang, leakage. Not muddy.

**CLEAR**—Easy to hear, easy to differentiate. Reproduced with sufficient high frequencies.

**COINCIDENT-PAIR**—A stereo microphone, or two separate microphones, placed so that the microphone diaphragms occupy approximately the same point in space. They are angled apart and mounted one directly above the other.

**COMB-FILTER EFFECT**—The frequency response caused by combining a sound with its delayed replica. The frequency response has a series of peaks and dips caused by phase interference. The peaks and dips resemble the teeth of a comb.

**COMBINING AMPLIFIER**—An amplifier at which the outputs of two or more signal paths are mixed together to feed a single track of a tape recorder.

**COMBINING NETWORK**—A resistive network at which the outputs of two or more signal paths are mixed together to feed a single track of a tape recorder.

**COMPACT DISC (CD)**—A read-only disc medium for storing digital audio programs up to 74 minutes long. The compact disc stores data in the form of a spiral groove of microscopic pits and is read optically by a laser. CD's digital audio format is 44.1 K sampling rate and 16-bit word length.

**COMPLEX WAVE**—A wave with more than one frequency component.

**COMPING**—Recording composite tracks.

**COMPOSITE TRACKS**—The process of recording several performances of a musical part on different tracks, so that the best segments of each performance can be played in sequence during mixdown.

**COMPRESSION**—1. The portion of a sound wave in which air molecules are pushed together, forming a region with higher-than-normal atmospheric pressure. 2. In signal processing, the reduction in dynamic range or gain caused by a compressor. 3. Data compression or data reduction is an encoding scheme to reduce the size of a data file by throwing away audio data deemed inaudible because of masking. ATRAC, MP3, MLP, AAC, RealAudio, and Microsoft Media are examples of compressed data formats.

**COMPRESSION RATIO (SLOPE)**—In a compressor, the ratio of the change in input level (in dB) to the change in output level (in dB). For example, a 2:1 ratio means that for every 2 dB change in input level, the output level changes 1 dB.

**COMPRESSOR**—A signal processor that reduces dynamic range or gain by means of automatic volume control. An amplifier whose gain decreases as the input signal level increases above a preset point.

**CONDENSER MICROPHONE**—A microphone that works on the principle of variable capacitance to generate an electrical signal. The microphone diaphragm and an adjacent metallic disk (called a backplate) are charged to form two plates of a capacitor. Incoming sound waves vibrate the diaphragm, varying its spacing to the backplate, which varies the capacitance, which in turn varies the voltage between the diaphragm and backplate.

**CONNECTOR**—A device that makes electrical contact between a signal-carrying cable and an electronic device, or between two cables. A device used to connect or hold together a cable and an electronic component so that a signal can flow from one to the other.

**CONSOLE**—*See* Mixing Console.

**CONTACT PICKUP**—A transducer that contacts a musical instrument and converts its mechanical vibrations into a corresponding electrical signal.

**CONTROLLER SURFACE**—A chassis with faders (and sometimes knobs) that resembles a mixer, used to adjust virtual controls that appear on-screen in computer editing software. Connected to the computer by USB, the controller surface might include analog and digital input/output connectors and MIDI connectors.

**CONTROL ROOM**—The room in which the engineer controls and monitors the recording. It houses most of the recording hardware.

**CROSSOVER**—An electronic network that divides an incoming signal into two or more frequency bands.

**CROSSOVER, ACTIVE (ELECTRONIC CROSSOVER)**—A crossover with amplifying components, used ahead of the power amplifiers in a biamped or triamped speaker system.

**CROSSOVER FREQUENCY**—The single frequency at which both filters of a crossover network are down 3 dB.

**CROSSOVER, PASSIVE**—A crossover with passive (nonamplifying) components, used after the power amplifier.

**CROSSTALK**—The unwanted transfer of a signal from one channel to another. Crosstalk often occurs between adjacent tracks within a record or playback head in a tape recorder, or between input modules in a console.

**CUE, CUE SEND**—In a mixing-console input module, a control that adjusts the level of the signal feeding the cue mixer that feeds a signal to headphones in the studio.

**CUE LIST**—*See* Edit Decision List.

**CUE MIXER**—A submixer in a mixing console that takes signals from cue sends as inputs and mixes them into a composite signal that drives headphones in the studio.

**CUE SHEET**—Used during mixdown, a chronological list of mixing-console control adjustments required at various points in the recorded song. These points may be indicated by tape-counter or ABS-time readings.

**CUE SYSTEM**—A monitor system that allows musicians to hear themselves and previously recorded tracks through headphones.

**DAMPING FACTOR**—The ability of a power amplifier to control or damp loudspeaker vibrations. The lower the amplifier's output impedance, the higher the damping factor.

**DAT (R-DAT)**—A digital audio tape recorder that uses a rotating head to record digital audio on tape.

**DATA COMPRESSION**—A data encoding scheme for reducing the amount of data storage on a medium. Same as Data Reduction. *See* Compression, ATRAC, *and* MP3.

**DAW**—Abbreviation for digital audio workstation.

**dB**—Abbreviation for decibel.

**DEAD**—Having very little or no reverberation.

**DECAY**—The portion of the envelope of a note in which the envelope goes from maximum to some midrange level. Also, the decline in level of reverberation over time.

**DECAY TIME**—*See* Reverberation Time.

**DECIBEL**—The unit of measurement of audio level. Ten times the logarithm of the ratio of two power levels. Twenty times the logarithm of the ratio of two voltages. dBV is decibels relative to 1 volt. dBu is decibels relative to 0.775 volt. dBm is decibels relative to 1 milliwatt. dBA is decibels, A weighted (*see* Weighted).

**DECODED TAPE**—A tape that is expanded after being compressed by a noise-reduction system. Such a tape has normal dynamic range.

**DE-ESSER**—A signal processor that removes excessive sibilance ("s" and "sh" sounds) by compressing high frequencies around 5 to 10 kHz.

**DELAY**—The time interval between a signal and its repetition. A digital delay or a delay line is a signal processor that delays a signal for a short time.

**DEMAGNETIZER (DEGAUSSER)**—An electromagnet with a probe tip that is touched to elements of the tape path (such as tape heads and tape guides) to remove residual magnetism.

**DEPTH**—The audible sense of nearness and farness of various instruments. Instruments recorded with a high ratio of direct-to-reverberant sound are perceived as being close; instruments recorded with a low ratio of direct-to-reverberant sound are perceived as being distant.

**DESIGN CENTER**—The portion of fader travel (usually shaded), about 10 to 15 dB from the top, in which console gain is distributed for optimum headroom and signal-to-noise ratio. During normal operation, each fader in use should be placed at or near design center.

**DESIGNATION STRIP**—A strip of paper taped near console faders to designate the instrument that each fader controls.

**DESK**—The British term for mixing console.

**DESTRUCTIVE EDITING**—In a digital audio workstation, editing that rewrites the data on disk. A destructive edit cannot be undone.

**DI**—Short for direct injection, recording with a direct box.

**DIFFUSION**—An even distribution of sound in a room.

**DIGITAL AUDIO**—An encoding of an analog audio signal in the form of binary digits (ones and zeros).

**DIGITAL AUDIO WORKSTATION (DAW)**—A computer, sound card, and editing software that allows you to record, edit, and mix audio programs entirely in digital form. Standalone DAWs include real mixer controls; computer DAWS have virtual controls on-screen.

**DIGITAL RECORDING**—A recording system in which the audio signal is stored in the form of binary digits.

**DIGITAL-TO-ANALOG CONVERTER**—A circuit that converts a digital audio signal into an analog audio signal.

**DIM**—To reduce the monitor volume temporarily by a preset amount so that you can carry on a conversation.

**DIRECT BOX**—A device used for connecting an amplified instrument directly to a mixer mic input. The direct box converts a high-impedance unbalanced audio signal into a low-impedance balanced audio signal.

**DIRECT INJECTION (DI)**—Recording with a direct box.

**DIRECTIONAL MICROPHONE**—A microphone that has different sensitivity in different directions. A unidirectional or bidirectional microphone.

**DIRECT OUTPUT, DIRECT OUT**—An output connector following a mic preamplifier, fader, and equalizer, used to feed the signal of one instrument to one track of a tape recorder.

**DIRECT SOUND**—Sound traveling directly from the sound source to the microphone (or to the listener) without reflections. Also, DirectSound is an audio driver for the Windows operating system, intended as an enhancement to MME (MultiMedia Extensions).

**DIRECTX**—A package of Windows audio, video, and game-controller drivers.

**DISTORTION**—An unwanted change in the audio waveform, causing a raspy or gritty sound quality. The appearance of frequencies in a device's output signal that were not in the input signal. Distortion is caused by recording at too high a level, using improper mixer settings, components failing, or vacuum tubes distorting. (Distortion can be desirable—for an electric guitar, for example.)

**DOLBY DIGITAL**—A perceptual coding method using AC-3 data compression, offering 6 discrete channels of digital surround sound. Dolby Digital uses a lossy encoding process to reduce the bit rate needed to transmit the six channels via a 2-channel bitstream. The standard audio format for DVD-Video.

**DOLBY PRO LOGIC**—A surround decoder that decodes the two channels of Dolby-Surround-encoded programs back into four channels (left, center, right, surround).

**DOLBY SURROUND**—A matrix encoding system that combines four channels (left, center, right, surround) into two channels. The Dolby Pro Logic decoder unfolds the two channels back into four. The surround channel, which is mono and limited bandwidth, is reproduced over left and right surround speakers.

**DOLBY TONE**—A reference tone recorded at the beginning of a Dolby-encoded tape for alignment purposes.

**DOUBLING**—A special effect in which a signal is combined with its 15- to 35-msec-delayed replica. This process mimics the sound of two identical voices or instruments playing in unison. In another type of doubling, two identical performances are recorded and played back to thicken the sound.

**DROP-FRAME**—For color video production, a mode of SMPTE time code that causes the time code to match the clock on the wall. Once every minute, frame numbers 00 and 01 are dropped, except every 10th minute.

**DROP-OUT**—During playback of a tape recording, a momentary loss of signal caused by separation of the tape from the playback head by dust, tape-oxide irregularity, etc.

**DRUM MACHINE**—A device that plays samples of real drums and includes a sequencer to record rhythm patterns.

**DRY**—Having no echo or reverberation. Referring to a close-sounding signal that has not yet been processed by a reverberation or delay device.

**DSD (Direct Stream Digital)**—A process that encodes a digital signal in a 1-bit (bitstream) format at a 2.8224 MHz sampling rate. Offers state-of-the-art sound quality; used in the Super Audio CD.

**DSP**—Abbreviation for digital signal processing, modifying a signal in digital form by doing calculations on the numbers. DSP is used for level changes, EQ, effects, and so on.

**DTS (Digital Theater System)**—A perceptual coding method using data compression, offering 6 discrete channels of digital surround sound. DTS uses a lossy encoding process to reduce the bitrate needed to transmit the 6 channels via a 2-channel bitstream.

**DVD**—Digital Versatile Disc. A storage medium the size of a compact disc that holds much more data. The DVD stores video, audio, or computer data. DVD-RAM and DVD-R are recordable; DVD-RW is rewritable, and DVD-A is audio only.

**DVD-AUDIO**—A DVD intended mainly for audio programs. It can use Dolby Digital or DTS encoded programs.

**DYNAMIC MICROPHONE**—A microphone that generates electricity when sound waves cause a conductor to vibrate in a stationary magnetic field. The two types of dynamic microphones are moving coil and ribbon. A moving-coil microphone is usually called a dynamic microphone.

**DYNAMIC RANGE**—The range of volume levels in a program from softest to loudest.

**EARTH GROUND**—A connection to moist dirt (the ground we walk on). This connection is usually done via a long copper rod or an all-metal cold-water pipe.

**EASI**—Enhanced Audio Streaming Interface, Emagic's sound card driver spec. EASI achieves low latency by interfacing the sound card directly with the audio application software.

**ECHO**—A delayed repetition of a signal or sound. A sound delayed 50 msec or more, combined with the original sound.

**ECHO CHAMBER**—A hard-surfaced room containing a widely separated loudspeaker and microphone, once used for creating reverberation.

**EDIT DECISION LIST (EDL)**—A list of program events in order, plus their starting and ending times.

**EDITING**—The cutting and rejoining of magnetic tape to delete unwanted material, to insert leader tape, or to rearrange recorded material into the desired sequence. Also, the same actions performed with a digital audio workstation, hard-disk recorder, or MiniDisc recorder–mixer—without cutting any tape.

**EDITING BLOCK**—A metal block that holds magnetic tape during the editing/splicing procedure.

**EFFECTS**—Interesting sound phenomena created by signal processors, such as reverberation, echo, flanging, doubling, compression, or chorus.

**EFFECTS BUS**—The bus that feeds effects devices (signal processors).

**EFFECTS LOOP**—A set of connectors in a mixer for connecting an external effects unit, such as a reverb or delay device. The effects loop includes a send section and a receive section. *See* Effects Send, Effects Return.

**EFFECTS MIXER**—A submixer in a mixing console that combines signals from effects sends, and then feeds the mixed signal to the input of a special-effects device, such as a reverberation unit.

**EFFECTS RETURN (AUX RETURN)**—In the output section of a mixing console, a control that adjusts the amount of signal received from an effects unit. Also, the connectors in a mixer to which you connect the effects-unit output signal. They might be labeled "bus in" instead. The effects-return signal is mixed with the program bus signal.

**EFFECTS SEND (AUX SEND)**—In an input module of a mixing console, a control that adjusts the amount of signal sent to a special-effects device, such as a reverberation or delay unit. Also, the connector in a mixer that you connect to the input of an effects unit. The effects-send control normally adjusts the amount of reverberation or echo heard on each instrument.

**EFFICIENCY**—In a loudspeaker, the ratio of acoustic power output to electrical power input.

**EIA**—Electrical Industries Association.

**EIA RATING**—A microphone-sensitivity specification that states the microphone output level in dBm into a matched load for a given sound pressure level (SPL). SPL + dB (EIA rating) = dBm output into a matched load.

**ELECTRET-CONDENSER MICROPHONE**—A condenser microphone in which the electrostatic field of the capacitor is generated by an electret—a material that permanently stores an electrostatic charge.

**ELECTROSTATIC FIELD**—The force field between two conductors charged with static electricity.

**ELECTROSTATIC INTERFERENCE**—The unwanted presence of an electrostatic hum field in signal conductors.

**ENCODED TAPE**—A tape containing a signal compressed by a noise-reduction unit.

**END-ADDRESSED**—Referring to a microphone whose main axis of pickup is perpendicular to the front of the microphone. You aim the front of the mic at the sound source. *See* Side-Addressed.

**ENVELOPE**—The rise and fall in volume of one note. The envelope connects successive peaks of the waves that make up the note. Each harmonic in the note might have a different envelope.

**EQUALIZATION (EQ)**—The adjustment of frequency response to alter the tonal balance or to attenuate unwanted frequencies.

**EQUALIZER**—A circuit (usually in each input module of a mixing console, or in a separate unit) that alters the frequency spectrum of a signal passed through it.

**ERASE**—To remove an audio signal from magnetic tape by applying an ultrasonic varying magnetic field so as to randomize the magnetization of the magnetic particles on the tape.

**ERASE HEAD**—A head in a tape recorder that erases the signal on tape.

**EXPANDER**—1. A signal processor that increases the dynamic range of a signal passed through it. 2. An amplifier whose gain decreases as its input level decreases. When used as a noise gate, an expander reduces the gain of low-level signals to reduce noise between notes.

**FADE-OUT**—To gradually reduce the volume of the last several seconds of a recorded song, from full level down to silence, by slowly pulling down the master fader.

**FADER**—A linear or sliding potentiometer (volume control), used to adjust signal level.

**FEED**—1. To send an audio signal to some device or system. 2. An output signal sent to some device or system.

**FEEDBACK**—1. The return of some portion of an output signal to the system's input. 2. The squealing sound you hear when a PA system microphone picks up its own amplified signal through a loudspeaker.

**FEED REEL**—The left-side reel on a tape recorder that unwinds during recording or playback.

**FILTER**—1. A circuit that sharply attenuates frequencies above or below a certain frequency. Used to reduce noise and leakage above or below the frequency range of an instrument or voice. 2. A MIDI filter removes selected note parameters.

**FLANGING**—A special effect in which a signal is combined with its delayed replica, and the delay is varied between 0 and 20 msec. A hollow, swishing, ethereal effect like a variable-length pipe, or like a jet plane passing overhead. A variable comb filter produces the flanging effect.

**FLETCHER–MUNSON EFFECT**—Named after the two people who discovered it, the psychoacoustical phenomenon in which the subjective frequency response of the ear changes with program level. Because of this effect, a program played at a lower volume than the original level subjectively loses low- and high-frequency response.

**FLOAT**—To disconnect from ground.

**FLUTTER**—A rapid periodic variation in tape speed.

**FLUTTER ECHOES**—A rapid series of echoes that occurs between two parallel walls.

**FLUX**—Magnetic lines of force.

**FLUXIVITY**—The measure of the flux density of a magnetic recording tape, per unit of track width.

**FLY-IN (LAY-IN)**—To copy part of a recorded track onto another recorder, then re-record that copy back onto the original multitrack tape in a different part of the song, in sync with other recorded tracks. For example, copy the vocal track from the first chorus of the song onto an external DAW or sampler. Re-record (fly-in) that copy onto the multitrack tape at the second chorus. Then the first and second choruses have identical vocal performances.

**FOLDBACK (FB)**—*See* Cue System.

**FREQUENCY**—The number of cycles per second of a sound wave or an audio signal, measured in hertz (Hz). A low frequency (for example, 100 Hz) has a low pitch; a high frequency (for example, 10,000 Hz) has a high pitch.

**FREQUENCY RESPONSE**—1. The range of frequencies that an audio device will reproduce at an equal level (within a tolerance, such as ± 3 dB). 2. The range of frequencies that a device (mic, human ear, etc.) can detect.

**FULL TRACK**—A single tape track recorded across the full width of a tape.

**FUNDAMENTAL**—The lowest frequency in a complex wave.

**GAIN**—Amplification. The ratio, expressed in decibels, between the output voltage and the input voltage, or between the output power and the input power.

**GAP**—In a tape-recorder head, the thin break in the electromagnet that contacts the tape.

**GATE**—1. To turn off a signal when its amplitude falls below a preset value. 2. The signal-processing device used for this purpose. *See also* Noise Gate.

**GATED REVERB**—Reverberation with the reverberant "tail" cut off before it fades out.

**GENERAL MIDI FILE (GM file)**—A MIDI file containing a standard set of musical instrument sounds. A General MIDI file produces the same sounds on any MIDI-capable instrument that supports the GM spec.

**GENERATION**—A copy of a tape or a bounce of a track. A copy of the original master recording is a first generation tape. A copy made from the first generation tape is a second generation, and so on.

**GENERATION LOSS**—The degradation of signal quality (the increase in noise and distortion) that occurs with each successive generation of a tape recording.

**GOBO**—A moveable partition used to prevent the sound of an instrument from reaching another instrument's microphone. Short for go-between.

**GRAPHIC EQUALIZER**—An equalizer with a horizontal row of faders; the fader-knob positions indicate graphically the frequency response of the equalizer. Usually used to equalize monitor speakers for the room they are in. Sometimes used for complex EQ of a track.

**GROUND**—The zero-signal reference point for a system of audio components.

**GROUND BUS**—A common connection to which equipment is grounded, usually a heavy copper plate.

**GROUNDING**—Connecting pieces of electronic equipment to ground. Proper grounding ensures that there is no voltage difference between equipment chassis. An electrostatic shield needs to be grounded to be effective.

**GROUND LOOP**—1. A loop or circuit formed of ground leads. 2. The loop formed when unbalanced components are connected together via two ground paths—the connecting-cable shield and the power ground. Ground loops cause hum and should be avoided.

**GROUP**—*See* Submix.

**GSIF**—GigaSampler Interface, Nemesys' Windows sound card driver that achieves low latency by interfacing directly between the sound card and the audio application software.

**GUARD BAND**—The spacing between tracks on a multitrack tape or tape head, used to prevent crosstalk.

**HALF-TRACK**—A tape track recorded across approximately half the width of a tape. A half-track recorder usually records two such tracks simultaneously in the same direction to make a stereo recording.

**HARD DISK**—A random-access storage medium for computer data. A hard-disk drive contains a stack of magnetically coated hard disks that are read by, and written to by, an electromagnetic head.

**HARD-DISK RECORDER**—A device dedicated to recording digital audio on a hard-disk drive. A hard-disk recorder–mixer includes a built-in mixer.

**HARMONIC**—An overtone whose frequency is a whole-number multiple of the fundamental frequency.

**HARMONIZER**—A signal processor that provides a wide variety of pitch-shifting and delay effects.

**HD**—Abbreviation for hard-disk drive.

**HEAD**—An electromagnet in a tape recorder that either erases the audio signal on tape, records a signal on tape, or plays back a signal that is already on tape.

**HEAD GAP**—*See* Gap.

**HEADPHONES**—A head-worn transducer that covers the ears and converts electrical audio signals into sound waves.

**HEADROOM**—The safety margin, measured in decibels, between the signal level and the maximum undistorted signal level. In a tape recorder, the dB difference between standard operating level (corresponding to a 0 VU reading) and the level causing 3% total harmonic distortion. High-frequency headroom increases with analog tape speed.

**HERTZ (Hz)**—Cycles per second, the unit of measurement of frequency.

**HIGHPASS FILTER**—A filter that passes frequencies above a certain frequency and attenuates frequencies below that same frequency. A low-cut filter.

517

**HISS**—A noise signal containing all frequencies, but with greater energy at higher octaves. Hiss sounds like wind blowing through trees. It is usually caused by random signals generated by microphones, electronics, and magnetic tape.

**HOT**—1. A high recording level causing slight distortion, maybe used for special effect. 2. A condition in which a chassis or circuit has a potentially dangerous voltage on it. 3. Referring to the conductor in a microphone cable that has a positive voltage on it at the instant that sound pressure moves the diaphragm inward.

**HUM**—An unwanted low-pitched tone (60 Hz and its harmonics) heard in the monitors. The sound of interference generated in audio circuits and cables by AC power wiring. Hum pickup is caused by such things as faulty grounding, poor shielding, and ground loops.

**HYPERCARDIOID MICROPHONE**—A directional microphone with a polar pattern that has 12 dB attenuation at the sides, 6 dB attenuation at the rear, and two nulls of maximum rejection at 110 degrees off-axis.

**IMAGE**—An illusory sound source located somewhere around the listener. An image is generated by two or more loudspeakers. In a typical stereo system, images are located between the two stereo speakers.

**IMPEDANCE**—The opposition of a circuit to the flow of alternating current. Impedance is the complex sum of resistance and reactance. Abbreviated as Z.

**INPUT**—The connection going into an audio device. In a mixer or mixing console, a connector for a microphone, line-level device, or other signal source.

**INPUT ATTENUATOR**—*See* Attenuator.

**INPUT MODULE**—In a mixing console, the set of controls affecting a single input signal. An input module usually includes an attenuator (trim), fader, equalizer, effects send, cue send, and channel-assign controls.

**INPUT SECTION**—The row of input modules in a mixing console.

**INPUT/OUTPUT (I/O) CONSOLE (IN-LINE CONSOLE)**—A mixing console arranged so that input and output sections are aligned vertically. Each module (other than the monitor section) contains one input channel and one output channel.

**INSERT JACKS**—*See* Access Jacks.

**JACK**—A female or receptacle-type connector for audio signals into which a plug is inserted.

**KEYBOARD WORKSTATION**—Several MIDI components in one chassis—a keyboard, a sample player, a sequencer, and perhaps a synthesizer and disk drive.

**KILO**—A prefix meaning one thousand. Abbreviated k.

**LATENCY**—The signal delay through an A/D, D/A converter, through a software program, or through a computer operating system. Monitoring latency is the delay between the time when a musician plays a note and when she hears the monitored signal of that note. Latency can make you play out-of-sync during overdubs.

**LAY-IN**—*See* Fly-In.

**LEADERING**—The process of splicing leader tape between program selections.

**LEADER TAPE**—Plastic or paper tape without an oxide coating, used for a spacer between takes (for silence between songs).

**LEAKAGE**—The overlap of an instrument's sound into another instrument's microphone. Also called bleed or spill.

**LEDE**—Abbreviation for Live-End/Dead-End, a type of control room acoustic treatment in which the front half of the control room prevents early reflections to the mixing position, while the back half of the control room reflects diffused sound to the mixing position.

**LED INDICATOR**—A recording-level indicator using one or more light-emitting diodes.

**LEVEL**—The degree of intensity of an audio signal—the voltage, power, or sound pressure level. The original definition of level is the power in watts.

**LEVEL SETTING**—In a recording system, the process of adjusting the input-signal level to obtain maximum level on the recording medium without distortion. A VU meter or other indicator shows recording level.

**LIMITER**—A signal processor whose output is constant above a preset input level. A compressor with a compression ratio of 10:1 or greater, with the threshold set just below the point of distortion of the following device. Used to prevent distortion of attack transients or peaks.

**LINE LEVEL**—In balanced professional recording equipment, a signal whose level is approximately 1.23 volts (+4 dBm). In unbalanced equipment (most home hi-fi or semipro recording equipment), a signal whose level is approximately 0.316 volt (−10 dBV).

**LIVE**—1. Having audible reverberation. 2. Occurring in real time, in person.

**LIVE RECORDING**—A recording made at a concert. Also, a recording made of a musical ensemble playing all at once, rather than overdubbing.

**LOCALIZATION**—The ability of the human hearing system to tell the direction of a real or illusory sound source.

**LOOP**—In a sampling program, to play the sustain portion of a sound's envelope repeatedly.

**LOUDSPEAKER**—A transducer that converts electrical energy (the signal) into acoustical energy (sound waves).

**LOWPASS FILTER**—A filter that passes frequencies below a certain frequency and attenuates frequencies above that same frequency. A high-cut filter.

**M**—Abbreviation for mega, or one million (as in megabytes).

**MAGNETIC RECORDING TAPE**—A recording medium made of magnetic particles (usually ferric oxide) suspended in a binder and coated on long strip of thin plastic (usually Mylar).

**MAGNETO-OPTICAL DRIVE (MO DRIVE)**—A drive that stores data (such as audio) on a 3.5-inch rewritable magneto-optical disk. The drive uses a laser and magnetic head to write data, and a laser to read data.

**MASK**—To hide or cover up one sound with another sound. To make a sound inaudible by playing another sound along with it. Masking is used in many data reduction schemes.

**MASTER FADER**—A volume control that affects the level of all program busses simultaneously. It is the last stage of gain adjustment before the 2-track recorder.

**MASTER TAPE**—A completed tape used to generate tape copies or compact discs.

**MD**—Abbreviation for MiniDisc.

**MDM**—Abbreviation for Modular Digital Multitrack.

**MEMORY**—A group of integrated circuit chips used to store digital data temporarily or permanently (such as an audio signal in digital format).

**MEMORY REWIND**—A tape-recorder function that rewinds the tape to a preset tape-counter position.

**METER**—A device that indicates voltage, resistance, current, or signal level.

**MIC**—An abbreviation for microphone.

**MIC LEVEL**—The level or voltage of a signal produced by a microphone, typically 2 millivolts.

**MIC PREAMP**—*See* Preamplifier.

**MICROPHONE**—A transducer or device that converts an acoustical signal (sound) into a corresponding electrical signal.

**MICROPHONE TECHNIQUES**—The selection and placement of microphones to pick up sound sources.

**MIDI**—Abbreviation for Musical Instrument Digital Interface, a specification for a connection between synthesizers, drum machines, and computers that allows them to communicate with and/or control each other.

**MIDI CHANNEL**—A route for transmitting and receiving MIDI signals. Each channel controls a separate MIDI musical instrument or synth patch. Up to 16 channels can be sent on a single MIDI cable.

**MIDI CONTROLLER**—A musical performance device (keyboard, drum pads, breath controller, etc.) that outputs a MIDI signal designating note numbers, note on, note off, and so on.

**MIDI/DIGITAL AUDIO SOFTWARE**—Software that combines a MIDI sequencer with a multitrack digital audio recorder/editor.

**MIDI IN**—A connector in a MIDI device that receives MIDI messages.

**MIDI INTERFACE**—A circuit that plugs into a computer and converts MIDI data into computer data for storage in memory or on hard disk. The interface also converts computer data into MIDI data.

**MIDI OUT**—A connector in a MIDI device that transmits MIDI messages.

**MIDI THRU**—A connector in a MIDI device that duplicates the MIDI information at the MIDI-In connector. Used to connect another MIDI device in the series.

**MID-SIDE**—A coincident-pair stereo microphone technique using a forward-facing unidirectional, omnidirectional, or bidirectional mic and a side-facing bidirectional mic. The microphone signals are summed and differenced to produce right- and left-channel signals.

**MILLI**—A prefix meaning one thousandth, abbreviated m.

**MIKE**—To pick up with a microphone.

**MINIDISC (MD)**—A rewritable, magneto-optical storage medium that is read by a laser. It resembles a compact disc in a 2.5-inch square housing. MD recorders use a data compression scheme called ATRAC.

**MIX**—1. To combine two or more different signals into a common signal. 2. A control on a delay unit that varies the ratio between the dry signal and the delayed signal.

**MIXDOWN**—The process of playing recorded tape tracks through a mixing console and mixing them to two stereo channels for recording on a two-track tape recorder.

**MIXER**—A device that mixes or combines audio signals and controls the relative levels of the signals.

**MIXING CONSOLE**—A large mixer with additional functions such as equalization or tone control, pan pots, monitoring controls, solo functions, channel assigns, and control of signals sent to external signal processors.

**MLP (Meridian Lossless Packing)**—Used in DVD-Audio discs, a data-reduction method that compresses six full-range channels of 24-bit, 96 kHz audio without data loss.

**MMC (MIDI Machine Control)**—A set of MIDI commands by which one device can control another. Some commands include Start, Stop, and Locate. MMC does not include sync information, but MTC does.

**MO DRIVE**—*See* Magneto-optical Drive.

**MODELER**—A device or software that simulates the sound of a microphone, guitar amp, or room.

**MODULAR DIGITAL MULTITRACK (MDM)**—A multitrack tape recorder that records 8 tracks digitally on a videocassette. Several 8-track modules can be linked together to add more tracks in sync. Two examples of MDMs are the Alesis ADAT and TASCAM DA-88.

**MONITOR**—A loudspeaker in a control room, or headphones, used for judging sound quality. Also, a video display screen used with a computer.

**MONITORING**—Listening to an audio signal with a monitor.

**MONAURAL**—Referring to listening with one ear. Often incorrectly used to mean monophonic.

**MONO, MONOPHONIC**—1. Referring to a single channel of audio. A monophonic program can be played over one or more loudspeakers, or one or more headphones. 2. Describing a synthesizer that plays only one note at a time (not chords).

**MONO-COMPATIBLE**—A characteristic of a stereo program, in which the program channels can be combined to a mono program without altering the frequency response or balance. A mono-compatible stereo program has the same frequency response in stereo or mono because there is no delay or phase shift between channels to cause phase interference.

**MOVING-COIL MICROPHONE**—A dynamic microphone in which the conductor is a coil of wire moving in a fixed magnetic field. The coil is attached to a diaphragm which vibrates when struck with sound waves. Usually called a dynamic microphone.

**MP3 (MPEG Level-1 Layer-3)**—A data compression format for audio. In an MP3 file (.mp3), the data has been compressed or reduced to $\frac{1}{10}$ its original size or less. Compressed files take up less memory, so they download faster. You download MP3 files to your hard drive, then listen to them. MP3 audio quality at a 128 kbps rate is nearly the same as that of CDs (depending on source material).

**MP3PRO**—A data-compression format for audio. MP3Pro is an improvement over MP3. Songs encoded at 64 kbps with MP3Pro are said to sound as good as songs encoded at 128 kbps with MP3. MP3Pro offers faster downloads and nearly double the amount of music you can put on a flash-memory player. MP3 and MP3Pro files are compatible with each other's players, but an MP3Pro player is needed to hear MP3Pro's improvement in sound quality.

**M-S RECORDING**—*See* Mid-side.

**MTC (MIDI Time Code)**—A form of time code transmitted over MIDI, used for synchronizing MIDI devices. Unlike SMPTE, MTC is not sample-accurate.

**MUDDY**—Unclear sounding; having excessive leakage, reverberation, or overhang.

**MULTIEFFECTS PROCESSOR**—*See* Multiprocessor.

**MULTIPLE-D MICROPHONE**—A directional microphone that has multiple sound-path lengths between its front and rear sound entries. This type of microphone has minimal proximity effect.

**MULTIPROCESSOR**—A signal processor that can perform several different signal-processing functions.

**MULTITIMBRAL**—In a synthesizer, the ability to produce two or more different patches or timbres at the same time.

**MULTITRACK**—Referring to a recorder or tape-recorder head that has more than two tracks.

**MUTE**—To turn off an input signal on a mixing console by disconnecting the input-module output from channel assign and direct out. During mixdown, the mute function is used to reduce tape noise during silent portions of tracks, or to turn off unused performances. During recording, mute is used to turn off mic signals.

**NEAR COINCIDENT**—A stereo microphone technique in which two directional microphones are angled apart symmetrically on either side of center and spaced a few inches apart horizontally.

**NEARFIELD MONITORING**—A monitor-speaker arrangement in which the speakers are placed very near the listener (usually just behind the mixing console) to reduce the audibility of control-room acoustics.

**NOISE**—Unwanted sound, such as hiss from electronics or tape. An audio signal with an irregular, non-periodic waveform.

**NOISE GATE**—A gate used to reduce or eliminate noise between notes.

**NOISE-REDUCTION SYSTEM**—A signal processor (Dolby or dbx) used to reduce tape hiss (and sometimes print-through) caused by the recording process. Some of these systems compress the signal during recording and expand it in a complementary fashion during playback.

**NONDESTRUCTIVE EDITING**—In a digital audio workstation, editing done by changing pointers (location markers) to information on the hard disk. A nondestructive edit can be undone.

**NONLINEAR**—1. Referring to a storage medium in which any data point can be accessed or read almost instantly. Examples are a hard disk, compact disc, and MiniDisc. *See* Random Access. 2. Referring to an audio device that is distorting the signal.

**OCTAVE**—The interval between any two frequencies where the upper frequency is twice the lower frequency.

**OFF-AXIS**—Not directly in front of a microphone or loudspeaker.

**OFF-AXIS COLORATION**—In a microphone, the deviation from the on-axis frequency response that sometimes occurs at angles off the axis of the microphone. The coloration of sound (alteration of tone quality) for sounds arriving off-axis to the microphone.

**OMNIDIRECTIONAL MICROPHONE**—A microphone that is equally sensitive to sounds arriving from all directions.

**ON-LOCATION RECORDING**—A recording made outside the studio, in a room or hall where the music usually is performed or practiced.

**OPEN TRACKS**—On a multitrack tape recorder, tracks that have not yet been used, or have already been bounced and are available for use.

**ORTF**—Named after the French broadcasting network (Office de Radiodiffusion Television Française), a near-coincident stereo mic technique that uses two cardioid mics angled 110 degrees apart and spaced 17 cm horizontally.

**OUTBOARD EQUIPMENT**—Signal processors that are external to the mixing console.

**OUTPUT**—A connector in an audio device from which the signal comes and feeds successive devices.

**OUTTAKE**—A take, or section of a take, that is to be removed or not used.

**OVERDUB**—To record a new musical part on an unused track in synchronization with previously recorded tracks.

**OVERHANG**—The continuation of a signal at the output of a device after the input signal has ceased. Sometimes called ringing.

**OVERLOAD**—The distortion that occurs when an applied signal exceeds a system's maximum input level.

**OVERTONE**—In a complex wave, a frequency component that is higher than the fundamental frequency.

**PAD**—*See* Attenuator.

**PAN POT**—Abbreviation for panoramic potentiometer. In each input module in a mixing console, a control that divides a signal between two channels in an adjustable ratio. By doing so, a pan pot controls the location of a sonic image between a stereo pair of loudspeakers.

**PARAMETRIC EQUALIZER**—An equalizer with continuously variable parameters, such as frequency, bandwidth, and amount of boost or cut.

**PATCH**—1. To connect one piece of audio equipment to another with a cable. 2. A setting of synthesizer parameters to achieve a sound with a certain timbre.

525

**PATCH BAY (PATCH PANEL)**—An array of connectors, usually in a rack, to which equipment inputs and outputs are wired. A patch bay makes it easy to interconnect various pieces of equipment in a central, accessible location.

**PATCH CORD**—A short length of cable with a coaxial plug on each end, used for signal routing in a patch bay.

**PEAK**—On a graph of a sound wave or signal, the highest point in the waveform. The point of greatest voltage or sound pressure in a cycle.

**PEAK AMPLITUDE**—*See* Amplitude, Peak.

**PEAKING EQUALIZER**—An equalizer that provides maximum cut or boost at one frequency, so that the resulting frequency response of a boost resembles a mountain peak.

**PEAK PROGRAM METER (PPM)**—A meter that responds fast enough to closely follow the peak levels in a program.

**PERIOD**—The time between the peak of one wave and the peak of the next. The time between corresponding points on successive waves. Period is the inverse of frequency.

**PERSONAL STUDIO**—A minimal group of recording equipment set up for one's personal use, usually using a 4-track cassette recorder–mixer. Also, a simple 4-track cassette recorder–mixer for one's personal use.

**PERSPECTIVE**—In the reproduction of a recording, the audible sense of distance to the musical ensemble, the point of view. A close perspective has a high ratio of direct sound to reverberant sound; a distant perspective has a low ratio of direct sound to reverberant sound.

**PFL**—Abbreviation for prefader listen. *See also* Solo.

**PHANTOM POWER**—A DC voltage (usually 12 to 48 volts) applied to microphone signal conductors to power condenser microphones.

**PHASE**—The degree of progression in the cycle of a wave, where one complete cycle is 360 degrees.

**PHASE CANCELLATION, PHASE INTERFERENCE**—The cancellation of certain frequency components of a signal that occurs when the signal is combined with its delayed replica. At certain frequencies, the direct and delayed signals are of equal level and opposite polarity (180 degrees out of phase), and when combined, they cancel out. The result is a comb-filter frequency response having a periodic series of peaks and dips. Phase interference can occur between the signals of two microphones picking up the same source at different distances, or can occur at a microphone picking up both a direct sound and its reflection from a nearby surface.

**PHASE SHIFT**—The difference in degrees of phase angle between corresponding points on two waves. If one wave is delayed with respect to another, there is a phase shift between them of $2\pi FT$, where $\pi = 3.14$, $F$ = frequency in Hz, and $T$ = delay in seconds.

**PHASING**—A special effect in which a signal is combined with its phase-shifted replica to produce a variable comb-filter effect. *See also* Flanging.

**PHONE PLUG**—A cylindrical, coaxial plug (usually ¼-inch diameter). An unbalanced phone plug has a tip for the hot signal and a sleeve for the shield or ground. A balanced phone plug has a tip for the signal hot signal, a ring for the return signal, and a sleeve for the shield or ground.

**PHONO PLUG**—A coaxial plug with a central pin for the hot signal and a ring of pressure-fit tabs for the shield or ground. Also called RCA plug.

**PICKUP**—A piezoelectric transducer that converts mechanical vibrations to an electrical signal. Used in acoustic guitars, acoustic basses, and fiddles. Also, a magnetic transducer in an electric guitar that converts string vibration to a corresponding electrical signal.

**PINCH ROLLER**—In a tape-recorder transport, the rubber wheel that pinches or traps the tape between itself and the capstan, so that the capstan can move the tape.

**PING-PONGING**—*See* Bouncing Tracks.

**PINK NOISE**—A noise signal containing all frequencies (unless band-limited), with equal energy per octave. Pink noise is a test signal used for equalizing a sound system to the desired frequency response, and for testing loudspeakers.

**PITCH**—The subjective lowness or highness of a tone. The pitch of a tone usually correlates with the fundamental frequency.

**PITCH CONTROL**—A control on a tape recorder that varies the tape speed, thereby varying the pitch of the signal on tape. The pitch control can be used to match the pitch of prerecorded instruments with that of an instrument to be overdubbed. It is also used for special effects, such as "chipmunk voices," and to play prerecorded tracks slowly so that fast musical passages can be overdubbed more easily.

**PITCH SHIFTER**—A signal processor that changes the pitch of an instrument without changing its duration.

**PLAYBACK EQUALIZATION**—In tape-recorder electronics, fixed equalization applied to the signal during recording to compensate for certain losses.

**PLAYBACK HEAD**—The head in a tape recorder that picks up a prerecorded magnetic signal from the moving tape and converts it to a corresponding electrical signal. The playback head is not the same as the sel-sync or sync head.

**PLAYLIST**—*See* Edit Decision List.

**PLUG**—A male connector that inserts into a jack.

**PLUG-IN**—Effects software which you load into your digital-editing program (called the "host"). The plug-in becomes part of the host program and can be called up from within the host. Some manufacturers make plug-in bundles, which are a variety of effects in a single package.

**POLAR PATTERN**—The directional pickup pattern of a microphone. A plot of microphone sensitivity plotted versus angle of sound incidence. Examples of polar patterns are omnidirectional, bidirectional, and unidirectional. Subsets of unidirectional are cardioid, supercardioid, and hypercardioid.

**POLARITY**—Referring to the positive or negative direction of an electrical, acoustical, or magnetic force. Two identical signals in opposite polarity are 180 degrees out-of-phase with each other at all frequencies.

**POLYPHONIC**—Describing a synthesizer that can play more than one note at a time (chords).

**POP**—1. A thump or little explosion sound heard in a vocalist's microphone signal. Pop occurs when the user says words with "p," "t," or "b" so that a turbulent puff of air is forced from the mouth and strikes the microphone diaphragm. 2. A noise heard when a mic is plugged into a monitored channel, or when a switch is flipped.

**POP FILTER**—A screen placed on a microphone grille that attenuates or filters out pop disturbances before they strike the microphone diaphragm. Usually made of open-cell plastic foam or silk, a pop filter reduces pop and wind noise.

**PORTABLE STUDIO**—A combination recorder and mixer in one portable chassis.

**POST-ECHO**—A repetition of a sound, following the original sound, caused by print-through.

**POWER AMPLIFIER**—An electronic device that amplifies or increases the power level fed into it to a level sufficient to drive a loudspeaker.

**POWER GROUND (SAFETY GROUND)**—A connection to the power company's earth ground through the U-shaped hole in a power outlet. In the power cable of an electronic component with a 3-prong plug, the U-shaped prong is wired to the component's chassis. This wire conducts electricity to power ground if the chassis becomes electrically hot, preventing shocks.

**PREAMPLIFIER (PREAMP)**—In an audio system, the first stage of amplification that boosts a mic-level signal to line level. A preamp is a stand-alone device or a circuit in a mixer.

**PREDELAY**—Short for pre-reverberation delay. The delay (about 30 to 150 msec) between the arrival of the direct sound and the onset of reverberation. Usually, the longer the predelay, the greater the perceived room size.

**PRE-ECHO**—A repetition of a sound that occurs before the sound itself, caused by print-through.

**PREFADER/POSTFADER SWITCH**—A switch that selects a signal either ahead of the fader (prefader) or following the fader (postfader). The level of a prefader signal is independent of the fader position; the level of a postfader signal follows the fader position.

**PREPRODUCTION**—Planning in advance what you're going to do at a recording session, in terms of track assignments, overdubbing, studio layout, and microphone selection.

**PRESENCE**—The audible sense that a reproduced instrument is present in the listening room. Some synonyms are closeness, definition, and punch. Presence is often created by an equalization boost in the midrange or upper midrange.

**PRESSURE ZONE MICROPHONE**—A boundary microphone constructed with the microphone diaphragm parallel with, and facing, a reflective surface.

**PREVERB**—A special effect in which the reverberation of a note precedes it, rather than follows it. Preverb is achieved by playing an instrument's track backwards while adding reverberation to it, and recording the reverberation on an unused track. When the tape is reversed so that the instrument's track plays forward, preverb is heard as the reverberation plays backwards.

**PRINT**—To record on tape or disc.

**PRINT-THROUGH**—The transfer of a magnetic signal from one layer of tape to the next on a reel, causing an echo preceding or following the program.

**PRODUCTION**—1. A recording that is enhanced by special effects. 2. The supervision of a recording session to create a satisfactory recording. This involves getting musicians together for the session, making musical suggestions to the musicians to enhance their performance, and making suggestions to the engineer for sound balance and effects.

**PROGRAM BUS**—A bus or output that feeds an audio program to a recorder track.

**PROGRAM MIXER**—In a mixing console, a mixer formed of input-module outputs, combining amplifiers, and program busses.

**PRO TOOLS**—The most popular digital audio editing platform for professional use. It offers computer multitrack recording, overdubbing, mixing, editing, effects, and a variety of plug-ins.

**PROXIMITY EFFECT**—The bass boost that occurs with a single-D directional microphone when it is placed a few inches from a sound source. The closer the microphone, the greater the low-frequency boost due to proximity effect.

**PULSE CODE MODULATION**—A method of analog-to-digital conversion. The analog signal voltage is measured several thousand times a second, and each measurement is a digital word (a string of 1s and 0s) of a certain word length or bit depth.

**PUNCH IN/OUT**—A feature in a multitrack recorder that lets you insert a recording of a corrected musical part into a previously recorded track by going into and out of record mode as the tape is rolling.

**PURE WAVEFORM**—A waveform of a single frequency; a sine wave. A pure tone is the perceived sound of such a wave.

**QUARTER-TRACK**—A tape track recorded across one-quarter of the width of the tape. A quarter-track recorder usually records two stereo programs (one in each direction).

**RACK**—A 19-inch-wide wooden or metal cabinet used to hold audio equipment.

**RADIO-FREQUENCY INTERFERENCE (RFI)**—Radio-frequency electromagnetic waves induced in audio cables or equipment, causing various noises in the audio signal.

**RANDOM ACCESS**—Referring to a storage medium in which any data point can be accessed or read almost instantly. Examples are a hard disk, compact disc, and MiniDisc.

**RAREFACTION**—The portion of a sound wave in which molecules are spread apart, forming a region with lower-than-normal atmospheric pressure. The opposite of compression.

**R-DAT**—*See* DAT.

**REALAUDIO G2**—A highly compressed audio file format used for streaming audio. Generally, RealAudio G2 has lower fidelity (less treble) than MP3, but the fidelity depends on modem speed. RealAudio files (.ra or .rm) are often used as short excerpts or previews of songs.

**REAL-TIME RECORDING**—1. Recording notes into a sequencer in the correct tempo, for later playback at the same tempo as recorded. 2. A recording made direct to lacquer disc or direct to 2-track without any overdubs or mixdown.

**RECIRCULATION (REGENERATION)**—Feeding the output of a delay device back into its input to create multiple echoes. Also, the control on a delay device that affects how much delayed signal is recycled to the input.

**RECORD**—To store an event in permanent form. Usually, to store an audio signal in magnetic form on magnetic tape. Recording is also possible on hard disk, on compact disc (CD-R), on magneto-optical disk, on MiniDisc, and in RAM.

**RECORD EQUALIZATION**—In tape-recorder electronics, equalization applied to the signal during recording to compensate for certain losses.

**RECORDER–MIXER**—A combination multitrack recorder and mixer in one chassis.

**RECORD HEAD**—The head in a tape recorder that puts the audio signal on tape by magnetizing the tape particles in a pattern corresponding to the audio signal.

**RECORDING/REPRODUCTION CHAIN**—The series of events and equipment that are involved in sound recording and playback.

**REFLECTED SOUND**—Sound waves that reach the listener after being reflected from one or more surfaces.

**REGENERATION**—*See* Recirculation.

**REGION**—In a digital audio editing program, a defined segment of the audio program.

**RELEASE**—The final portion of a note's envelope in which the note falls from its sustain level back to silence.

**RELEASE TIME**—In a compressor, the time it takes for the gain to return to normal after the end of a loud passage.

**REMIX**—To mix again; to do another mixdown with different console settings or different editing.

**REMOTE RECORDING**—*See* On-Location Recording.

**REMOVABLE HARD DRIVE**—A hard-disk drive that can be removed and replaced with another, used in a digital audio workstation to store a long program temporarily.

**RESISTANCE**—The opposition of a circuit to a flow of direct current. Resistance is measured in ohms, abbreviated ω, and may be calculated by dividing voltage by current.

**RESISTOR**—An electronic component that opposes current flow.

**RETURN-TO-ZERO**—*See* Memory Rewind.

**REVERBERATION**—Natural reverberation in a room is a series of multiple sound reflections that make the original sound persist and gradually die away or decay. These reflections tell the ear that you're listening in a large or hard-surfaced room. For example, reverberation is the sound you hear just after you shout in an empty gymnasium. A reverb effect simulates the sound of a room—a club, auditorium, or concert hall—by generating random multiple echoes that are too numerous and rapid for the ear to resolve. The timing of the echoes is random, and the echoes increase in number with time as they decay. An echo is a discrete repetition of a sound; reverberation is a continuous fade-out of sound.

**REVERBERATION TIME (RT60)**—The time it takes for reverberation to decay to 60 dB below the original steady-state level.

**REVERSE ECHO**—A multiple echo that precedes the sound that caused it, building up from silence into the original sound. This special effect is created in a manner similar to preverb.

**RFI**—*See* Radio Frequency Interference.

**RHYTHM TRACKS**—The recorded tracks of the rhythm instruments (guitar, bass, drums, and sometimes keyboards).

**RIBBON MICROPHONE**—A dynamic microphone in which the conductor is a long metallic diaphragm (ribbon) suspended in a magnetic field.

**RIDE GAIN**—To turn down the volume of a microphone when the source gets louder, and turn up the volume when the source gets quieter, in an attempt to reduce dynamic range.

**RINGING**—*See* Overhang.

**RMF (Rich Music Format)**—A format for a MIDI file with General MIDI sounds plus custom sounds. Designed to be played on a Beatnik player.

**ROOM MODES**—*See* Standing Wave.

**RT60**—*See* Reverberation Time.

**SACD**—*See* Super Audio CD.

**SAFETY COPY**—A copy of the master tape, to be used if the master tape is lost or damaged.

**SAFETY GROUND**—*See* Power Ground.

**SAMPLE**—1. To digitally record a short sound event, such as a single note or a musical phrase, into computer memory. 2. A recording of such an event.

**SAMPLING**—Recording a short sound event into computer memory. The audio signal is converted into digital data representing the signal waveform, and the data is stored in memory chips, tape, or disc for later playback.

**SATURATION**—Overload of magnetic tape. The point at which a further increase in magnetizing force does not cause an increase in magnetization of the tape oxide particles. Distortion is the result.

**SCENE AUTOMATION**—A form of console automation in which the static console settings are stored in memory. A "snapshot" or reading of many of the settings is taken and stored for later recall. In contrast, dynamic automation continuously follows the fader and knob moves, and the automation data is usually stored as a MIDI file.

**SCMS (Serial Copy Management System)**—An anti-copy scheme in consumer digital audio devices (those with S/PDIF connectors). SCMS circuits read flags in the data stream that allow users to make only first-generation copies, not copies of copies.

**SCRATCH VOCAL**—A vocal performance that is done simultaneously with the rhythm instruments so that the musicians can keep their place in the song and get a feel for the song. Because it contains leakage, the scratch-vocal recording is usually erased. Then the singer overdubs the vocal part that is to be used in the final recording.

**SCRUB**—To manually move an open-reel tape slowly back and forth across a recorder playback head in order to locate an edit point. Some digital editing software has an equivalent scrubbing function.

**SCSI**—Small Computer Systems Interface, a standard spec for high-speed computer input and output. Commonly used for hard drives, CD-ROM drives, and CD-R recorders. Supports up to seven devices.

**SENSITIVITY**—1. The output of a microphone in volts for a given input in sound pressure level. 2. The sound pressure level a loudspeaker produces at one meter when driven with 1 watt of pink noise. *See also* Sound Pressure Level.

**SEQUENCE**—A MIDI data file of musical-performance note parameters, recorded by a sequencer.

**SEQUENCER**—A device that records a musical performance done on a MIDI controller (in the form of note numbers, note on, note off, etc.) into computer memory or hard disk for later playback. A computer can act as a sequencer when it runs a sequencer program. During playback, the sequencer plays synthesizer sound generators or samples.

**SESSION**—1. A time period set aside for recording musical instruments, voices, or sound effects. 2. On a CD-R, a lead-in, program area, and lead-out.

**SHELVING EQUALIZER**—An equalizer that applies a constant boost or cut above or below a certain frequency, so that the shape of the frequency response resembles a shelf.

**SHIELD**—A conductive enclosure (usually metallic) around one or more signal conductors, used to keep out electrostatic fields that cause hum or buzz.

**SHOCK MOUNT**—A suspension system that mechanically isolates a microphone from its stand or boom, preventing the transfer of mechanical vibrations.

**SIBILANCE**—In a speech recording, excessive frequency components in the 5 to 10 kHz range, which are heard as an overemphasis of "s" and "sh" sounds.

**SIDE-ADDRESSED**—Referring to a microphone whose main axis of pickup is perpendicular to the side of the microphone. You aim the side of the mic at the sound source. *See also* End-Addressed.

**SIGNAL**—A varying electrical voltage that represents information, such as a sound.

**SIGNAL PATH**—The path a signal takes from input to output in a piece of audio equipment.

**SIGNAL PROCESSOR**—A device that is used to alter a signal in a controlled way.

**SIGNAL-TO-NOISE RATIO (S/N)**—The ratio in decibels between signal voltage and noise voltage. An audio component with a high S/N has little background noise accompanying the signal; a component with a low S/N is noisy.

**SINE WAVE**—A wave following the equation $y = \sin x$, where $x$ is degrees and $y$ is voltage or sound pressure level. The waveform of a single frequency. The waveform of a pure tone without harmonics.

**SINGLE-ENDED**—1. An unbalanced line. 2. A single-ended noise reduction system is one that works only during tape playback (unlike Dolby or dbx, which work both during recording and playback).

**SINGLE-D MICROPHONE**—A directional microphone having a single distance between its front and rear sound entries. Such a microphone has proximity effect.

**SLAP, SLAPBACK**—An echo following the original sound by about 50 to 200 msec, sometimes with multiple repetitions.

**SLATE**—At the beginning of a recording, a recorded announcement of the name of the tune and its take number. The term is derived from the slate used in the motion-picture industry to identify the production and take number being filmed.

**SMPTE TIME CODE**—A modulated 1200 Hz square-wave signal used to synchronize two or more recorders or MIDI devices. SMPTE uses the format HH:MM:SS:FF (hours, minutes, seconds, frames) to specify locations in the recorded program. SMPTE is an abbreviation for the Society of Motion Picture and Television Engineers, who developed the time code.

**SNAKE**—A multipair or multichannel mic cable. Also, a multipair mic cable attached to a connector junction box.

**SNAPSHOT AUTOMATION**—*See* Scene Automation.

**SOLO**—On an input module in a mixing console, a switch that lets you monitor that particular input signal by itself. The switch routes only that input signal to the monitor system.

**SOUND**—Longitudinal vibrations in a medium (such as air) in the frequency range 20 Hz to 20,000 Hz.

535

**SOUND CARD**—A circuit card that plugs into a computer and converts an audio signal into computer data for storage in memory or on hard disk. The sound card also converts computer data into an audio signal.

**SOUND MODULE (SOUND GENERATOR)**—1. A synthesizer without a keyboard, containing several different timbres or voices. These sounds are triggered or played by MIDI signals from a sequencer program, or by a MIDI controller. 2. An oscillator.

**SOUND PRESSURE LEVEL (SPL)**—The acoustic pressure of a sound wave, measured in decibels above the threshold of hearing. The higher the SPL of a sound, the louder it is. $\mathrm{dB\,SPL} = 20\log(P/P_{ref})$, where P = the measured acoustic pressure and $P_{ref} = 0.0002\,\mathrm{dyne/cm^2}$.

**SOUND WAVE**—The periodic variations in sound pressure radiating from a sound source.

**SPACED-PAIR**—A stereo microphone technique using two identical microphones spaced several feet apart horizontally, usually aiming straight ahead toward the sound source.

**SPATIAL PROCESSOR**—A signal processor that allows images to be placed beyond the limits of a stereo pair of speakers—even behind the listener or toward the sides.

**S/PDIF**—Sony Philips Digital Interface (IEC 958 Type II). A 2-channel digital signal interface format that uses a 75-ohm coaxial cable with RCA connectors, or an optical cable with TOSLINK connectors. *See also* AES/EBU.

**SPEAKER**—*See* Loudspeaker.

**SPECIAL EFFECTS**—*See* Effects.

**SPECTRUM**—The output versus frequency of a sound source, including the fundamental frequency and overtones.

**SPL**—*See* Sound Pressure Level.

**SPLICE**—To join the ends of two lengths of magnetic tape or leader tape with tape. Also, a splice is the taped joint between two lengths of magnetic tape or leader tape.

**SPLICING BLOCK**—*See* Editing Block.

**SPLIT CONSOLE**—A console with a separate monitor-mixer section. *See also* In-Line Console.

**SPLITTER**—A transformer or circuit used to divide a microphone signal into two or more identical signals to feed different sound systems.

536

**SPOT MICROPHONE**—In classical music recording, a close-placed microphone that is mixed with more distant microphones to add presence or to improve the balance.

**STANDING WAVE**—An apparently stationary waveform, created by multiple reflections between opposite room surfaces. At certain points along the standing wave, the direct and reflected waves cancel, and at other points the waves add together or reinforce each other.

**STEM**—A submix in ProTools lingo—a drums submix, keys submix, left-front submix, etc.

**STEP-TIME RECORDING**—Recording notes into a sequencer one at a time without regard to tempo, for later playback at a normal tempo.

**STEREO, STEREOPHONIC**—An audio recording and reproduction system with correlated information between two channels (usually discrete channels), meant to be heard over two or more loudspeakers to give the illusion of sound-source localization and depth.

**STEREO BAR, STEREO MICROPHONE ADAPTER**—A microphone stand adapter that mounts two microphones on a single stand for convenient stereo miking.

**STEREO IMAGING**—The ability of a stereo recording or reproduction system to form clearly defined audio images at various locations between a stereo pair of loudspeakers.

**STEREO MICROPHONE**—A microphone containing two mic capsules in a single housing for convenient stereo recording. The capsules usually are coincident.

**STREAMING AUDIO**—Audio sent over the Internet in real time. A streaming file plays as soon as you click on its title. A downloaded file doesn't play until you copy the entire file to your hard disk. Streaming audio is heard almost instantly, but usually sounds muffled and can be interrupted by Net congestion. With downloaded audio, you must wait up to several minutes to hear the song, but the sound is high-fidelity and continuous.

**STUDIO**—A room used or designed for sound recording.

**SUBMASTER**—1. A master volume control for an output bus. 2. A recorded tape that is used to form a master tape.

**SUBMIX**—A small preset mix within a larger mix, such as a drum mix, keyboard mix, vocal mix, etc. Also a cue mix, monitor mix, or effects mix.

**SUBMIXER**—A smaller mixer within a mixing console (or standalone) that is used to set up a submix, a cue mix, an effects mix, or a monitor mix.

**SUPER AUDIO CD (SACD)**—An alternative to DVD-Audio, Super Audio CD was developed by Sony and Philips. It is the size of a CD but offers higher sound quality and 5.1 surround sound. SACD uses the Direct Stream Digital (DSD) process, which encodes a digital signal in a 1-bit (bit-stream) format at a 2.8224 MHz sampling rate. This system offers a frequency response from DC to 100 kHz with 120 dB dynamic range.

**SUPERCARDIOID MICROPHONE**—A unidirectional microphone that attenuates side-arriving sounds by 8.7 dB, attenuates rear-arriving sounds by 11.4 dB, and has two nulls of maximum sound rejection at 125 degrees off-axis.

**SUPPLY REEL**—*See* Feed Reel.

**SURROUND SOUND**—A multichannel recording and reproduction system that plays sound all around the listener. The 5.1 surround system uses the following speakers—front-left, center, front-right, left-surround, right-surround, and subwoofer.

**SUSTAIN**—The portion of the envelope of a note in which the level is constant. Also, the ability of a note to continue without noticeably decaying, often aided by compression.

**SWEETENING**—The addition of strings, brass, chorus, etc., to a previously recorded tape of the basic rhythm tracks.

**SYNC, SYNCHRONIZATION**—Aligning two separate audio programs in time, and maintaining that alignment as the programs play.

**SYNC, SYNCHRONOUS RECORDING**—Using a record head temporarily as a playback head during an overdub session, to keep the overdubbed parts in synchronization with the recorded tracks.

**SYNC TONE**—*See* Tape Sync.

**SYNC TRACK**—A track of a multitrack recorder that is reserved for recording an FSK sync tone or SMPTE time code. This allows audio tracks to synchronize with virtual tracks recorded with a sequencer. A sync track also can synchronize two audio tape machines or an audio recorder and a video recorder, and can be used for console automation.

**SYNTHESIZER**—A musical instrument (usually with a piano-style keyboard) that creates sounds electronically and allows control of the sound parameters to simulate a variety of conventional or unique instruments.

**TAIL-OUT**—Referring to a reel of tape wound with the end of the program toward the outside of the reel. Tape stored tail-out is less likely to have audible print-through.

**TAKE**—A recorded performance of a song. Usually, several takes are done of the same song, and the best one—or the best parts of several—becomes the final product.

**TAKE SHEET**—A list of take numbers for each song, plus comments on each take.

**TAKE-UP REEL**—The right-side reel on a tape recorder that winds up the tape as it is playing or recording.

**TALKBACK**—An intercom in the mixing console for the engineer and producer to talk to the musicians in the studio.

**TAPE**—*See* Magnetic Recording Tape.

**TAPE LOOP**—An endless loop formed from a length of recording tape spliced end-to-end, used for continuous repetition of several seconds of recorded signal.

**TAPE RECORDER**—A device that converts an electrical audio signal into a magnetic audio signal on magnetic tape, and vice versa. A tape recorder includes electronics, heads, and a transport to move the tape.

**TAPE SYNC**—A frequency-modulated signal recorded on a tape track, used to synchronize a tape recorder to a sequencer. Tape sync also permits the synchronized transfer of sequences to tape. *See also* Sync Track.

**TDIF**—TASCAM Digital Interface, an interface protocol for connecting digital audio signals to and from TASCAM DTRS multitrack recorders, such as the DA-78 and DA-88.

**3-PIN CONNECTOR**—A 3-pin professional audio connector used for balanced signals. Pin 1 is soldered to the cable shield, pin 2 is soldered to the signal hot lead, and pin 3 is soldered to the signal return lead. *See also* XLR-Type Connector.

**THREE-TO-ONE RULE (3:1 Rule)**—A rule in microphone applications. When multiple mics are mixed to the same channel, the distance between mics should be at least three times the distance from each mic to its sound source. This prevents audible phase interference.

**THRESHOLD**—In a compressor or limiter, the input level above which compression or limiting takes place. In an expander, the input level below which expansion takes place.

**TIE**—To connect electrically, for example, by soldering a wire between two points in a circuit.

**TIGHT**—1. Having very little leakage or room reflections in the sound pickup. 2. Referring to well-synchronized playing of musical instruments. 3. Having a well-damped, rapid decay.

**TIMBRE**—The subjective impression of spectrum and envelope. The quality of a sound that allows us to differentiate it from other sounds. For example, if you hear a trumpet, a piano, and a drum, each has a different timbre or tone quality that identifies it as a particular instrument.

**TIME CODE**—A modulated 1200-Hz square-wave signal used to synchronize two or more tape or disc transports. *See also* Tape Sync, Sync Track, SMPTE.

**TONAL BALANCE**—The balance or volume relationships among different regions of the frequency spectrum, such as bass, midbass, midrange, upper midrange, and highs.

**TOSLINK (Toshiba Link)**—A fiber optic cable connection for S/PDIF data transfers.

**TRACK**—A path on magnetic tape containing a single channel of audio. A group of bytes in a digital signal (on tape, on hard disk, on compact disc, or in a data stream) that represents a single channel of audio or MIDI. Usually one track contains a performance by one musical instrument.

**TRANSDUCER**—A device that converts energy from one form to another, such as a microphone or loudspeaker.

**TRANSFORMER**—An electronic component made of two magnetically coupled coils of wire. The input signal is transferred magnetically to the output, without a direct connection between input and output.

**TRANSIENT**—A short signal with a rapid attack and decay, such as a drum stroke, cymbal hit, or acoustic-guitar pluck.

**TRANSIENT RESPONSE**—The ability of an audio component (usually a microphone or loudspeaker) to follow a transient accurately.

**TRANSPORT**—The mechanical system in a reproduction device that moves the medium past the read/write heads. In a tape recorder, the transport controls tape motion during recording, playback, fast forward, and rewind.

**TRIM**—1. In a mixing console, a control for fine adjustment of level, as in a Bus Trim control. 2. In a mixing console, a control that adjusts the gain of a mic preamp to accommodate various signal levels.

**TRS (Tip Ring Sleeve)**—A phone-plug connector used for send/return, stereo, or balanced mono connections.

**TUBE**—A vacuum tube, an amplifying component made of electrodes in an evacuated glass tube. Tube sound is characterized as being "warmer" than solid-state or transistor sound.

**TWEETER**—A high-frequency loudspeaker.

**UNBALANCED LINE**—An audio cable having one conductor surrounded by a shield that carries the return signal. The shield is at ground potential.

**UNIDIRECTIONAL MICROPHONE**—A microphone that is most sensitive to sounds arriving from one direction—in front of the microphone. Examples are cardioid, supercardioid, and hypercardioid.

**USB (Universal Serial Bus)**—A Mac/PC computer serial interface for connecting external devices such as MIDI interfaces and audio interfaces. Faster than a standard serial port but slower than SCSI.

**VALVE**—British term for vacuum tube. *See* Tube.

**VBR**—Variable Bit Rate MP3 encoding. The bit rate varies with the audio signal.

**VIRTUAL CONTROLS**—Audio-equipment controls that are simulated on a computer monitor screen. You adjust them with a mouse.

**VIRTUAL TRACK**—A sequencer recording of a single musical line, recorded as data in computer memory. A virtual track is the computer's equivalent of a tape track on a multitrack tape recorder. Also, a recording of a single take of one instrument or vocal on a random-access medium.

**VU METER**—A voltmeter with a specified transient response, calibrated in VU or volume units, used to show the relative volume of various audio signals, and to set recording levels.

**WAV (.WAV)**—A computer audio file format for Windows. It encodes sound without any data reduction, using pulse code modulation. Audio resolution is 16-bit, 44.1 kHz, or higher.

**WAVEFORM**—A graph of a signal's sound pressure or voltage versus time. The waveform of a pure tone is a sine wave.

**WAVELENGTH**—The physical length between corresponding points of successive waves. Low frequencies have long wavelengths; high frequencies have short wavelengths.

541

**WEBER**—A unit of magnetic flux.

**WEIGHTED**—Referring to a measurement made through a filter with a specified frequency response. An A-weighted measurement is taken through a filter that simulates the frequency response of the human ear.

**WINDOWS MEDIA**—*See* WMA.

**WINDSCREEN**—*See* Pop Filter.

**WMA (Windows Media Audio)**—A popular compressed audio file format for streaming audio and for downloads. Windows Media 8 promises performance similar to that of MP3Pro—near-CD quality at 48 kbps and CD quality at 64 kbps.

**WOOFER**—A low-frequency loudspeaker.

**WORD LENGTH**—*See* Bit Depth.

**WORKSTATION**—A system of MIDI- or computer-related equipment that works together to help you compose and record music. Usually, this system is small enough to fit on a desktop or equipment stand. *See also* Keyboard Workstation *and* Digital Audio Workstation.

**WOW**—A slow periodic variation in tape speed.

**XLR-TYPE CONNECTOR**—An ITT Cannon part number that has become the popular definition for a 3-pin professional audio connector. *See also* Three-Pin (3-Pin) Connector.

**X-Y**—*See* Coincident-Pair.

**Y-ADAPTER**—A cable that divides into two cables in parallel to feed one signal to two destinations.

**Z**—Abbreviation for impedance.

**ZONE**—*See* Region.

# INDEX